TWENTIETH CENTURY
INTERPRETATIONS
OF

LIGHT IN AUGUST

TWENTIETH CENTURY INTERPRETATIONS

OF

LIGHT

IN AUGUST

A Collection of Critical Essays

Edited by

DAVID L. MINTER

Prentice-Hall, Inc. A SPECTRUM BOOK   *Englewood Cliffs, N.J.*

PRENTICE-HALL INTERNATIONAL, INC. (*London*)
PRENTICE-HALL OF AUSTRALIA, PTY. LTD. (*Sydney*)
PRENTICE-HALL OF CANADA, LTD. (*Toronto*)
PRENTICE-HALL OF INDIA PRIVATE LIMITED (*New Delhi*)
PRENTICE-HALL OF JAPAN, INC. (*Tokyo*)

Contents

TWENTIETH CENTURY
INTERPRETATIONS
OF

LIGHT IN AUGUST

Introduction

by David L. Minter

In about 1914, when he was seventeen, William Faulkner began writing verse. Several of his early poems (and drawings as well) appeared, beginning in 1917, in the University of Mississippi yearbook, *Ole Miss,* and in the University newspaper, *The Mississippian.* In 1919 and 1922 single poems appeared in *The New Republic* and *The Double Dealer,* a "little magazine" based in New Orleans; and in 1924 Faulkner's first book, *The Marble Faun,* a small volume of verse, was privately printed. Attracting few sales and little attention, *The Marble Faun* taught Faulkner to speak of himself as a "failed poet" and encouraged him to turn to fiction.[1]

Faulkner's apprenticeship in fiction, prepared for as it was by his experiments with poetry, was brief, yielding but two works, *Soldiers' Pay* (1926) and *Mosquitoes* (1927). The publication of *Sartoris* in 1929 marked both his move from apprenticeship toward maturity and the emergence of his mythical kingdom, Yoknapatawpha County. "With *Soldiers' Pay* and *Mosquitoes,*" Faulkner later remarked,

> I wrote for the sake of writing because it was fun. Beginning with *Sartoris* I discovered that my own little postage stamp of native soil was worth writing about and that I would never live long enough to exhaust it, and that by sublimating the actual into the apocryphal I would have complete liberty to use whatever talent I might have to its absolute top. . . . [S]o I created a cosmos of my own.[2]

The multilayered discovery that Faulkner made during the writing

---

[1] William Faulkner, "Interview with Jean Stein vanden Heuvel," in *Lion in the Garden: Interviews with William Faulkner, 1926–1962,* ed. James B. Meriwether and Michael Millgate (New York: Random House, Inc., 1968), p. 238. On Faulkner's life, see the chronology below, pp. 111–15, and Michael Millgate, *The Achievement of William Faulkner* (New York: Random House, Inc., 1966), pp. 1–57.

[2] *Ibid.,* p. 255.

of *Sartoris* did in fact prove inexhaustible. The publication of his last Yoknapatawpha novel, *The Reivers*, preceded his death on July 6, 1962, by but one month and two days. The discovery of Yoknapatawpha also proved immediately generative. It issued, with astonishing speed, in a series of major works. Begun in August 1931 and published in October 1932,[3] *Light in August* was the fourth and last of the important novels (the others being *The Sound and the Fury, As I Lay Dying,* and *Sanctuary*) published by Faulkner in the four years following *Sartoris*.[4] These years, years that taught Faulkner to speak of the poet as "a creature driven by demons," [5] we have come to call "the time of genius" or "the great years." [6] In American fiction, to take an immediate context, Faulkner's first great period is now ranked with the great years of Herman Melville and the major phase of Henry James.[7]

Following a brief respite, Faulkner began, in 1936, a second period of remarkable achievement. Between October 1936 and May 1942 he published five novels, including *Absalom, Absalom!, The Hamlet,* and *Go Down, Moses.* Faulkner's third, and final, period of significant activity, which also followed a brief respite, began with *Intruder in the Dust* (1948), included *The Town* and *The Mansion,* and ended with *The Reivers* (1962). This last, and perhaps least remarkable, phase in Faulkner's literary career brought with it both public recognition, including the Nobel Prize in 1950, and critical acclaim. Both recognition and acclaim have, of course, met with resistance. But the frequent attacks of the late 20's and early 30's and the relative neglect of the

[3] *Light in August* was first published in the United States by Harrison Smith and Robert Haas (New York, 1932). The first British edition was published by Chatto & Windus Ltd. (London, 1933). Later the novel was issued by New Directions (Norfolk, Connecticut, 1947). The texts of these three editions are impressions, direct or by photo-offset, from the original plates and are reliable. Later a new edition, containing errors and changes, was published in the Modern Library series (New York, 1950). More recently Modern Library has issued a reliable text reproduced photographically from the first printing (New York, n.d.).

In the selections that follow Millgate uses one of the three early reliable editions; Abel, Brooks, Lamont, Longley, Slabey, Slatoff, and Vickery use the first (1950) Modern Library edition; and the remaining writers do not specify edition.

[4] A collection of stories, *These Thirteen* (1931), also belongs to this period.

[5] William Faulkner, "Interview with Jean Stein vanden Heuvel," p. 239.

[6] See Frederick J. Hoffman, *William Faulkner,* 2nd ed. (New York: Twayne Publishers, Inc., 1961), p. 19; Richard Chase, *The American Novel and Its Tradition* (Garden City, New York: Doubleday & Company, Inc., 1957), pp. 205-36.

[7] See Millgate, *The Achievement of William Faulkner,* pp. 42-57, 279-92.

late 30's and early 40's have, since 1946, given way to attention of very considerable magnitude.[8]

The critical consensus that proclaims Faulkner's greatness is important primarily because it enables us more adequately, if still tentatively, to define the nature and extent of his achievement—to distinguish its qualities and fix its boundaries. Less drastically experimental than *The Sound and the Fury* and *As I Lay Dying, Light in August* is more "conventional" in structure and technique and is therefore less perplexing to approach, although it clearly does not represent "a return" by Faulkner "to the traditional novel." More substantial and compelling, more clearly "a major work" than *Sartoris* or *Sanctuary, Light in August* is more fully suggestive of Faulkner's greatness.[9] In short, it is a good place for serious, inquisitive readers to begin to know the magnitude and order of Faulkner's created world and to begin to locate the critical problems appropriate to it.

The shorter excerpted statements that make up the second part of this collection present contrasting positions on those aspects of the novel that have proved most problematical—the status and significance of the major characters of each of the novel's three main strands and the roles in the novel of religion, sex, and women. The essays that constitute the first part of the collection represent a variety of approaches to the novel as a whole. Richard Chase ties *Light in August* to an American literary tradition. Michael Millgate points to basic affinities between the novel and major traditions of British and Continental fiction of the nineteenth century, affinities he sees enriching rather than compromising both the unusual emotional and moral engagement that Faulkner demands and the unconventional techniques that he employs. Cleanth Brooks sees in the pervading force of the community a clue to the novel's central structure. Darrel Abel seeks to define the nature of its fluid reality and to describe the poetic techniques used in capturing and creating that fluid reality in a literary form. Olga Vickery traces three patterns of imagery, the circle, the shadow, and the mirror, which work in the novel to

[8] For a discussion of the critical reception of Faulkner's fiction, see Robert Penn Warren, "Introduction: Faulkner: Past and Present," *Faulkner: A Collection of Critical Essays,* Twentieth Century Views Series (Englewood Cliffs, N. J.: Prentice-Hall, Inc., 1966), pp. 6–19. On 1946 and the publication of Malcolm Cowley's *The Portable Faulkner* as the "great watershed for Faulkner's reputation in the United States," see p. 10.

[9] See Michael Millgate, *William Faulkner,* Evergreen Pilot Books (New York: Grove Press, Inc., 1961), p. 44; and Olga W. Vickery in this collection.

ate isolated individual consciousnesses to one another and to a shared public world and which work, too, to suggest how reason and imagination together integrate individual need and communal need, private realm and public arena. Such variety in itself testifies to the rich complexity of *Light in August*.

II

Among those of Faulkner's qualities that have impressed all of his better readers are the fecundity of his imagination, the range of his compassion, and the reach of his courage as artist. Not only within his fictional kingdom of Yoknapatawpha County, population 15,611, area 2400 square miles, "William Faulkner, sole owner and proprietor," [10] but within his individual novels as well, we find an "abundance of representation," scores of compelling, unforgettable characters, and an "abundance of narrative incident," a wealth of action in language.[11] Faulkner possessed, in short, fecundity of the rare sort that we associate in the novel with Balzac, Dickens, and James. Commensurate with his fecundity was the range of his interest and compassion. Reaching beyond those he grandly termed "the unvanquished," those who remain impervious even to final defeat, his interest and compassion touch the terrible, like Percy Grimm of *Light in August*'s brutal climax, and the small, those "who stand a little in the background," [12] like the furniture repairer and dealer of *Light in August*'s last chapter. Equal, too, to Faulkner's fecundity was the reach of his courage as artist, his willingness, or as some would have it, his compulsion, to expose and explore every aspect of each of his novelistic worlds.

Such courage, at least in Faulkner's case, was not without its dangers: on occasion the difficulties we encounter stem less from profundity of vision than "from the fact that his mind is so astonishingly energetic, his sensibility so vividly aroused by all the issues present to his mind, that he is . . . leaping from one [possibility] to the other in excited discovery." [13] But Faulkner's world is finally an ordered world, and

[10] Malcolm Cowley, "Introduction," *The Portable Faulkner,* The Viking Portable Library (New York: The Viking Press, 1946), p. 5.

[11] Irving Howe, *William Faulkner: A Critical Study* (New York: Random House, Inc., 1952), p. 154; and Michael Millgate in this collection.

[12] Cowley, "Introduction," *The Portable Faulkner,* p. 20.

[13] Alfred Kazin, "Faulkner in His Fury," *The Inmost Leaf: A Selection of Essays* (New York: Harcourt, Brace and Company, 1955), pp. 266–68.

it is, accordingly, big rather than swollen with significance. Faulkner possessed to remarkable degree the coherence of imagination that marks novelists of the first rank: "the ability to sustain details in so long and dynamic a single period that they finally compose a single order of progression." [14] In his determination to move toward the largest possible extension of meaning, Faulkner frequently employs big, familiar devices and motifs—most noticeably, in *Light in August,* the odyssey motif and elements of the Passion story.[15] But his world is a world of the immediate and the actual, of small, specific sounds and colors, through which he endows even the most familiar and universal of conventions with a local habitation. Albert Camus, one of Faulkner's early admirers, once remarked that what he liked most about Southern fiction was "the dust and the heat." [16] In Faulkner's world "the actual," the land and the ways of the land that he knew, its dust, its heat, its humor, not only precede and prepare for but become (in Faulkner's term, are sublimated into) "the apocryphal."

Faulkner's determination to expose every aspect of each of his imagined worlds meant, among other things, that his fictions frequently would defy even such familiar and useful distinctions as that between comic and tragic modes. In *Light in August,* even more, say, than in the predominantly comic *As I Lay Dying* or the predominantly tragic *Absalom, Absalom!,* the two mingle. To Cleanth Brooks, the mode of the novel is finally "that of comedy"; to Olga Vickery and John L. Longley, it is finally tragedy.[17] But to these and all other

[14] *Ibid.,* p. 268. See Darrel Abel, Cleanth Brooks, Norman Holmes Pearson, and Olga W. Vickery in this collection.

[15] On the odyssey motif, see Michael Millgate in this collection; and Alfred Kazin's splendid essay, "The Stillness of *Light in August*," which, because it has been several times reprinted and is available in Robert Penn Warren, ed., *Faulkner: A Collection of Critical Essays,* Twentieth Century Views Series (Englewood Cliffs, N. J.: Prentice-Hall, Inc., 1966), pp. 147–62, has not been reprinted here. On Faulkner's use of the Passion story, see Faulkner and Brooks in this collection and C. Hugh Holman, "The Unity of Faulkner's *Light in August*," PMLA, LXXIII (March, 1958), 155–66. On Faulkner's use of such motifs, compare his description of the inception of *As I Lay Dying*: "I simply imagined a group of people and subjected them to the simple universal natural catastrophes which are flood and fire with a simple natural motive to give direction to their progress." ("Interview with Jean Stein vanden Heuvel," p. 244.)

[16] Quoted in Kazin, "The Stillness of *Light in August*," p. 149.

[17] See Brooks, Vickery, and Longley in this collection. John L. Longley's fine discussion of "Joe Christmas: the Hero in the Modern World" has not been reprinted in full in this collection only because it is readily available in Robert Penn Warren, ed., *Faulkner: A Collection of Critical Essays,* Twentieth Century Views Series (Englewood Cliffs, N. J.: Prentice-Hall, Inc., 1966), pp. 163–74.

careful readers it is clear that in this several-stranded story the two modes are mixed. The novel begins with Lena Grove and ends with Lena, her child, and Byron Bunch. In this strand, in which Lucas Burch is a supporting character, a villain to be precise, the mode is comedy. And in this strand the comic heroine, Lena Grove, is dominant, and the comic hero, Byron Bunch, subordinate. Between the first and last chapters (the novel's framing chapters, and the only chapters in which Lena is dominant), we encounter two other stories: first, at considerable length, the story of Joe Christmas, in which Doc Hines and Mr. McEachern, together with Lucas Burch and Percy Grimm, are subordinate villains, and Joanna Burden something of a subordinate heroine, and in which the mode is tragedy; and second, more briefly, the story of Gail Hightower, in which the comic and the tragic very much mingle. All of which is to say, first, that the novel's dominant hero and heroine pull it in different directions (which in turn is to suggest why, appropriately, they never meet), and second, that, in addition to being counterpointed, the hero's tragic story and the heroine's comic story are interlaced by the story of Gail Hightower.

Joe Christmas' desperate, violent search for "peace"—"That was all I wanted," he says[18]—his search for a sense of his own identity and a sense of place in his world, is a "tragic and essentially modern story." The journey, the frantic circling, of this "doomed, deracinated, terribly alone" man is not merely futile but extravagantly destructive. In clear juxtaposition is the "steady imperturbable onward linear progress" of Lena Grove, through whose life, and through the birth of whose child, the "barren and ruined" (p. 385) world of the novel is partially renewed. Gail Hightower, who witnesses the terrible death of Joe Christmas and attends the calm childbearing of Lena Grove, is by the conjunction of the two, by the suffering of the one and the renewing generation of the other, moved "from rigidity into life." [19] The issue that has troubled even the most careful readers of *Light in August* is the relation of the novel's three strands and particularly the success of Hightower's unifying strand, the dynamics and the significance, the how and the so what, of Hightower's renewal.[20]

[18] *Light in August* (New York: Harrison Smith and Robert Haas, 1932), p. 313. All page references in the text of this introduction are to this edition of *Light in August*.

[19] Millgate, *William Faulkner*, pp. 44–49. On Joe Christmas' isolation, compare Alfred Kazin's discussion in "The Stillness of *Light in August*," p. 151, of him as "the most solitary character in American fiction."

[20] See Howe, *William Faulkner*, pp. 148–49. Even Kazin, in "The Stillness of

The link between Lena Grove and Joe Christmas that provides a basis for their unwitting cooperation in Gail Hightower's emergence resembles the link Hannah Arendt has described between the saint and the criminal: "the one [the saint] being for, the other [the criminal] against, all men," she writes, both "remain outside the pale of human intercourse and are, politically [and otherwise], marginal figures." [21] At first glance, Joe Christmas may seem a pure instance of the criminal. He commits, after all, among other things, a terrible murder. Several critics, including Malcolm Cowley, one of Faulkner's best readers, have linked Joe Christmas and Popeye, the grotesque villain of *Sanctuary*, as willing agents, dehumanized, deliberate extenders, of destruction.[22] The far simpler Lena Grove might seem at first to support such a view: to confirm that it is her hand that is for and Joe Christmas' that is against all men. But Lena Grove is after all too finely, even too traditionally, drawn a comic heroine in the pastoral mode to be in any simple sense a saint. Furthermore, in keeping with Faulkner's superbly controlled compulsion toward complexity, Lena, as an unwed mother in a traditional society, is something of an outcast as well as something of a saint.[23]

Allied as she is with everything that is permanent and enduring, with everything that is natural, simple, certain, Lena is able to comprehend the whole of her world with "a single glance all-embracing, swift, innocent and profound" (p. 5); she is at home in it endlessly, from day to dark and dark to day again. A man with no authentic name and with none to come, Joe Christmas is, in Melville's term an "isolato." Whereas Lena moves slowly, purposefully across the face of her world, Joe Christmas circles furiously, ever hesitating and alone, forever gray and indefinite as a shadow. Whereas Lena's linear odyssey brings forth life, Joe Christmas' circular flight ends in death. Yet, just as Lena is outcast as well as saint, Joe Christmas is something more than criminal; at least in his last moments, as he lies on the floor conscious, unmoving, accepting death, he becomes an emblem of terrible and yet hopeful sacrifice.

Light in August," p. 148, is troubled by Faulkner's "attempt to will his painful material into a kind of harmony that it does not really possess."

[21] Hannah Arendt, *The Human Condition* (Chicago: University of Chicago Press, 1958), p. 180. Compare R. W. B. Lewis, *The Picaresque Saint: Representative Figures in Contemporary Fiction* (Philadelphia: J. B. Lippincott Company, 1959).

[22] Cowley, "Introduction," *The Portable Faulkner*, p. 15.

[23] See p. 4, where we learn that to her brother Lena is "a whore," and compare pp. 7–8.

He just lay there, with his eyes open and empty of everything save consciousness, and with something, a shadow, about his mouth. For a long moment he looked up at them with peaceful and unfathomable and unbearable eyes. Then his face, body, all, seemed to collapse, to fall in upon itself, and from out the slashed garments about his hips and loins the pent black blood seemed to rush like a released breath. It seemed to rush out of his pale body like the rush of sparks from a rising rocket; upon that black blast the man seemed to rise soaring into their memories forever and ever. They are not to lose it, in whatever peaceful valleys, beside whatever placid and reassuring streams of old age, in the mirroring faces of whatever children they will contemplate old disasters and newer hopes. It will be there, musing, quiet, steadfast, not fading and not particularly threatful, but of itself alone serene, of itself alone triumphant. (pp. 439–40)

The strange story of Joe Christmas demands of us disturbing flexibility. For it requires that we entertain a disquieting possibility: that in a world which so easily accommodates itself to the cruelty of a sheriff who beats defenseless others, to "the insensitive, life-denying rigidity" of McEachern, and to the "principled inhumanity" of Doc Hines and Percy Grimm,[24] that in a world in which absurdity and injustice so resoundingly reside, the furious and confused response of Joe Christmas, no less than the calm and purposeful response of Lena Grove, is necessary and even heroic. Since we see Lena primarily as a pastoral creature, and not as an outcast, and since we associate her not only with everything that is natural, simple, fertile, but also with that triumph of artifice, Keats' bride of quietness and slow time, we know that she must endure.[25] Similarly, since we see Joe Christmas as isolated and hollow, and even, in clothes and manner, as strangely urban, since we associate him with everything that is barren and artificial, we know that he must die. "Something is going to happen to me," we hear him quietly think; "I am going to do something" (p. 97; compare p. 110). We know, in short, that it is Joe Christmas and not Lena Grove whom some terrible fatality awaits. But *Light in August* nonetheless stands among those works of modern literature, including the entire literature of hipsterism, in which we see, and must ourselves accommodate, a blurring of the line between saint and criminal, suppliant and murderer.[26]

---

[24] Millgate, *William Faulkner*, p. 49. See, too, Millgate's discussion of tension in *Light in August* between masculine adherence to "clear-cut patterns of crime and punishment" and feminine "tendency to blur" those patterns (p. 46).

[25] See Darrel Abel and Norman Holmes Pearson in this collection.

[26] See the works cited in note 20 above.

The movement of Joe Christmas' story is from what he has done (his killing of Joanna Burden), first, to the history lying behind and illuminating what he has done, back to what he has done, and finally to what happens to him. What Faulkner achieves by thus defying, almost obliterating, the distinction between passivity and activity, between what the world does to shape Joe Christmas and what he does to shape his world, between everything that happens to Joe (injustice, violence, and death) and every act that he commits, is to suggest that in the case of Joe Christmas the two are not only inter-related but inseparable. The death Joe Christmas meets at the hands of Percy Grimm is prefigured in the death he inflicts on Joanna Burden. The pistol that Joanna Burden holds, the pistol that misfires, delaying the death of Joe Christmas, later has its dual counterpart in the scene of Joe Christmas' death—first in the pistol that Joe Christmas holds but does not fire and second in the pistol that Percy Grimm holds and empties into the body of Joe Christmas, thus completing the destruction that Joanna Burden attempted and that, long before her, Hines and McEachern began. Similarly, the razor with which Joe Christmas grotesquely kills Joanna Burden has its counterpart in the bloody knife Percy Grimm wields in mutilation. The death Joe Christmas meets is thus anticipated by, is thus implicit in, the death he inflicts.

What is most strikingly clear in the relation between the death Joe Christmas inflicts and the death he suffers is true, too, of his whole life. At virtually every point he is both active and passive, both agent and victim. In describing and attempting to account for the final, futile run that culminates in Joe Christmas' death, Gavin Stevens sees and articulates in racial terms a fundamental conflict within Joe Christmas: [27]

". . . his blood would not be quiet, let him save it. It would not be either one or the other and let his body save itself. Because the black blood drove him first to the Negro cabin. And then the white blood drove him out of there, as it was the black blood which snatched up the pistol and the white blood which would not let him fire it. And it was the white blood which sent him to the minister, which rising in him for the last and final time, sent him against all reason and all reality, into the embrace of a chimera, a blind faith in something read in a printed Book. Then I believe that the white blood deserted him for the moment. Just a second, a flicker, allowing the black to rise in its final moment and make him turn upon that on which he had postulated his hope of salvation.

[27] See the discussions of Joe Christmas as hero in this collection.

It was the black blood which swept him by his own desire beyond the aid of any man, swept him up into that ecstasy out of a black jungle where life has already ceased before the heart stops and death is desire and fulfillment. And then the black blood failed him again, as it must have in crises all his life. He did not kill the minister. He merely struck him with the pistol and ran on and crouched behind that table and defied the black blood for the last time, as he had been defying it for thirty years. He crouched behind that overturned table and let them shoot him to death, with that loaded and unfired pistol in his hand." (pp. 424–25)

Some such conflict is indeed the basic conflict not only within Joe Christmas but within his world. But it is a conflict rather between life and death than between "white blood" and "black blood." The two figures representing opposite poles in the world of *Light in August*, Lena Grove, the source of life, and Percy Grimm, the instrument of death, are both white.[28] What Faulkner does in *Light in August* is to revise and extend, through poetic context and action, the conflict described, but miscast, by Stevens.

The struggle Joe Christmas wages with his world is a struggle for peace and life, for repose and creation, against fury and death. His defeat, though neither simple nor full, is certain in part because he lives in a world he never made, a world too large and too hostile for him to conquer or even withstand. He is, in short, overmatched. A part of what we see in him, therefore, is man as victim. His suffering, at once concentrated, large, and representative, is in part imposed and inflicted. To Joe Christmas as victim, pity is the proper response; to him we say what Gail Hightower says: "Poor man. Poor mankind" (p. 93). But, as John L. Longley has suggested, we feel, before Joe Christmas' terrible ordeal, not only pity but terror.[29] And it is this that suggests that Joe Christmas is more than either victim or villain, that he is tragic hero as well, that in him Faulkner renders not merely individual man as enemy and victim of man but individual man as enemy and victim of himself. What we learn in the story of Joe Christmas' early years is how, in the orphanage and in the home of the McEacherns, he has become, *in part,* an ally of his world against himself. The ambiguity that is his heritage and his identity, his defining quality, touches more than race, parentage, and place; it touches

[28] Note that Stevens assumes what in the novel remains in doubt: that Joe Christmas is part Negro. Note, too, how small a role Negroes, apart from whites' preoccupation with them, actually play in the novel.

[29] See John L. Longley in this collection; see, too, the fuller piece by Longley as cited in note 16 above.

his basic disposition toward life. What we see in Joe Christmas' circular flight, in his attitude toward women, in his fear of progeny, and in his failure, by firing at Percy Grimm, to resist death, is the deep division within him between the forces of life and the forces of death. Both the Christmas who resists and flees death and the Christmas who serves and welcomes death are present to the end. Joe Christmas the ally of death not only refuses to oppose Percy Grimm, that ally of racism, perverse religion, militarism, and fear of sex; he even embraces the death Percy Grimm offers as peace, as release from the pain, ambiguity, and suffering that are his life.[30] But the Joe Christmas who flees and defies death, too, is present to the end. It is he who refuses to permit his perverted self to kill Hightower; it is he who stills the hand so long turned against man and life, the hand that would destroy, in Hightower, the one man so moved by his ordeal as again to become, despite fear, an ally (albeit an ineffectual ally) of life. And it is this Christmas who endures the death his other self embraces, who accepts it, who suffers it, not as release but as means of becoming, for all who see him, an emblem of sacrifice.[31] It is because of the continuing presence of this self, which is at the end "of itself alone serene, of itself alone triumphant," that Joe Christmas is able to speak to us not merely of "old disasters" but of "newer hopes" (p. 440).

The shadows and the grayness that we associate with Joe Christmas point to the division within him between the forces of death, the impulse toward it, the yearning to inflict and to suffer it, and the forces of life, the impulse toward peace, not as escape but as repose and generation. The shadows and the grayness accordingly suggest that to the end Joe Christmas belongs neither to Lena's world nor to Hines's, McEachern's, and Grimm's, but to both. His triumph is that, despite everything that is done to him, he remains in part dedicated to life. That dedication we see, moreover, not only in the suffer-

---

[30] On Percy Grimm, see William Faulkner, Letter to Malcolm Cowley [September 20, 1945], *The Faulkner-Cowley File: Letters and Memories, 1944–1962*, ed. Malcolm Cowley (New York: The Viking Press, 1966), p. 32. Faulkner describes Grimm as a "Fascist galahad who saved the white race by murdering Christmas." "I didn't realize," Faulkner adds, "until after Hitler got into the newspapers that I had created a Nazi before he did." See Olga Vickery and Maxwell Geismar in this collection; and Ilse D. Lind, "The Calvinistic Burden of *Light in August*," *New England Quarterly*, XXX (1957), 307–29.

[31] Compare Millgate, *William Faulkner*, p. 47: "The main function of the much-discussed Christ-imagery which clusters around Christmas, especially at the moment of his death, is not to make him a 'Christ-figure'—an unnecessarily portentous term —but to underline his role as a sacrificial victim."

ing that defines his acceptance of death but also in the fury and violence that ironically define and undermine his doomed search for peace in life.

Because Joe Christmas finally speaks complexly of "newer hopes" as well as more simply of "old disasters," he can join Lena Grove as occasion and instigator of Hightower's emergence into life. In Hightower's preoccupation with the past we see not mere withdrawal from life but denial of it. We see, that is, something very close to the tension and struggle that are Joe Christmas' drama. By choosing to live in the non-world of his empty illusions, Hightower has become, for his wife in her Memphis hotel room and for himself in his morbid mausoleum, an agent of death. For him vision has been illusion, not dream, an instrument of death rather than of life. His story in *Light in August*, however, is the story of his reluctant move toward reentering life. Before we witness his futile effort to save Joe Christmas, we see him successfully deliver Lena's child. When we move from Chapter 19, which centers on the death of Joe Christmas, to Chapter 20, which culminates in Hightower's vision, we move to a style that begins in elegy and moves toward epiphany. Through attending Lena in the birth of her child and Joe Christmas in the ordeal of his death, Gail Hightower is renewed. He perceives the primal hope which Lena represents in her "tranquil obedience to . . . the good earth['s]" command that she renew and replenish her "barren and ruined" world (pp. 384–85). And he apprehends the complex hope that Joe Christmas bespeaks. Prepared as he is by the logic of his own life, by his own deep ambivalence toward life, Hightower is in fact enabled not only to apprehend but to appropriate that hope, to make it the very substance of his final vision. The fruit of his renewal, the sign of his emergence "from rigidity to life," is his move from vision as illusion to vision as illumination. After he has given up his distortions of the past, after he has admitted the truth regarding his grandfather's death and has accepted responsibility for his wife's death, he discovers in the relation he discerns between Joe Christmas and Percy Grimm that the struggle between life and death is a struggle waged not only among men but within man. It is only after we have shared Hightower's vision that we fully understand the hope as well as the disaster that defines the drama of Joe Christmas.

Hightower's illusion, the illusion he comes so reluctantly to see as illusion, is in one of its aspects a denial of life. But it is in another aspect a token of his desire that death, if it must triumph over life, triumph with the sound of drums and the clash of swords, not with the screech of a man whose sleep has been disturbed by chicken thieves and with the blast of a fowling piece, that least discriminate and most inglorious of weapons. What Hightower finally sees—and what through him we see—is that the struggle between life and death is, not merely in the case of Joe Christmas but characteristically in his world, a struggle in which glory and degradation are profoundly mixed and are so precisely because man is deeply ambivalent toward life itself. But Hightower sees, too, that death's triumph is neither simple nor full; he sees that through continued refusal simply to choose death, refusal that defies the force of everything his world does to him, Joe Christmas is enabled to express hope as well as disaster. In his continued, though mixed, allegiance to life, maintained as it is despite the violence that besets, partially corrupts, and finally destroys him, Joe Christmas becomes an emblem, not of mere terror, but of terrible hope.

Light in August ends with Lena, her child, and her would-be lover and husband. The rich styles of the nineteenth and twentieth chapters give way to the calm, detached, colloquial, humorous voice of a furniture repairer and dealer, a simple man in bed telling his wife the story of what he has seen on his travels. But the vitality and endurance of Lena surely are not, in any simple way, commensurate with the terrible stories of Joe Christmas and Gail Hightower. Lena endures, and her endurance permits her to end the novel she has begun. But she does not prevail. Her tranquillity lasts to the end—her voice remains to the last scene "quiet, tranquil, stubborn" (p. 18). But it does not bring tranquillity to its world. Lena remains fascinated with life, wondering at how a body gets around. But her repose and fascination are weaknesses as well as strengths. They are born of her energy and vitality, her instinctive engagement with and love of life. But they are limited by her obliviousness to the suffering of Joe Christmas, whose last home she inherits but whom she somehow essentially cannot meet, and to the suffering of Gail Hightower, upon whom she depends but whom she never understands. She endures as easily as she does only by being inured to the hardship and privation of her own life and only by remaining impervious to the sufferings of those destroyed by a world in which she lives and thrives. Her comic story, centering on the birth of her child, a birth that in many details parallels what we know about the birth of Joe Christmas, thus frames the very different stories that dominate *Light in August*. But it does not balance the bleakness of the stories juxtaposed to it. For the final meaning of *Light in August* we must look beyond the simple

story of Lena, first, to the complex stories of Gail Hightower and
Joe Christmas, whose lives, save for the meaning they yield, are
altogether grim and barren. And we must also look to the relations
that the novel establishes among its three principal characters rather
than to the very different relations that it depicts as informing the
lives those characters live. In brief, we must look for meaning to the
novel as a formal whole. In the life the novel renders, Lena Grove
touches and alters but never comprehends Gail Hightower, and she
remains almost totally oblivious to Joe Christmas. Only through the
novel's structure does the inadequate hope of Lena's comic story en-
close and embrace the terrible hope of the tragic stories of Joe Christmas and Gail Hightower.

III

Two very different works published in 1942, Maxwell Geismar's
Writers in Crisis and Alfred Kazin's *On Native Grounds*, seriously
challenged Faulkner's claim to our attention. To Geismar, Faulkner's
career reflected increasing fascination with "the perverse and the
pathological." Further, Faulkner's tendency to see "humanity only
in terms of its aberrations" seemed to Geismar to culminate in the
displayed "variety of perversions which the writer contrives for his
characters" in *Light in August*. As though to complement Geismar's
work, Kazin attacked not the stuff but the style and form of Faulkner's
work, describing Faulkner's complicated techniques as springing rather
"from an obscure and profligate confusion . . . than from an elaborate and coherent aim." [32] Increasingly, however, we have come to
see in Faulkner's work, not simple fascination with the perverse and
the pathological, but complex devotion to the "poet's . . . duty" as
he saw and defined it: the duty to write of "the human heart in conflict with itself," of man torn and debased by hate, greed, and fear,
yet "capable of compassion and sacrifice and endurance." [33] Gradually,
too, as Kazin's own career suggests, we have made peace with Faulkner's "solitary" style and strange formal experiments.[34] For we have

[32] Maxwell Geismar, *Writers in Crisis: The American Novel, 1925–1940* (Boston:
Houghton Mifflin Company, 1942), pp. 167–68. Alfred Kazin, *On Native Grounds:
An Interpretation of Modern American Prose Literature* (New York: Reynal and
Hitchcock, 1942), p. 457.
[33] William Faulkner, "Nobel Prize Address," *Faulkner Reader* (New York: Random House, Inc., 1954), pp. 3–4.
[34] Compare Kazin, *On Native Grounds*, pp. 453–68; "Faulkner in His Fury," pp.

come to see what Conrad Aiken saw quite early: that the "uncompromising and almost hypnotic zeal" with which Faulkner insists on his style is a token of his dedication to his art, and that, if we are to understand Faulkner, we must understand the "functional reason and necessity" of the elements and structure of his style[35]—of his seemingly indiscriminate fondness for big words like *imponderable*, smaller ones like *outrage* and *amaze*, and strange ones like *avatar* and *apotheosis*,[36] and of his seemingly indefensible use of sentences that seem "needlessly involved" and "perversely thick with parentheses, [and] even with parentheses within parentheses." [37]

Full understanding of the significance of Faulkner's famous "Protestant" rhetoric must await fuller knowledge of the literary models and oral traditions that helped inspire it. But we may begin to understand its purpose by noting that Faulkner's most famous and problematical words are used in relation "to individuals of every type and in every class" and in relation "to houses, hills, roads, [and] dogs" as well. "These words are not merely interjections"; they are essential. They create the dominant "atmosphere" in which Faulkner's characters, "Negro . . . white, Southern . . . Northern, old settlers . . . new exploiters," move.[38] What most of Faulkner's characters and all of his readers essentially must feel, sooner or later in one way or another, is "outrage" and "fury" before the terrible violence and injustice that foil man's efforts to remake and perfect the living state of his world, and "outrage" and "astonishment" before the constant motion that defies full, final understanding of the why and wherefore of that violence, injustice, and failure. The structure as well as the elements, the form as well as the content, of Faulkner's "strangely fluid and slippery and heavily mannered prose"—those "queer sentences" that at first so often seem "monsters of grammar or awkwardness"—prove in the end "extraordinarily effective" in rendering a basically violent

---

257–73; and "The Stillness of *Light in August*," pp. 147–62. And compare Clifton Fadiman, "Faulkner, Extra-Special, Double-Distilled," *William Faulkner: A Collection of Critical Essays,* Twentieth Century Views Series, ed. Robert Penn Warren (Englewood Cliffs, N. J.: Prentice-Hall, Inc., 1966), pp. 289–90; Conrad Aiken, "William Faulkner" [1939], *A Reviewer's ABC: Collected Criticism of Conrad Aiken* (New York: Meridian Books, Inc., 1958), pp. 201–2; and Cowley, "Introduction," *The Portable Faulkner,* pp. 3–4.

[35] Aiken, "William Faulkner," pp. 200, 202.

[36] For more complete lists, see Kazin, "Faulkner in His Fury," p. 259; and Cowley, "Introduction," *The Portable Faulkner,* pp. 3–4.

[37] Kazin, "Faulkner in His Fury," p. 259.

[38] *Ibid.,* pp. 262–63.

and endlessly problematical reality.[39] For Faulkner's style forces us to stand before and enter his created world in the only attitude proper to it, an attitude, moreover, that is close to one we see again and again displayed in his characters' disposition toward life. Before the violence and injustice that torture Faulkner's world we must feel not only outrage and fury but also astonishment and bafflement, and we must do so precisely because the source and the end of that violence and injustice are problematical.

It was through his "peculiar" style and his "elaborate method[s] of deliberately withheld meaning, of progressive and partial and delayed disclosure" that Faulkner found in art an adequate mistress to his terrible, complex, and inexhaustible vision of outraged and baffled man, man who knows himself immersed and committed yet ambivalent toward his terrible world, who knows, too, that his efforts to find and perfect the life he seeks must fail and that his efforts to understand both his world and his failure must forever remain imperfect. In the "fierceness and openness" of the prose of *Light in August* we see reflected Faulkner's sense of outrage at the implications of his vision.[40] But in the novel's calm stress upon the beatitude of its own formal achievement, its stress upon its triumph in creating in art relations and fulfillment missed and lost in life, we see reflected Faulkner's sense of pride that at least in art, in the anguish of imaginative contemplation and the labor of aesthetic translation, man triumphs over the terrible failures that define his life.

[39] Aiken, "William Faulkner," pp. 202–3.
[40] *Ibid.*, pp. 200–203; and Kazin, "Faulkner in His Fury," p. 265.

PART ONE

Interpretations

Faulkner's *Light in August*

by Richard Chase

There could hardly be a more characteristically American novel than *Light in August*—with its realism; its loose structure; its few characters who though vividly presented are never quite convincingly related to each other; its tendency to become a romance by taking on a legendary quality and by alternating violent melodramatic actions with comic interludes and scenes of pastoral idyl; its concern with the isolated self; its awareness of contradictions, racial and other; its symbolism of light and dark. Generally speaking, *Light in August* is in these respects akin to books apparently as diverse as *The Prairie*, *The House of the Seven Gables*, *Moby Dick*, *The Grandissimes*, and *Huckleberry Finn*, not to mention *Uncle Tom's Cabin* and many others, including such novels of more recent vintage as Robert Penn Warren's *Night Rider* and Ralph Ellison's *Invisible Man*.

In *Light in August* things are perceived in space rather than temporally as they are in *The Sound and the Fury*. Except for the Reverend Hightower, one of Faulkner's characters who are ruined by time, no one is particularly aware of time; and the surviving, enduring character, Lena Grove, lives in a timeless realm which seems to be at once eternity and the present moment. The Mississippi landscape spreads out before us and the faculty of vision becomes very important as we are shown the town of Jefferson, the houses of Hightower and Miss Burden, or the smoke on the horizon as Miss Burden's house burns. There is much use of the painter's art (even the sculptor's, as when Faulkner makes a wagon slowly passing through the countryside

"Faulkner's Light in August" *(Editor's title). From* The American Novel and Its Tradition *by Richard Chase (Garden City, New York: Doubleday & Company, Inc., 1957), pp. 210–19. Copyright © 1957 by Richard Chase. Reprinted by permission of Doubleday & Company, Inc.*

look like part of a frieze, or a seated person—Lena Grove or High-tower—resemble a statue). The art style is not cubist or otherwise modernist as it sometimes is in Faulkner's writing (*Pylon*, for example); it is serene, harmonious, and always aware, even in the midst of dark and violent actions, of a luminousness and spatial harmony that suggest an eternal order.

A simple and somewhat disconnected story emerges from the "abundance of representation," which, as Irving Howe correctly says, constitutes the splendor of *Light in August*. Lena Grove, a poor and ignorant farm girl from Alabama, painfully wends her way into northern Mississippi in pursuit of Lucas Burch, with whose child she is pregnant. Hearing that her ne'er-do-well lover has got a job at a sawmill near Jefferson, she goes there and finds Byron Bunch and Joe Christmas. But Burch has left; as the story goes on, Lena has her child and at the end is still on the road, an example apparently of perpetual motion. Now she is accompanied not by Burch but by Bunch; which one accompanies her she seems to regard as a matter of indifference.

Meanwhile in a long and exhaustive flash-back we are told the history of Joe Christmas, an orphan and (as everyone including himself assumes) part Negro. We are told how Christmas murders Miss Burden, a descendant of New England abolitionists, and how he is caught, escapes, and is finally murdered himself in the Reverend Hightower's kitchen by Percy Grimm. We are also told a good deal about the life of Hightower, particularly how he ruined his career and lost his wife because of his fantasy of identification with his Confederate grandfather, an officer in the army who had been killed in Jefferson during the Civil War. As the story unfolds, Hightower is now an old man isolated from the world, but before he dies he gets more or less involved with Lena and Joe Christmas and serves rather loosely as the unifying figure and center of intelligence of the last sections of the novel. There are thus three separate strands of narrative in *Light in August*, each having its central character. The book makes a kind of triptych.

Lena Grove is one of those intensely female females we meet in Faulkner's books, like Eula Varner in *The Hamlet*. A somewhat bovine earth mother, she has all those womanly qualities which, as Faulkner likes to point out, baffle, fascinate, outrage, and finally defeat men. According to Faulkner's gynecological demonology (it constitutes a sort of Mississippi Manichaeism) men are more interesting and valuable than women but the dark or Satanic principle of the universe decrees that they are the weaker sex and are doomed to be frustrated and ephemeral. Faulkner appears to agree both with folk superstition and Henry Adams that compared with women men are in Adams's word "epiphenomenal."

The bovine woman brings to Faulkner's mind echoes of ancient myth and ritual (hence the name, Lena Grove . . .) and he treats her alternately with gravity and with a measure of humorously grandiose fantasy and mockery. Lena's placidity is not only that of the cow but unmistakably that of the gods in their eternity. Hence Faulkner has given her a ritual office by associating her with the religious procession depicted in Keats's "Ode on a Grecian Urn," a favorite poem of Faulkner of which there are several echoes in *Light in August*. In Lena's unvarying inner harmony (and here Faulkner is serious rather than mocking) all opposites and disparates are reconciled or perhaps rendered meaningless. In the words of Keats's poem, beauty is truth and truth beauty. By implying that Lena Grove somehow symbolizes this ideal unity Faulkner suggests no metaphysical reconciliation. He merely praises again the quiet enduring stoicism and wisdom of the heart which he finds among the poor whites, Negroes, and other socially marginal types.

The first thing to be said about Joe Christmas is that he is not a villain, as is sometimes thought. Nor, except in a distantly symbolic way, is he a tragic hero or a "Christ-figure." He has many of the qualities Faulkner admires. He suffers, he is a divided man, he is marginal and bereaved; he is "outraged." He asks merely to live, to share the human experience, and to be an individual. Like the slave in "Red Leaves," he "runs well"—he has in other words some power of giving his doomed life meaning by insisting as long as he can on his right to be human. All this outbalances his being a criminal. It even outbalances his being a murderer.

It is the custom of some traditionalist critics to say, in the words of one of them, that "sentimentalists and sociologists are bound to regard Christmas solely as a victim," whereas actually he is a tragic figure akin to Oedipus. But the main difference between Joe Christmas and Oedipus (or any other tragic hero in the full classic sense) is that Christmas really *is* a victim; he never has a chance, and a chance, or at least the illusion of a chance, a tragic hero must have. It is true that in *The Sound and the Fury* and perhaps elsewhere Faulkner achieves a genuine tragic vision of life and evokes the profound and harmonious emotions that tragedy evokes. But on the whole his vision of things is more akin to that of "sentimentalists and sociologists" than to that of Sophocles—if by this we mean that, like many modern novelists, he takes a rather darkly naturalistic view of things but finds a saving grace in the simplest sentiments of men. Joe Christmas, as Faulkner presents him, is a character conceived not in the manner of the tragedian but of the naturalistic novelist. There is no mystery, no disastrous choice, no noble action, no tragic recognition. Instead there are heredity, environment, neurotic causation, social maladjustment. What happens later to Joe Christmas is made inevitable by the circumstances of his boyhood in the orphanage. In fact one may be very specific about the origin of the train of causes. Christmas's life is given its definitive bias by his encounter with the dietitian, described near the beginning of Chapter 6. Hiding in a closet and eating toothpaste, he has seen the dietitian making illicit love. When she discovers this, Christmas expects, and *desires,* to be whipped. Instead she offers him a silver dollar:

> He was waiting to get whipped and then be released. Her voice went on, urgent, tense, fast: "A whole dollar. See? How much you could buy. Some to eat every day for a week. And next month maybe I'll give you another one."
> He did not move or speak. He might have been carven, as a large toy: small, still, round headed and round eyed, in overalls. He was still with astonishment, shock, outrage.

What the boy wants is recognition, acceptance as a human being, if only through physical punishment. A whipping would establish the passionate, human contact. Instead he is given a silver dollar, and he sees his doom in its adamant, abstract, circular form. He has now been given an irresistible compulsion to destroy every human relationship that he gets involved in. And this compulsion includes the suicidal desire to destroy himself.

Joe Christmas thus joins the long procession of isolated, doomed heroes that begin to appear in the American novel with Brockden Brown, Hawthorne, and Melville. This is not the place to discuss the complex picture of Protestantism that emerges from *Light in August*; yet one may note that in the isolation of Christmas (and others in the book) Calvinism is still strongly felt as an influence, despite the fact that the psychology Faulkner has applied is generally "Freudian," in the popular behavioristic sense. Apparently nothing appears to our American novelists to be more terrible than to have become isolated or to have fallen victim to a cold, abstract hatred of life—nor, we must admit, does any doom call forth a more spontaneous admiration or require a more arduous repudiation.

But if Christmas has his American ancestors, Faulkner has also made some attempt at modernizing him by making him in effect a Conradian or postromantic, existentialist hero. The portrait of Kurtz, the ultimately lost, rootless, and alienated man in Conrad's *Heart of Darkness*, is a distant model for Christmas. The Reverend Hightower, too, is a kind of Marlow (the narrator of Conrad's story), if only in the tone of his voice and in his physical appearance ("Hightower sits again in the attitude of an Eastern idol, between his parallel arms on the armrests of the chair"). And it is clear that Faulkner has learned some of his more florid rhetoric from Conrad. The following passage might have come from the pen of either Conrad or Faulkner; it is from *Heart of Darkness*:

> And in the hush that had fallen suddenly on the whole sorrowful land, the immense wilderness, the colossal body of the fecund and mysterious life seemed to look at her, pensive, as though it had been looking at the image of its own tenebrous and passionate soul.

This sort of thing has its own rhetorical magnificence, although both Conrad and Faulkner are perhaps a little too easily moved by the fecund, the pensive and the tenebrous. And there is no doubt that these authors—melodramatists both—tend to construct a rhetoric of doom and darkness in excess of what the occasion demands.

The Reverend Hightower is one of Faulkner's best characters. He appeals to us in many ways—first and most importantly in the sad everyday conditions of his life: the decaying house with the weather-beaten sign in front saying "Art Lessons Christmas Cards Photographs Developed"; the swivel chair in which he sits before the desk with the green shaded reading lamp as he gazes fixedly out the window; his moving colloquies with Byron Bunch, who, though his companion, is so different from him in heritage and intellect—as different as Sancho Panza is from Don Quixote (a parallel which is very much in Faulkner's mind). Only because Hightower is established in novelistic detail do we become interested in the fantastic obsession that has ruined his life. Like Quentin Compson and Horace Benbow (see *Sartoris* and *Sanctuary*), Hightower is one of Faulkner's intellectuals— he is fastidious, genteel, frightened by life. Haunted by the glory and crime of the past, he is incapable of living in the present. Like Quentin Compson he tries willfully to impose a kind of order on the irrational flow of time and nature. His view of things, however, is not metaphysical or theological like Quentin's; it is purely mythic and aesthetic, the product of a mind immersed in Keats and Tennyson. A careful reading of the pages at the end of Chapter 20 will show that Hightower does not return to his earlier Christian belief in his moment of ultimate insight before he dies. The turn of his mind is to grasp truth aesthetically; truth is for him an ecstatic perception of a supreme moment in the natural, historical order, a moment in which, to employ the Keatsian vocabulary Faulkner encourages us to use, beauty is grasped as truth and truth as beauty. Before he dies he sees the truth about himself—"I have not been clay"—which is merely a way of admitting finally that neither truth nor beauty can be perceived by the mind that remains inverted and solipsistic and denies man's common fate in nature and time. This is the truth that finally comes to Hightower; and it is what allows him to see for the first time, and pathetically for the last, the full beauty of the myth he has lived by. For a moment he can now be free, for the first time and the last. The progression of his views has thus taken him beyond his Christianity and his pure aestheticism to a full, profound, perhaps tragic naturalism (to use the word in its philosophical rather than strictly novelistic reference).

A good deal has been written about the symbolism of *Light in August,* and although much of this criticism has been predictably beside the main points, it remains true that this novel has in it a much more complicated symbolism than *The Sound and the Fury* or *As I Lay Dying.* The most obviously conscious and willed symbolism is the least successful—such as the attributes of Christ Faulkner associates with Joe Christmas; these have an artificial, inorganic, even an arty quality about them. The symbolism that seems most profoundly organic with the action and meaning of the book is that of the circle, and I would judge that, like any interesting symbol, this was half consciously intended by the author but has implications within the book of which he was probably not entirely conscious when he wrote it.

Three circles should be kept in mind; they are associated with the three main characters. Remembering the theme of solitude vs. society, alienation vs. community . . . in *As I Lay Dying,* we remember also that Faulkner spoke of Addie Bundren's aloneness as a circle that had to be violated in order to be made whole. Although this is a literary idea that Faulkner might have absorbed from many sources, among them Yeats, the symbol of the circle of selfhood may be taken as an archetype of the modern imagination, and especially wherever Puritanism has made itself felt. Lena Grove's circle, then, since she is a kind of earth goddess, is simply that of the death and renewal of nature. She is also associated with the urn of Keats's ode and the ritual procession of its encircling frieze. In the circle of her being truth and beauty are perpetually absorbed into each other. In Lena selfhood is whole; it is congruous with experience, with nature and with time.

The circle associated with Joe Christmas is the fatalistic, repetitive pattern of his life; in actual symbolization it varies from the silver dollar the dietician gives him to the pattern of his flight from the sheriff and his dogs. He wants, of course, to break out of his circle—"to define himself as human," in the words of Robert Penn Warren. Yet whenever this becomes possible, usually in relation to a woman he has become involved with, he succumbs to the irresistible compulsion to preserve his isolation. Finally, virtual suicide is the only solution. One might add that his circle is also racial; he is doomed to oscillate helplessly between the white world and the black.

If Christmas's imprisoning circle is imposed on him by circumstance, the Reverend Hightower's is imposed by himself, forged by his own intellect and neurotic fantasy. Only at the end when for a moment he is released from the isolation and stagnation of his life does the wheel that is a part of his obsessive fantasy finally spin free:

> The wheel whirls on. It is going fast and smooth now, because it is freed now of burden, of vehicle, axle, all. In the lambent suspension of August into which night is about to fully come, it seems to engender and surround itself with a faint glow like a halo. The halo is full of faces. The faces are not shaped with suffering, not shaped with anything: not horror, pain, not even reproach. They are peaceful, as though they have escaped into an apotheosis; his own is among them.

Despite the religious overtones of the language, this ultimate vision of Hightower seems to be a purely naturalistic intuition of his own solidarity with the other people he has known. It is this intuition that finally frees him.

The symbolism we have been noticing runs fairly deep, but it remains of the natural order, as, on the whole, does similar symbolism having to do with the self and its isolation in the writings of Hawthorne, Melville, and James. The specifically Christian symbolism in *Light in August* is not made deeply significant. It seems impossible to be much impressed with the fact that Faulkner calls one of his characters "Joe Christmas," and that he is thirty-three years old, has his feet votively bathed, and is in a manner crucified. The symbolism of the circle would certainly, if we had here a specifically Christian novel, include the traditional symbolism of death and the newborn spiritual life. But this central mystery of Christianity is not present. And *Light in August* reminds us that Faulkner's imagination is not characteristically stirred by incarnation, catharsis, and harmony, but rather by separation, alienation, and contradiction. If *Light in August* were a Christian novel it might use the symbolism of the book as it stands —the circle, the opposition of light and dark, and so on. But in some way it would have to employ the idea that life comes about *through* death, that in some way a new spiritual life had come to the community of Jefferson through the death of Joe Christmas. But this does not happen; there is no new life, no transfiguration anywhere that would not have occurred without Joe Christmas. There is no new religious consciousness or knowledge. In Joe Christmas we do not celebrate the death and rebirth of the hero.

Light and dark, good and evil, life and death, Eros and Thanatos are postulated in *Light in August* as eternal and autonomous contradictions. There is no possibility of absorbing and reconciling these contradictions in a whole view of life that is in any specific sense religious, or, for that matter, tragic. There are only two courses open: 1) to commit some transcendent act of horror or violence or suicide, 2) to find reattachment to the simple concrete conditions of life, through love, stoic patience, or humor, for in this way one may, as it were, temporarily step aside from the eternal contradictions in which humanity is involved and give the world the appearance of harmony.

The Shadow and the Mirror: *Light in August*

by Olga W. Vickery

Despite Faulkner's use of a clearly defined plot, *Light in August* is by no means a return to the traditional novel. Rather it constitutes his attempt to integrate certain experimental features of his earlier novels into a conventional narrative frame, thereby carrying one step further his use of structure to clarify theme. In both *The Sound and the Fury* and *As I Lay Dying* the public world serves merely as a frame for events which the reader is engaged in seeing from different perspectives. In *Light in August,* however, we are no longer concerned with examining the particular nature and limits of the individual consciousness but rather with its relation to other minds and to the public world of events, statements, and mass responses.

Because of the interpenetration and interdependence of the private and public worlds, each character is multidimensional. He is at once subject and object, observer and observed, creator and created. Thus, Joe Christmas as well as the Reverend Hightower and Joanna Burden are both self-crucified and crucified by others, both villain and victim. The interplay of these polar aspects of the human being produces much of the dramatic tension and the grotesque quality in the novel. There is a continual movement from one world to another, each with its own kind and degree of distortion. Depending upon who is acting as observer, this distortion provides a mirror image of the particular world of the observer or of the public world as represented by the town of Jefferson. In a sense, the individual and the community are obverse reflections of each other. Yet because the reflection is obverse, each fails to recognize himself, and so reacts with instinctive fear and

"The Shadow and the Mirror: Light in August." *From* The Novels of William Faulkner: A Critical Interpretation [*1959*], *rev. ed., by Olga W. Vickery (Baton Rouge: Louisiana State University Press, 1964), pp. 66–83. Reprinted with the permission of the publisher.*

anger which ultimately lead him to destroy his own image. In short, each is the victim of the other.

The nature of the private world and its relation to others is indicated by a threefold pattern of interlocking imagery—the circle, the shadow, and the mirror. All the main characters in *Light in August* are strangers to Jefferson and they remain strangers no matter how long their stay or how deep their roots. Their isolation is suggested by the image of the circle which achieves its clearest expression and greatest significance in the episode of Joe Christmas' flight and his sudden realization: "It had been a paved street, where going should be fast. It had made a circle and he is still inside of it. . . . 'And yet I have been farther in these seven days than in all the thirty years,' he thinks. 'But I have never got outside that circle.' " (296) In the midst of that jostling, noisy intercourse which is society and to which all men contribute, each is alone, unable to break through the circumference of his own circle or to admit anyone into it. Because of the solipsistic quality of the private world, each individual sees others and is himself seen as a shadow, ghostlike and unreal. Walking the streets of Jefferson, Joe Christmas, for example, looks like "a phantom, a spirit, strayed out of its own world, and lost." (99) The images of the circle and the shadow are linked in the description of Byron Bunch and Brown, passing "one another as though on opposite orbits and with an effect as of phantoms or apparitions." (386) It is Hightower, however, who extends the insight provided by these images with his recognition that other people are simply "mirrors in which he watches himself." (427)

Yet no matter how isolated and impenetrable the private world of an individual, he still has a physical and social existence in the public world which makes its demands of him. His comfort, if not his life, depends on his accepting and exemplifying in his own life those stereotypes which represent society's vision of itself and its past. And since withdrawal or rebellion are as much public acts as is affirmation, no one can escape. Society has myths not only of the hero but also of the antagonist, and it has evolved rituals to deal with each. Collectively, Jefferson is Southern, White, and Elect, qualities which have meaning only within a context which recognizes something or someone as Northern or Black or Damned. This antithesis is periodically affirmed through the sacrifice of a scapegoat who represents, in fact or popular conviction, those qualities which must be rejected if Jefferson is to maintain its self-defined character.

Miss Burden, Hightower, and Christmas serve as such scapegoats and serve willingly, almost eagerly, since they too have accepted the absolute necessity and validity of the dichotomies in whose names they are destroyed. Thus, Miss Burden, despite her birth in Jefferson, is a "Northerner" in the eyes of the town, and hence she is automatically aligned with the "Negro" and the "Damned." Hightower, on the other hand, offends not by being a Northerner but by refusing to play the role of "Reverend" in the manner established by custom and tradition. He becomes "Gail Hightower Done Damned in Jefferson." (52) This judgment is then in part justified and in part explained by the town's accusation of Hightower's unnatural relationship with a Negress. Out of this judgment his ritualistic punishment by masked men and his ostracism follow inevitably. Joe Christmas, of course, represents the third category, that of the Negro, and it is this assumption that predetermines the manner of his pursuit and lynching. But at the same time he constitutes an omnipresent threat to all categories: he cannot say with certainty whether he is Negro or white; he is a Southerner with too many Northern ideas; and he seems quite indifferent to salvation or damnation.

Accordingly, Christmas has a dual function in the novel. As an individual, he explores his own relation to the myth of the Negro, while as a part of society, he is identified with the myth. Through his oscillation between repudiation and affirmation of his black blood, he reveals his own uncertainty and his need to resolve the dilemma posed to him by the old Negro gardener: " 'You dont know what you are. And more than that, you wont never know. You'll live and you'll die and you wont never know.' " (336) He is obsessed with the idea that he must choose, yet his every action emphasizes his inability to do so. In the world of Jefferson, however, after Brown's accusation has taken root, he is treated as if he were in actual fact a Negro. The varying responses, ranging from Gavin Stevens' cool, impersonal analysis to Gail Hightower's anguished sympathy to the mob's violence, are directed at the concept of the Negro with which he is identified. Inescapably Joe is forced into the ritual of pursuit and lynching performed almost casually by a society which has been elaborating it for generations.

The basis of this pattern is Jefferson's conviction that the individual can only become a member of society by permitting himself to be classified according to race, color, geographic origin, and so on. Created by man, these categories become creators of man insofar as they establish social identification as the necessary prerequisite to human existence. The sheer weight of generations, each in its turn conforming to and therefore affirming this process of public labelling, establishes the labels not only as a matter of tradition but as a kind of revealed truth. What starts as a verbal pattern of classification thus becomes a social order not to be challenged or changed. And what starts as a category becomes a myth, for certainly the word "Negro" is a compressed myth just as the stock response to that word is a compressed ritual. The result is that men like Joe Christmas or Velery Bon, who can neither fit nor be fitted into these categories, are either sacrificed to or driven out of the society whose cherished beliefs they threaten.

Certainly there is no one set of categories which can claim Christmas or be claimed by him. He is indeed the "disaccommodated man," with "something definitely rootless about him, as though no town nor city was his, no street, no walls, no square of earth his home." (27) Yet he cannot ignore the concept of race which assigns men to one of two separate worlds, each with its traditions and modes of thinking and acting. The irony of Joe's position is that what seems to be a choice is in reality a delusion: Negro or white—to choose one is to affirm the existence of the other. His awareness of this dichotomy makes him take up the role of antagonist in all situations. In the presence of whites he becomes Negro; among Negroes he feels himself to be white. The result is that series of tensions and conflicts for which he himself is at least partly responsible. The Joe Christmas who is finally lynched as "Negro" is the joint creation of his private world and of the larger public universe.

In this respect Mrs. Hines's account of his birth becomes significant, for it reveals that Joe is born into a myth created for him by others. Since Millie's pregnancy is considered an unforgivable sin by Hines, he looks for a scapegoat who will bear the guilt and punishment. By calling her lover a "nigger," he can transform a commonplace seduction into the horror of miscegenation. That is his justification, moral and religious, for the brutally inhuman treatment of his daughter, her lover, and her child. His reasons for regarding Christmas with malevolence and hatred remain personal, but his actions and statements help formulate that confused and violent myth which is Joe's particular agony. His brooding watchfulness having isolated Joe from the other children at the orphanage, Hines then provides the three year old with an explanation: " 'Why dont you play with them other children like you used to? . . . Is it because they call you nigger?' " (335) The awareness of something strange or different about Joe is thus simultaneously impressed on Joe and on others.

The identification of Joe with Negro receives additional and unexpected support from the dietitian. Surprised in the midst of her clandestine love affair, she lashes out at Joe calling him a "little rat" and a "little nigger bastard." In the days of frenzied uncertainty and fear which follow, she links the carelessly spoken invective with Hines's attitudes and with the meaningless taunts of the children. Though she had never considered Joe to be a Negro, "she believed that she had, had known it all the while, because it seemed so right: he would not only be removed; he would be punished for having given her terror and worry." (113) At cross purposes, each speaking a strange, private language, and each motivated by personal reasons, the dietitian and Hines, nevertheless, combine to extend and intensify Joe's awareness of himself as a different kind of being and to force the matron to act on the assumption that he is indeed a Negro.

Although the "taint" of Negro blood is never revealed to McEachern, Joe himself is imbued with its possibility. For a time, however, it lies quiescent in his consciousness while he endeavors to assimilate yet another aspect of his life. To the social pattern of black and white, the implications of which he is yet to realize, is added the religious pattern of the elect and the damned. His vague, emotional response to God is replaced by the creed and discipline of a particular church. And the spiritual relationship of father and son is submerged in an intricate and deadly game of good and evil, reward and punishment. McEachern's religious discipline is accepted eagerly by Joe because it makes his life completely predictable, relieving him of the necessity for self-judgment and responsibility. Accordingly, he rejects Mrs. McEachern's awkward and uncertain attempts to establish a more purely human relationship with him.

Ultimately, however, he seeks and finds such a relationship in his love for Bobbie, the waitress. It is this love which prompts him to rebel against McEachern's Calvinistic ritual of confession and penance and to resist the customary punishment which McEachern seeks to inflict on him at the dance. But this achievement is short-lived, for Bobbie's later shrieks of rage signal the destruction of the last of Joe's natural, spontaneous emotions. Her betrayal, which impels him into the long, lonely street of his life, is not only sexual but religious and racial, for all three are involved in the idea of miscegenation into which their affair is suddenly transformed. So long as their affair proves satisfactory and trouble free, Bobbie simply ignores Joe's confession that " 'I think I got some nigger blood in me.' " (171) In a moment of crisis, however, and in order to save herself, she, like the dietitian, finds it convenient not only to believe but to act upon that belief. All blame, all possible punishment is shifted to Joe as "Negro" who significantly enough has himself provided the material for this accusation. Suddenly conscious of her white blood, Bobbie has no compunctions about abandoning a "nigger" whom she had naively mistaken for a white man nor about watching that "nigger" beaten senseless by her friends.

The beating establishes the antithesis of black and white in Joe's own physical experience and thereby intensifies his awareness of it. His life becomes a series of episodes in which he provokes racial violence from Negro and white alike, a violence which constitutes an almost joyful affirmation of the Negro-white pattern in which both Joe and his opponents are trapped. That someone could simply ignore that pattern fills him with an indignant amazement and outrage. He beats the prostitute who refuses to be horrified by his Negro blood, thus forcing her to initiate that ritual of violence which he expects. His reaction is understandable, for her indifference challenges the validity of the premise on which he has built his whole life. Whether or not he himself is a Negro may remain in doubt, but that there is something called Negro which demands certain attitudes and actions on the part of all white people must not be denied.

During his relationship with Joanna Burden, Joe's preoccupation with such categories becomes especially acute since he recognizes the same obsession in her. In fact, her concern with racial, geographical, and religious myths serves as a complement and antithesis to his own. Not even their frenzied and insatiable love-making can destroy their ingrained awareness of what each believes the other to represent. While her body surrenders completely to his, Joanna still mutters "Negro! Negro! Negro!" And Joe, on his way to her bedroom, still pauses to smash the dishes of food prepared by the white woman and left for him in the kitchen. Thus, even miscegenation is powerless to erase their concern with racial differences and indeed serves only to intensify it.

Joe's wild hope, as he holds her letter in his hand, that they can escape from their own preconceptions into a world where " 'She is still she and I am still I' " (238) is doomed from its very inception. For what he visualizes is a return to the natural world where the only meaningful categories are male and female and the only meaningful relationship is sexual. But Joanna, her physical need for him exhausted, demands of him that choice which he has spent his whole life evading. She insists that he ignore his uncertainty and accept once and for all the role of Negro as modified by the North together with that of repentant sinner. The violence between them is inevitable, but signifi-

cantly it is both impersonal and unimpassioned. Joanna's act of raising the pistol and Joe's use of the razor are both projected as shadows
against the wall—phantom weapons directed at phantom opponents.
For each sees embodied in the other that racial myth which has dominated their lives and which they must destroy if they are to be free.

Yet in the very act of gaining his freedom, Joe loses it. The act of
murder leaves him vulnerable to society's judgments and actions. The
fire at Miss Burden's and her decapitated body generate a tension in
the milling crowd which needs only the proper spark to explode it into
violence. That spark is supplied by Brown, a man whose parentage is
as obscure as Joe's own. The pattern made familiar by Hines, the
dietitian, and Bobbie is repeated as the cry of "Negro" and the suggestion of miscegenation channel the restless and undirected energy
of the observers away from the accuser. Three times Brown repeats
" 'Accuse the white man and let the nigger go free' " until the crowd
grasps the significance of that contrast and prepares itself for action.
Once he pronounces the word "Negro," the actual guilt of Joe Christmas, the circumstances, and the motivation, all become irrelevant, for
the connection between "Negro" and "murder" is part of the public
myth. At the same time Joanna Burden loses all individuality, becoming simply a white woman and hence an innocent victim who must be
avenged. Accusation, conviction, and punishment constitute a single
simultaneous belief-act as "Joe, the son of Joe" becomes Joe, the son of
a Negro.

The compelling nature of the pattern evoked by Brown is indicated
by the fact that no one thinks to question his premise. The mob is, of
course, wholly absorbed in the idea of revenge, but even those who
sympathize with Joe never doubt that he is a Negro. Though he has
ample evidence of Brown's character, Byron still takes his word and in
his turn convinces Hightower. The intense shock felt by the latter is
occasioned by his sickening realization that a public myth is once more
demanding its victim, that the ritualistic sequence of the chase, the
pursuit, and the final immolation is now inevitable. Even the cos-
mopolitan Gavin Stevens, with his Harvard and Heidelberg studies behind him, is not able to see Joe Christmas except through a filter of
preconceptions. Though he recognizes that Hines is quite mad, he,
nevertheless, accepts his contention that Joe's father was actually a
Negro. More important: despite his disinterested rationalism and objectivity, he assigns definite though arbitrary moral values to black and
white blood, claiming that it was the former which made Joe strike
Hightower and the latter which enabled him to die heroically.

As these stock reactions and attitudes crystallize in Jefferson, Joe Christmas himself is able if only temporarily to escape their coercive pressure. At the outset he is still sufficiently obsessed with the fictions he has spent his life affirming through endless challenges to pause in a Negro church. Standing in the pulpit and cursing God, he assumes, possibly in his own mind and certainly in the minds of the congregation, the terrifying form of anti-Christ. But the body's need for food and rest erases all the illusions that the mind creates and perpetuates. The stage beyond, where even food becomes unnecessary, gives to Christmas the human dignity all his violence could not seize. For the first time, he sees his life not in terms of "black" and "white" but simply of the human race. Inevitably his new found awareness of himself as man causes him to be rejected by both the Negroes and the whites. Negro fear is balanced by white outrage at the fact that " 'He never acted like either a nigger or a white man. That was it. That was what made the folks so mad.' " (306)

Ironically, as Christmas transcends the categories of black and white and of good and evil, thus resolving his own personal dilemma, he is once more forced to exemplify them in the sequence of flight and pursuit, capture and death, begun by his own act of murder but given shape by Brown's accusation of "nigger." Dazedly he half-comprehends that he has given himself up to the public world by his act and that he can no longer refuse the role it has given him to play. Since he is a "nigger" murderer, each gesture, even each emotion which he is permitted to feel, is already established. Sardonically he reflects on his unsuccessful attempts to give himself up: " 'Like there is a rule to catch me by, and to capture me that way would not be like the rule says.' " (294) As Christmas recognizes the inevitability of this pattern and of his own part in it, he visualizes himself sinking "at last into the black abyss which had been waiting, trying, for thirty years to drown him and into which now and at last he had actually entered, bearing now upon his ankles the definite and ineradicable gauge of its upward moving." (289) Significantly, he becomes aware of the borrowed shoes as a symbol of his acceptance of "the black abyss" only when he is in the wagon on his way to Mottstown to give himself up and thus to assume the role of Negro which Jefferson has prepared for him.

It is, then, as "Negro" that Christmas is lynched in a scene that echoes and intensifies all the earlier acts of his life. In the "cloistral dimness" of Hightower's house Christmas resembles "a vengeful and furious god pronouncing a doom" (406) on the men whose "faces seemed to glare with bodiless suspension as though from haloes." (405)

Saints and sinners, the elect and the damned, the victim and the persecutors become strangely confused with one another. Through Percy Grimm, the "young priest" of the occasion, the elect and white of Jefferson castrate and slay the Negro according to ancient custom, but instead of purification, they are left with a sense of their own guilt and self-doubt. Through his castration, Christmas finally does escape society's categories. Having made him a "Negro" in order to crucify him, society, by its own passion for affirming the reality of its myths in actual living experience, in the end explodes both those myths and the categories out of which they were evolved. It is no longer the Negro murderer or even Joe Christmas but simply "the man" who rises "soaring into their memories forever and ever." (407)

In the moment of Christmas' death, then, there occurs a final violent fusion of the public and private myths of the "Negro," a fusion developing out of the interaction of these myths as charted in the actual chronological sequence of the novel. Moreover, in the process of unfolding this interaction the chronological sequence has shown the gradual identification of the individual, Joe Christmas, with this public myth. Through Joanna Burden and Gail Hightower that identification is given historical perspective, not only because they themselves are conscious of the historical origins of the particular myths which dominate Joe Christmas and themselves alike, but because they have virtually stopped living in the public world where their beliefs might be modified by further interaction. At the same time they represent the two remaining categories, one geographical and the other religious, in terms of which the South establishes its identity. The Negro, the Yankee, the Apostate—these are the key figures in a society which defines itself by exclusion.

Like Joe Christmas, Joanna Burden presents an obverse reflection of one aspect of the South. For though she is excluded from the community as a Northerner, she too is obsessed with the myth of the Negro. Despite the apparently irreconcilable opposition of their attitudes which led them to actual war, both North and South are concerned with the problem of the Negro, a concern which gives form and substance to a concept but which takes no cognizance of individuals as individuals. In both, this concept, bolstered by the legends of history as seen from their own particular perspective, engenders a set pattern of beliefs and actions. Eventually, these acts and beliefs involving the "Negro" are transformed into a kind of religion, a distorted version of Calvinism in which black and white replace or are identified with evil and good. Each holding this extreme view, Joanna Burden, the scion of New England, is scarcely distinguishable from McEachern or even Hines.

Joanna's increasing awareness of this myth parallels Joe's, though without his tormenting uncertainty as to his own relationship to it. As a child, she simply accepts that fact that certain people have darker skins than her own. But this innocence or naïveté is not permitted to continue. Her father, Nathaniel Burden, slowly transforms the physical black and white she sees into a moral and religious order. She is made aware of "Negro" " 'not as people, but as a thing, a shadow in which [she] lived, we lived, all white people, all other people.' " (221) The shadow becomes a "black cross" to which she is a martyr, a phantom priestess immolating herself on a phantom altar. Consequently, her whole life is devoted to perpetuating and giving substance to a metaphor: " 'You must struggle, rise. But in order to rise, you must raise the shadow with you.' " (222)

To this belief in her martyrdom, Joanna Burden sacrifices all her natural impulses, thereby creating a bifurcated individual. Thus, Joe sees her as "a dual personality: the one the woman at first sight of whom in the lifted candle . . . there had opened before him, instantaneous as a landscape in a lightningflash, a horizon of physical security and adultery if not pleasure; the other the mantrained muscles and the mantrained habit of thinking born of heritage and environment with which he had to fight up to the final instant." (205) His entrance into her life signals an overt conflict between these two aspects of her being. The sex-starved body conquers for a time "the mantrained habit of thinking" and expresses itself in a desperate and imperious need to experience every possible sensation and every possible emotion that physical love can suggest. Acting out of a world of fantasies, she quickly passes "through every avatar of a woman in love": (226) the lover's pursuit, secret trysts, baseless accusations and jealousy, seduction, and even rape.

Yet even in the midst of these exaggerated manifestations of her long suppressed desires, she is not entirely free of her intellectual heritage. She can only seek to postpone its mastery over her: " 'Don't make me have to pray yet. Dear God, let me be damned a little longer, a little while.' " (231) The implicit identification of sex with sin prepares the way for the corruption of her relationship with Joe and for her own final perversion in which he ceases to be the means of satisfying her physical demands and comes to symbolize the sexual superstitions associated with the Negro. In this last phase, she is not having intercourse with a man but with an image of her own creation, with the idea of "Negro" for which she has given up her life. Accordingly, she emerges from the affair with her instincts once more subdued and with her obsessions once more crystallized and intensified.

No longer driven by her desire to sin, Joanna is left free to brood over the fact that she has sinned. In retrospect she naturally sees all the facets of her relationship with Christmas in the light of her old "man-trained habits of thinking" and the result is a reaffirmation of Calvinism and rededication of herself to the black cross. Nor can she leave Christmas alone, for he is the Negro, the symbol of her responsibility, her sin and damnation, and most important, her salvation. Her pleading, bribes, and threats are her attempt to make him translate into living flesh and act her concept of the Negro. He is to ignore his own uncertainty, admit his black blood, his sinfulness, and his dependence for salvation on her and her God. Joe's refusal to submit himself to that formula threatens that myth for the sake of which she has continued to draw breath. She reacts to his recalcitrance, as the mob does later, by resorting to violence. Ironically the transformation of Joe Christmas into a Negro which she does not accomplish in her life is effected through her death.

Gail Hightower is, of course, rejected by Jefferson because he has proved himself unworthy of directing its religious, spiritual life. Like Joe Christmas and Joanna Burden, he is an impure element of which society must purge itself; and like them, he too mirrors yet another aspect of the South: its preoccupation with the legends of its own past. The exploits of the gallant Confederate forces are part of the inheritance of every Southern boy as well as an article in the belief of every Southern community. Such legends, provided they are accepted as legends, remain as valuable and harmless as the stories of Charlemagne. Hightower, however, sees a kind of revealed truth in the vision of his grandfather, compounded of an old Negress' storytelling and his own boyish imagination. The imagination is given full scope because there is nothing and no one to contradict his fictions. With an equal opportunity for deifying his father who also had a share in the glorious war, young Gail is unable to place the mantle of heroism on his shoulders. Thus, the dead grandfather becomes the symbol of "that fine shape of eternal youth and virginal desire which makes heroes," (423) while the living father evokes only the grim brutality and carnage of battle.

Eventually the legends of the past become the only truth and the only reality for Hightower, rendering his connection with the public world precarious at best. For unlike his father, he cannot function as "two separate and complete people, one of whom dwelled by serene rules in a world where reality did not exist." (415) And since nothing can compare with his vision, the people he meets and the tasks he is forced to perform become annoying interruptions of the commonplace and trivial. What destroys Hightower is not the fact that he has a dream, but that for the sake of the dream, he becomes insensitive and indifferent to the quality of his actual experience. Thus, he ignores his wife and her needs because the affection due her has already been pre-empted by her counterpart so that "when he did see her he did not see her at all because of the face which he had already created in his mind." (420) Dominated by his vision, he stands in the pulpit, fusing religion, the galloping cavalry, and his dead grandfather into one incoherent rhapsody, while he remains sublimely indifferent to the growing uneasiness of his parish and to the suicide of his wife.

As if recognizing that he has no place in Jefferson, that indeed his dream-world is threatened by it, Hightower deliberately provokes the violence which will ensure his isolation. For he can only justify and safeguard his withdrawal by "making it appear that he was being driven, uncomplaining, into that which he did not even then admit had been his desire since before he entered the seminary." (428) Each of his actions becomes a defiance, a calculated incentive to public outrage and retribution. Thus he, like Christmas, is at least partially responsi-ble for his own isolation and for the violence he suffers. In his self-chosen role of antagonist, he experiences a fierce exultation, momen-tarily revealed by his demonic grin hidden by the prayer book. As passive victim, he suffers the threats and beating by the K.K.K. "with that patient and voluptuous ego of the martyr," (429) since it merely confirms his contemptuous judgment of society.

Safe at last in his lonely house, unvisited and undisturbed, High-tower yet retains one tenuous connection with the external world in the person of Byron Bunch. And it is Byron who ultimately forces him to re-examine his world and his life. Compelled by Byron to attend the birth of Lena's child, he becomes for the occasion a participant in rather than a spectator of life. But more important, through the birth he is initiated into the world of nature and discovers that life itself is a source of human value. Reversing his former opinion of Lena, he sees her as a symbol of life and a new paradise: *"That will be her life, her destiny. The good stock peopling in tranquil obedience to it the good earth."* (356)

Byron's plea that he at least attempt to save Joe Christmas is much more difficult to deal with. For though Hightower is willing to accept the natural world, he is not prepared to re-enter the social world. From the moment he hears of Christmas' Negro blood and of the murder, he knows beyond any doubt the sequence of events which must culminate in violence and death. He knows because he himself had been caught in a similar pattern. And though he feels pity, compassion even horror, he waits passively for the mob to turn once more "with insult and violence upon those who like them were created by the same God and were driven by them to do that which they now turn and rend them for having done it." (319–20) To interfere with the beliefs and rituals of society would be to admit his responsibility for that society. It would, in effect, expose the futility of a life devoted solely to the worship of a dream and to a world "intact and on all sides complete and inviolable, like a classic and serene vase, where the spirit could be born anew sheltered from the harsh gale of living." (419)

Nevertheless, when the escaped and fleeing Christmas rushes into his house, Hightower does make the one gesture which could give substance to his vision. Ironically, this one fumbling but heroic attempt to save Christmas at the risk of his own life, this one act which so far transcends practical considerations that it contains the germ of another legend, is nullified by a younger version of himself. Percy Grimm, engrossed in his own vision of military gallantary which has been fostered by a more recent war, sees nothing in Hightower's words but another example of the degrading crudeness of the non-military world. Too much has happened to Hightower and to Jefferson since the day he abandoned his chosen calling for him to be able to sway or influence the lynch-mob in any way. The past is irremediable.

Jarred out of his complacency and self-righteousness by Joe's death, Hightower sees his past with a new clarity. The image of the great wheel, which gives form to his memories, echoes and passes judgment on all the other solitary circles that have collided violently without ever establishing contact with one another. What he finally comes to recognize is the interdependence of the individual and society, of the private and public worlds, and, more important, the interdependence of individuals within the public world. He, Joe Christmas, and Joanna Burden have all been self-created martyrs to an idea and to that idea they have sacrificed others beyond themselves. Society, no less deluded, attacks and sacrifices them in the name of the same ideas. Their personal histories, like the history of Jefferson, consist of a perpetual denial of life for the sake of empty rituals, each of which enshrines some abstraction. Hightower has the intelligence to attain this bitter self-knowledge and to realize that the responsibility rests with the individual, but he does not have the strength to live with it. As his head falls to the window sill, he hears once again the thunderous cavalry charge peopling Jefferson with the old insubstantial phantoms.

Compared with the embattled lives and specter-haunted thoughts of Hightower, Christmas, and Miss Burden, the calm journey of Lena Grove with a willing Byron Bunch in her wake seems almost an impertinence. Yet it is through her presence that we achieve a final perspective on the action. Into the schematic world of Jefferson she introduces, by virtue of her own intellectual limitations and her pregnancy, the world of nature with its total indifference to both moral and social categories. This provides a significant contrast to Joe Christmas' painful initiation and absorption into society. Both are strangers to Jefferson; but while Joe comes bearing death for himself and others, Lena comes bearing life. The ritual in which she involves others is the natural one of pregnancy and birth. Thus, while the one crystallizes the obsessions of society, the other dispels them. The same almost anonymous figures who attach the label of Negro to Christmas in order to lynch him also forget the social stigma of Lena's pregnancy in order to help her.

Like Joe Christmas, Lena herself is a center for the actions and reactions of various characters and the object of a clearly defined public attitude. Each person she meets sees not her but an image of what he believes her to be, and that image is at least partly predetermined by the convention that identifies virginity with virtue. For Mrs. Armstid she is the fallen woman; for the men at the store, a foolish virgin to be treated with mingled pity and scorn; and for Byron, who loves her, she is the innocent victim of a scoundrel. Each of these images, grounded in a concern with Lena's unmarried state, conveys more information about the observers and their society than they do about her, for unlike Christmas, she does not mirror or share the preconceptions of the community. From the moment we see her delicately licking the sardine oil from her fingers, she is wholly absorbed in the new sensations with which her leisurely travels provide her. Even her search for a father for her child is more a matter of instinct than of morality. What she is looking for is security not respectability. Once Byron assumes this responsibility, she shows no great haste to marry and so to remove the social stigma from herself and her child.

Though Lena is judged harshly, she is consistently treated with kindness. The reason is that she offends against the mores of society without challenging its very foundations as Joe Christmas does. In a sense, the community's convictions and actions operate independently. Mrs. Armstid or the men who offer Lena a ride preserve the myth of virginity in which they share by revealing their contempt for the unmarried Lena, but at the same time they respond to her needs as a woman about to give birth to a child. Here the pressing demands of nature take precedence over social convention.

Thus Lena's arrival signals the breaking up of the old compulsive patterns which match action to judgment. Mrs. Armstid's tight-lipped offer of food, shelter, and money prepares us for Byron's quick abandonment of his routine of overtime work and weekly trips to the country church when Lena appears. He too acts "contrary to all the tradition of his austere and jealous country raising which demands in the object physical inviolability." (42) It is not, however, until Mrs. Hines calls him to the cabin where Lena is in labor that he fully realizes and admits to himself that she is not a virgin. Hightower, despite his distrust of Lena and his fear of Byron, disrupts the pattern of his life and leaves his sanctuary to attend the birth of her child. The sheriff, momentarily overlooking the letter of the law, recognizes her need and therefore her right to use Miss Burden's cottage. Even the anonymous truck driver is trapped into kindness towards Lena and gives up his bed, though not the right to grumble about it.

In each of these cases, the separation of judgment and action is made possible by Lena's own indifference to the former. The relationship between society and the individual is reciprocal as the lives of Hightower, Miss Burden, and Christmas amply illustrate. But Lena refuses or rather is incapable of acting in the light of society's preconception of her. Accordingly, where Joe Christmas intensifies, she destroys the barriers between herself and others; where he forever threatens life with extinction, she becomes the means of its renewal and continuance. This difference is made explicit by the incidents involving food. Lena herself is indifferent to the spirit in which it is offered so long as it sustains her and her child. And her acceptance of it invariably fosters a more personal, human relationship with the giver. Christmas, on the other hand, is forever rejecting the food offered him because of his abnormal sensitivity to the thoughts and attitudes of the giver. He is able to share food with Bobbie, believing that she loves him, but he consistently rejects meals offered by Mrs. McEachern, Byron Bunch, or Miss Burden. The food which sustains Lena in her world of physical experience proves poisonous to Christmas, who lives largely in a world of obsessive ideas which he projects, rightly or wrongly, into every situation. Joe and Lena thus present two contrasting attitudes to experience and to society, and these in turn evoke sharply different responses from society.

Both make a claim on Byron Bunch, the one uncommitted character in the novel, since he has isolated himself from both nature and society. But it is his love for Lena and his sudden and unexpected initiation into the world of nature which she represents that makes Byron willing and eager to help Christmas. Her needs destroy those protective barriers of meaningless routine which he has built around himself. As Hightower points out, Byron, by loving her, becomes vulnerable, for he has allowed himself to be caught up in a chain of events and circumstances over which he can exercise no control. At the same time, however, he has gained in some measure a self-respect, a dignity, and a courage which was lacking in his isolated safety and which gives promise of being a sufficient shield against whatever catastrophes he may encounter. His romantic desire to protect Lena, to convert Hightower, and to save Christmas appear, at first sight, exaggerated reactions to his former passivity and belief in non-inter-ference. But the important thing is that he does not rest in these attitudes or treat his vision of Lena as immutable. He is still neces-sarily the creator of his own world, but now he is willing to recognize when he has built awry and to reshape it with an eye to reality.

His ability to do so is dependent, to a large extent, on his eventual discovery of the resources of humor. His love for Lena, itself an irra-tional act, makes him realize the comic aspect of his own behavior. By laughing at his own follies and gullibility, he is able to continue acting irrationally which, in this case, is also humanely; for laughter is one means of re-examining the shibboleths of society and of placing the individual and his world once more in perspective. Though Byron is still sustained by illusions, he is no longer blindly ruled by them. Instead he endeavors through them to establish his kinship with other men. Though he continues to believe in Lena's chastity, Hightower's wisdom, and Joe's black blood, nevertheless, he arranges for the con-finement, argues for the first time with Hightower, and does what little he can to help Joe. His illusions are thus more nearly centered on humanity and grounded in the immediacy of living experience. It is man's nature to dream and dreams by their very essence are both distortions of reality and desires for a new shape to experience.

Certainly, the real Lena, more than slightly stupid and more than slightly selfish, and the real Confederate Hightower, who found an inglorious death in a chickencoop, are both unworthy of the dreams and the devotion they inspire. The responsibility, however, lies not with them but with the Byron Bunches and Gail Hightowers who can be moved to save or to deny Joe Christmas because of their dreams. Reason and imagination can prove an integrative force, identifying the interest of the individual with those of the community and establishing a link between the private and public worlds. They can also be destructive insofar as they enable man to invent infinitely various excuses which permit him to live while ignoring life itself. Rationally conceived categories and myths may render morality simpler and clearer by providing formulas of universal applicability, but in the process they destroy those essential motives for morality which must be found by the individual in life itself. This is the truth that Hightower could only know; it is also the truth which Byron, in fumbling and often farcically inadequate fashion, seeks to live.

Frozen Movement in *Light in August*

by Darrel Abel

I. Symbol

Faulkner's *Light in August* does not (except within the arbitrary perspective of any given character in the novel) delineate a single complete action with a beginning, a middle, and an end. For Faulkner's reality, like Bergson's, is a "becomingness"—not static, but dynamic; not formed, but fluid. To Faulkner, "The present does not exist, it becomes. . . . "[1] According to Bergson, "Reality is mobility. There do not exist *things* made, but only things in the making, not *states* that remain fixed, but only states in process of change."[2]

A writer . . . escape[s] from the static and particular into the vital and general . . . [through] the poetic faculty alluded to in "Tintern Abbey," by which "the heavy and the weary weight / Of all this unintelligible world is lightened" and "We see into the life of things." . . . [In short, the poet's] technique must master a paradox: in order to fix reality in a literary construct, it must freeze movement. "Faulkner appears to arrest the motion at the very heart of things; moments

---

"Frozen Movement in Light in August*" by Darrel Abel. From* Boston University Studies in English, *III (1957), 32–44. Condensed and reprinted with the permission of the author and the publisher.*

[1] Jean-Paul Sartre, "Time in Faulkner: *The Sound and the Fury*," trans. Martine Darmon, in Frederick J. Hoffman and Olga W. Vickery, *William Faulkner: Two Decades of Criticism* (East Lansing, Michigan: Michigan State College Press, 1954), p. 183. Reprinted from *Situations,* I, "Le Bruit et la fureur" (Paris: Gallimard, 1947), pp. 70–81.

[2] Quoted by permission of the publishers, The Philosophical Library, from Henri Bergson, *The Creative Mind,* trans. Mabelle L. Andison (New York: The Philosophical Library, 1946), p. 222. All subsequent quotations cited by page numbers enclosed in parentheses in the text refer to this edition.

erupt and freeze, then fade, recede and diminish, still motionless." [3] . . .

In *Light in August* Faulkner attempts to contrive through symbols an immobile representation of mobility, and at the same time to suggest how "relative" and arbitrary any distinct and arranged version of mobile reality must be. He endeavors to represent a fluid reality in the static terms "necessary to common sense, to language, to practical life"; and at the same time to disclose that the static images through which he makes the fluid reality visible are merely arrested and discontinuous blinks—what Bergson calls "snapshots" or "cuttings made out of the becoming" (pp. 227, 222, 39).

Such a symbolic shuttering of reality controls the narration from the opening pages, which offer an image, immediately augmented into a symbol,[4] of the mule-drawn country wagons in which Lena Grove made her enchanted, ineluctable progress from Alabama into Mississippi; "back-rolling now behind her a long monotonous succession of peaceful and undeviating changes from day to dark and dark to day again, through which she advances in identical and monotonous and deliberate wagons as though through a succession of creak-wheeled and limp-eared avatars, like something moving forever and without progress across an urn." [5]

In this figure the countryside across which Lena travels is, like the "silent form" of Keats's urn,[6] a designated image or visible metaphor of eternity. The stories of Lena Grove and Joe Christmas constitute the "legend" (or "brede" or "frieze") seen against this immutable image of eternity. A legend is both an inscription and an old story, especially an "old story" in the colloquial sense of something happening over and

[3] Sartre, "Time in Faulkner," p. 182.

[4] I use the terms "image," "symbol," and "figure" in this paper in the different senses which I think they usually carry: "image"—a distinct, unified sense-impression of an object; "symbol"—an image which is the nucleus and sign of a congeries of not readily explicable meanings and sensations; "figure"—pattern or design, possibly a configuration of images in time or space; also, any kind of trope.

[5] Quoted by permission of the publishers, Random House, from William Faulkner, *Light in August* (New York: Modern Library, 1950), Chap. I. All subsequent quotations cited by chapter numbers enclosed in parentheses in the text refer to this book.

[6] For more explicit allusions by Faulkner to Keats's "Ode to a Grecian Urn" which show how persistently Keats's urn-symbol has haunted Faulkner's imagination, see Faulkner's article "Verse Old and Nascant: A Pilgrimage," *Double-Dealer,* VII (1925), 130; and "The Bear," *Go Down, Moses* (New York: Modern Library, 1955), p. 297. Norman Holmes Pearson has commented on Keats's urn-symbol as employed in *Light in August* in "Lena Grove," *Shenandoah,* III (1951), 3–7.

over again from time immemorial. Against the background of countryside which is Faulkner's equivalent of the "silent form" of Keats's
urn, the comic and pathetic leaf-fring'd [7] legends of Lena Grove and
Joe Christmas are seen to be, although interesting as individual histories, even more significant as expressions, moments, postures, phases
of a human reality into which all personal realities fade. The stillness
of urn and countryside represent, not immobility itself, but "deserts
of vast eternity"—so vast that in such perspective all particulars and
moments are lost.

Faulkner's somewhat peculiar use of the word "avatar," in characterizing the progressive appearances or apparent progress of both
Lena Grove and Joe Christmas through space and time, makes their
stories legends of arrested human striving like the "brede / Of marble
men and maidens" on the urn. Lena "advances as though through a
succession of avatars"; Joe, "as in numberless avatars" (Chaps. I, X).
The main signification in Faulkner's use of the term "avatar" is of
course simply "embodiment." [8] The avatar-figure, which converts personal histories into a mere succession of envisagements of a continuous
and moving process of human "becoming," determines the conception
of the other characters in the novel too. In Faulkner's sense of "avatar,"
Hightower's whole inert existence is a kind of prolonged or aborted
avatar, in consequence of his belief "that I skipped a generation. . . .

---

[7] Professor Pearson ("Lena Grove," p. 6) remarks that Lena's family name
(Grove) alludes to the "leaf-fring'd"; probably, despite the change of vowel, Burch's
name also has this reference. That *Light in August* is "a kind of pastoral" has been
noted by Cleanth Brooks in "Notes on Faulkner's 'Light in August,'" *Harvard
Advocate*, CXXXV (1951), 27.

[8] Thus, for example, Faulkner calls the old mulatto Lucas Beauchamp in *Intruder
in the Dust* an "avatar" ("Lucas in ten thousand Sambo-avatars") of the Negro in
a position of moral superiority to the white man who has injured him (*Intruder
in the Dust* [New York: New American Library, "Signet Books"], Chap. IX). In the
"Appendix" to *The Sound and the Fury* which he wrote for *The Portable Faulkner*,
ed. Malcolm Cowley (New York: Viking Press, 1946), Faulkner speaks of old Brig-
adier General Jason Lycurgus Compson II as "now completing the third of his
three avatars—the one as son of a brilliant and gallant statesman, the second as
battle-leader of brave and gallant men, the third as a sort of privileged pseudo-
Daniel Boone-Robinson Crusoe." In the same "Appendix" Faulkner tells of Jefferson's mousy librarian spending "her life trying to keep *Forever Amber* in its or-
derly overlapping avatars . . . out of the hands of highschool juniors and seniors":
the "avatars" of *Forever Amber*, that is, are the whole succession of forbidden sexy
novels which titillate feverish adolescent fancy. "Avatar," in these various instances,
seems to signify a periodic succession of embodiments of an essentially identical
reality—or, as in "ten thousand Sambo-avatars," perhaps multiple simultaneous
embodiments.

I had already died one night twenty years before I saw light" (Chap. XX). Even Byron Bunch philosophically questions his own determinateness as a self, his own identity: *"You just say that you are Byron Bunch. . . . You are just the one that calls yourself Byron Bunch today, now, this minute"* (Chap. XVIII). Faulkner apparently uses the avatar-figure to indicate that a person's sense of distinct and stable identity is simply a hypostatization of the streaming subjective life in which he transiently exists and which his private consciousness defines for him as *his* life.

A less conspicuous device of Faulkner's for indicating that the "fixed" is only an arbitrary arrest of the "moving" is his frequent mention of the omnipresent muted hum of natural life,[9] furnishing a vague, monotonous, repetitive, generalized accompaniment to foreground action. Thus Joe Christmas, voicing his finally definite intention to murder Joanna Burden, heard around him "a myriad sounds, . . . voices, murmurs, whispers: of trees, darkness, earth, people: his own voice; other voices evocative of names and times and places . . ." (Chap. V). As he entered the house later, to commit the deed, "The dark was filled with voices, myriad, out of all time that he had known, as though all the past was a flat pattern. And going on: tomorrow night, all the tomorrows, to be a part of the flat pattern, going on" (Chap. XII). After Christmas' capture, as Hightower hears from Mrs. Hines the story of his early life, "through the open window there comes now only the peaceful and myriad sounds of the summer night" (Chap. XVI). And later, as Hightower is alone in his house, struggling to suppress his humane impulse to sympathize with and help "poor mankind": "Beyond the open window the sound of insects has not ceased, has not faltered" (Chap. XVI). These generalized, remote, anonymous voices of changing, enduring reality constitute an audible image of the continuous and moving, just as urn and countryside are its visible image.

If, then, *Light in August* eschews classical form—lacks a single complete action with a beginning, a middle, and an end—it does so because there is no alpha or omega in Faulkner's alphabet of reality. His novel ends, but his story does not: it is merely a harsh and prolonged suspiration swelling out of and subsiding into the "myriad voices, out of all time." Faulkner's story is about convergent or con-

---

[9] Faulkner's "myriad voices, out of all time" correspond to what Bergson calls "the uninterrupted humming of life's depths" (pp. 176–177). Faulkner externalizes and objectifies the concept by finding an "objective correlative": the summertime chorus of insect-sounds.

nected human destinies, which have as their nexus the burning of the Burden house, an event which any individual character views as a fixed and understood reality, but which is in fact a symbol capable of as many significances as the various individuals who view it are enabled to read into it from their own experience, their own ideas. To the stranger who brings Lena to Jefferson, it is merely "a house burning" (Chap. I). But as a crucial moment in each of the human histories which converge in it, it is variously interpreted. To each, it brings "light in August" in a different way, provides a glaring but transient interval of illumination and realization.

II. Story

"There is at least one reality which we all seize from within, by intuition and not by simple analysis. It is our own person in its flowing through time, the self which endures" (p. 191). "If, instead of claiming to analyze duration . . . , one first installs oneself in it by an effort of intuition, one has the feeling of a certain well-defined *tension,* whose very definiteness seems like a choice between an infinity of possible durations" (p. 218). The central perception offered to readers of *Light in August* is expressed in Bergson's sentence, "The higher the consciousness, the stronger is this tension of its own duration in relation to that of things" (p. 105). Such a "tension" requires a consciousness of at least two "possible durations": the intuition of our own duration, "which we all seize from within"; and the intuition of some possible duration more comprehensive than our own. Duration consists of "the addition to the present feeling, of the memory of past moments" (p. 211). "The distinction between our present and past is . . . , if not arbitrary, at least relative to the extent of the field which our attention to life can embrace" (p. 179). Thus, intuitions grasp "durations" which vary infinitely in comprehensiveness. They may include awareness of immediate and instant reality, or of our whole lives since birth, or of generations of our family, or of the continuing life of the human species, or of the vast transcendent flux in which the *élan vital* endlessly reshapes reality in novel and more complex forms.

Of the major characters in *Light in August,* the one with least awareness of "this tension of its own duration in relation to that of things" is Lena Grove, for her intuition of her own duration is a very contracted one, and she has no intuition of any other duration. Her "attention to life" embraces only what immediately confronts her; there is little addition to her present feeling "of memory of past events." She cares nothing for her own past or for her family, and never thinks of them; she is fully content with the moment which she occupies, and with the bliss of being in it. As the book opens, she reflects, *"Although I have not been quite a month on the road I am already in Mississippi";* and as it ends, she says, "Here we aint been coming from Alabama but two months, and now it's already Tennessee" (Chaps. I, XXI). The brief span of her attention to the past is clearly marked in such reflections: the only past she ever speaks of is a very recent one, and she speaks of it only as the antecedent of the present in which she is almost wholly engrossed. Her consciousness has "an inward-lighted quality of tranquil and calm unreason" (Chap. I). "The duration of things" is not measured for her by the tides of God or the clocks and calendars of man, but solely by the elemental urges and responses of her nature to her immediate surroundings. She knows no reality beyond her subjective moment. She represents ordinary naive mankind, inviolably innocent because it cannot enter the realm of ideas. To Hightower she stands for *"the good stock peopling in tranquil obedience to it the good earth"* (Chap. XVII). She is too unsophisticated to comprehend good and evil. Faulkner assigns her the first and last speeches of the novel because, just as hers is the least conscious and sophisticated, so is it the most elemental and enduring, aspect of humanity. She is one of Sandburg's "people who live on," a primitive character like Hardy's "man harrowing clods."

If *Light in August* at all anticipates Faulkner's later statement, in his Nobel Prize acceptance speech, that "man will not merely endure; he will prevail," it does so by identifying the "crucified" Joe Christmas with Lena's child, and by exhibiting her calm and confident onward travel at the end of the story. The hate, mistrust, and evil will which impel mankind to crucify some of its members are counterbalanced by the love, trust, and good will tendered to Lena and her child. Lena prevails, not by her understanding, but by her complacent trust in others, a trust amounting almost to obstinacy and stupidity. Although her story is a comedy of rustic innocence, a comic pastoral, Faulkner dignifies instead of disparaging her.

In contrast, Joe Christmas' story is tragic, or at least pathetic. Although Lena is hardly more than an expression of the will to live of the species, Joe is a person struggling to establish his selfhood, and aware of overwhelming influences extending into his life from a long reach of time and a broad range of human relationships. He saw his own history as a struggle to gain status in white society, or, failing that, to revert to primitivism. A long passage near the end of Chapter V serves as figure for his life. It relates how, on the night before he murdered Joanna Burden, he wandered into the Negro section of Jefferson, Freedman Town, "like a phantom, a spirit, strayed out of its own world and lost. . . . It was as though he and all other manshaped life about him had been returned to the lightless hot wet primogenitive Female." He ran in frantic revulsion "out of the black hollow," but became calm when he reached a white neighborhood with "clustered lights: low bright birds in stillwinged and tremulous suspension." He said of the white life around him, "That's all I wanted. . . . That dont seem a whole lot to ask." As he walked on, he saw behind him "the far bright rampart of the town . . . and the black pit from which he had fled . . . black, impenetrable, in its garland of August-tremulous lights. It might have been the original quarry, abyss itself" (Chap. V).

In retrospect Christmas saw his career as a vain striving to emerge from the black, primitive, earthly, female, passionate "allmother of obscurity and darkness" (Chap. X) into light, civilization, manliness, volition, identity. In the course of this vain striving, his hatred of the "lightless hot wet primogenitive Female" grew into a complex obsession. His first indelible impressions, at the orphanage, were of females, sex, guilt, and the rejection of Negroes as inflictions divinely and irrevocably decreed. At the McEacherns', throughout his boyhood, these impressions were all confirmed and deepened. His first experience of sex made it for him thereafter simply an overmastering lust: "something liquid, deathcolored and foul" (Chap. VIII). After his young innocence and affection had been outraged by the malformed whore Bobbie Allen (an episode grotesquely caricaturing love's young dream), he tried to coerce by injury and hate the world into which he could not find a way by generosity and love. Even at the age of five in the orphanage he had learned to believe that *"I am different from the others"* (Chap. VI), and he never was able to surmount the difference.

After his decisive rejection by the white world, he tried to return to primitive black life. In Detroit

> he lived with Negroes, shunning white people. . . . He now lived as man and wife with a woman who resembled an ebony carving. At night he would lie in bed beside her, . . . trying to breathe into himself the dark

odor, the dark and inscrutable thinking and being of Negroes, with each suspiration trying to expel from himself the white blood and the white thinking and being. And all the while his nostrils at the odor which he was trying to make his own would whiten and tauten, his whole being writhe and strain with physical outrage and spiritual denial. (Chap. X)

Christmas failed to recover "the dark and inscrutable thinking and being of Negroes," not because they refused to accept him, but because his upbringing had conditioned him against it. He had not gained a place in the white world, but he had been unfitted for a place in the black world. His was the tragedy of "black blood" in a "pale body" (Chap. XIX), an antagonism of two possibilities so equal in strength that each negated the other. Thus Gavin Stevens summed up his tragedy:

> It was not alone all those thirty years [of his personal existence] . . . , but all those successions of thirty years before that which had put that stain either on his white blood or his black blood, whichever you will, and which killed him. . . . His blood would not be quiet. . . . It would not be either one or the other. (Chap. XIX)

Thus Faulkner shows that the conviction of his outcast fate which dogged "Christmas, the son of Joe" (Chap. XVI) grew in his mind like a fatality. When he anticipated murdering Joanna Burden, he did not acknowledge that he willed to do it, but that he was fated to do it: *"Something is going to happen to me"* (Chap. V). When he murdered her, he "believed with calm paradox that he was the volitionless servant of the fatality[10] in which he believed that he did not believe" (Chap. XII). He transvaluated murder into something like a creative act, however, since it was for him a symbolic annihilation of the world which had denied his claims to selfhood and status. Joanna Burden was his appropriate victim, for she combined in one person the three elements of coercion which Joe had experienced: femaleness, Calvinism, and obsession with color-difference.[11]

Since Christmas could not find a secure life anywhere, his only al-

[10] Most of the principal characters in the novel (Grimm, McEachern, Joanna Burden, and even Gail Hightower) act as if their wills were determined by some overruling necessity. For an excellent brief discussion of the theme of fatality in Faulkner, see Rabi, "Faulkner and the Exiled Generation," in *William Faulkner: Two Decades of Criticism,* especially pp. 132–134.

[11] For discussion of the conjoined Negro-sex motifs in *Light in August* see Phyllis Hirshleifer, "As Whirlwinds in the South: An Analysis of *Light in August*," *Perspective,* II (1949), 237–238.

ternative was to die: to accept and hasten the doom that he thought was determined for him. After the murder, as he looked at his feet in the black Negro shoes that he had put on to throw the pursuing bloodhounds off the scent, it "seemed to him that he could see himself being hunted by white men at last into the black abyss, which had been waiting, trying, for thirty years to drown him and into which now and at last he had actually entered, bearing upon his ankles the definite and ineradicable gauge of its upward moving" (Chap. XIV).

Just as Lena represents the comedy of ordinary life, so does Joe represent the tragedy of extraordinary life. Hated, corrupted, and persecuted from the hour of his birth, he was not only accused of being evil by those who "crucified" him for righteousness' sake (Hines in the name of God, Grimm in the name of patriotism and society); he *was* evil, for he had been imbued with all the sin and corruption of humanity; he was a scapegoat burdened with the accumulated evils of his generation. But even his persecutors were not responsible for the tragedy. Although Hines and Grimm were persecutors rather than victims, although Lucas Burch was Judas rather than Christ, all alike were servants of the general and traditional obsessions which assigned their roles in the tragedy. Byron Bunch's opinion about the town of Jefferson's long harassment of Hightower applies equally well to Christmas' "crucifixion": "The entire affair had been a lot of people performing a play and . . . now and at last they had all played out the parts that had been allotted to them" (Chap. III).

III. Coda

"Installed in universal mobility, . . . consciousness contracts in a quasi-instantaneous vision an immensely long history which unfolds outside it. The higher the consciousness, the stronger is this tension of its own duration in relation to that of things" (p. 105). Gail Hightower is the most significant character in *Light in August* because only he attained the higher consciousness which "contracts in a quasi-instantaneous vision an immensely long history which unfolds outside it." Hightower suffered even more than Joe Christmas, for he who experiences most suffers most. Hightower tried to maintain that he had "bought immunity" (Chap. XIII) from involvement in the affairs of living men, but his long-suppressed humanity impelled him "to come back into life" (Chap. XIII) to assist at a birth and try to prevent a death. His identification with the human beings whose fates, when he was forced to sympathize with them, illustrated both the hopeful and tragic possibilities of the life he had evaded, made him comprehend the general fate of mankind, which is to serve the compulsive ideas which are its inheritance. Hightower's own story is an exaggerated rendering of the truth that all men are directed by ancestral ghosts and do not fully possess their own realities. He had chosen to withdraw into his ancestral ghost, rather than to let the human past summed up in him enter the present; but his story, like Joanna Burden's and Joe Christmas', shows the persistence through generations of a pattern of transmitted ideas and tendencies which effectually make each inheritor their instrument, because they are not externally dictated to him but are constitutive of his own character.

Because Hightower had so long lived a "dead life in the actual world," "dissociated from mechanical time" (Chap. XVI), had not enacted a vital role in the present, he was able, like God in a high tower in a medieval mystery play, to see that present with detachment. He had breadth of understanding and depth of compassion, and rose to contemplation of those principles of human action, those conditions of human life, which are so recurrent in time that they seem ulterior to time, and "tease us out of thought/As doth eternity." . . . Lena Grove, a pagan generatrix, is mankind aware of its existence only through participation in the burgeoning life of nature; Joe Christmas lives and dies in a world of ideas of good and evil; but Gail Hightower, by his intuition of "universal mobility," philosophically transcends both the natural and moral worlds.

The concluding revery of Hightower (to whom light in August comes more effulgently than to any other character, although all the witnesses of Christmas' death . . . have a half-comprehended enlightenment) shows him in an instant when "consciousness contracts in a quasi-instantaneous vision an immensely long history which unfolds outside itself." In his agony of comprehension, of realization, Hightower sits "in the lambent suspension of August into which night is about fully to come," and all the faces of the recent past rise before him, but "not shaped with suffering, not shaped with anything: not horror, pain, not even reproach. They are peaceful, as though they have escaped into an apotheosis" (Chap. XX). The figure which structures his revery is a rapidly revolving wheel of thought,[12] or consciousness, which slows

---

[12] Faulkner, in representing what Bergson calls "intuition of duration," generally uses cyclic figures. Movement across an urn is of course cyclic movement. Joe Christmas feels that for thirty years he has been running "inside a circle" (Chap. XIV). Lena thinks of her movement along a country road as being "like measured

and stops to focus the static images and characters which perception distinguishes in the continuous, moving reality. But the wheel in rapid revolution is a halo full of faces that "all look alike, composite of all the faces that he has ever seen" (Chap. XX).

In this apocalyptic instant in Hightower's vision the faces of Christmas and Grimm, in mortal life obsessed and murderous opponents, "fade and blend." "Then it seems to [Hightower] that some ultimate dammed flood within him breaks and rushes away. He seems to watch it, feeling himself losing contact with earth, lighter and lighter, emptying, floating. . . . [He thinks,] 'With all air, all heaven, filled with the lost and unheeded crying of all the living who ever lived, wailing still like lost children among the cold and terrible stars. . . .' " (Chap. XX). Thus, for an instant, Hightower escapes from the static and discontinuous appearances which constitute reality to ordinary perception: leaves the temporal world of frieze and legend and enters the eternity of the urn-world itself. When, by philosophic intuition, man is able to "arise from a frozen vision of the real . . . to perceive all things *sub specie durationis,*" "all things acquire depth,—more than depth, something like a fourth dimension. . . . What was immobile and frozen in our perception is warmed and set in motion. Everything comes to life around us. . . . A great impulse carries beings and things along. We feel ourselves uplifted, carried away, borne along by it" (p. 186). In the Dionysian dance of life there comes a serene moment of Apollonian vision.

The climactic symbol of *Light in August,* the lambent wheel which Hightower sees in his highest moment of vision as an image of eternity, is an archetypal symbol whose richness can be best apprehended in comparison with literary parallels. The most obvious is Dante's recurrent conjunction of images of light and a rapidly revolving wheel in the *Paradiso* (e.g., Cantos, i, xii, xxviii), especially the elaborate image of the circle of fire, or rapidly whirling wheel haloed with

---

thread being rewound onto a spool" (Chap. I). This simile is also used by Bergson to suggest the sense of "our own person in its flowing through time" (p. 191): "It is, if you like, like the unrolling of a spool. . . . But it is just as much a continual winding, like that of thread into a ball" (pp. 192–193). Richard Chase has discussed the contrasting significances of what he calls "linear discreteness and curve" in "The Stone and the Crucifixion: Faulkner's *Light in August,*" *Kenyon Review,* X (1948), 539–551 (reprinted in *William Faulkner: Two Decades of Criticism*). I think that his argument, although perceptive and valuable, miscarries somewhat because he thinks in terms of the form of Faulkner's cyclic images, instead of noting that they are essentially images of duration.

light, which Dante views in the ninth heaven (Canto xxviii). Dante quotes in connection with this image a passage from Aristotle's *Meta-physics* on the *primum mobile,* the "unmoved mover" which is the center and source of this dazzle of cyclic movement. Similarly, Plato's *Timaeus* designates the stars in their courses as "a moving image of eternity"—a passage which may be the source of the famous opening stanza of Henry Vaughan's poem "The World":

> I saw Eternity the other night
> Like a great ring of pure and endless light,
> All calm, as it was bright,
> And round beneath it, Time, in hours, days, years,
> Driven by the spheres
> Like a vast shadow moved, in which the world
> And all her train were hurl'd.

I think it likely that such reminiscences, whether conscious or not, have contributed to Faulkner's symbol of the haloed wheel of High-tower's vision. If Hightower, like Dante, is regarded as one who, while still in mortal life, is afforded a vision of eternity in all its phases, his experience exhibits something of hell, of purgatory, and of heaven. His inferno consists of his witnessing and participating in the com-plicated tragedy of human evil and mortality which is consummated in the "crucifixion" of Joe Christmas. His purgatory is the initial stage of his revery after Christmas' death, when finally, in "a consternation which is about to be actual horror," he admits his guilt as an "in-strument of [his wife's] despair and shame," while "sweat begins to pour from him, springing out like blood" (Chap. XX). He sees, beyond his own guilt, the determinism which fixed this complicity in evil upon him: "If I am the instrument of her despair and death, then I am in turn instrument of someone outside myself" (Chap. XX). Purged by his abandonment of delusion, his admission of truth, he enters his paradise, his moment of perception of an eternal truth which leaves his stale and corrupt "body empty and lighter than a forgotten leaf and even more trivial than flotsam lying spent and still . . . ; so that it can be now Now" [13] (Chap. XX).

But, although *Light in August* contains a *Divina commedia,* a *Comédie humaine* encompasses it: Lena, the almost primitive embodi-

[13] Faulkner's "now Now" is a verbal device for signaling the moment of High-tower's passage from a temporal now to the Eternal Now. Compare "yesterday to-day and tomorrow are Is: Indivisible: One" (*Intruder in the Dust,* Chap. IX).

ment of the human species' persistent effort to seek attachments and find durable satisfactions in local, temporal, and personal terms, is presented to us first and last. Her primacy in the story does not mean, I think, that Faulkner rejects Hightower's vision of reality for her view of it, but rather that he regards Lena's reality as the almost universally and constantly available one, and Hightower's as a difficult, fleeting, and rarely attainable one.

The Community and the Pariah

by Cleanth Brooks

. . . [N]early all the characters in [*Light in August*] are drawn from the ranks of the plain people and most of them exhibit a Puritan ethic. They are in tension with nature, and some have even been deformed and perverted in a struggle against it. The theme of man strained away from nature, however, is only one of several significant Faulknerian themes to be found in *Light in August*. . . . The community . . . is the powerful though invisible force that quietly exerts itself in so much of Faulkner's work. It is the circumambient atmosphere, the essential ether of Faulkner's fiction. But for many a reader, the community is indeed invisible and quite imperceptible: it exerts no pressure on him at all—and lacking any awareness of this force, he may miss the meaning of the work. Such readers find *Light in August* quite baffling simply because they are unaware of the force of community that pervades it and thus miss the clue to its central structure.

Yet a little reflection will show that nearly all the characters in *Light in August* bear a special relation to the community. They are outcasts—they are pariahs, defiant exiles, withdrawn quietists, or simply strangers. Miss Burden, the daughter of carpetbagger intruders, has lived for years within what can be described only as a kind of cultural cyst. The community has tried its best to expel the Reverend Mr. Hightower, though having failed in the attempt it has finally accorded him a sort of grudging acceptance. Joe Christmas is, of course, Ishmael himself, actively defying the community. Even Byron Bunch fits into this pattern of alienation. Byron, with his methodical earnestness and his countrified asceticism, is regarded as a kind of eccentric—a "charac-

"*The Community and the Pariah*." *From* William Faulkner: The Yoknapatawpha Country *by Cleanth Brooks (New Haven and London: Yale University Press, 1963), pp. 47–74. Copyright © 1963 by Yale University. Condensed and reprinted with the permission of the publisher.*

ter." For "seven years [he] had been a minor mystery to the town"
(p. 369).

But the community itself, the great counterforce to which these
characters are attracted or against which they are reacting, has no
special representatives in the novel and need have none. For the
community, everywhere in the novel, is visible to the reader who is
prepared to see it. It expresses itself through Mrs. Armstid emptying
her china bank and knotting the coins into a sack for Lena; through
the sheriff kicking the ineffectual bloodhounds or ordering the thrill-
seekers away from his examination of the Negro witness; through the
second-hand furniture dealer who relates the closing episode of the
novel; and through a dozen other minor or anonymous characters.

Sometimes the author makes an explicit comment upon the community, as he does in the long and brilliantly handled account of
Gail Hightower in Chapter 3. After Mrs. Hightower's shameful death,
the community is sure that Hightower will resign his church. When
he does so at last, after persistent moral pressure, the town is glad.
"Then the town was sorry with being glad, as people sometimes are
sorry for those whom they have at last forced to do as they wanted
them to" (p. 60). But Hightower still would not leave the town, and
the community was furious with him for his stubbornness. Finally,
some men took him out and beat him, and the townspeople, now
horrified, offered "to prosecute the men who had done it" (p. 62). But
Hightower refused to tell who his assailants were. "Then all of a
sudden the whole thing seemed to blow away, like an evil wind. It
was as though the town realized at last that he would be a part of its
life until he died, and that they might as well become reconciled."
Neighbors once more began to leave baskets of food upon his porch—
"though they were the sort of dishes which they would have sent to a
poor mill family. But it was food, and wellmeant" (p. 63).

. . . The plight of the isolated individual cut off from any community of values is of course a dominant theme of contemporary literature. But by developing this theme in a rural setting in which a powerful sense of community still exists, Faulkner has given us a kind of
pastoral—that is, he has let us see our modern and complex problems
mirrored in a simpler and more primitive world. *Light in August* is,
in some respects, a bloody and violent pastoral. The plight of the lost
sheep and of the black sheep can be given special point and meaning
because there is still visible in the background a recognizable flock
with its shepherds, its watchdogs, sometimes fierce and cruel, and its
bellwethers.

Yet the reader of *Light in August* may still question the relation of the fact of community to the meaning of the novel. Granted that the community is a living force, what does that have to do with the meaning of the novel? And he can scarcely be blamed if he goes on to ask whether *Light in August* is a novel at all. What possible relation is there between the two main characters, Lena and Joe Christmas, who never meet and who go their separate ways, the one placidly, the other violently? There is obviously the bare fact of contrast; but is there anything more? Do not these characters between them rend the book in two? [1]

Both questions are in order. A proper answer to the first (the relation of the community to the meaning of this novel) will suggest an answer to the second (the unity of the novel). But the answer to the first cannot be succinct, and in any case we must begin by considering more fully the relations of the various characters—to each other and to the world around them.

Lena and Joe Christmas, as everyone has seen, stand in obvious contrast to each other. Their very likenesses stress their basic differences. Both are orphans; both escape from home by crawling out a window; both are betrayed by their first loves; both in the course of their wanderings come to Jefferson. But how different they are in relation to society! Every man's hand is sooner or later lifted against Joe Christmas; he demands that it be so. But Lena, heavy with child, on an obviously ridiculous quest to find the father of her child, leads a charmed life. Even the women who look upon her swollen body with evident disapproval press their small store of coins upon her, and the community in general rallies to help her. As Mrs. Beard remarks to Byron Bunch: "Aint you and that preacher and ever other man that knows about her already done everything for her that she could think to want?" (p. 368). In the person of Bunch, her quixotic errand actually raises up for her an authentic though clumsy knight-errant, who becomes her protector and fights her battles.

Joe repels, Lena attracts the force of the community into which they both come as strangers. But the point is not that Lena is "good" and Joe "bad." Joe's alienation from the community is not simply "willed" —there are deep-seated reasons for it, and, moreover, his is only the most extreme of a whole series of such alienations.

Faulkner has documented each history of alienation rather carefully,

---

[1] See, for example, Richard Rovere's introduction to the [1950] Modern Library edition.

and has done so in great detail with those of Joe Christmas and Gail Hightower. Hightower, because of certain warping influences in childhood, becomes fettered to the past. Because of certain traumatic experiences in childhood, Christmas is cut off from any meaningful past. Hightower toward the end of the novel comes to the bitter realization that he has hardly lived at all. The son of middle-aged parents (his father fifty, his mother forty), brought up in an austere house, he came as a child to dote upon the memory of his Confederate cavalryman grandfather, who represented all that his father was not. Hightower regards his father as an enemy. As he puts it, "I skipped a generation" (p. 418). He is able to invest his grandfather's death (he was shot while robbing a henhouse on some foraging expedition) with romantic glamour. His sermons mix up in an incredible farrago the charging cavalry with the word of God. Late in the novel he comes to admit to himself that "for fifty years" he has "not even been clay: I have been a single instant of darkness in which a horse galloped and a gun crashed. . . . my dead grandfather on the instant of his death" (p. 430). But his friend Byron Bunch has realized the truth about him long before, thinking to himself: "it's the dead folks that do him the damage. It's the dead ones that lay quiet in one place and dont try to hold him, that he cant escape from" (p. 65).

But Christmas has no "dead ones" to hold him, no family, no past. The orphanage, where he was conscious that the grim old man was watching him "all the time," and life with his foster father, the dour Calvinist McEachern, lock him into himself. He is cut off from ties of any sort, and he learns to suspect and resent any appeal to sentiment or tenderness. Part of that suspicion of tenderness comes from his experiences with sex. Faulkner has most skillfully traced this development through the well-known toothpaste episode, the experience with the Negro girl, and the affair with the prostitute-waitress Bobbie, but he has not forced the development to extremes. Joe is not made into an overt homosexual. But his distaste for women and his fear of them is accounted for, and this antifeminine attitude becomes, as we shall see, a meaningful part of the novel. It is parallel to the attitude of Hightower, who does not understand women and comes to shrink from them and all that they represent. Doubtless the community was viciously wrong in accusing Hightower of homosexual practices; yet there is a latent tendency in him just as there is in Christmas. There is this much justice in Grimm's bitter accusation when Hightower, attempting to give Christmas the alibi for which Bunch had pleaded, says "He was with me the night of the murder" (p. 406).

It is Joe's latent homosexuality that involves him with Joanna Burden. When he forces himself upon her, there is "no feminine vacillation, no coyness of obvious desire. . . . It was as if he struggled physically with another man for an object of no actual value to either, and for which they struggled on principle alone" (p. 205). It is when Joanna's masculinity finally dissolves into nymphomania and that in turn gives way to feminine religiosity that Joe kills her. He cannot bear having her pray over him.

Joanna Burden is one of the most interesting of Faulkner's characters. . . . She is lonely, cut off from her kind, shunned by the community; and she has been crippled (very much as Hightower has been) by her personal inheritance. But she has courage, a quiet power of endurance, and a remarkable lack of bitterness at her plight. . . .

Joanna has been warped by the pressure of events away from the fulfillment of her nature. She has been forced to bury a part of herself; but the needs and desires are there, and when they are awakened too late for normal fulfillment in children and a home, something very terrible happens to her. Joe Christmas is perceptive enough on this point. He says to himself early in their relationship: "At least I have made a woman of her at last" (p. 207), though later, less certain of the fact, he thinks: "She's trying to be a woman and she dont know how" (p. 210). But Joe is not prepared for the torrent that is released when the "New England glacier [is] exposed suddenly to the fire of the New England biblical hell" (p. 225). Later he observes, when she sometimes stares at him "with the wild, despairing face of a stranger," that "she wants to pray, but she dont know how to do that either" (p. 228).

Faulkner is pitiless in recounting the details of Joanna's sexual discovery of herself and in indicating the man's revulsion from her—his feeling that he was "being sucked down into a bottomless morass" (p. 227). But there is never any question that Joanna is essentially the victim—of sex too long repressed, of sex driven up into the head—or of her being compelled to her actions by a self that she had scarcely known existed. To witness Joanna's one love affair is like watching a stunted autumnal plant frantically trying to bloom and seed itself before the killing frosts—"something of dying summer spurting again like a dying coal" (p. 228). Compare also: "hair just beginning to gray drawn gauntly back to a knot as savage and ugly as a wart on a diseased bough" (p. 241).

At the end, Joanna reverts to her ancestral religion—as in some sense she has known all the time that she must. "Don't make me have to pray yet," she prays. "Dear God, let me be damned a little longer, a little while" (p. 231). When she becomes once more the religious woman, the solicitous mother figure, the woman who would counsel the child and do him good, Joe finds that he has to kill her, and does —though not before Joanna has tried to kill him, for she serves a just God who will not be mocked, whose judgments are very sure, and she is ready to be that God's instrument. The last point is very important: Joanna's final gesture is not the spiteful reaction of a jilted woman. There is something almost impersonal about it. As she has told Joe when she asked him for the last time to kneel and pray with her, "It's not I who ask it" (p. 247). She is the dedicated instrument of her God, whether in saying "kneel with me" or in pulling the trigger.

Joanna Burden's frantic exploration of sex contrasts with Joe's attitude toward sex. Joe's life, as the author observes, had been, "for all its anonymous promiscuity . . . conventional enough, as a life of healthy and normal sin usually is" (p. 227). And on another level, Joanna is contrasted with Lena in her attitude toward sex, for Lena, with her uncomplicated urge to foster life, is not so much normal as an embodiment of the very norm itself.

Most of all, however, Joanna invites comparison with Hightower. Faulkner has pointed to the parallels between these two characters in a number of ways. Both are recluses. Both have been rejected by the community for good and sufficient reason. Both are dominated by the past, since the family past has impinged upon both of them in a special way. Because of all this, the incautious reader might even leap to the conclusion that it was something in the personal heritage of these two people that destroyed them, leaving them unfulfilled and incomplete. In contrast to Joe Christmas, who has no roots in anything, Joanna and Hightower may seem too deeply rooted, helplessly fettered by their personal traditions—the one of militant abolitionism, the other of the galloping Confederate cavalry leader. But neither's is a live tradition. It does not connect past with present. It is absurdly doctrinaire and abstract or absurdly romantic. That, incidentally, is how the community judges both these obsessions.

The ancestors of both Gail Hightower and Joanna Burden were able to fulfill themselves. Calvin Burden, Joanna's grandfather, was lusty, full-blooded, completely alive. He was a fire-eating abolitionist, coming home "especially on Saturday nights . . . still full of straight whiskey and the sound of his own ranting. . . . [But he] was no proselyter, [no] missionary" (p. 212). His peer is Hightower's grandfather, a "hale, bluff, rednosed man with the moustache of a brigand chief" (p. 412), triumphantly at home in his world.

Joanna's father Nathaniel, after an exciting youth spent in the Southwest, becomes an austere grizzled man who settles in Jefferson immediately after the Civil War. There his father and his son are shot down in a Reconstruction period election. But with all his justification for bitterness, and though isolated as a hated alien, he has an understanding of the values of the community. As Joanna herself reconstructs it: "We were foreigners . . . that thought differently from the people whose country we had come into without being asked or wanted. And [father] was French, half of him. Enough French to respect anybody's love for the land where he and his people were born and to understand that a man would have to act as the land where he was born had trained him to act" (p. 223).

Like Joanna's father, Hightower's father was an abolitionist, though a Southern abolitionist. But he entered the Confederate army and "took an active part in a partisan war and on the very side whose principles opposed his own" (p. 414). He taught himself surgery during the war, retained his idealism, and, as Faulkner puts it, "the other part of him, which lived in the actual world" (p. 415), was as successful as any man and more successful than most. Thus, though Joanna's and Hightower's fathers were as unlike their own fathers as they could be, they too were able to fulfill themselves. Both the grandfathers and the fathers of Joanna and Hightower were whole men, fully related to the world outside them, fully alive. The issue is not that of a Northern or Southern heritage or even that of a sensual or ascetic temperament: both traditions and both temperaments are represented in their ancestors. The real issue is whether one's relation to one's heritage permits participation in life or isolates one from life— whether it connects past with present or is simply a private obsession.

The most fascinating instance of the alienated person that occurs in the novel is that of Percy Grimm. Faulkner says: "I wrote [*Light in August*] in 1932 before I'd ever heard of Hitler's Storm Troopers," [2] and thus had described a storm trooper without knowing it. Faulkner's claim that he had described the breed without help from the newspapers is quite justified; but because of hazy and inaccurate notions of the rise of Nazism, some readers will not realize just how accurate

---

[2] See Frederick L. Gwynn and Joseph L. Blotner, eds., *Faulkner in the University* (Charlottesville: The University of Virginia Press, 1959), p. 41.

Faulkner's account is. In the first place, it may seem strange to them that one should regard Percy Grimm as an alienated character at all. Yet Faulkner has gone to great pains to show that Grimm is cut off from the community and is thoroughly conscious of being cut off from it. Indeed, Faulkner has been almost as careful in working up the background of Percy Grimm's spiritual starvation and alienation as he has with that of Gail Hightower.

Grimm had been born too late to take part in the First World War. Because he had missed out on being a soldier, the boy had received a kind of psychic blow. As Faulkner puts it: "The boy was suffering the terrible tragedy of having been born not alone too late but not late enough to have escaped first hand knowledge of the lost time when he should have been a man instead of a child" (p. 394). At another point, Faulkner makes the comment that Grimm had no one "to open his heart to." In short, Percy Grimm is a man who needs desperately to be felt a part of the community. He needs it so much that he attempts to seize the community values by violence. He yearns to wear a uniform marking him as the community's representative and defender. Whereas Christmas repudiates the customs and institutions of the community, Grimm insists upon seeing them in peril and demanding the right to take up arms in their defense. We shall miss the point badly if we entertain any doubts as to Percy Grimm's sincerity of motives in trying to prevent a lynching. He wants to ensure that Joe Christmas, murderer though he be, shall have a fair and proper trial.

So much for Grimm's conscious motives. What his unconscious motives are becomes plain enough when he confronts Joe Christmas at the end of the chase. Faulkner makes it clear that only in the heat of the chase does Grimm suddenly feel released, happy, fulfilled. Grimm runs "with a kind of fierce and constrained joy." Later, "above the blunt cold, rake of the automatic, his face had that serene, unearthly luminousness of angels in church windows" (p. 402). It is probably only at the very end that the dammed-up sadism is revealed even to Grimm himself, bursting forth in a full tide as he fires the shots into the overturned table and seizes the butcher knife.

A lesser artist would have made of Grimm a kind of caricature, merely brutalized and bestial. It is a mark of Faulkner's insight that even in his "Storm Trooper" he sees lurking beneath the fury and brutality the emotionally starved, lonely, terrified little boy.

In a sense we may say that Joe Christmas and Percy Grimm are closely akin—mirror images of each other in their relation to the community. This is why it makes good artistic sense that the stricken and wounded Hightower, in a final moment of truth about himself, should see the faces of Christmas and Grimm blurred together. In this vision there appear to him the faces of his wife, the townspeople, the members of his congregation, and those of Byron Bunch, Lena, and Joe Christmas. But one "face alone is not clear. It is confused more than any other, as though in the now peaceful throes of a more recent, a more inextricable, compositeness. Then he can see that it is two faces which seem to strive . . . in turn to free themselves one from the other, then fade and blend again" (p. 430). Suddenly, he realizes whose the second face is: " 'Why, it's . . .' he thinks. 'I have seen it, recently . . . Why, it's that . . . boy. . . . who fired the . . .' " (p. 431).

The theme of alienation from the community is in this novel closely connected with an emphasis on a kind of hellfire Protestantism. In much of his work Faulkner reveals himself to be a Protestant anticlerical, fascinated and also infuriated by some of the more violently repressive features of the religion that dominates his part of the country. But in *Light in August* his criticism of the harsher Protestantism is not a gratuitous gesture that disturbs the work of art: it is absorbed into the total pattern of meaning. . . .

In *Light in August* some of the characters who have become cut off from the community—and from life—become reintegrated with it, fully or partially. Such a character is Byron Bunch. He has suffered no traumatic experience in his youth; he has received no special conditioning from the past; nor has he violently rebelled or been violently rejected by the community. He is rather the methodical little "settled" man with no vices, the perpetual bachelor, who is somewhat withdrawn from the tides of life. We are told how he came to fall in love and, through this love, became involved in matters of life and death, crime and scandal. We are also told how Hightower, who had tried so desperately hard to avoid involvement ("I have brought immunity") is also drawn back into decision and responsibility. Hightower, as Bunch's confidant and in some sense his spiritual adviser, fears that Bunch is risking his "freedom," and counsels him to avoid involvement. But finally, through Bunch, he himself once more becomes involved in life and death; he delivers Lena's baby, since the doctor has not got to her in time, and he makes a desperate last-minute attempt to save Joe Christmas just before he is shot to death in the next room.

The involvement of Bunch comes through a woman, and that fact itself is significant. For the alienation of many of those separated from the community has come about through their attitudes toward

woman and sex—or at least reveals itself in those attitudes. It is so
with Christmas, with Hightower, and with Byron Bunch. One might
include Joanna Burden here, for though she is a woman, her mas-
culinization is the badge of her loneliness and the means through
which she is destroyed. Hightower makes the connection very definitely. As he passes the charred timbers of her house he says: "Poor,
barren woman. To have not lived only a week longer, until luck returned to this place. [Lena's child has just been born in a cabin on her
place.] Until luck and life returned to these barren and ruined acres"
(p. 357). Joanna's own barrenness is precisely to the point, and con-
versely Lena's fertility is connected not only literally with life but
also with luck, good fortune.

Lena, by the way, is the only one of the strangers—the outsiders
who have come into the community—who does not suffer from frustration and alienation. The others suffer from the characteristic disease
of modern life, its sick hurry and divided aims. One can recognize in
the situation of Christmas or Hightower themes characteristic of
other writers of our time such as Eliot and Joyce. To all of them one
might apply John Crowe Ransom's telling description of modern man
as a being unable "to fathom or perform his nature." Since Christmas
does not know who he is, he can express himself only in fits of compulsive violence. Gavin Stevens thinks that perhaps just before his death,
Christmas did come to know who he was, and there are rather clear
indications that Hightower fathoms his nature at the end, but this
knowledge comes very late. Lena is almost alone in not suffering from
this modern defect. She can perform her nature because she does not
need to fathom it: she *is* nature.

Lena (along with Eula of *The Hamlet*) has sometimes been called
an "earth goddess." The description does have a certain aptness when
applied to Eula, especially in some of the more rhapsodic passages of
The Hamlet. But it is a little highfalutin for Lena. It is more accurate
to say that Lena is one of Faulkner's several embodiments of the
female principle—indeed, one of the purest and least complicated of
his embodiments. Her rapport with nature is close. She is never baffled
as to what course of action to take. She is never torn by doubts and
indecisions. There is no painful introspection. This serene composure
has frequently been put down to sheer mindlessness, and Lena, to be
sure, is a very simple young woman. But Faulkner himself undoubtedly attributes most of Lena's quiet force to her female nature. Faulkner may indeed have had a rather romantic idea of woman. He certainly had an old-fashioned idea of her. In the Faulknerian world men

have to lose their innocence, confront the hard choice, and through a process of initiation discover reality. But women are already in possession of this knowledge, naturally and instinctively. That is why in moments of bitterness Faulkner's male characters—Mr. Compson in *The Sound and the Fury,* for example—assert that women are not innocent and have a natural affinity for evil. It would be more accurate to say that Faulkner's women lack the callow idealism of the men, have fewer illusions about human nature, and are less trammeled by legalistic distinctions and the niceties of any code.

In *Light in August,* however, the male-female contrast is stressed in a rather different way. Here, the principal male characters suffer alienation. They are separated from the community, are in rebellion against it—and against nature. But Lena moves serenely into the community and it gathers itself about her with protective gestures. Its response to her, of course, is rooted in a deep and sound instinct: Lena embodies the principle upon which any human community is founded. She is the carrier of life, and she has to be protected and nurtured if there is to be any community at all.

A basic theme in *Light in August* is man's strained attempt to hold himself up in rigid aloofness above the relaxed female world. Many of the men in the novel take up this stance, notably Hightower and Christmas. The crazed fanatic Doc Hines and the dour Presbyterian McEachern are to be numbered here too; perhaps also, though with an obvious difference, Hightower's father, Joanna Burden's father, and Joanna (as masculinized woman) herself. Byron Bunch, when we first see him, is aligned with this group. He is timid with women, and his religiousness has just a hint of the anchorite in it. Even Lucas Burch ought to be mentioned in this company—if only for comic relief (though he does have a quite literal claim to be admitted: in his own terms, he is not the marrying kind, and we last see him frantically escaping from Lena and her baby and his responsibilities to them).

Lena's function in the novel ought now to be clear. Faulkner uses her to affirm a kind of integrity and wholeness by which the alienated characters are to be judged. But Lena has more than a symbolic function. She is the means through which Byron Bunch is redeemed from his pallid half-life and brought back into the community. And she is the indirect means through which Hightower is redeemed. This coming back into the community is an essential part of their redemption. Unless the controlling purposes of the individual are related to those that other men share and in which the individual can participate, he is indeed isolated and is forced to fall back upon his personal values, with all the risk of fanaticism and distortion to which such isolation is liable.

The community is at once the field for man's action and the norm by which his action is judged and regulated. It sometimes seems that the sense of an organic community has all but disappeared from modern fiction, and the disappearance accounts for the terrifying self-consciousness and subjectivity of a great deal of modern writing. That Faulkner had some sense of an organic community still behind him was among his most important resources as a writer.

If in Faulkner's work the community can still serve as a positive norm, does that mean that in his fiction there is no room for the roles of the prophet and the saint? Can one ever find implicit approval of the individual's effort to amend or transcend the values held by the community? The answer is yes, and often. Faulkner was always fascinated by rebels and has usually accorded them a full measure of dramatic sympathy. But his fiction also reveals keen awareness of the perils risked by the individual who attempts to run counter to the community. The divergent individual may invite martyrdom; he certainly risks fanaticism and madness. In *Light in August* Faulkner's emphasis is primarily on the distortion and perversion and sterility which isolation from the community entails, though even here there is a clear recognition of a heroic element in Hightower, Joanna Burden, and Joe Christmas.

The term "redemption" may seem to claim too much for Hightower. Yet by the end of the novel he has been powerfully changed. After he has successfully delivered Lena's baby, he feels "a surge of something almost hot, almost triumphant" and thinks "I showed them! . . . Life comes to the old man yet" (p. 355). And he goes home to read not Tennyson but *Henry IV*, "food for a man" (p. 355). When he hears that Byron has left, he says to himself: "So he departed without coming to tell me goodbye" (p. 363). And then, with a conscious and purposed inversion of the usual phrase, "After all *he* has done for *me*. Fetched to me. Ay; given, restored, to me" (italics mine). Later, it is true, Hightower has to experience Christmas' attack upon him, the futile attempt to stop Grimm with a lie offered too late to save Christmas' life, and the blood-letting in his own house. But he has dared the opprobrium and told the generous lie, and in the long reverie which closes Faulkner's account of him he has admitted to himself that he "was the one who failed" (p. 426), that he was responsible for his wife's death, that he has been "a charlatan preaching worse than heresy" (p. 427), and that, bound by his romantic fixation on his grandfather's death, he has himself been neither dead nor alive. In this hour of truth he has his vision of the faces, and sees them for what they are, and he hears once again the phantom cavalry, the mystic experience with which he has sustained himself in the past, but this time he hears with a difference "the clashing sabres and the dying thunder of hooves," for he himself has finally dared something and has broken out of his self-centered dream.

Most readers have assumed that Hightower, old and exhausted, his head bandaged after Christmas' blows, dies as he hears "the dying thunder of hooves." But Faulkner, in his University of Virginia discussions, indicated that Hightower "didn't die." [3] This is obviously highly interesting; but as far as the larger scheme of the book is concerned, it hardly matters: whether Hightower died or lived on, he had broken out of the circle in which we find him at the opening of the story.

And what of Byron Bunch? Is he also "redeemed?" Can we say so in view of the curious and somewhat ambiguous ending of the novel in which Lena has not accepted marriage with Byron but, with Byron in tow, pursues her ridiculous quest for the father of her child, the unspeakable Lucas Burch? An answer to this question necessarily brings up for consideration Faulkner's attitude—not only to the characters in this episode but to all the happenings in the book. What shall we call the predominant mode? Tragic or comic or neither?

Finally and generally, I believe, the mode is that of comedy. To say so in the light of some of the terrible episodes may seem perverse. But Faulkner's comedy is frequently a makeweight to the terrible. The tender-minded reader may feel that Faulkner frequently uses a savage humor; but his is never a cynical and nihilistic humor. Its function is to maintain sanity and human perspective in a scene of brutality and horror. For example, there is the wonderful passage in which the countryman who has discovered the fire in Miss Burden's house enters and finds her body with the head almost severed, a condition which presents him with a problem in getting the dead woman downstairs. He is afraid to try to pick her up and carry her out "because her head might come clean off." But the fire forces the issue and he has to pick her up and bring her out as best he can. When he deposits the body on the ground, however, the cover in which

[3] *Ibid.*, p. 75.

he had hastily wrapped her "fell open and she was laying on her side, facing one way, and her head was turned clean around like she was looking behind her. And he said how if she could just have done that when she was alive, she might not have been doing it now" (p. 8o).

This is comic and we may call it a grotesque and savage comedy, but we miss the point if we think that the countryman is being rude or cynical. It does not occur to him to leave the body in the burning house, and he has done his best under the circumstances to observe the decencies. His wry and sardonic humor is not disparaging or irreverent, though it speaks to the issue and keeps, amid the horror, a tenacious grip on common sense. Faulkner's work is full of this kind of comedy. *The Hamlet* and *As I Lay Dying* abound in it, and there is not a little of it in *Light in August*.

One can look at Faulkner's comedy in still another way. We may say that Faulkner tends to take the long view in which the human enterprise in all its basically vital manifestations is seen from far off and with great detachment. If the view is long enough and the perspective full enough, the basic attitude is almost inevitably comic. James Joyce comes to mind. His *Ulysses*, though it has much pathos and horror in it, is also finally a comic work. In *Light in August* Faulkner observes even the tragic events that involve Joanna Burden with detachment and in a full perspective. It is Lena and her instinct for nature, Lena and her rapport with the community, Lena as a link in the eternal progression from mother to daughter who provides the final norm for our judgment. In this connection Faulkner's abiding concern with man's endurance and his ability to suffer anything— compare the Nobel Prize speech—is worth remembering. Tragedy always concerns itself with the individual, his values, his tragic encounter with the reality about him, and the waste which is suffered in his defeat. Comedy involves, on the other hand, the author's basic alignment with society and with the community.

In calling *Light in August* a pastoral we have already suggested something of the comic mood. The pastoral, on the whole, aligns itself with comedy, not with tragedy. The suggestion made earlier that *Light in August* is a kind of pastoral has not been made whimsically. The last chapter of the book, with the adventures of Byron Bunch and Lena, is almost conventionally pastoral, and pastoral with an authentic comic note, for Byron is comically balked of his reward. The little man has done quite nobly. He has befriended and protected Lena, and now Lena obviously should marry him; but as the book closes, Lena is still hitchhiking across Tennessee in pursuit of Lucas Burch. Yet Byron finds it impossible to abandon her.

Our last glimpse of Lena is given through the eyes of a character whom we have not met before in the novel. Faulkner introduces him most casually. The last chapter simply opens to the statement that there lives in the eastern part of the state a furniture repairer and dealer "who recently made a trip into Tennessee to get some old pieces of furniture which he had bought by correspondence." On this trip the furniture dealer picked up the hitchhikers Lena, her baby, and her strange little bachelor companion. The oddity of the group piques his curiosity. Later he senses what is going on and the situation stirs his amusement, though it is an amusement not without insight into Lena's coquetry and not without a trace of pity for Byron's abashed devotion.

The reader may resent the casual and last-minute introduction of the new narrator and he may be disposed to dismiss this incident as simply another of Faulkner's tricky fictional devices. Yet if he has been able to see the importance of the community in this novel, he should have little difficulty in hearing and recognizing the voice of the community once more in the furniture dealer's narration. It is not important that we do not know his name or that we have not met him before or that we shall not meet him again. He can be for us the anonymous, earthy, genial, experienced, tough-minded representative of a corporate body of values, insights, and beliefs.

As such a representative, he finds Byron's plight amusing, and he obviously enjoys having so good a story to relate to his wife when he gets home. But his humor is not cruel and his insights into the relation of man and woman, the nature of chivalry, and the connection of love with honor are not untouched by a certain wisdom. In any case, we can observe that this last chapter of *Light in August,* with its comic overtones, does not really represent an abandonment of the theme that I ventured earlier to characterize in a phrase borrowed from John Crowe Ransom. For Byron Bunch too is a man unable "to fathom or perform his nature"—still unable, that is, in our last glimpse of him, to bring Lena to terms. He has acted unselfishly and gallantly, but he cannot do now what the furniture dealer knows that he ought to do: force the issue and persuade Lena to accept him as lover and husband.

On the first night they camp out together, the furniture dealer thinks that Byron has nerved himself to the act. He watches Byron quietly entering the truck where Lena is sleeping and, as he observes to his wife, "I says to myself, 'Old boy, if you'd a just done this last night, you'd a been sixty miles further south than you are now, to my knowledge" (p. 440). But Lena repels Byron's advances with the exclamation: "Why, Mr. Bunch. Aint you ashamed. You might have woke the baby, too." And the furniture dealer tells his wife: "I be dog if I dont believe she picked him up and set him back outside on the ground like she would that baby if it had been about six years old" (p. 441).

Byron had retired in confusion, but when the furniture dealer started the next day's journey with the imperturbable Lena and her child, Byron was waiting around the next curve in the road, and got back in the truck with the explanation: "I done come too far now. . . . I be dog if I'm going to quit now." Lena answers him with: "Aint nobody never said for you to quit" (p. 443).

The furniture dealer evidently has no doubt that eventually Lena will marry Byron. He says to his wife, in explaining Lena's continuation of her obviously foolish quest, "I think she was just traveling. I dont think she had any idea of finding whoever it was she was following. I dont think she had ever aimed to, only she hadn't told him [Byron] yet. . . . I reckon she knew that when she settled down this time, it would likely be for the rest of her life. That's what I think" (p. 444).

Gail Hightower, too, had earlier made the same prophecy when he imagined that Lena would continue to bear children, fulfilling her nature, but, in the future, children sired by Byron. Eventually, one supposes, Byron came to realize that Lena wanted to be possessed and mastered. For though Faulkner counsels that man should stand in awe of nature, and, loving and respecting it, should forbear to violate it, he does not expect man to stand perpetually aloof from nature, completely passive and lacking a field for action. Byron needs to learn the mean between a rape and Platonic love. But Faulkner did not choose to give us here the story of the marriage of Byron and Lena. He preferred to end his novel on the dominant theme of man's inability to fulfill himself, though the theme is treated here not tragically but with humor and amused irony—even as social comedy.

Faulkner's *Light in August*

by *Michael Millgate*

By comparison with *The Sound and the Fury* and *As I Lay Dying* the opening pages of *Light in August* display a much closer approximation to the techniques and progressions of "conventional" fiction. The first chapter, with its image of Lena Grove pursuing her tranquil way steadily across the face of Mississippi, immediately recalls the opening of such Hardy novels as *The Mayor of Casterbridge* or *The Return of the Native,* and even the abrupt transitions to apparently unrelated material in the second and third chapters will not disturb anyone familiar with Dickens—with, say, *Bleak House,* or *Our Mutual Friend.* Throughout *Light in August,* indeed, we are aware of an essential affinity with the major traditions of the nineteenth-century novel and especially with the work of Hardy and Dickens, and the initial impression of the relative conventionality of *Light in August* to some degree remains to the end of the book. But the demands the novel makes of its readers are by no means of a wholly conventional nature; this is especially true of the kind of moral and emotional engagement which Faulkner extorts, but it is also true of the narrative technique, which is much less straightforward than might appear at first sight.

The "time present" of the novel, as defined by the opening account of Lena's meeting with Armstid, begins on a Friday afternoon. In a sense, however, Lena's relationship with Armstid and his wife lies outside the action of the novel proper; it is a framing episode, a prelude, linked with the epilogue or coda provided in the final chapter

"Faulkner's Light in August*" (Editor's title). From* The Achievement of William Faulkner *by Michael Millgate (New York: Random House, Inc., 1966; London: Constable & Co. Ltd., 1966), pp. 124–37. Copyright © 1963, 1964, 1966 by Michael Millgate. Excerpted and reprinted with the permission of Random House, Inc., and A. D. Peters & Company.*

of the book. The point at which the main action of the novel is
engaged is at the very end of the first chapter, when Lena arrives on
the outskirts of Jefferson and sees the smoke rising from the ruins of
Miss Burden's home. This is about midday on the Saturday, and it
is important to note that, for all the novel's abundance of narrative
incident, many of the major events have by this time already taken
place. One major event—indeed, it is one of the three crucial events
in the immediate action of the novel—has taken place during the
night which Lena spent at the Armstids': this is the death of Joanna
Burden. The two other crucial events both take place on the ninth
day following Lena's arrival in Jefferson; that Monday morning Lena
gives birth to her child, and that afternoon Percy Grimm hunts down
Joe Christmas and kills him. A very considerable proportion of the
novel is taken up with extended "flashbacks" which recount the history
of various characters up to the point at which they become involved
in the present action. . . .

. . . We first see Christmas, for example, as he appears to Mooney,
the foreman at the planing mill, to Byron Bunch, and to the people
of Jefferson generally: only later are we given those details of Christmas's birth and upbringing which force us radically to amend our judgment of a man whom we, like the people of Jefferson, have already condemned on sight as inherently vicious and worthless. . . . If, on the
other hand, we are given Lena Grove's history the moment she appears,
that is primarily because she and her background are so simple and
so easily explained, and because she seems not so much a character
in the book, with possibilities of development and unanticipated
variety, as a kind of impersonalised catalytic force, effecting change
but itself unchanging. She provides a steady, imperturbable ground-
note, an onward linear progression that offers a constant contrast to
the desperate contortions—moral, emotional, and physical—of the
other characters.

It seems possible to speak almost in diagrammatic terms of this novel,
rich as it is in symbolic potentialities, disposed in large and readily
distinguishable blocks of material, and with whole scenes presented
almost in the form of tableaux, as formalised, even frozen, action:[1]
Lena traversing the face of Mississippi "like something moving forever and without progress across an urn" (p. 5); Christmas and Mc-
Eachern waiting in rigid immobility during the intervals of their

[1] See Darrel Abel, "Frozen Movement in *Light in August*," *Boston University Studies in English*, III (Spring 1957), 32–44 [this volume, pp. 42–54]; Norman Holmes Pearson, "Lena Grove," *Shenandoah*, III (Spring 1952), 3–7.

hourly ritual of command, refusal, and punishment; Percy Grimm pursuing Christmas "with that lean, swift, blind obedience to whatever Player moved him on the Board" (p. 437). It is remarkable that a great deal even of the present action of the novel is not directly recounted but reflected in the minds and memories of witnesses who were not themselves involved in the action: Gavin Stevens giving his interpretation of the events leading to Christmas's death; the furniture dealer telling his wife of his encounter with Lena and Byron Bunch; the impersonal "they" of the latter part of Chapter 15, recounting "about supper tables in electrically lighted rooms and in remote hill cabins with kerosene lamps" (p. 330) the story of Christmas's arrest in Mottstown and the curious behaviour of Doc Hines and his wife. It is almost as though Faulkner were seeking to "domesticate," to incorporate within the structure of a conventional novel, the technique of multiple reflection which he had earlier employed in *As I Lay Dying,* and it is certainly clear that in *Light in August* he is concerned not merely to tell the stories of Joe Christmas, Lena Grove and Gail Hightower but also, and perhaps primarily, to show the impact of these stories upon the people of Jefferson.

One cannot avoid speaking in the plural of the stories of Christmas, Lena and Hightower, for there are quite unmistakably three distinct strands in the novel. They are not, however, entirely separable strands, and critics have become steadily more aware of the essential unity of the novel, a unity secured through various forms of thematic interrelation and ironic reflection rather than through the more familiar kinds of narrative link—though even these links are stronger and more numerous than has often been allowed, as Malcolm Cowley discovered when he attempted to separate one of the strands for inclusion in *The Portable Faulkner*.[2] Joanna Burden, in the corruption of a sensuality discovered too late and pursued too far, offers an obvious contrast to the healthy animality of Lena Grove; Lena herself, travelling down her "peaceful corridor paved with unflagging and tranquil faith and peopled with kind and nameless faces and voices," (p. 4) is at the opposite pole from Joe Christmas, who for fifteen years has travelled down a street which "ran on in its moods and phases, always empty: he might have seen himself as in numberless avatars, in silence, doomed

[2] Malcolm Cowley to William Faulkner, September 17, 1945. The Faulkner-Cowley correspondence is deposited in the Yale University Library. Faulkner's letters are, with one exception, undated but have been numbered and catalogued in the sequence in which Malcolm Cowley placed them. Future references will give simply this number.

with motion, driven by the courage of flagged and spurred despair."
(p. 213) Faulkner himself spoke of Hightower as the antithesis of
Christmas, in that he "escaped into his past," [3] presumably an allusion
to the way in which Christmas, bereft of all certainty about his past,
cannot rest from his passionate engagement with the present. On a
more comic level, there is the utter dichotomy between the conscien-
tious Byron Bunch and his shiftless "rival" and near-namesake, Lucas
Burch. . . .

Running throughout the book is that fundamental irony which
Faulkner explores to a greater or lesser degree in almost all of his
novels: the gulf between appearance and actuality, the contrast between the public and the private self. We have already noted the contrast between the outward face of Joe Christmas and the inner reality
with which the reader becomes increasingly familiar as the book pro-
gresses. Another character whom we apprehend on two levels in this
way is Joanna Burden, inwardly a chaos of sensuality, outwardly a
woman of mature wisdom, dispensing "advice, business, financial and
religious, to the presidents and faculties and trustees, and advice personal and practical to young girl students and even alumnae, of a
dozen negro schools and colleges through the south." (p. 20) Hightower and Byron Bunch are other characters in whom we become aware
of such a duality, while again and again we realise that the characters
themselves are seeing their fellow men and women not as they actually
are but as they wish them to be: so Miss Burden sees Christmas as
"negro"; so Hightower discerns in his wife, as Joe Christmas discerns
in Bobbie Allen, a non-existent quality of love.

These ironic patterns are clearly related to that theme in the novel
which critics have often, and rightly, identified as being of major significance: the demand of organised society and organised religion that
the human individual act in strict accordance with prescribed abstract
patterns. At the hands of religious authoritarians such as Hines and
McEachern, Christmas has suffered all his life from this demand, and it
is in response to the same rigid requirement that he is finally hunted
down according to the rules prescribed in Jefferson for the treatment of
"nigger murderers." There are, too, several passages in the novel which
seem to imply a general social denunciation. After the death of Miss
Burden, for instance, the people of Jefferson refused to let her body
lie in peace but preferred to believe that it "cried out for vengeance"
(p. 273) . . . It is interesting, however, that Faulkner's criticism of

[3] Frederick L. Gwynn and Joseph L. Blotner, eds., *Faulkner in the University*
(Charlottesville: The University of Virginia Press, 1959), p. 45.

Jefferson is relatively mild. After the arrest of Christmas it is the peace and quiet of the town which is insisted upon: Percy Grimm walks across "the quiet square empty of people peacefully at suppertables about that peaceful town and that peaceful country," (p. 430) and Faulkner makes it entirely clear in this deeply imagined and superbly evoked episode that it is Percy Grimm alone who provokes the town to that course of ritual action of which he himself inevitably becomes the final instrument. The men who share Grimm's pursuit of Christmas do not necessarily share his savagery, for one of them vomits at the sight of the castration, and it is clear that, in his presentation of Grimm, Faulkner was not especially concerned to portray a specifically Southern type of violence: years later he wrote to Malcolm Cowley of having created a Nazi before Hitler did.[4] Although it would be an exaggeration to say that in its conduct towards Christmas the society of Jefferson appears at its collective worst, it might at least be said that the occasion permitted the worst elements in Jefferson to emerge and take command. But in any case a counterbalance is supplied by Lena Grove: she brings out—not always readily, but eventually—the best in Jefferson, and it is with Lena, in her familiar role as the calm recipient of kindness, that the book begins and ends.

There is, however, little qualification or amelioration of the book's rejection of organised religion and religious fanaticism. The bigotry of several characters, in the past as well as the present, is closely examined and shown to be self-condemned by its own rigidity and inhumanity, and it is a final astringent touch in Faulkner's treatment of this theme that as Percy Grimm hunts down Joe Christmas his face displays "that serene, unearthly luminousness of angels in church windows," (p. 437) and his voice sounds "clear and outraged like that of a young priest." (p. 439) All these characters, so assured in their narrow faith, are in contrast to Joe Christmas himself, a man engaged in unceasing introspection, a persistent and desperate search for personal identity and for a meaning in life.[5] He is several times likened to a monk, and Faulkner, answering a question put to him at the University of Virginia, spoke revealingly of Christmas's self-isolation from the world . . .[6] For all his confusion, however, it is Christmas who discovers one of the two

---

[4] Malcolm Cowley, Editor's Note, *The Portable Faulkner* (New York: The Viking Press, 1946), p. 652. Compare Faulkner to Cowley, 9.

[5] See Alfred Kazin, "The Stillness of *Light in August*," in Frederick J. Hoffman and Olga W. Vickery, eds., *William Faulkner: Three Decades of Criticism* (New York and Burlingame: Harcourt, Brace and World, Inc., 1963), pp. 252–53.

[6] Gwynn and Blotner, eds., *Faulkner in the University*, p. 72. [See Faulkner's own discussion of Joe Christmas on pp. 93–94, 95 of this volume.]

forms of religious and moral experience which Faulkner appears to
offer as valid. Christmas, who becomes godlike in his last agony, discovers the way of suffering, of passive acceptance, the path of crucifixion. The opposite but complementary figure in the novel is Lena
Grove, who, in her simple and unquestioning acceptance of a kind of
natural religion, seems to embody those simple and permanent values
which Faulkner so frequently and so powerfully affirmed, the values of
endurance, patience, fecundity, and simple faith. *"That will be her life,
her destiny,"* Hightower recognises: *"The good stock peopling in tranquil obedience to it the good earth; from these hearty loins without
hurry or haste descending mother and daughter."* (p. 384)

The opposition, and indeed counterpoint, of Lena Grove and Joe
Christmas is clear and apparent throughout the novel, and its validity
is readily acceptable. The disturbing figure, morally and structurally, is
that of Hightower. He has seemed to many critics a shadowy and in-
determinate figure, lacking a sufficiently substantial stake in the plot
or an adequately defined role in the moral or symbolic patterns of the
book as a whole. But such a judgment may result from a failure to distinguish Hightower's functions from Faulkner's deliberate characterisa-
tion of him as a non-participator, a man withdrawn from life and its
sufferings. . . .

* * *

. . . The "idea" in forming Faulkner's presentation of Hightower is
clear; it is, indeed, sufficiently implied in the obvious symbolism of his
name.[7] But Hightower . . . has . . . more than a merely narrative
connection with the Byron Bunch-Lena Grove relationship. He is more
than once described as an eastern idol, and for Byron Bunch he is initially a repository of wisdom; it is Byron who interprets the stale smell
of Hightower's house as the odour of goodness. Byron at the opening
of the book is Hightower's disciple, his imitator in silence, withdrawal, isolation from life; but Byron is converted by his love for
Lena to a new concern for humanity which soon extends beyond his
relationship with Lena herself and overflows into a compassionate if
hopeless attempt to aid Joe Christmas. What vitiates so many of the
relationships in the novel—between Joanna Burden and Joe Christmas,
for example, between Christmas and his various women, between Hightower and his wife—is their selfishness and lack of generosity: the

---

[7] Mr. Albert Erskine has pointed out to me, however, that the name is not uncom-
mon in Mississippi.

partners use those whom they claim to love primarily as a means of attacking some personal problem. As Hightower comes eventually to realise of his own married life, such relationships remain on an abstract level rather than a human one, and they are effectively criticised in terms of the warm, humane, and outward-going quality of Byron's love for Lena. Byron not only breaks with his earlier discipleship but actually becomes his master's teacher, showing him the way to that recognition of value in life, in human involvement, which Hightower finally achieves. It is, however, too late for Hightower to be effectively reborn. Lena does not name her baby after him, and his mind cannot rest in the vision of human solidarity and interdependence which he has with such agony achieved but returns ineluctably to that obsessive image of his grandfather which has haunted him throughout his life— though Faulkner himself reminded us that this image was not in itself an ignoble one: "[Hightower] had to endure, to live, but that was one thing that was pure and fine that he had—was the memory of his grandfather, who had been brave." [8]

Faulkner said more than once that he began *Light in August* with nothing clearly in mind save the image of Lena Grove—"knowing no more about it than a young woman, pregnant, walking along a strange country road." [9] . . . The suggestion that "Light in August" is a countryman's expression used of a cow or mare due to drop her calf or foal in that month might tend to confirm the primacy of the Lena Grove element, but it seems unlikely that in choosing a title for so various a novel Faulkner would have such a narrow range of relevance in mind.[10] In any case, discussion of this point has to some extent diverted attention from other substantial justifications for the title which appear within the book itself. Many critics have noticed the frequency in the novel of images of light and dark, for example, and Faulkner spoke very interestingly of a special quality of light which he had in mind:

[I]n August in Mississippi there's a few days somewhere about the middle of the month when suddenly there's a foretaste of fall, it's cool, there's a lambence, a luminous quality to the light, as though it came not from just today but from back in the old classic times. It might have fauns and satyrs and the gods and—from Greece, from Olympus in it some-

[8] Gwynn and Blotner, eds., *Faulkner in the University*, p. 75; see also p. 45.

[9] Typescript of an unpublished autobiographical piece in the Alderman Library, pp. 2–3.

[10] The manuscript in the Alderman Library seems originally to have been entitled "Dark House" . . . possibly an allusion to section VII of Tennyson's *In Memoriam*.

where. It lasts just for a day or two, then it's gone, but every year in
August that occurs in my country, and that's all that title meant, it was
just to me a pleasant evocative title because it reminded me of that time,
of a luminosity older than our Christian civilization.[11]

It is this light which shines on the day of Christmas's death and at the
moment when Hightower finally recognises the truth about himself and
the extent of his responsibility both for his own suffering and for that
of his dead wife: "In the lambent suspension of August into which
night is about to fully come, it [the wheel of his thinking] seems to engender and surround itself with a faint glow like a halo." (p. 465) But
Faulkner seems to hint at some wider meaning in his references to "the
old classic times . . . fauns and satyrs and the gods" and the "pagan
quality" of Lena Grove. The "earth-mother" qualities in Lena Grove
are clearly hinted at in her name, and have long been recognised. But
given Faulkner's undoubted familiarity with these stories of classical
mythology and with the works of Joyce and Eliot, and his probable
acquaintance with Frazer's *The Golden Bough,* it would not be surprising if he had further analogies in mind: not necessarily a complex
and carefully articulated pattern of analogy such as Joyce evolved in
Ulysses, but perhaps some slightly opportunistic exploitation of an
available source such as he had shown in his allocation of three sections
of *The Sound and the Fury* to the dates of Easter 1929 or in the various
hinted analogies in *Light in August* itself between Joe Christmas and
Jesus Christ, between Lena Grove and the Virgin Mary, and between
Byron Bunch and Mary's husband, Joseph.[12]

Any search for underlying patterns in *Light in August* might well
begin with a consideration of the extensive series of parallels and sub-
stitutions which appear in the course of the novel and which again
and again establish thematic and even narrative links between its different strands. An obvious example is Mrs. Hines's confused identification of Lena's baby with Joe Christmas when he was a child, and her
further reference to the baby as being actually Christmas's son.[13] One
thinks also of the similarities between the apparently opposed back-
grounds of Hightower and Miss Burden, fanatics of the South and of

[11] Gwynn and Blotner, eds., *Faulkner in the University,* p. 199.

[12] See Robert M. Slabey, "Myth and Ritual in *Light in August,*" *Texas Studies in
Literature and Language,* II (Autumn 1960), 328–49 [this volume, pp. 91–92], for
an extremely interesting discussion of mythic elements in the novel.

[13] Kazin, "The Stillness of *Light in August,*" p. 249, speaks of this incident as
"virtually an annunciation."

the North; of the parallelism between the tragic encounter of Joe
Christmas with Percy Grimm and the primarily comic encounter of
Byron Bunch with Lucas Burch, which takes place at the same moment in time; of the reverberations set up in the reader's mind by the
incident of Christmas breaking into a Negro church like an impersonation of the devil, recalling as it does both the mad forays into Negro
churches made by his grandfather, Doc Hines, and the moment of
Satanic glee caught by the camera as Hightower leaves his empty
church.

Most important of all, however, is the relationship between Miss
Burden and Lena Grove and Lena's replacement of Miss Burden at
the plantation after the latter's death, and there are reasons for thinking that Faulkner may have intended a series of allusions to the goddess Diana and to the sacred groves where she was worshipped. Lena
Grove's name is an obvious hint leading in this direction, and the
Burden house itself is several times described as standing almost hidden among a grove of trees, a grove which still stands even when the
house itself has gone; the place, too, is one to which Negro women
have come for many years as to a shrine or to a "wise woman"—"approaching the house in a manner not exactly secret, yet purposeful,
. . . emerging again and returning down the radiating paths not fast
and yet not loitering." (p. 243) Miss Burden, the original mistress of
the grove, is not on the face of it an especially Diana-like character, but
she has certain characteristics in common with the Roman Diana—
notably her masculinity, her reputation for virginity, and her moon-
like ebb and flow of passion as she and Christmas pass through all the
different phases of their relationship—and it is she whom the Negro
women have consulted in their troubles, especially, it appears (p. 251),
in those troubles of pregnancy and childbirth which were Diana's special province. Lena Grove, on the other hand, with her name, her air
of timeless permanence, and her fecundity, has much in common with
that Ephesian Diana who was specifically an earth-mother, fertility
figure.

Is there, perhaps, some sense in which Faulkner intended the ritualistic murder of Joanna Burden, carried out as Lena Grove pauses over-
night on the outskirts of the town, to be an act preparatory to the
replacement of Miss Burden's alien, outmoded, and sterile influence
by the natural vitality and fecundity embodied in Lena? Certainly
something more than the mere establishment of a weak narrative link
seems to be involved in Lena's occupation of the cabin on the Burden

estate and the birth there of her child. Hightower, in particular, makes
it clear that new life has come to the run-down plantation, the "ruined
garden," (p. 264) that some kind of symbolic rebirth has been enacted:

> He emerges from the woods at the far side of the pasture behind the
> cabin. Beyond the cabin he can see the clump of trees in which the
> house had stood and burned, though from here he cannot see the charred
> and mute embers of what were once planks and beams. "Poor woman,"
> he thinks. "Poor, barren woman. To have not lived only a week longer,
> until luck returned to this place. Until luck and life returned to these
> barren and ruined acres." It seems to him that he can see, feel, about
> him the ghosts of rich fields, and of the rich fecund black life of the
> quarters, the mellow shouts, the presence of fecund women, the pro-
> lific naked children in the dust before the doors; and the big house
> again, noisy, loud with the treble shouts of the generations. (p. 385)

Hightower sees the pathos of Miss Burden's passing, but the reader
may sense that her death has in some way been a precondition of the
rebirth which is here so eloquently evoked. The death seems fated,
like so much else in the novel, and, like the death of Joe Christmas
nine days later, it is certainly executed in ritualistic fashion: Miss
Burden herself prepares for it in prayer and Christmas prepares for it
by performing what can perhaps be best described as the quasi-rituals
of stripping himself of the last woman-sewn button and showing himself naked in the lights of a passing car, by shaving at the spring,
and by temporarily immersing himself in the "thick black pit" (p. 107)
of the Negro district.

Immediately before Christmas goes in to kill Miss Burden, at midnight on the Friday, we are given this insight into his thoughts:

> Now it was still, quiet, the fecund earth now coolly suspirant. The dark
> was filled with the voices, myriad, out of all time that he had known,
> as though all the past was a flat pattern. And going on: tomorrow night,
> all the tomorrows, to be a part of the flat pattern, going on. He thought
> of that with quiet astonishment: going on, myriad, familiar, since all
> that had ever been was the same as all that was to be, since tomorrow
> to-be and had-been would be the same. Then it was time. (p. 266)

This is as precise a verbal definition as can be found in the novel of
the kind of representative significance embodied by Lena Grove:
Christmas here realises, in a flash of insight, the fundamental permanence of the earth and of human experience which lies beneath and
beyond the immediate present of agonised searching and violent experience in which he is himself so inextricably engaged. Also signifi-

cant, however, is the final statement: "Then it was time." This is the
moment on which, in a very real sense, the whole novel turns, the
moment of midnight on the Friday night which Lena spends at the
Armstids'. It is on this point of time that the entire long flashback recounting Christmas's previous experiences is poised, and since the
flashback begins on page 111 and occupies only a few pages short of a
third of the novel, it must be considered one of Faulkner's most extended experiments in suspended time.

The statement, "Then it was time," may thus be in the nature of an
announcement that the moment has been released from its suspension,
that the action is henceforward immersed once more in the flow of
time. This is, however, a novel in which the course of present events is
very carefully charted and in which many of the characters display an
extraordinary awareness of time: Byron meticulously keeps his own
time when working alone; Hightower always knows the time although
he has no clock; while Christmas is being pursued he is driven to speak
to people not by any need for food but by his need to know what day
it is. It seems probable that Faulkner had some kind of deliberate time
scheme in mind as he wrote the book, and since the ancient festival of
Diana used to be celebrated in August it is conceivable that he intended some allusion to it.[14] The fact that fire was especially important
in the celebration of the festival would then give additional significance to the fire at the Burden house and to the title of the novel itself. There are several more hints of this kind, and there are even a
number of features in the account of Christmas's pursuit and murder by
Percy Grimm—most notably, the comparison of Grimm to a young
priest—which tempt one to wonder whether Faulkner's imagination
may not initially have been seized by Frazer's description in the opening pages of *The Golden Bough* of the "barbarous custom" followed in
Roman times to decide the succession to the priesthood of Diana's
sacred grove and sanctuary at Nemi.[15]

These suggested correspondences between *Light in August* and the
mythology and anthropology surrounding the figure of Diana may be
entirely accidental. Alternatively, such correspondences, like those

[14] J. G. Frazer, *The Golden Bough: A Study in Magic and Religion* (London,
1911), Part I, Vol. 1, pp. 12–14. The present action of *Light in August* apparently
takes place in 1932 (see William H. F. Lamont, "The Chronology of *Light in August*,"
Modern Fiction Studies, III [Winter 1957–1958], 360–361), and it is perhaps worth
noting that in that year August 13, the date of Diana's festival, fell on a Saturday:
Joe Christmas waits for midnight on the Friday night before going into the house
to kill Miss Burden in the early moments of the Saturday.

[15] Frazer, *The Golden Bough*, Part I, Vol. 1, pp. 8–11.

linking characters in the book with the members of the Holy Family, may represent only one among several patterns of analogy which Faulkner pursued in the course of the novel, and it is possible that he intended a symbolic substitution of Lena as a Holy Mother figure (an aspect in her presentation which is particularly stressed in the final chapter) for the barren Diana figure of Miss Burden.[16] But one thing is clear: the structure of *Light in August* cannot be adequately defined as a loose combination and conflation of three separate stories. As other critics have argued, there are in effect three quite distinct conclusions to the novel, each containing a bare minimum of references to the other two, and it would have been extremely simple for Faulkner, had he so wished, to establish a much closer texture of purely narrative links between the three strands. He did not so choose, however, and the structure of *Light in August* which we have already remarked as harking back in certain important respects to *As I Lay Dying* may also be said to look forward to the divided "double-novel" structure of *The Wild Palms*. But in reading *Light in August* we are not especially aware of the discreteness of the different narrative strands. Much of the novel's cohesion derives from its interconnecting patterns of reflection, repetition, substitution, and contrast. Something is also gained by Faulkner's use of recurrent images, such as that of the circle, and of analogical patterns. But the great and unifying strength of the book remains its most obvious one: the sheer force and passion of its presentation of Joe Christmas, the quintessential victim, and the way in which we, like all the characters in the book, are irresistibly swept into the vortex of Christmas's restless life and agonising death.

[16] Compare *ibid.*, p. 14: "The Christian Church appears to have sanctified this great festival of the Assumption of the Blessed Virgin on the fifteenth of August." This first chapter of *The Golden Bough* offers many extremely suggestive points of comparison with *Light in August*.

PART TWO

View Points

THE BROADER DESIGN
OF FAULKNER'S FICTION

William Faulkner

As regards any specific book, I'm trying primarily to tell a story, in the most effective way I can think of, the most moving, the most exhaustive. But I think even that is incidental to what I am trying to do, taking my output (the course of it) as a whole. . . .

From William Faulkner, Letter to Malcolm Cowley [Nov. 1944], in Malcolm Cowley, The Faulkner-Cowley File: Letters and Memories *(New York: The Viking Press, Inc., 1966), p. 14. Copyright © 1966 by The Estate of William Faulkner. All rights reserved. Excerpted and reprinted with the permission of The Viking Press, Inc., and Chatto & Windus, Ltd.*

Malcolm Cowley

Faulkner's mythical kingdom is a county in northern Mississippi, on the border between the sand hills covered with scrubby pine and the black earth of the river bottoms. Except for the storekeepers, mechanics, and professional men who live in Jefferson, the county seat, all the inhabitants are farmers or woodsmen. Except for a little lumber, their only product is baled cotton for the Memphis market. A few of them live in big plantation houses, the relics of another age, and more of them in substantial wooden farmhouses; but most of them are tenants, no better housed than slaves on good plantations before the Civil War. Yoknapatawpha County—"William Faulkner, sole owner and proprietor," as he inscribed on one of the maps he drew—has a population of 15,611 persons scattered over 2,400 square miles. It sometimes seems to

From "Introduction," The Portable Faulkner. *Revised and expanded edition edited by Malcolm Cowley (New York: The Viking Press, Inc., 1946), pp. 5, 8. Copyright 1946 by the Viking Press, Inc. Reprinted by permission of The Viking Press.*

me that . . . all the people of the imaginary county, black and white, townsmen, farmers, and housewives, have played their parts in one connected story. . . .

All his books in the Yoknapatawpha saga are part of the same living pattern. It is this pattern, and not the printed volumes in which part of it is recorded, that is Faulkner's real achievement. Its existence helps to explain one feature of his work: that each novel, each long or short story, seems to reveal more than it states explicitly and to have a subject bigger than itself.

THE UNITY OF *Light in August*

Malcolm Cowley

"Light in August" I now feel is the best of your novels. . . . I thought when I first read it that it dissolved too much into the three separate stories of Lena Grove (wonderful), Hightower and Joe Christmas—but I read it [again] with the idea that Lena or Joe might be picked out of the text and found that they were too closely interwoven with the others. It would be easy for you to *write* Joe Christmas into a separate novel, but the anthologist can't pick him out without leaving bits of his flesh hanging to Hightower and Lena.

From Malcolm Cowley, Letter to William Faulkner [September 17, 1945], in Malcolm Cowley, The Faulkner-Cowley File: Letters and Memories *(New York: The Viking Press, Inc., 1966), pp. 28–29. Copyright © 1966 by Malcolm Cowley. Excerpted and reprinted with the permission of The Viking Press, Inc., and Chatto & Windus Ltd.*

Lawrance Thompson

One element of form has been saved for a final consideration. It is the structural antithesis of counterpoint established between the story of what happened to Joe Christmas and the story of what happened to

From William Faulkner: An Introduction and Interpretation, *by Lawrance Thompson, Second Edition. Copyright © 1963, 1967 by Holt, Rinehart and Winston, Inc. Excerpted and reprinted by permission of Holt, Rinehart and Winston, Inc.*

Lena Grove. One aspect of theme acquires implicit illumination from Faulkner's arrangement of those two narratives in such a way that the action starts and ends with Lena Grove. Here, as in *The Sound and the Fury*, the structural arrangement lets the positives bracket and contain the negatives. Lena Grove is another of Faulkner's primitive and pagan characters; a social outcast who has made herself vulnerable to social criticism because she has violated certain moral conventions. At first glance, her innocent attitudes toward love and hate appear to be merely naïve. Yet from the start Lena Grove is represented as having a peculiar power to evoke from others various reflections of her own gentleness, kindliness, and compassion. Implicitly, Faulkner establishes an important counterpoint between Lena Grove's capacity for placing herself in accord with "the old earth of and with and by which she lives," and Joe Christmas' placing himself at odds with "the very immutable laws which earth must obey." If interpreted within the framework of Faulkner's moral vision, those "laws" have to do with the "verities of the heart." They include an awareness of the practical necessity implicit in positive expressions of courage, endurance, compassion, aspiration, sacrifice, pride, and love. Faulkner begins by establishing her pagan kinship with Mother Earth and with the fruitful light of August: "swollen, slow, deliberate, unhurried and tireless as augmenting afternoon itself . . . with that providential caution of the old earth of and with and by which she lives." The analogies implied between her inner light and the outer light of August becomes reinforced when Hightower says of her, after her child has been born on the morning of the day Joe Christmas is to die, "That will be her life, her destiny. The good stock peopl[ing], in tranquil obedience to it, the good earth; from these hearty loins without hurry or haste descending mother and daughter." Those passages suggest why Faulkner chose to bracket, structurally, the negations and hatreds of the Joe Christmas story within the affirmations of the Lena Grove story.

PROTESTANTISM AS ANTAGONIST IN
Light in August

William Van O'Connor

[William Faulkner saw the] Protestant or puritan spirit as . . . one of the most significant factors, even the key factor, in the tragedy of

Negro and white relationships. This theme [is] . . . explicitly worked
out and elaborated in . . . *Light in August.* If one does not perceive
that the Calvinist spirit is the central issue of *Light in August,* the
novel of necessity will seem confused in theme. It is episodic in structure, but the meaning is clear. The Civil War and the black shadow of
slavery do, as some critics insist, suffuse the book. It is proper enough to
observe the position of Hightower in the story, to relive with him the
imagined scenes of galloping horses, burning buildings, the wounded
and dead of the Civil War—these do live on into the 1920's, even in
the minds of those less crippled by such memories than the defrocked
old minister. But the greater force, in which the War and the black
shadow are caught up, is Calvinism, and, larger than it, rigidity of
principle and harshness of spirit; and it is this force that menaces Joe
Christmas, the putative Negro, and that persecutes Hightower. Byron
Bunch and Lena Grove are more than comic relief; they are proof
that one need not succumb to such a force.

From "Protestantism in Yoknapatawpha County" by William Van O'Connor,
The Hopkins Review, *V (Spring, 1952), 31. Excerpted and reprinted with the permission of the publisher.*

Hyatt H. Waggoner

In one of Gail Hightower's final meditations he pronounces an often
quoted judgment on Southern Protestant Christianity. The music he
hears coming from the church seems to him to have "a quality stern
and implacable, deliberate and without passion so much as immolation,
pleading, asking, for not love, not life, forbidding it to others, demanding in sonorous tones death, as though death were the boon, like all
Protestant music." "Puritanism," or punitive religious moralism, is perhaps the chief intended antagonist in *Light in August,* as it is the immediate antagonist in *Sanctuary.*

"Pleasure, ecstasy," Hightower thinks, "they cannot seem to bear."
Hines and McEachern could be his illustrations, the two most obviously pious people in the story and the two most responsible for the
fate of Joe Christmas. He does not think of them because he does not
know what we know about Christmas's past, but we, reading, supply

From William Faulkner: From Jefferson to the World *by Hyatt H. Waggoner
(Lexington: University of Kentucky Press, 1959), pp. 100–101. Excerpted and reprinted with the permission of the publisher.*

them for him. And when we have finished the novel we feel that events have proved Hightower right when he pictures a crucifixion inflicted not despite but because of the religion of his fellow townsmen:

> *And so why should not their religion drive them to crucifixion of them-*
> *selves and one another?* . . . It seems to him that the past week has
> rushed like a torrent and that the week to come, which will begin to-
> morrow, is the abyss, and that now on the brink of the cataract the
> stream has raised a single blended and sonorous and austere cry, not
> for justification but as a dying salute before its own plunge, and not to
> any god but to the doomed man in the barred cell within hearing of
> them and of the two other churches, and in whose crucifixion they too
> will raise a cross. "And they will do it gladly," he says, in the dark
> window.

Hightower's thoughts constitute a terrible indictment of Southern Christianity, charging that it has become so distorted that it leads men toward hatred and destruction and death, crucifying Christ all over again, and "gladly." A great deal of the substance of the book has the effect of leading us to accept this judgment, and *Light in August* is Faulkner's most fully documented statement on what he sees as the religious errors and the racist guilt of his region. The grim fanatical fundamentalism of McEachern and the mad fundamentalist racism of Hines are judged in negative terms and without any shadow of qualification.

Lawrance Thompson

[A]ny statement of Faulkner's major thematic concerns in *Light in August* should point out that in none of his other novels does Faulkner unburden himself quite so furiously as to what he believes to be certain aberrations in Christian practice. He might even be giving conscious support to Nietzsche's claim that Christianity has found ways for poisoning human strength and dignity through preaching excessive self-contempt and self-immolation. A careful reading of *Light in August* should clarify the fact that the basic antithesis or counterpoint or polarity, here, is derived from Faulkner's rebellious insistence on contrasting certain pagan attitudes with certain Christian attitudes for

From William Faulkner: An Introduction and Interpretation, *by Lawrance Thompson, Second Edition. Copyright © 1963, 1967 by Holt, Rinehart and Winston, Inc. Excerpted and reprinted by permission of Holt, Rinehart and Winston, Inc.*

purposes of honoring the pagan. Whatever concepts Faulkner here salvages from his own Christian heritage he reinterprets, as a means of separating them from those meanings in Christian dogma. If he chose largely to define the positive elements of his themes in terms of negatives, he may have done so because once again he wanted to shock, hurt, and upset Christian complacencies.

Sex and Women in *Light in August*

Maxwell Geismar

. . . Faulkner's eroticism is in the end hardly erotic. The underlying view is not sexual, but a distaste for sex. It retards rather than arouses the sensual impulses, throws its blight, in fact, over all the natural passions . . . [with its] emphasis on necrophilia and cannibalism, on misogynists and miscegenation, . . . [on] murderers and their dangling corpses, . . . "Light in August" appears to synthesize all the strains of Faulkner's discontent.

In its scope "Light in August" is certainly one of Faulkner's big novels. Here he has again penetrated more deeply into his people and created a more complex scene than that of "As I Lay Dying." Here too, in a curious way, Faulkner is closer to the central figures of his novel, though it is not easy at first for us to recognize just who the central figures of the novel are. Written as objective narrative rather than interior monologue, "Light in August" is still not without complexity in its exposition. Through the story of Lena, another poor-white mountain girl, again pregnant, again wandering, again seeking the father of her child, and again, we are inclined to believe, mentally deficient, we come to Byron Bunch who falls in love with her. Through Byron's story, we come to Hightower, the minister, betrayed by his wife, driven out of his parish by his congregation, living in disgrace with the town and among his memories of the Civil War. Caught by the dead who had conceived him, the son "who grew to manhood among phantoms" dies among them—

From "William Faulkner: The Negro and the Female," Writers in Crisis: The American Novel, 1925–1940 *by Maxwell Geismar (Boston: Houghton Mifflin Company, 1942), pp. 162–64. Excerpted and reprinted with the permission of the publisher.*

He hears above his heart the thunder increase, myriad and drumming. Like a long sighing of wind in trees it begins, they sweep into sight, borne now upon a cloud of phantom dust. They rush past, forwardleaning in the saddles, with brandished arms, beneath whipping ribbons from slanted and eager lances; with tumult and soundless yelling they sweep past . . . are gone; the dust swirls skyward sucking, fades away into the night which has fully come. Yet . . . it seems to him that he still hears them: the wild bugles and the clashing sabres and the dying thunder of hooves.

From the story of Hightower, held by that moment of thundering hooves and wild bugles in which his life, Faulkner tells us, had begun and ended, we come at last (I am simplifying the exposition, since these narratives within narratives are also broken in time and place) to the murder in Jefferson. Working backward in time from that, we reach the relationship of Joe Christmas and the Miss Burden of "Light in August." And what a romance this is, the central love affair of Faulkner's maturity—this colored Romeo and abolitionist Juliet of Jefferson, Mississippi; the amoral mulatto and the starved spinster; the brutal criminal and the aging nymphomaniac. We come at last to the vicious conjunction in Faulkner's work of the Negro and the Female, the twin furies of Faulkner's deep southern Waste Land; but a waste land, quite unlike Eliot's, of demons and incubae rather than pallid clerks, one which is built on diseased fury and ends, indeed, not with a whimper but a bang.

Which of these entwined partners of evil seems to earn more of Faulkner's opprobrium? It is the woman, Faulkner implies, who has been responsible for the fate of Joe Christmas, the new Faulknerian hero, orphan and outcast, hunted by the world and venting his own hatred on it, semblance of a white man who carried the taint of his own knowledge that he is negro. It is worth while noticing the sequence of female actions which have conditioned the history of Christmas.

Leslie A. Fiedler

In the work of William Faulkner, the fear of the castrating woman and the dis-ease with sexuality present in the novels of his contem-

From Love and Death in the American Novel *by Leslie A. Fiedler (New York: Stein & Day Publishers, 1966), pp. 320–22. Copyright © 1966, 1960 by Leslie A. Fiedler. Excerpted and reprinted with the permission of Stein & Day Publishers, and Jonathan Cape Ltd.*

poraries, Fitzgerald and Hemingway, attain their fullest and shrillest expression. Not content with merely projecting images of the anti-virgin, he insists upon editorializing against the woman he travesties in character and situation. No Jiggs and Maggie cliché of popular anti-feminism is too banal for him to use; he reminds us (again and again!) that men are helpless in the hands of their mothers, wives, and sisters; that females do not think but proceed from evidence to conclusions by paths too devious for males to follow; that they possess neither morality nor honor; that they are capable, therefore, of betrayal without qualm or quiver of guilt but also of inexplicable loyalty; that they enjoy an occasional beating at the hands of their men; that they are unforgiving and without charity to other members of their own sex; that they lose keys and other small useful articles with maddening regularity but are quite capable of finding things invisible to men; that they use their sexuality with cold calculation to achieve their inscrutable ends, etc., etc.

Until his last books, Faulkner treated with respect only females, white ladies or colored women, past the menopause. The elderly maiden or widowed aunt is the sole female figure in his fiction exempt from travesty and contempt. Up to the very verge of her climacteric, woman seems to Faulkner capable of the most shameless concupiscence, like Miss Burden in *Light in August,* cowering naked in the garden of the decaying house waiting to be captured and possessed in an obscene game of hide-and-seek. Faulkner sometimes gives the impression of the village misogynist swapping yarns with the boys at the bar in order to reveal a truth about women which shocks even himself. Like old Varner in *The Hamlet,* he keeps assuring his readers that he "cheerfully and robustly and undeviatingly" declines to accept "any such theory as female chastity other than as a myth to hoodwink young husbands. . . ." But there is little robust or cheerful about his attitudes, however undeviatingly he may assert them; he is less like Varner fundamentally than like Hightower, the scared and stinking refugee from life in *Light in August,* who cries out in despair that "the husband of a mother, whether he be the father or not is already a cuckold . . . what woman has ever suffered from any brute as men have suffered from good women?"

Pubescent or nubile women, for Faulkner, fall into two classes, roughly corresponding to those of Hemingway, though for the former both are terrifying: great, sluggish, mindless daughters of peasants, whose fertility and allure are scarcely distinguishable from those of a beast in heat; and the febrile, almost fleshless but sexually insatiable daughters of the aristocracy. Not the women he observes but those he dreams inhabit Faulkner's novels, myths of masculine protest: the peasant wench as earth goddess (Lena Grove in *Light in August,* Dewy Dell in *As I Lay Dying,* Eula Varner in *The Hamlet*), or the coed as nymphomaniac Venus (Cecily of *Soldiers' Pay,* Patricia in *Mosquitoes,* Temple Drake in *Sanctuary*). Their very names tend toward allegory, "Dewy Dell," for instance, suggesting both a natural setting and woman's sex, her sex as a fact of nature, while "Temple Drake" evokes both a ruined sanctuary and the sense of an unnatural usurpation: woman become a sexual aggressor—more drake than duck.

Unlike the natural women of Hemingway, Faulkner's dewiest dells turn out to be destroyers rather than redeemers, quicksands disguised as sacred groves. In his portrayal of Lena Grove, he relents for once into something like admiration; but his Eula Varner is more typical. Faulkner begins by describing Eula, the goddess who presides over the revels of *The Hamlet* and is married off in the end to its Devil, Flem Snopes, in terms of a pagan dithyramb to Aphrodite: "Her entire appearance suggested some symbology out of the old Dionysic Times, honey in sunlight and bursting grapes, the writhen bleeding of the crushed fecundated vine beneath the hard rapacious trampling goat-hoof." What begins as a pre-Christian eulogy to the inarticulate manifestation of sheer fertility imperceptibly slips over into a puritan cry of distress and distaste before unredeemed, burgeoning life.

Robert M. Slabey

The sex polarity in *Light in August* is most vividly detailed in three descriptions of Joe's "descent into the abyss"; each time the experience is twofold: first, the dark pit itself, followed by an awareness of its opposite, the street, thus making it possible to view their polarity in juxtaposition. Joe's first experience was at the age of fourteen with the Negro girl in the dark barn; he felt himself "enclosed by the woman-shenegro"; (p. 137) leaning over her, "he seemed to look down into a black well and at the bottom saw two glints like reflection of dead stars." After the girl has fled his beating and he is engaged in fighting his comrades, there "was no She at all now . . . it was as if a wind

From *"Myth and Ritual* in Light in August" *by Robert M. Slabey,* Texas Studies in Literature and Language, *II (1960–61), 339–341. Excerpted and reprinted with the permission of the author and the publisher.*

had blown among them, hard and clean." Joe's terrifying night walk through Freedman Town (the Negro section) before he murders Joanna is related first in the anti-chronology of the novel and most fully. (pp. 99–101) He is enclosed by the cabinshapes and the women voices talking and laughing in a strange language: "It was as though he and all other manshaped life about him had been returned to the lightless hot wet primogenitive Female . . . It might have been the original quarry, abyss itself." Fleeing the "thick black pit," he ascends, panting and his heart thudding, into the main street and "the cool hard air of white people." During Joanna's nymphomania "It was as though he had fallen into a sewer"; (p. 224) "he was at the bottom of a pit in the hot wild darkness"; (p. 235) he "began to see himself as from a distance, like a man being sucked down into a bottomless morass." What he longed for was "the street lonely, savage, and cool." (pp. 227–228) The symbolic antithesis is between the images of the pit and the images of the breeze and the street, between female and male, wet, flaccid, hot darkness and dry, rigid, cool light. Pit and breeze are archetypes of female and male respectively: the pit is the primordial womb symbol; the procreative wind and the solar phallus symbolize the creative element in the source of the wind.

Joe rejects the Female on other occasions. An autoerotic assertion of his white masculinity is accomplished in a ritualistic fashion. Standing under Joanna's window he curses her "with slow and calculated obscenity," slashes the last button of his undergarment (recalling that a woman had sewed buttons on his clothes), walks naked across the yard feeling "the dew under his feet as he had never felt dew before." As he stands by the road in the thigh-tall weeds, the headlights of an approaching car shine on his body which becomes "white out of the darkness like a kodak print emerging from the liquid," and as the car passes a white woman shrieks. He spends the night in the deserted but still faintly ammoniac stable, thinking "It's because [horses] are not women. Even a mare horse is a kind of man." (pp. 93–95)

In contrast with these experiences there is the account of Joe's arrival at Miss Burden's in the spring—an earth ritual and a return to the womb. Lying in the copse, Joe can feel "the neversunned earth strike, slow and receptive, against him through his clothes" and is able to breathe in "the damp rich odor of the dark and fecund earth." (p. 199) Climbing through the kitchen window, he was "a shadow returning without a sound and without locomotion to the all-mother of obscurity and darkness." (p. 200) His early relations with Joanna are described in similar Freudian terms: "it had been as though he were outside a house where snow was on the ground, trying to get into the house." (p. 235) Joe's homosexuality has been accepted by several critics; his hermaphroditism (and there is a tradition that Adonis was a Hermaphrodite) is fundamentally psychic and his bisexual urges are symbolic of his opposing impulses. Freudian critics have been justified in citing as evidence the magazine which Joe reads—"of that type whose covers bear *either* pictures of women in underclothes *or* pictures of men in the act of shooting one another with pistols" (p. 96, *italics* added)—but they do not note the implications of an essentially indifferent correlative statement. They also fail to realize the strength of the comparative in Joe's thoughts on the McEacherns: "It was the woman: that soft kindness which he believed himself doomed to be forever victim of and which he *hated worse than* he did the hard and ruthless justice of men." (p. 147, *italics* added) Joe's revulsions at "womanfilth" and sex are balanced by his numerous anonymous promiscuities ("And always, sooner or later, *the street* ran through cities, through an identical and well-nigh interchangeable section of cities without remembered names, where beneath *the dark and equivocal and symbolical archways of midnight* he bedded with the women and paid them when he had the money, and when he did not have it he bedded anyway and then told them that he was a Negro"). (p. 196, *italics* added)

JOE CHRISTMAS: CHRIST FIGURE, VILLAIN, OR TRAGIC HERO

William Faulkner

Q. Mr. Faulkner, did you intend any Christ symbolism in *Light in August* in Joe Christmas?

A. No, that's a matter of reaching into the lumber room to get out something which seems to the writer the most effective way to tell what he is trying to tell. And that comes back to the notion that there are so few plots to use that sooner or later any writer is going to use some-

From Faulkner in the University, *ed. Frederick L. Gwynn and Joseph L. Blotner (Charlottesville: The University Press of Virginia, 1959), p. 117. Excerpted and reprinted with the permission of the publisher.*

thing that has been used. And that Christ story is one of the best stories that man has invented, assuming that he did invent that story, and of course it will recur. Everyone that has had the story of Christ and the Passion as a part of his Christian background will in time draw from that. There was no deliberate intent to repeat it. That the people to me come first. The symbolism comes second.

William H. F. Lamont

I believe that the desire to prove Joe Christmas to be a symbol of Jesus Christ has lured some scholars into assuming that Joe was the same age as Christ (thirty-three) at the time of his death. In the Introduction to the Modern Library edition of *Light in August,* Richard H. Rovere says: "There is Joe's uncertain paternity, the virginity of his mother, the spasmodic introduction of ideas of blood and sacrifice and crucifixion, and the fact that Christmas was lynched at the age Christ was when he was crucified" (xiii). The same kind of statement is made by Beekman W. Cottrell in the Winter 1956–57 *Modern Fiction Studies:* "There is the name of Joe Christmas, with its initials J. C. There is the fact of his uncertain paternity and his appearance at the orphanage on Christmas day. Joe is approximately thirty-three years of age at his lynching" (207).

William Faulkner himself tells us, however, that Joe was already thirty-three when he first arrived in Jefferson (197[1]) and that he lived there for three years. Therefore, he must have been thirty-six, not thirty-three, at the time of his death.

Furthermore, the mere addition of the number of years which Joe spent in different institutions and homes indicates that he was thirty-six when he died. He was an infant of three months when he was abandoned at the doorway of the home for foundlings (332, 335). He spent five years in the home (124). He spent thirteen years (from the ages of five to eighteen) on the farm of the McEacherns (180, 186). He spent the next fifteen years (from eighteen to thirty-three) drifting

---

From "The Chronology of Light in August," *by William H. F. Lamont,* Modern Fiction Studies, *III (1957–1958), 360–61. © 1958 by Purdue Research Foundation, Lafayette, Indiana. Reprinted with the permission of the publisher.*

[1] All page references are to the Modern Library edition of *Light in August.*

around the highways of the United States (195). He spent the last three years of his life (thirty-three to thirty-six) in Jefferson (81).

*   *   *

Limiting this brief note to the main facts of Joe's chronology, I think that I can safely say that as far as specific time references are concerned, Joe does not follow the Christ parallel at all. Joe was *not* born in December (Christmas) but in September; he was *not* crucified on a Friday (Good Friday), but on a Monday; he was *not* thirty-three when he died, but thirty-six.

William Faulkner

. . . Joe Christmas . . . didn't know what he was. He knew that he would never know what he was, and his only salvation in order to live with himself was to repudiate mankind, to live outside the human race. And he tried to do that but nobody would let him, the human race itself wouldn't let him. And I don't think he was bad, I think he was tragic. And his tragedy was that he didn't know what he was and would never know, and that to me is the most tragic condition that an individual can have—to not know who he was.

From Faulkner in the University, *ed. Frederick L. Gwynn and Joseph L. Blotner (Charlottesville: The University Press of Virginia, 1959), p. 118. Excerpted and reprinted with the permission of the publisher.*

John L. Longley, Jr.

—Aristotle has not defined pity and terror—said Stephen Dedalus—I have. Pity is the feeling which arrests the mind in the presence of whatsoever is grave and constant in human sufferings and unites it with the human sufferer. Terror is the feeling which arrests the mind in the presence of whatsoever is grave and constant in human sufferings and unites it with the secret cause.—

From The Tragic Mask: A Study of Faulkner's Heroes *by John L. Longley, Jr. (Chapel Hill: The University of North Carolina Press, 1963), pp. 192–204. Excerpted and reprinted with the permission of the publisher.*

It is appropriate that Joyce's Stephen Dedalus should formulate this definition, for, different as he is from Joe Christmas, they are alike in being heroes who are distinctly modern and who must make their way in a cosmos that is violent, chaotic, and absurd. Stephen's plight is only slightly less desperate than Christmas', and Stephen's motto *non serviam* is very close to Christmas' rigid determination not to submit to those forces that compulsively attempt to shape him to their will. . . .

Little else in modern literature has the speed and inevitable onward sweep of the chapter in which Percy Grimm pursues Christmas and kills him. Taken merely as evocative realism, the writing is superb: the shots, the shouting; the blind rushes and clotted confusion of the mob; the added detail of the fire siren, a characteristic sound of our time, screaming the rise and fall of its meaningless message; the early resolution of the pursuit into a personal contest between Christmas and Grimm. The rendition of Grimm as a type is as merciless as anything else of the sort ever done. Grimm is as the embodiment of pure force so often is: his rather colorless personality and appearance are in ghastly disproportion to his ability to produce evil and violence. He is Faulkner's equivalent of the classic Nemesis of the Furies— machine-like, unerring, impersonal, mindless. Here the problem of belief is no problem at all.

Still guided perhaps by his irrational hope, Christmas runs into Hightower's house holding the pistol he has snatched up on the way. He could kill Grimm easily, but with nothing to lose by another killing, he does not; this is his final gesture of human reconciliation. Grimm empties the magazine of his automatic into Christmas' body, but this is not all.

When the others reached the kitchen they saw the table flung aside now and Grimm stooping over the body. When they approached to see what he was about, they saw that the man was not dead yet, and when they saw what Grimm was doing one of the men gave a choked cry and stumbled back into the wall and began to vomit. Then Grimm too sprang back, flinging behind him the bloody butcher knife. "Now you'll let white women alone, even in hell," he said. But the man on the floor had not moved. He just lay there, with his eyes open and empty of everything save consciousness, and with something, a shadow, about his mouth. For a long moment he looked up at them with peaceful and unfathomable and unbearable eyes. Then his face, body, all, seemed to collapse, to fall in upon itself, and from out the slashed garments about his hips and loins the pent black blood seemed to rush like a released breath. It seemed to rush out of his pale body like the rush of sparks from a rising rocket; upon that black blast the man seemed to rise soaring into their memories forever and ever. They are not to lose it, in whatever peaceful valleys, beside whatever placid and reassuring streams of old age, in the mirroring faces of whatever children they will contemplate old disasters and newer hopes. It will be there, musing, quiet, steadfast, not fading and not particularly threatful, but of itself alone serene, of itself alone triumphant. Again from the town, deadened a little by the walls, the scream of the siren mounted toward its unbelievable crescendo, passing out of the realm of hearing.

They are not to lose it, nor, I think, are we. In Stephen Dedalus' terms, we feel pity and terror to a degree that is almost unbearable. One does not know why we feel these emotions or even less why the tragic spectacle is so compelling. It may be that it is better that we don't know. Certainly, as Nietzsche claimed, the tragic emotions lurk in the dark, irrational part of the blood, and very likely the rational mind wants no part of them. "Pity is the feeling which arrests the mind in the presence of whatsoever is grave and constant in human sufferings and unites it with the human sufferer." This part at least is no problem. We unite with Joe Christmas because he is the modern Everyman. In a cosmos where the only constants are absurdity and instability, we have the right to expect anything except rationality. Any one of us could become the victim. His suffering far transcends the time and place and means Faulkner has used and comes to stand for everything that is grave and constant in the human condition.

"Terror is the feeling which arrests the mind in the presence of whatsoever is grave and constant in human suffering and unites it with the secret cause." The union with the secret cause is almost as terrible as the suffering itself, because it gives a moment of true insight into ourselves. Part of this insight is perfectly symbolized in *Light in August* when the injured Hightower, in a scene that might have come straight out of Dostoyevsky, is working himself toward complete self-knowledge. As the wheel of his memory turns on and on, he comes to realize that his own cold selfishness, his absorption in the Confederate grandfather, has caused his wife's disgrace and death. As the crowd of faces in his memory struggles to come into focus, one of them becomes the dead face of Christmas, but the focus is not clear; another face is struggling with that face, struggling to become clear and be recognized. Suddenly it emerges: it is the face of Percy Grimm, gunman, mutilator, avenging fury, lyncher extraordinary. Hightower never saw either of them before the lynching, but their terrible failure and terrible guilt are somehow directly related to his own failure to live up to his humanity. Somewhere at the root of the secret cause of things as they are, we are all related; we are all involved. We are all responsible because we are all a part of mankind. So far as the rational mind goes, the union with the secret cause is a moment of awareness, of realizing that grave and constant human suffering is truly constant. Once we achieve this awareness, the acceptance of the tragic human situation, with all its absurdity and irrationality, becomes possible, and with the acceptance come the emotions of peace and tranquility.

LENA GROVE AND BYRON BUNCH

Irving Howe

Beyond a doubt Lena is the most harmoniously drawn character in the book. . . . But despite this elemental perfection, Lena is less interesting than Christmas or Hightower; she may indeed possess, as one critic writes, a "holistic consciousness" which shields her from the suffering of the other characters, but it remains a very limited sort of consciousness. So meager an intelligence must qualify, though not eliminate, our feeling for her. Those critics who see in Lena a triumph of traditional health and in Christmas the self-destructiveness of "modernism"—who see this and nothing else—do not really grant Faulkner's mind its due. . . . Is he not suggesting rather that Christmas and Hightower are destroyed because they accept, each in his inadequate way, the challenge of their humanity, the first by seeking selfhood and the second by a fanatical immersion in history, while Lena, the good unruffled vegetable Lena, survives them in her stupidity? Such a reading . . . invokes an observable truth: the price of effort often *is* self-destruction, and equally often the reward for animal calm is safety. One may be fond of Lena but one identifies with Hightower or, in a somewhat different way, with Christmas. To think of Lena as an agent of traditional morality is to graze the notion that goodness is contingent upon a low level of intelligence.

From William Faulkner: A Critical Study *by Irving Howe (New York: Random House, Inc., 1952), pp. 150–51. Copyright 1952 by Irving Howe. Excerpted and reprinted by permission of Random House, Inc.*

Walter J. Slatoff

The story of Lena Grove, with which the book begins and ends, has generally been seen as a pastoral frame for the novel, and Lena and Byron have usually been viewed as providing a norm of sanity and natural behavior against which the violence and perversions of the other stories can be measured. Certainly there is much to compel such a view. Lena's full-bodied health, serenity, and faith in the natural order of things, and her pleasure in life, are in sharp contrast to the fanaticism, barrenness, anguish, or despair that mark most of the other major characters. Hightower, "remembering the strong young body from out whose travail even there shone something tranquil and unafraid" thinks that she will have many more children—*"The good stock peopling in tranquil obedience to it the good earth; from these hearty loins without hurry or haste descending mother and daughter. But by Byron engendered next"* (p. 356)—and he goes on to suggest that obedience and relation to earth is perhaps equivalent to prayer. Byron, until the last chapter of the book at least, is clearly a norm, if not an ideal, of generosity and unpretentious decency, perhaps the most clearly virtuous of any of Faulkner's characters. His religion, unlike that of McEachern, Hines, and Hightower, is a peaceful modest affair; each Sunday he quietly and unobtrusively goes to a country church to lead the choir.

On the other hand, there is much which works in opposition to this view. Lena unquestionably has a kind of wisdom, but she is deeply mistaken about the character and intentions of Lucas, whose emptiness and falseness are completely and immediately apparent to everyone else who encounters him. When Mrs. Armstid warns her that Lucas will run away if she finds him, she answers, "I reckon a family ought to be all together when a chap comes. Specially the first one. I reckon the Lord will see to that" (p. 18). About this, too, she is terribly wrong, unless one is to consider as a being together the forced and brief encounter between Lena and Lucas just before he flees.

Numerous critics have seen Lena as a sort of earth-mother symbolizing the basic natural order, and Faulkner has said recently, "It was her

Reprinted from Walter J. Slatoff: Quest for Failure: A Study of William Faulkner, *pp. 175–78.* © *1960 by Cornell University. Excerpted and used by permission of Cornell University Press.*

destiny to have a husband and children and she knew it, and so she went out and attended to it without asking help from anyone. . . . She was never for one moment confused, frightened, alarmed." [1] There is, however, another, far more trivial side to Lena. One of the first things we learn about her is that on trips to town she would ask her father to stop the wagon at the edge of town so she could walk the rest of the way in "because she believed that the people who saw her and whom she passed on foot would believe that she lived in the town too" (p. 3). After breakfast at the Armstids she is very proud of the fact that she "et polite." Nor is her treatment of Byron in the last chapter particularly natural or admirable, especially when one remembers her easy acceptance and high valuation of the worthless Lucas. Nor is it true that she was never for one moment confused, frightened, or alarmed. She is distinctly confused and frightened by Mrs. Hines' confusion and her own confusion about the identity of her child and its father (p. 359), and she is very much alarmed when she believes Byron has gone away for good. While it is true that she didn't explicity ask help from anyone, she is not unlike Anse Bundren in her dependence on others and her expectation that help will be provided. This expectation is not completely unself-conscious, Faulkner suggests several times. [2]

It can be argued, of course, that without some of the characteristics I have just pointed to Lena would lose all verisimilitude and become pure symbol, much as Eula Varner is in *The Hamlet*. This is true, but it is important to recognize these aspects of her character when one proposes her as a norm or ideal.

But Faulkner undermines this view of her in a more important way —by reducing her to a flat comic character at two crucial points in the book. At the end of the first chapter as she approaches Jefferson, where she hopes to find the father of her child, her only response is: "My, my, . . . here I aint been on the road but four weeks, and now I am in Jefferson already. My, my. A body does get around" (p. 26). And at the very end of the book, after having tormented Byron terribly with her apparent indifference to him, and seemingly unconcerned about his clearly visible pain, she comments: "My, my. A body does get around. Here we aint been coming from Alabama but two months, and now it's already Tennessee" (p. 444).

[1] Jean Stein, "The Art of Fiction XII: William Faulkner," *Paris Review*, No. 12 (Spring, 1956), 50.
[2] See, for example, the description of the way she passes and notes the Armstid wagon and then waits for it (pp. 6–10).

We are left finally, I think, with the kind of ambiguity about her which is suggested by the description of her face as having "either nothing in it, or everything, all knowledge" (p. 379), an ambiguity often encountered in Faulkner in the phrase "at once empty and profound."

Even harder to reconcile with the view of Lena and Byron as norm is the reduction of Byron in the last chapter to a purely comic character. Not only has he been presented as the highest representative of man and conscience throughout the book, but in the latter part he has grown in stature by taking more responsibility for the people around him than he ever had before. Moreover, more than any other character, he has been involved in all three stories. Yet in the final chapter Faulkner makes us see him chiefly as an ineffectual and ridiculous little man, so defeated and humiliated by Lena that the narrator of the section becomes "downright ashamed to look at him, to let him know that any human man had seen and heard what happened" (p. 441). It is true that both we and the narrator continue to feel sympathetic toward him, but we can hardly feel respect.

Norman Holmes Pearson

. . . Who is [Byron] Bunch? He is, as Faulkner describes him, "the kind of a fellow you wouldn't see at the first glance if he was alone by himself in the bottom of an empty concrete swimming pool." Looked at thematically, his is, as a student of mine once wrote, the situation of the great bunch (mass) of people who have not the tragic intensity of Joe, Joanna, or Hightower, but could follow their lead. We think of men like Byron Bunch in terms of where they place their loyalty. Bunch had believed that he could injure no man so long as he kept working at the lumberyard outside the city. His only social connection was with a parish in another town, which he left each week when Sunday was over. His nearest affinity was with Hightower, though he still stumbled when he entered Hightower's door. But when Byron first sees Lena he falls in love, completely and fully. His isolation is broken. He is sure of himself, he no longer stumbles, and he is ready to care for Lena and her unborn illegitimate child. He has found someone to belong to.

From The American Writer and the Feeling for Community, *by Norman Holmes Pearson, American Studies Inaugural Lecture, University of Alabama, March 20, 1962. Excerpted and reprinted with the permission of the author.*

When the book closes we see him and Lena and the child setting out again on an endless journey. The child is the future. Look at his heritage: he is a bastard by Burch, the foster son of Bunch, the godson of Hightower, and the apparent child of Joe Christmas (in the eyes of Joe's grandmother who would claim the baby for her own, and also of Lena who says, "and I think that his pa is that Mr.—Mr. Christmas too"). The nameless one is the heir of all these persons and of their solutions to life. He is a native of Jefferson. One remembers Joanna with her Calvin ancestry and the "white race's doom and curse for its sins." "The curse of every white child that ever was born and that ever will be born," her father said. "None can escape it." "Not even me?" Joanna asked. "And he said, 'Not even you. Least of all, you.' " Joanna speaks for the strain, when, in her words:

> I thought of all the children coming forever and ever into the world, white, with the black shadow already falling upon them even before they drew breath.

But yet this child of Lena is quiet at his mother's breast, and he is quiet because she is there with her timelessness and innocence, her repose in a troubled world of estrangement. He is a token of community. He, not Joe Christmas, is a Christ-child, related to all mankind. "A family ought to be together when a chap comes," a character has said early in the book, "Specially the first one. I reckon the Lord will see to that." The family is indeed now together, and is defined on the broader terms of the human community of all those who have willy-nilly, sinful or innocent, become involved.

And who is Lena? Hightower in his final scene remembers: "When he believed that he had heard the call it seemed to him that he could see his future, his life, intact and on all sides complete and inviolate, *like a classic and serene vase*, where the spirit could be born anew sheltered from the harsh gale of living and die so, peacefully, with only the far sound of the circumvented wind, with scarce even a handful of rotting dust to be disposed of." Joe Christmas vomits when the dietitian and the intern were in bed together. Later he again vomits when he learns from Bobbie about woman's "periodic filth": "In the notseeing and the hardknowing as though in a cave he seemed to see a diminishing *row of suavely shaped urns* in the moonlight, blanched. And not one was perfect. Each one was cracked and from each crack there issued something liquid, deathcolored and foul." Now, reminded of the classicly serene and suavely shaped urn as an ideal, we can remember with more symbolic significance the first description of Lena on her travels, seen at the beginning of the novel as we also see her at the end: "backrolling now behind her a long monotonous succession of peaceful and undeviating changes from day to dark and dark to day again, through which she advanced in identical and deliberate wagons as though through a succession of creakwheeled and limpeared avatars, *like something moving forever and without progress across an urn*." It is Lena's progress in the book as though across the frieze of an urn, across the Grecian urn of Keats' poem, the endless line of the composed frieze, which having been contemplated, is "all ye know on earth, and all ye need to know."

> Thou still unravish'd bride of quietness,
>> Thou foster-child of silence and slow time,
> Sylvan historian, who canst thus express
>> A flowery tale more sweetly than our rhyme: . . .
>> What men or gods are these? What maidens loth?
> What mad pursuit? What struggle to escape?
>> What pipes and timbrels? What wild ecstasy?

Now, reflected from Keats' poem, we can see Lena Grove whose family name suggests the "leaf-fring'd legend." She is the "still unravish'd bride of quietness," the "foster-child of silence and slow time." Contrasted with her placid progress are the mad pursuit and the struggles of others to escape from social involvement. What struggling men or gods are these, we might indeed ask: what workmen, ne'er-do-wells, preachers, twisted similitudes of Christ? What way is offered against the egotistical ways of flight, vengeance, and withdrawal which destroy community? *Light in August* is the tale and the legend to serve as an example of the way of beauty and truth.

And what of Byron Bunch?

> Fair youth, beneath the trees, thou canst not leave
>> Thy song, nor ever can those trees be bare;
>> Bold lover, never, never canst thou kiss,
> Tho winning near the goal—yet, do not grieve;
>> She cannot fade, tho thou hast *not* thy bliss,
>> For ever wilt thou love, and she be fair!

The vision of the book and its established community is a final vision, "all breathing human passion far above." It is spiritualized. Yet it is evidenced on the basis of man's expressed relationship to man's fellow men.

GAIL HIGHTOWER

John L. Longley, Jr.

The usual flaw among [Faulkner's] tragic figures is pride, which quite often takes the form of insistence upon privilege or prerogative. . . .

The Reverend Gail Hightower's difficulties grow out of . . . concern with his own obsessions. His isolation from his fellow men and his denial of his responsibilities toward them grow out of his single-minded determination to have what he wants. What he wants is the right to live in Jefferson where his grandfather, a Confederate cavalryman, was shot dead from his horse in a raid. He is obsessed with the idea of the grandfather and is preoccupied with reconstructing an imaginary life built around the grandfather's accidental presence in Jefferson long ago. He has no real concern or interest other than being present at the window of his study late each afternoon when he imagines he hears the horses of the troop galloping through the town. His church members are bewildered and shocked by his concern with his grandfather, and his neglect of his wife drives her to nymphomania and eventually to a scandalous death. When he refuses to leave the town, he is taken into the woods by masked men and beaten unconscious. But he proves more stubborn than his attackers and in the long run the town decides to ignore him.

His one friend is Byron Bunch, and it is Byron who comes to Hightower and asks him to swear that Christmas was at Hightower's house the night of the murder. Hightower will not do it, even though it may save Christmas from the mob. "I've paid! I won't! I've bought immunity!" is his cry. Too late, when Percy Grimm is pursuing Christmas into Hightower's house, Hightower shouts out the lie that, told earlier, might have saved Christmas' life. But it comes too late, and Christmas is killed in Hightower's kitchen.

Later, when the violence is over and Hightower is going through an agonizing reappraisal of his life, he realizes that his own selfishness has brought on the death of his wife, that his own cowardice and his failure to save Christmas are somehow part and parcel of the guilt of

---

From The Tragic Mask: A Study of Faulkner's Heroes *by John L. Longley, Jr. (Chapel Hill: The University of North Carolina Press, 1963), pp. 227–29. Excerpted and reprinted with the permission of the publisher.*

Percy Grimm. In his arrogance, his selfishness and pride, his persistence
in his line of conduct, and the fall from the high calling of his office,
he is authentically tragic.

Carl Benson

What we have to deal with in *Light in August* is the peculiar collo-
cation in Jefferson, Mississippi, of various lives whose stories cannot
be accounted for on the basis of narrative alone. If, however, we see
that the thematic conflict is between rigid patterns of self-involvement
on the one hand and commitment to a solidarity that transcends self
on the other, we must see that the chief character, the moral protagonist . . . is Gail Hightower, the old unchurched minister who is,
as we open the story, ironically "Done Damned in Jefferson." It may
be that at the end he is still damned as far as Jefferson is concerned,
but through him the reader who inhabits a larger, though not dissimilar, community is enabled to estimate the relative moral worth
of the other characters and the fixations which inhibit or limit their
participation in society.

Actually, it might reasonably be argued that Hightower is also the
central figure in a strict narrative sense and that far too many readers
have been misled by the seemingly simple opposition of the violent
Joe and the placid Lena. After all, Byron brings to Hightower the
problems of Lena and Joe as well as his own. Joe's grandmother also
comes to the old minister for assistance. Indeed, a good part of the
action of the entire book seems designed to evoke the action or the
response of Hightower. But it is his function of moral hero with which
we are principally concerned. My argument is that he is a Yoknapatawpha Heyst who, like Conrad's hero, achieves a victory by traveling the moral distance from selfish immunity to redemption by the
conviction that immunity cannot be bought. We have hints that his
redemption is of major importance almost from the beginning. As soon
as Byron Bunch brings him the problem of helping Lena, he breaks
into a sweat of fear of being drawn from the isolation he thinks he
had paid for. Thereafter, as Byron continues to ask his aid, though
he replies, "I won't," and "I have paid," his compassionate nature

From "Thematic Design in Light in August," *by Carl Benson,* The South Atlantic
Quarterly, *LIII (1954), 542–46. Excerpted and reprinted with the permission of the
author and Duke University Press.*

gradually asserts its mastery; by the end he is so involved with "poor mankind" that he has delivered Lena's child and has tried to save Joe Christmas from Percy Grimm.

If it be objected that Hightower is no fit candidate for the role of moral hero, it may be said that Faulkner is aware of this irony, because he made it. Indeed, Faulkner's profound pessimism and his ultimate idealism both find witness in the use of Hightower as moral standard: pessimism, because we are given no better than Hightower as the slide rule for solidarity; idealism, because Hightower rises from the most foolish and inhumane illusion of all to tremendous heights by the abnegation of the illusion. He achieves moral stature in the only way possible for him—by descending into the pit of himself and ripping from his heart his dearest sin.

It is significant that Hightower's recognition of the true nature of his cherished illusion should be saved for the magnificent penultimate chapter . . . In this last scene we finally understand the childhood obsession that formed the original cause of his desire for immunity: the growing-up in a house populated by three phantoms (the sick mother, the harshly rigorous yet tame father, the old Negro woman) and a ghost, the heroic grandfather about whom the Negro woman told him stories, who was shot with a fowling piece while he was engaged in the very unmilitary, and yet somehow grand, prank of robbing a chicken coop. Brooding over this image of selfless, magnificent folly has caused the young Gail Hightower to become convinced that "I had already died one night twenty years before I saw light," and has compelled him to believe that "My only salvation must be to return to the place to die where my life had already ceased before it began." To this freakish illusion he has subordinated his entire life. . . . He uses the call to the ministry, the influences of the seminary and of his wife, to "shun the harsh gale of living," to get the pastorship in Jefferson, where his grandfather had died. Now, in his last revery as he sits dying . . . Hightower is finally beginning to see the enormity of his moral shortcomings . . . Here Faulkner introduces his effective turning-wheel imagery. Hightower's awakened moral consciousness turns slowly, like a wheel in heavy sand, as he unwillingly accepts the implications of his misspent life. . . . Thus, in the moment of final recognition, Hightower sees destroyed his cheating martyrdom, his justification for his behavior to his wife and the church, his immunity, and the cherished ghost itself.

In order to accentuate the significance of Hightower's moral struggle and victory, resulting in the abnegation of the illusion, Faulkner says,

"The wheel, released, seems to rush on with a long sighing sound.
. . . It is going fast and smooth now, because it is freed now of burden,
of vehicle, axle, all. In the lambent suspension of August [here perhaps
is the moral significance of the title] into which night is about to fully
come, it seems to engender and surround itself with a faint glow like
a halo." The function of the wheel imagery shifts. The wheel is dis-
engaged from the private conscience of Hightower and spins before
him carrying on its circumference the faces of the people who have
populated the novel. It is as if the old minister, freed at last of his
morally debilitating illusion, has earned the right to pass judgment on
the people he has ignored, misunderstood, or wronged. He sees all the
chief figures of the novel and even some individually insignificant
members of his congregation. And in the compassion he has attained
by his acknowledgment of the ubiquity of human responsibility, he
perceives that the faces of all suffering humanity are pretty much
alike. . . .

Appendix: An Outline of the Narrative Structure of *Light in August*

by B. R. McElderry, Jr.

The Narrative Structure of Faulkner's Light in August

Day	Ch.	Forward Action / Immediate Past / Remote Past
Sat.	1	Lena's arrival in Jefferson. Burden fire sighted.
Sat.	2	Brown's association with Joe Christmas explained. Byron identifies Brown as Burch (Lena's seducer).
	3	Hightower's life in Jefferson. His wife's scandalous death. Loss of his church. His delivery of the Negro baby.
Sun.	4	Byron tells Hightower of Lena's search for Brown (Burch), of the fire, of the murder of Joanna Burden.
Fri.	5	Christmas quarrels with Brown, goes to town, returns: "Something is going to happen to me."
	6–7–8–9	Christmas at orphanage, adopted by McEacherns, meets waitress and tells her he is part Negro, beats up McEachern at dance, is himself beaten by waitress's friends.
	10	Christmas, three years before the murder, enters Joanna Burden's kitchen.

From "The Narrative Structure of **Light in August**," *by B. R. McElderry, Jr.,* College English, *XIX (1957–1958), 206–7. Excerpted and reprinted with the permission of the National Council of Teachers of English and B. R. McElderry, Jr.*

	11	Christmas seduces Joanna Burden.
		Story of the Burden family, abolitionists settled in the South.
	12	Christmas resents Joanna's increasing domination.
Fri.		Christmas murders Joanna when she draws a pistol.
Fri.		Christmas commandeers a car to further his escape.
Sat.	13	Sheriff investigates murder.
Tues.		Byron tells Hightower he is moving Lena to Brown's cabin at Burden Place.
Wed.		Hightower learns that Christmas's trail has been found.
Wed.		Hightower urges Byron to leave Lena.
Wed.	14	Deputy reports Lena staying at Brown's cabin.
Tues.		Christmas disturbs Negro church.
Fri. after murder		Christmas captured at Mottstown.
Fri.	15	Hineses learn of Christmas's capture.
Sun.	16	Through Byron, Mrs. Hines asks Hightower to give false alibi for her grandson, Christmas. Hightower refuses. Byron takes Hineses to Lena's cabin.
Mon.	17	Lena's baby born. Byron, previously refused by Lena, quits his job.
Mon.	18	Brown, taken by deputy to see Lena, escapes.
Mon.		Brown, pursued by Byron, beats him up.
Mon.		Byron learns Christmas has been killed.
Mon.	19	Lawyer Stevens puts Hineses on train, promising to send Christmas's body for burial.
Mon.		Christmas escapes, is shot and castrated by Percy Grimm.
	20	Hightower's early life—his Civil War father and grandfather, his invalid mother, his marriage to the minister's daughter.
Mon.		Hightower's death.
	21	The traveling furniture dealer's story of Byron's dog-like faithfulness to Lena, and her eventual acceptance of him.

Chronology of Important Dates

	Faulkner	*The Age*
1896		McKinley defeats Bryan for the Presidency.
1897	William Faulkner born, September 25, New Albany, Mississippi.	
1898		United States declares war on Spain.
1902	The family of Murry C. and Maud Butler Faulkner moves to Oxford, Mississippi.	
1907		Henry Adams, *Education*.
1913		Robert Frost, *A Boy's Will*.
1914	Phil Stone begins to recognize and encourage Faulkner's literary talents and interests.	World War I begins. Sir J. G. Frazer completes *The Golden Bough*, begun in 1890.
1916		Henry James dies. James Joyce, *A Portrait of the Artist as a Young Man*.
1917	Faulkner's first published work, a drawing, appears in the 1916–17 volume of *Ole Miss,* the University of Mississippi annual.	United States enters World War I. T. S. Eliot, *Prufrock and Other Observations*.

1918	April: Faulkner visits Phil Stone in New Haven. July: Faulkner leaves Oxford to begin training in the Royal Air Force in Toronto, Canada.	Henry Adams dies.
1919	Faulkner's "L'Après-Midi d'un Faune," appears in *The New Republic*. Faulkner enrolls in the University of Mississippi and works on *The Marble Faun*.	Sherwood Anderson, *Winesburg, Ohio*.
1920	Faulkner resigns from the University and goes to New York.	F. Scott Fitzgerald, *This Side of Paradise;* Ezra Pound, *Hugh Selwyn Mauberley;* Sinclair Lewis, *Main Street;* English translation of Freud's *A General Introduction to Psychoanalysis*.
1921	Faulkner returns to Oxford and becomes postmaster at the University.	
1922	Faulkner publishes a poem in *The Double Dealer*.	Marcel Proust dies. Eliot, *The Waste Land;* Joyce, *Ulysses;* E. E. Cummings, *The Enormous Room*.
1923		Harding dies and Coolidge becomes President. Wallace Stevens, *Harmonium*.
1924	*The Marble Faun* (poems), Faulkner's first book, published.	Nikolai Lenin, Woodrow Wilson, and Joseph Conrad die.
1925	Faulkner moves to New Orleans and begins association with *The Double Dealer* group, including Sherwood Anderson; writes *Soldiers' Pay*. July: sails for Europe. December: returns to Oxford.	Fitzgerald, *The Great Gatsby;* Theodore Dreiser, *An American Tragedy;* John Dos Passos, *Manhattan Transfer;* Ernest Hemingway, *In Our Time*.
1926	February: *Soldiers' Pay*, Faulkner's first novel, published.	Hemingway, *The Sun Also Rises*.

1927	April: *Mosquitoes.*	Publication of Proust's *A la recherche du temps perdu*, begun in 1908, completed.
1929	January: *Sartoris.* October: *The Sound and the Fury.* Faulkner marries Estelle Oldham and settles in Oxford.	Thomas Wolfe, *Look Homeward, Angel;* Hemingway, *A Farewell to Arms.* October: The Wall Street Crash.
1930	October: *As I Lay Dying.*	D. H. Lawrence dies. *I'll Take My Stand,* by "Twelve Southerners."
1931	February: *Sanctuary* revised and published. August: *Light in August* begun. September: *These Thirteen* (stories).	
1932	February: *Light in August* finished. May: Faulkner begins work in Hollywood. October: *Light in August* published.	Erskine Caldwell, *Tobacco Road.*
1933	April: *A Green Bough* (poems).	Nathanael West, *Miss Lonelyhearts;* W. B. Yeats, *Collected Poems.* Hitler becomes Chancellor of Germany; Roosevelt becomes President of the United States; Prohibition is repealed.
1934		Fitzgerald, *Tender Is the Night;* J. T. Farrell, *The Young Manhood of Studs Lonigan;* Henry Miller, *Tropic of Cancer.*
1935		Stevens, *Ideas of Order.*
1936	October: *Absalom, Absalom!*	
1938	February: *The Unvanquished.*	Thomas Wolfe dies. Dos Passos, *U. S. A.;* Allen Tate, *The Fathers.*
1939	January: *The Wild Palms.* Faulkner elected to the National Institute of Arts and Letters.	W. B. Yeats dies. John Steinbeck, *The Grapes of Wrath.* Italy invades Albania; Franco wins in Spain; Germany in-

		vades Poland; World War II begins.
1940	April: *The Hamlet.*	F. Scott Fitzgerald and Nathanael West die.
1941		United States enters World War II. James Joyce and Sherwood Anderson die.
1942	May: *Go Down, Moses.*	
1943		Eliot completes *Four Quartets.*
1945		Roosevelt dies and Truman becomes President; United States bombs Hiroshima and Nagasaki; World War II ends.
1946	April: *The Portable Faulkner,* edited by Malcolm Cowley.	Robert Penn Warren, *All the King's Men.*
1948	September: *Intruder in the Dust.* Faulkner elected to the American Academy of Arts and Letters.	Pound, *The Pisan Cantos;* Norman Mailer, *The Naked and the Dead.*
1949	November: *Knight's Gambit* (stories).	Robert Frost, *Complete Poems.*
1950	May: Faulkner awarded the Howells Medal for Fiction by the American Academy. August: *Collected Stories.* November: The Nobel Prize.	
1951	March: National Book Award for *Collected Stories.* September: *Requiem for a Nun.* October: Legion of Honor.	William Styron, *Lie Down in Darkness.*
1952		Ralph Ellison, *Invisible Man.*
1953		Saul Bellow, *The Adventures of Augie March.*
1954	August: *A Fable.*	Stevens, *Collected Poems.*
1955	National Book Award and Pulitzer Prize for *A Fable.* State Department trip to Japan.	Wallace Stevens and Thomas Mann die. Vladimir Nabakov, *Lolita.*

1957	Writer-in-Residence, University of Virginia. State Department trip to Greece. May: *The Town.*	
1958	Writer-in-Residence, University of Virginia.	Theodore Roethke, *Words for the Wind.*
1959	November: *The Mansion.*	
1961	State Department trip to Venezuela.	Ernest Hemingway dies.
1962	June 4: *The Reivers.* July 6: Faulkner dies in Oxford. July 8: Faulkner is buried.	E. E. Cummings dies.
1963		Robert Frost and Theodore Roethke die.
1965		T. S. Eliot dies.

Notes on the Editor and Contributors

DAVID L. MINTER teaches at Rice University. He has published essays on Jane Austen and F. Scott Fitzgerald and is the author of *The Interpreted Design*.

DARREL ABEL teaches at Purdue University. An Advisory Editor of *Modern Fiction Studies,* he is the author of several distinguished essays on American literature.

CARL BENSON teaches at Auburn University.

CLEANTH BROOKS teaches at Yale University. He is the author of several widely influential works, including *The Well Wrought Urn, Modern Poetry and the Tradition,* and *William Faulkner: The Yoknapatawpha Country.*

RICHARD CHASE formerly taught at Columbia University. His books include *Quest for Myth, Herman Melville, Emily Dickinson, Walt Whitman Reconsidered,* and *The American Novel and Its Tradition.*

MALCOLM COWLEY is a distinguished man of letters. He is the author of *Exile's Return, After the Genteel Tradition,* and *The Literary Situation.* In 1946 he edited *The Portable Faulkner,* a record of the compilation of which can be found in *The Faulkner-Cowley File: Letters and Memories, 1944–1962.*

LESLIE A. FIEDLER teaches at the State University of New York at Buffalo. A novelist and critic, he is the author of *Love and Death in the American Novel, No! In Thunder,* and *Waiting for the End.*

MAXWELL GEISMAR, a literary critic and historian, is the author of *Writers in Crisis, The Last of the Provincials, Rebels and Ancestors,* and other books.

IRVING HOWE teaches at Hunter College. He is the author of *Sherwood Anderson, Politics and the Novel, A World More Attractive,* and other books, as well as *William Faulkner: A Critical Study.*

WILLIAM H. F. LAMONT teaches at Rutgers, the State University, New Jersey, and has published articles and checklists in a number of American and European journals.

117

JOHN L. LONGLEY, JR., teaches at the University of Virginia. He is the author of *The Tragic Mask: A Study of Faulkner's Heroes.*

BRUCE R. McELDERRY teaches at the University of Southern California. He is the author of essays on English and American literature of the nineteenth and twentieth centuries.

MICHAEL MILLGATE teaches at University College, University of Toronto. He is the author of *William Faulkner, American Social Fiction: James to Cozzens,* and *The Achievement of William Faulkner.*

WILLIAM VAN O'CONNOR formerly taught at the University of California at Davis. He wrote numerous essays and several books, including *The Tangled Fire of William Faulkner.*

NORMAN HOLMES PEARSON teaches at Yale University. He edited, with William Rose Benét, the *Oxford Anthology of American Literature,* and with W. H. Auden, *Poets of the English Language,* and he has written many essays on American literature of the nineteenth and twentieth centuries.

ROBERT M. SLABEY teaches at the University of Notre Dame. He is the author of several essays on modern literature.

WALTER J. SLATOFF teaches at Cornell University. He is the author of *Quest for Failure: A Study of William Faulkner.*

LAWRANCE THOMPSON teaches at Princeton University. He is the author of *Fire and Ice: The Art and Thought of Robert Frost, Melville's Quarrel with God,* and *William Faulkner: An Introduction and Interpretation.*

OLGA W. VICKERY teaches at the University of Southern California. She is co-editor of *William Faulkner: Three Decades of Criticism* and is the author of *The Novels of William Faulkner: A Critical Interpretation.*

HYATT H. WAGGONER teaches at Brown University. He is the author of *The Heel of Elohim, Hawthorne,* and *William Faulkner.*

Selected Bibliography

In addition to the essays by Alfred Kazin and John L. Longley mentioned in the Editor's Introduction and to the fuller original texts of the essays and excerpted statements included in this collection, the reader will find useful the following:

Backman, Melvin. *Faulkner: The Major Years.* Bloomington: Indiana University Press, 1966, pp. 67–87. A general study useful especially for its study of Gail Hightower.

Chase, Richard, "The Stone and the Crucifixion: Faulkner's *Light in August*," *Kenyon Review,* X (1948), 539–51. A perceptive study of several important patterns of imagery.

Hirshleifer, Phyllis, "As Whirlwinds in the South: An Analysis of *Light in August*," *Perspective,* II (1949), 225–39. Particularly useful for its discussion of religious and sexual motifs.

Holman, C. Hugh, "The Unity of Faulkner's *Light in August*," *PMLA,* LXXIII (1958), 155–66. A thorough but unsatisfactory examination of the relationship between the Passion Story and *Light in August*.

Kirk, Robert W., "Faulkner's Lena Grove," *Georgia Review,* XXI (1967), 57–64. A useful study to compare with Howe, Slatoff, and Pearson in this collection.

Lind, Ilse Dusoir, "The Calvinistic Burden of *Light in August*," *New England Quarterly,* XXX (1957), 307–29. One of the fuller treatments of religious motifs, and particularly of Southern "Puritanism" or "Calvinism," in *Light in August*.

Nemerov, Howard, "Calculation Raised to Mystery: The Dialectics of *Light in August*," in *Poetry and Fiction: Essays,* pp. 246–59. New Brunswick, New Jersey: Rutgers University Press, 1963. An essay interesting particularly with regard to Faulkner's technique.

Pearson, Norman Holmes, "Lena Grove," *Shenandoah*, III (1952), 3–7. An earlier version of the essay reprinted in this collection, but with more exclusive focus on Lena Grove and the urn imagery.

Slabey, Robert M., "Joe Christmas, Faulkner's Marginal Man," *Phylon*, XXI (1960), 266–77. An interesting essay to compare with Longley's treatment of Joe Christmas in this collection.

West, Ray B., Jr., "Faulkner's *Light in August:* A View of Tragedy," *Wisconsin Studies in Contemporary Literature*, I (1960), 5–12. An important treatment of *Light in August* as basically tragic in mode.

LIONEL TRILLING

Edward Joseph Shoben, Jr.

FREDERICK UNGAR PUBLISHING CO.
NEW YORK

Library of Congress Cataloging in Publication Data

Shoben, Edward Joseph.
  Lionel Trilling.

  (Modern literature series)
  Bibliography: p.
  Includes index.
  1. Trilling, Lionel, 1905–1975—Criticism and
interpretation. I. Title. II. Series:

PS3539.R56Z9   818′.5209   81–40472
ISBN 0–8044–2815–8   AACR2

Acknowledgments

The obligations which I have incurred in the writing of this little volume exceed the space available for their acknowledgment. A few, however, simply cannot go unmentioned. I owe the first expression of gratitude to Diana Trilling, Lionel's wife for forty-six years and a critic, in her own right, of considerable dimension. One of the joys of this rewarding task has been the renewal of my acquaintance with her, and both her warmth and her helpfulness have exceeded all reasonable expectations. She also is the main source of biographical information about her husband, whose social grace and interpersonal accessibility clothed an intense sense of privacy. Second, my heartfelt appreciation goes to numbers of students with whom I have shared these chapters in various drafts and who have both identified in a kindly and helpful fashion my tendencies toward opacity and at least some of my lapses from either logic or accuracy. What defects remain are certainly not their fault but mine. Third, a number of friends have read one or more sections of this book and provided me with aid and comfort for which I simply lack the wit to thank them adequately. I count on their forgiveness as I have been able to count on their help. They include Ilena Dunlap, Johanna Gallers, Richard S. Goldberg, Harvey Goldstein, Sharon Milan, and Lois Parker. They all have a proper claim to credit for much of what may be of merit here, but they have no responsibility for

errors or stupidities. Both, despite grim efforts to avoid
or to eliminate them, may appear.

One final word: I have dedicated this essay to my
wife and to my granddaughter. The inscription to the
former has a bald literalness that masks private and rich
complexities and intensities that I pray she fully understands. The inscription to the latter, who was born
while this little work was in progress, grows out of the
unexpected hopes and loving yearnings that new grand-
fatherhood quickens. I shall be particularly proud if
this book of mine provides a bridge by which Abigail
may one day cross the years to become acquainted with
Lionel Trilling's mind and character.

Contents

Preface

When a clinical psychologist writes a book about a literary critic, some explanation obviously is in order. In the present case, the necessary explanation entails three statements that I am delighted to put on the public record.

In the first place, I have been bewildered and troubled for years by the great gulf that yawns between psychology and serious reflections on literature, between the social sciences and the humanities. Both concern themselves with human functioning and with the qualities of human experience; both aim at increasing our understanding of ourselves and our relationships to others and to the realities of culture, and both reflect the uses of the mind and the imagination in our efforts to achieve that always deficient comprehension of our status and our conduct as human beings. Lionel Trilling stands out as a literary figure who, if he did not bridge that chasm in the enterprise of thought, certainly narrowed it. Committed to Freud, skeptical but sympathetically informed about Marx, and intimately familiar with the contemporary efforts of such social scientists as David Riesman and Daniel Bell, he insisted that the self defines the central subject matter of literature, and that the conflict between the self, ever seeking a greater degree of autonomy and free expression, and the culture, at once nurturant and nay-saying, lies at the heart of the human drama. As one whose professional des-

1

tiny it is to hold frequently the damp hand of other
people's misfortune, I agree. In the unshared reflections
in which I occasionally indulge in my consulting room,
I often am terrified by the perception of how fragile is
the skin of civilization that covers the idiosyncratic and
self-serving drives, impulses, and passions of my pa-
tients. Just as frequently, I find both my compassion
and my rage aroused by the ways in which the influences of society have cruelly cabined the spontaneity,
the emotional capabilities, and the imaginations of the
people with whom I work.

What may seem odd is that a great deal of the
understanding I may possess of these poignant matters
derives as much from the literary record of human destiny as from my own discipline of psychology. This
state of affairs may issue from nothing more than the
fact that my personal intellectual awakening, if it ever
occurred, took place during my undergraduate years
under the auspices of some stimulating teachers of literature. I am more inclined to believe, however, that
writers like Shakespeare and Melville understood more
of the vicissitudes of the human heart, more of the
subterranean forces that color our experience for good
or ill, than most (which is *not* a synonym for "all")
psychologists. The superiority of outstanding literary
insight stems, I think, from the capacity of the disciplined and informed imagination to perceive experience
in its essence and as a totality, a whole, whereas psychologists typically content themselves with more precise but fractional forms of comprehension, eschewing
great leaps of the imaginative reason in favor of an inch-
worm's units of progress, in the faith that these small
increments will profitably cumulate. Both procedures
strike me as essential. What I regret is that they so
seldom enter into an enriching dialogue with one another.

In the mind of Lionel Trilling, something, at least,
of that dialogue went on for half a century. In his es-

says and books, the extensions of a remarkable mind, that dialogue becomes available to any who can read. As a participant in that interchange, I have learned much that puts me in Trilling's debt. In a very real sense, this effort of mine represents an acknowledgment of that debt and a desire to share with others my considerable benefits as Trilling's debtor.

Second, a clinician cannot escape the great puzzles: about the meaning of that dream of happiness human beings are heir to; about how life's contradictions can be managed with a measure of contentment and its buffets sustained without breaking the spirit; about the sources of enjoyment and pride we can find even in the face of our own mortality and our own curious and damaging self-destructive and socially disruptive tendencies. Neither could Trilling. His concern for the complexities of personal experience and for the quality of life as people encounter it on a day-to-day basis underlay all his reflections on the authors, works, and issues to which he turned his attention. That concern, always immediate and warm, coupled with the creativity with which he mined the literary veins available to him, make him, for me, a model and an exemplar in the twentieth century of the tradition that deserves to be called humanistic. In addition to the fertility and provocative power of his mind, Trilling exhibits in his published work a *character*—a set of reflected-upon values in action—that, I confess, I envy to a degree and that I admire enormously. The world, I believe, would be a more engaging place if it were populated by a few more Lionel Trillings.

Finally, I spent the years from 1950 to 1965 as a faculty member at Columbia University. Trilling, thirteen years my senior, had already achieved the acclaim due him for the work culminating in *The Liberal Imagination* when I arrived on Morningside Heights, still a bit callow, a trifle brash, and marked by levels of ignorance that time has done too little, I'm afraid, to reduce. Although I never knew him well, Trilling was extraordinarily generous and sweetly responsive to me, and his friendliness and occasional gentle guidance meant a good deal to me personally and to my intellectual development. I've rarely enjoyed such comfortably stimulating talk as at our infrequent lunches together at the Faculty Club or during occasional gentle discussions in his office or mine. Neither a full-fledged friend nor a disciple (Trilling wanted no disciples), I found my affections almost as much invoked as my respect for his personal qualities and my esteem for his intellectual powers. If (as I hope is the case) my admiration shows in the pages that follow, I make no apologies and simply quote Trilling himself: "objectivity . . . begins with what might be called a programmatic prejudice in favor of the work or author being studied." The point is that, once again, Trilling's character figures as largely in his work as does his mind, and both his mind and his character have something of worth to say to our much-chivied civilization.

1

∿∿∿∿∿∿∿∿∿∿∿∿∿∿∿∿∿∿∿∿∿∿∿∿∿∿

Lionel Trilling:
The Opposing Self

White-haired, his deep-set eyes characteristically haunted, Lionel Trilling roamed the front of his Columbia College classroom. The magisterial reputation as literary and social critic that he brought with him evoked an atmosphere of formality. Yet, without attempting to deny it and with an all but articulate and quietly insistent pleasure in decorum, he colored the climate of formality with a relaxed ease. Appearing (but only appearing) to turn randomly through the pages of James Joyce's *Dubliners*, he read aloud in a softly modulated baritone: "He lived at a little distance from his body." The always evanescent smile warmed the haunted eyes, and there was a sudden joyous glow that every undergraduate in the class felt, whether or not he understood it in some more intellectual sense. "Marvelous phrase," Trilling exclaimed. "Isn't that the essence of alienation?" He then commented, still moving in his leisurely fashion about the room, on an association between the habit of one of the characters in *Dubliners* of keeping a rotting apple in his desk and Friedrich Schiller's statement that he could only write poetry if a rotting apple were emitting its fragrance from his tabletop. And that led to a typical, good-humored but thoroughly serious warning against preciousness and too academic an approach to literature. "If anyone connects any of these rotting apples to the

Fall," Trilling grinned, "he immediately loses twenty points on the next exam."

Representative as it is, this commonplace vignette catches many of the central qualities of Trilling as a human being—his courtly combining of formality and relaxation, the mystery of the hag-ridden eyes, and the ready smile that always failed to realize itself fully. The story reflects his love of fun that clearly exceeded an intellectual's taste for sheer wit, and it at least suggests the delight he found in seriousness without solemnity. It hints at his sense of the richness and crucial value of linkages between the experience of literature and the experience of life. It vibrates with his refusal to burden works of art with imposed symbols, to force them onto procrustean beds of aesthetic or literary theory, as against investing the effort to see each of them as, in the phrase of Matthew Arnold's that he so prized, "an object as in itself it really is."

If *mind* was and remains the dominant motif in Trilling as teacher and as writer, what accounts for his influence and his importance is the intimacy with which mind married passion. When he wrote of E. M. Forster's "two ideals" of truth and passion, the first symbolized by "some vaguely ancient pagan time" in Greece, and the second by the "ruffianism of the Renaissance" in Italy,[1] he spoke in significant part from self-knowledge and a felt commonality. In quoting Forster's "those ghosts who are still clothed with passion or thought are profitable companions," he reveals something vital and distinctive in himself.

Such self-revelation didn't happen often. Trilling was a deeply private person. His use of "I" in his essays is far more an acknowledgment of responsibility for the ideas and judgments he advances than it is a means of self-disclosure, and, in his relationships, he was at once highly available but essentially inaccessible. Most people who knew him only casually or only in his roles as professor, colleague, or co-participant in a professional conference, were quite aware that to talk with him was to command his full attention, that to ask his help was to receive it. Few, however—probably no more than his wife Diana and perhaps such rare and old friends as Jacques Barzun and James Grossman—caught more than glimpses of an intense inner life. Nevertheless, one cannot read him, just as one could not know him at any distance, without realizing that Trilling's feelings surged powerfully within him and that he was a man who cared profoundly about people, values, and ideas.

Indeed, his capacity for enjoyment was basically a function of his large capacity for feeling and for caring. While he was too much a born-and-bred New Yorker to qualify as an outdoorsman or to respond to nature after the manner of the Wordsworth he so deeply admired, he liked to wade a trout stream, and he appreciated the skills that a fly rod requires. Although without the cultivation of a true gourmet, he enjoyed a variety of foods and wines. Cordially and genuinely interested in a remarkably wide range of people, his fascination with personalities quite different from his own and with their distinctive ways of fraternizing was only partly professional. A reflection of his preoccupation with manners, with what he called the "hum and buzz of implication" that informally but fundamentally "draw the members of a culture together," it also emerged from his committed concern for human "variousness and possibility."[2]

For closely related reasons, he sometimes found an uncomplicated and joyful pleasure in mindless movies, and his fondness for what he regarded as second-rate literature seemed based in a contented suspension of his critical faculties and a resultant freedom, almost a license, to toy with ideas and forms that levied little on his seriousness. Laughter, including his own, so long as it was without derision, was important to him. It occurred often and sometimes memorably. During the course that Trilling taught jointly with Barzun in cultural history, a student once mentioned, while the class was discussing Malthus, the famous motto of the Order of the Garter: *Honi soit qui mal y pense.* Barzun immediately quipped, "*Honi soit qui Malthus pense,*" which evoked from Trilling a wry, "*Honi soit qui mal thus puns.*" On another occasion, bewildered by students' boredom with Stendhal's *The Red and the Black*, he asked if Julien Sorel did not evoke their empathy through mirroring their own drives and aspirations. Overwhelmingly, they replied that they had little use for Julien's self-serving ambitions; what they wanted was decent, socially useful work to do. "I felt," he said, "like an aging Machiavelli among the massed secretariat of the U.N."[3] In the middle of the fifth of the Charles Eliot Norton lectures, which were to become *Sincerity and Authenticity*, the book into which Trilling most fully and most openly poured his most passionate convictions, he observed that "Irony is one of those words, like love, which are best not talked about if they are to retain any force of meaning." Looking up from his text, he grinningly commented, "Other such words are sincerity and authenticity."[4] More than most of us, Trilling understood the sense of personal ease and even gaiety that results from not taking oneself *too* seriously.

But his passionate nature also had its raspy side. Although controlled, it defined in his eyes a virtue for which, therefore, there was no need for apology. He appears never to have quoted Cardinal John Henry Newman's concept of the gentleman as one who refrains from hurting others, but that notion was deeply and functionally rooted in his own code, his own courtliness. It lent fire to those occasions when he deliberately went on the attack. His virtual demolition of V. L. Parrington and Theodore Dreiser illustrates this seldom-exercised capability.[5] When he makes his pox-o'-both-your-houses case against C. P. Snow and F. R. Leavis for their roles in the "two cultures" controversy, he directs the white heat of his outrage with a laser beam's

precision and controlled destructiveness.[6] The intensity
of his assault is even greater when he charges the likes
of Norman O. Brown, R. D. Laing, and David Cooper
with cant and hypocrisy, with being neither sincere nor
authentic.[7] At other times, his assaults had the quality
of irritability, a touch of gentled and justified snide.
While praising James Pope-Hennessy's life of Moncton
Milnes, for example, Trilling cannot inhibit a few "objections . . . of a . . . carping kind":

I do not know who . . . instructed the English writers of
nineteenth-century biographies that Wordsworth is the
very type of sentimentality and taught them that whenever
they refer to sentimentality they should call it "Words-
worthian sentimentality." Mr. Pope-Hennessy has not freed
himself of this bad practice. . . . He [tells] us that a certain
Mrs. Twistleton had been born Ellen Dwight, "the daughter of a member for the Province of Massachusetts in the
House of Representatives." The best opinion holds that by
the nineteenth century Massachusetts was already what in
this country we call a State. . . . Mr. Pope-Hennessy refers
to (Hawthorne) as the author of . . . *The House With
the Seven Gables,* which is not unlike referring to *The Mill
Upon the Floss,* or a *Tale About Two Cities,* or *Much Ado
Concerning Nothing.* . . . he speaks of [Hawthorne's *English Notebooks*] as having been "very sanely edited" by
Professor Randall Stewart, as if the *Notebooks* were a natural temptation to editorial frenzy, an impression which he
confirms by speaking of them as having been "sponsored"
in England by the Oxford University Press; in my experience, the O.U.P. publishes rather than sponsors books, and
I cannot understand why it should have changed its practice on this one occasion.[8]

Good fun, but fun with a decided bite in it.

The biting fun has its rationale. Favoring and finding value in David Riesman's concept of the inner-
directed character, those persons who have internalized the ideals of adult authority, especially the
aspirations and demands of "good" parents, Trilling
cites the conventional Latin tag that so often has

served as the motto of the inner-directed personality: *Ad astra per aspera* ("to the stars through difficulty"). He also suggests the translation, "To the heights by means of asperity," for, he says, "a kind of asperity marks the dealings of the inner-directed man with the world, his fellow men, and himself."

The man of business as well as the scientific or artistic genius, or the religious leader, or the philosopher, were all at one in their submission to inner-direction. The belief that energy, self-control, and self-reverence would achieve miracles was held not only by the dullest spirits of [the nineteenth century] but also by the noblest. We must think of the Alger books as being the expression not merely of a strenuous philistinism but of a general culture in which strenuousness was valued in all walks of life. There was a connection between the passions of a Bounderby and a Beethoven.[9]

For all his charm and gentlemanliness, for all his genuine sweetness, Trilling thrived on controversy and strenuously involved himself in it. As he remarked of William James, he "hated war but he loved the idea of fighting," and he often quoted James's statement that, "If this life be not a real fight in which something is eternally gained for the universe by success, it is no better than a game of private theatricals from which one may withdraw at will. But it *feels* like a fight."[10]

And yet there is a tension, a profound and disturbing ambivalence, that constitutes the engine powering Trilling's work, both as writer of fiction and as critic. In evaluating George Saintsbury, "a critic in whom I find it hard to discover merit," he said of his response to literature that, "almost by its very lack of ideas and of interest in ideas, by the very indiscriminateness of its voracity, it expresses an emotion that might seem to pass for an idea—for it affirms the swarming, multitudinous democracy of letters, and testifies to the rightness of loving civilization and culture in and for themselves and of taking pleasure in human communi-

cation almost for its own sake and of the order and peace in which men may listen to each other and have time and generosity enough to listen even to those who do not succeed in saying the absolutely best things." And Trilling's celebration of Edmund Wilson rests on Wilson's "awareness that what constitutes the matter of literature is the discordant and destructive reality that threatens the peace which makes literature possible."[11]

If life feels like a fight, the legitimate purpose of the battle is to achieve and to maintain those forms and that degree of peace essential to creative effort, and the context always strains, always challenges, always threatens: ". . . no cultural situation is ever really good, culture being not a free creation but a continuous bargaining with life."[12] For one who prizes individuality, who struggles unremittingly for the increased autonomy of the self, who delights in the human "variousness and possibility" that only *persons* can embody, it is not easy "to love civilization and culture in and for themselves," when one knows only too well how civilization and culture cabin and shape and restrict the growth of selfhood. This, however, was the tension with which Trilling lived and with which he concerned himself, both as a literary figure and as a man.

Accounting for this abiding ambivalence on the basis of publicly available knowledge is hard to do. Much has been made, undoubtedly correctly, of his being a New Yorker and a Jew, but no other New York Jew became Lionel Trilling. He was born on the Fourth of July, 1905, in New York City, the only son of David W. and Fannie Cohen Trilling. His father was a native of Bialystok, then in Lithuania, now a city in northeastern Poland, always a place dominated by first Czarist and later Soviet Russia. Although the English-sounding name suggests one conferred by immigration authorities when David arrived, a boy in his early teens, at Ellis Island, it is entirely authentic. Relatively late in his life, Trilling discovered namesakes in many places,

all tracing their lineage from a distinguished rabbi of Bialystok.

That passage through Ellis Island, according to Diana Trilling, is associated with a cloud of disgrace and failure under which Lionel's father lived all his life, and about which his son learned only in his mid-twenties. Displaying a degree of precocity as a child, David Trilling seems to have been destined for a scholarly career, probably as a member of the rabbinate. At his Bar Mitzvah, however, the ceremony of his entry into manhood, he somehow broke down. It seems likely that he stumbled and forgot, despite the prompters all around him, the prayer and the chant from the Haf-Torah required of him. Apparently embarrassed to the point of humiliation, his family appears to have shipped him off to the United States, an unwanted exile.

In response to his rejection and his shame, he somehow acquired at least the veneer of a gentleman, even a touch of the dandy. Diana Trilling recalls that his wife spoke of his having been an excellent and enthusiastic dancer, and that his son remembered him as a strong swimmer. His English was fluent and unaccented; and outside his family, he maintained an attitude of warmth, courtesy, and charm. Inside it, he was intensely hypochondriacal, and his emotions occasioned anxiety by virtue of both the ease with which they could be touched off and their intensity once unleashed. Occupationally, he established himself as a moderately successful custom tailor, but because, he said, he wanted his son to think of himself as the offspring of a manufacturer rather than a workman, he at some point went into business as a wholesale furrier.

A long series of mistakes culminated in the late 1920s in his disastrous decision to make handsome and expensive raccoon coats—for chauffeurs. Closed automobiles had by then almost universally replaced the older open models, but Mr. Trilling was sure that they were a short-lived fad. While the passengers in open

"touring" cars could protect themselves against the cold with rugs, drivers enjoyed no such option; the costly coats were virtual essentials for their health as well as their comfort, and they were sure to sell. When Lionel expressed doubts and asked his father why he didn't cultivate college students as potential customers, David condescendingly explained that students could hardly afford expensive garments like his. No one could shake his curious and characteristically wishful faith in the economic resources of chauffeurs. Meanwhile, as members of his family arrived in America, he took care of them for various periods of time, performing a duty that never freed him, through adequate expiation, from the severe embarrassment that he had caused or the shaming sense of failure that he lived with.

Fannie Trilling, on the other hand, was a sturdy and protective presence in her son's life. Although her parents were also East Europeans, she had been born and spent her early girlhood in London's East End. Her Anglophilia ran deep. She read omnivorously until her eyes failed in her late eighties, and she deeply impressed her daughter-in-law by the growth and adaptiveness she displayed during the last thirty years of her life, when she steadily and thoughtfully modified her views and values. When Lionel was apparently no more than four or five, his mother shared with him her dream of his taking a PhD at Oxford; and when, because of a deficiency in mathematics, he was not admitted in good standing as a freshman at Columbia in 1921, she unhesitatingly and successfully called on the appropriate university officer to have the decision altered. To her confidence, to her loving support, and to her stimulating aspirations for him, her son quite directly attributed much of the drive, the tenacity, and the fundamental self-respect that carried him through dark years and crises to the degree of eminence that he eventually achieved.

Lionel Trilling's parents, then, were middle-class,

respectable, and affectionately respectful of the potentials for progress they perceived in their adopted America. His father bore the considerable burden of managing a guilty secret, but was a distinctive and colorful if highly trying figure. On one occasion, while living at home as a student, Lionel returned to the house to find his father rifling his desk and reading his mail. In response to his son's not-often-expressed fury, the elder Trilling explained in hurt tones, "I'm not reading your mail. I'm just interested in your life." His mother, ambitious for her boy, protected him against his father's communicable anxieties and peculiar fantasies. When Lionel, for example, won a part in a school play, she kept her husband out of the room while she heard his lines. If the family lived a somewhat restricted life socially and culturally, rarely eating in restaurants or going to the theatre, they never felt excluded because of their Jewishness, and his mother especially could deal comfortably with gentiles. Fannie Trilling maintained a kosher household, but she was entirely acceptant of her husband's taste—away from home—for ham and shellfish; and Friday-night suppers, featuring Sabbath candles, apparently represented more a compound of tradition and habit than a matter of piety or conviction.

The extent, then, to which Lionel absorbed a Jewish element into his self-concept remains unclear. In his essay on "Wordsworth and the Rabbis,"[13] he disclaims any talent as a Hebraist, either as a boy attending Hebrew school in essentially a pro forma fashion or as an adult. He speaks of his knowledge of the Jewish tradition as "all too slight," and he characterizes as "primitive" his account of the world view, the values, and the distinctive propensity for mysticism of the rabbis in the *Pirke Aboth* or *Sayings of the Fathers*. Yet his familiarity with the *Aboth* is obviously intimate, and he records his admiration for Max Kadushin's *The Rabbinical Mind* with greater warmth than sheer scholarly brilliance could provoke, or than even his acknowledg-

MODERN LITERATURE SERIES

GENERAL EDITOR: Philip Winsor

In the same series:

S. Y. AGNON   *Harold Fisch*
SHERWOOD ANDERSON   *Welford Dunaway Taylor*
LEONID ANDREYEV   *Josephine M. Newcombe*
ISAAC BABEL   *R. W. Hallett*
JAMES BALDWIN   *Carolyn Wedin Sylvander*
SIMONE DE BEAUVOIR   *Robert Cottrell*
SAUL BELLOW   *Brigitte Scheer-Schäzler*
JORGE LUIS BORGES   *George R. McMurray*
BERTOLT BRECHT   *Willy Haas*
ANTHONY BURGESS   *Samuel Coale*
ALBERT CAMUS   *Carol Petersen*
TRUMAN CAPOTE   *Helen S. Garson*
WILLA CATHER   *Dorothy Tuck McFarland*
JOHN CHEEVER   *Samuel Coale*
COLETTE   *Robert Cottrell*
JOSEPH CONRAD   *Martin Tucker*
JULIO CORTÁZAR   *Evelyn Picon Garfield*
JOAN DIDION   *Katherine Usher Henderson*
JOHN DOS PASSOS   *George J. Becker*
THEODORE DREISER   *James Lundquist*
FRIEDRICH DÜRRENMATT   *Armin Arnold*
WILLIAM FAULKNER   *Joachim Seyppel*
F. SCOTT FITZGERALD   *Rose Adrienne Gallo*
FORD MADDOX FORD   *Sondra J. Stang*
JOHN FOWLES   *Barry N. Olshen*
MAX FRISCH   *Carol Petersen*
ROBERT FROST   *Elaine Barry*
GABRIEL GARCÍA MÁRQUEZ   *George R. McMurray*
MAKSIM GORKI   *Gerhard Habermann*
GÜNTER GRASS   *Kurt Lothar Tank*
ROBERT GRAVES   *Katherine Snipes*
PETER HANDKE   *Nicholas Hern*
LILLIAN HELLMAN   *Doris V. Falk*
ERNEST HEMINGWAY   *Samuel Shaw*
HERMANN HESSE   *Franz Baumer*
CHESTER HIMES   *James Lundquist*
HUGO VON HOFMANNSTHAL   *Lowell W. Bangerter*
CHRISTOPHER ISHERWOOD   *Claude J. Summers*
SARAH ORNE JEWETT   *Josephine Donovan*
UWE JOHNSON   *Mark Boulby*
(continued on last page of book)

LIONEL TRILLING

ment of fondness for an old teacher makes appropriate. Four observations suggest that once again ambivalence defines a major motif in Trilling's life.

To consider effectively these four instances, we must understand something of Elliot Cohen and *The Menorah Journal*, and the role that the man and the magazine played in Trilling's youth. Cohen, after demonstrating outstanding talent as a literary scholar and critic at Yale, gave up on graduate work when he realized that a Jew in the 1920s was simply not going to be appointed to an American university post in English. Charismatic, witty, and endlessly energetic, he became managing editor of *The Menorah Journal* and gathered around him a clever and strikingly capable group of young people as staff and contributors. The *Journal* had been founded by Henry Hurwitz as a kind of extension of the Menorah Society that he had started at Harvard. His purpose was to deal with the sense of exclusion felt by Jewish students and by Jews of an intellectual disposition generally from a wide range of educational and cultural opportunities. Although the magazine was his creation, and although he maintained it through his stubborn and successful insistence that it be financed by the Jewish community, Hurwitz was too solemn, too stiff, and too sedate in both manner and outlook to determine the *Journal*'s character. The mercurial Cohen, at once glittering and substantial, dominated it and, from 1923 to 1931, gave it a quality of irreverent liveliness that embarrassed Hurwitz but made it deeply attractive to youthful and aspiring artists, writers, and social critics. Little older than his animated young staff, Cohen established unchallenged seniority and leadership by his drive, his wit, his wide range of knowledge, and his almost smothering attentiveness to the development of each of his junior colleagues. Some years later, on the strength of the same qualities, Cohen founded *Commentary*, a magazine of somewhat broader appeal but still conceived as a Jewish publication serving the Jewish community and reflecting primarily its needs, interests, and concerns.

Trilling was one of the little group that came under Cohen's strong influence, and it was in *The Menorah Journal* that, still an undergraduate and not quite twenty, he published in 1925 a story entitled "Impediments."[14] It deals with the relationship between the first-person narrator, himself an undergraduate, and a fellow student named Hettner. Hettner is "a scrubby little Jew with shrewd eyes and full, perfect lips that he twisted out of their crisply cut shape." Hettner wants talk, acceptance, friendship. The narrator hides behind "the convenient barrier" that he is erecting "against men who were too much of my own race and against men who were not of my own race and hated it." He fears that Hettner will "attempt to win into the not-too-strong tower that I had built myself, a tower of contemptible ivory perhaps, but very useful." One night, Hettner visits the narrator in the latter's dormitory room. Drinking gin and tea, the two "engage in battle" until morning, Hettner driving for relationship, for the acknowledgment of Jewish commonality, the narrator repelling him with flippancies. At last, Hettner goes to the door; "not very loud, as though he were prefacing a long tirade that must begin low to reach its height of fury, [he] said, 'What a miserable dog you are.'" The accusation and the hatred are deserved and are understood so, but it is quite clear that the tower of contemptible ivory will remain intact. A protective fortress is equally necessary against the fully committed Jew and against the anti-Semite. Complexity marks the ambivalence, but the ambivalence is undeniable.

Second, we have Trilling's own oblique comments on his Jewish childhood and associations. They are made in the context of a tribute to Robert Warshow, a brilliant movie critic and student of popular culture, who died suddenly at thirty-seven. Trilling reflects on the nature of Warshow's involvement with the Jewish community during the years that the younger man worked under Cohen in an editorial capacity at *Commentary*. "I should say," Trilling writes, "that it was essentially not very different from my own." Warshow, presumably following a pattern very much like Trilling's, "acknowledged, and with pleasure, the effect that a Jewish rearing had had upon his temperament and mind, and he was aware of, and perhaps surprised by, his sense of connection with Jews everywhere—and found that the impulses of his intellectual life came from sources that were anything but Jewish, that the chief objects of his thought and feeling were anything but Jewish. At the same time, he had, and thought he should have, a very considerable awareness of the life of 'the Jewish community' and a genuine if detached interest in it."[15] If this statement has the ring of genuineness, it also carries strong overtones of limitation. The protective personal fortress has lost some of its obvious armament and proclaimed impregnability, but its functions still are exercised, although more generously and more suavely.

Third, this impression is reinforced by Trilling's account of his refusal of an invitation from Elliot Cohen to serve on an advisory board for *Commentary* at the time the magazine was just beginning. Trilling wrote to Cohen, explaining that he "had had his experience of the intellectual life lived in reference to . . . the Jewish community" and that he had no desire to repeat it. Others might affiliate with the new publication for all sorts of legitimate reasons; "for me it could now only be a posture and a falsehood."[16] Despite the anger and expressed contempt that his letter evoked from many of the members of *Commentary*'s staff, he resolutely held to it. Indeed, the episode marked one of the barriers that Trilling's friendship with Warshow had to surmount.

Finally, there are Trilling's recollections of the period from about 1923 to 1931, when he was one of those clever young people clustered with such verve around Elliot Cohen at *The Menorah Journal*. What gave that group its coherence, what stimulated and supported its high morale, was "the idea of Jewishness." That idea had no religious significance; "we were not religious." It had no connections with Zionism; "we were inclined to be skeptical about Zionism and even opposed to it . . . during the violence that flared up in 1929 some of us were on principle pro-Arab." What was sought was "authenticity . . . a sense of identity." What authenticity and a sense of identity meant was "that the individual Jewish person recognizes naturally and easily that he *is* a Jew and 'accepts himself' as such, finding pleasure and taking pride in the identification, discovering in it one or another degree of significance. From which there might follow an impulse to kinship with others who make the same recognition, and perhaps the forming of associations on the basis of this kinship." The sincerity of this formulation can remain entirely beyond challenge, but it appears quite inconsistent with the view expressed in "Impediments," with the notion that the impulses of one's intellectual life and the objects of one's thought and feeling are "anything but Jewish," or with Trilling's refusal to serve on *Commentary*'s advisory board because to do so would amount to "a posture and a falsehood." That inconsistency and its implication of ambivalence seem intensified by the mild and somewhat covert hostility, or at least the negative self-criticism, in the activities of *The Menorah Journal*'s young, clever, liberal, and secular staff—satirizing "the sodden piety" in so much of Jewish literature, teasing Jewish life generally, writing "vivacious stories of modern sensibility in which the protagonists were Jewish," etc. Nor is either the inconsistency or the implied ambivalence lessened as a function of the purpose of these vigorous efforts—"to help create a consciousness that could respond to the com-

plexities of the Jewish situation with an energetic un-
abashed intelligence."

But the reference to "the Jewish situation" provides a useful clue. For the first four decades of the
twentieth century, whatever pride in their culture,
whatever strengthening perception of belonging to an
ancient and honorable tradition of dignity and accom-
plishment, that American Jews could bring to their own
self-definition, they could hardly avoid that toxic frag-
ment in their identity that was thrust upon them by a
profoundly prejudiced and anti-Semitic society.[17] That
external identification not only entailed an exclusion,
both deeply felt and entirely actual, from many aspects
of American life; because of its massiveness and per-
vasiveness, it carried the force of an accusation that
seemed somehow justified. The emotional and spiritual
effects of this experience were typically debilitating and
frequently ruinous. The interest of Cohen and the
young people gathered around him at *The Menorah
Journal* was less in the phenomena of anti-Semitism
than in these "emotional or characterological effects,
which they undertook at least to neutralize."[18]

In many important ways, Trilling's Jewishness
seems far less a central component of his self-concept
than a crucial exigency imposed by the bigotry of the
culture: *Ad astra per aspera* once again. Helped in one
fashion by the example of his parents, especially his
mother, when he was small, in quite a different fashion
by his peers and by Elliot Cohen in the decade of his
twenties, Trilling learned to respond to that exigency
with tenacity, courage, and intelligence. Jewishness was
for him a part of his "hard inheritance," the mastery of
which shaped his character and gave direction to some
of his key concerns. It was the basis for his response to
the line from Goethe with which Freud closed his posthumous *Outline of Psychoanalysis*: "What you have
inherited from your fathers, truly possess it so as to
make it your very own." In making his Jewishness his

very own in the context of American society in the
twenties and thirties, Trilling sensitized himself to
Freud's conception of the eternal warfare between the
self, straining after its own realization, and the nay-
saying culture, and he laid the groundwork for his interest in tragedy, with its entailment of "some meaningful relation between free will and necessity."[19] We are
almost certainly touching here the roots of his sense of
the intransigeance of social reality, and of the value of
imagination in coping with it. Similarly, his distrust of
panaceas, of Utopias and fanaticisms—his insistence
on confronting issues in all their complexity—found its
base in his coming to grips, at the historical moment in
which he did it, with his Jewish identity. As it did for
others, it created large and threatening problems for
him, and he maintained a constant awareness that those
problems could not be successfully, appropriately, or
decently solved by denying or otherwise attempting to
escape that identity. The tension could not be resolved;
it could only be managed.

The processes for its management were enlarged
and honed by his education at Columbia College.
When Trilling enrolled at Morningside Heights, he
entertained literary ambitions. He dreamed of being a
novelist and even had plans in that direction. Looking
back on his career shortly before his death, he wrote,
"I am always surprised when I hear myself referred to
as a critic . . . It always startles me, takes me a little
aback . . . and raises an internal grin . . . Criticism . . .
was always secondary, an afterthought; in short, not a
vocation but an avocation." Even as an undergraduate,
he was manifesting his lifelong concern "not with
aesthetic questions, except secondarily, but rather with
moral questions, with the questions raised by the
experience of quotidian life and by the experience of
culture and history." Out of this concern emerged his
tendency, for which many of his literary colleagues have
found it hard to forgive him, "to be a little skeptical of

literature, impatient with it, or at least with the claims of literature to be an autonomous, self-justifying activity." What mattered when he first went to college (and what continued to matter) was the possibility of changing and correcting the structure of society and the dynamics of culture through conscious intention and the application of intelligence.

"Intelligence" in 1921 at Columbia College was a great and special word. It had been given a banner and something of a creed by the title essay of John Erskine's *The Moral Obligation to Be Intelligent*; and it was Erskine who had instituted and directed, over the intense opposition of many of his faculty colleagues, the General Honors program that had a profound impact on Trilling and many others. A virtually forgotten man in America's cultural life, Erskine enjoyed a zestful and distinguished career marked by the publication of over forty books. Many of his novels, such as *The Private Life of Helen of Troy, Galahad,* and *Adam and Eve* retain both their readability and their merit. His autobiographical volumes, especially *My Life as a Teacher* and *My Life in Music,* continue to illuminate entertainingly some of the central tendencies in the intellectual and artistic life in America from shortly after the turn of the century through the Second World War. He wrote verse, social commentary, literary scholarship and criticism, opera libretti and music criticism, and a history of the New York Philharmonic Society and its distinguished orchestra. After he was forty, he won a minor but favorable reputation as a concert pianist; and between 1928 and 1937 he took leave from his professorship in the English department at Columbia to serve as the president of the Juilliard School of Music. More than anyone else, it was he who built that institution into the great cultural resource that it is today.

Above all else, Erskine was a teacher, fully committed to the notion that education is or should be a special form of companionship over generations, serving two purposes. One is the personal development of "courage, without which no one ever speaks out," "determination to go through to the end," and a "firmness of purpose" that emerges from and is disciplined by a sense of how one's life is inevitably and necessarily shared with others. The other purpose is citizenship, both the informed capability and the readiness to participate in the affairs of society, in the shaping of the polity. Here are the moral bases of the obligation to be intelligent about oneself and about one's social world, and the method of acquiring intelligence, conceived in this way, lies through a "delighted" and intimate familiarity with the great intellectual and artistic works of the past, primarily books but not excluding music and the visual arts. Erskine's General Honors program, which embodied his faith, consisted simply in having relatively small groups of undergraduates meet for two hours (which often stretched spontaneously into much longer periods) each week to discuss one of the great works of Western culture with two faculty members "selected for their disposition to disagree with each other." There were no lectures and no surround of literary scholarship. The *Odyssey*, the *Aeneid*, Dante's poem, or a play by Shakespeare was read as if it had just appeared on a best-seller list and was dealt with on the basis of its direct meaning for contemporaries. What Erskine was reaching for was partly an analogue to the spirit with which the "audience thronged the ancient theatre to enjoy a new work by Aeschylus or Sophocles." They "were not classical scholars [but] merely the human beings for whom the play was written." Partly, Erskine was attempting to provide students with the bases for a common intellectual life. Overwhelmingly, he was seeking an experience of "delight" that would promote the growth of intelligence in his special sense. Obviously, this enterprise at Columbia was the father of such Great Books ventures as have taken form at St. John's College in Annapolis and in Santa Fe, at the University of Chicago under the presidency of Robert Hutchins, and under the auspices of the Encyclopaedia Britannica.[20]

When Trilling entered General Honors, he was a participant in a heady and controversial project to which he brought his novelistic ambitions. "I did not count myself among those who were intelligent," he says:

I would have been the first to say that I was observant, even perceptive, of certain things, that I was intuitive; and I rather prided myself on a quality that went by the name of subtlety. But intelligence I scarcely aspired to: it did not seem to me that this was a quality that a novelist needed to have, only a quick eye for behavior and motive and a feeling heart. But . . . I was seduced into bucking to be intelligent by the assumption which was prepotent in Columbia College that intelligence was connected with literature and that it was advanced by literature.[21]

The intelligence that he was "seduced into aspiring toward" had three central informing ideas. The first lay at the heart of the humanistic tradition: that "men who were in any degree responsible for the welfare of the polity and for the quality of life that characterized it must be large-minded men, committed to great ends, devoted to virtue, assured of the dignity of the human estate and dedicated to enhancing and preserving it; and that great works of the imagination could foster and even institute this large-mindedness, this magnanimity." The second bore on the question of background and social-class membership: "The Columbia *mystique* was directed to showing young men how they might escape from the limitations of their middle-class or their lower-middle-class upbringings by putting before them great models of thought, feeling, and imagination, and great issues which suggested the close interrelation of the private and personal life with the public life, with life in society."[22] The third expressed itself in the faith that great works of thought and imagination were *accessible*, that their value lay in the stimulus that they provided not merely to specialized scholars but to the human beings for whom they had been written. Shot through the fabric of Columbia College and the General Honors program was the great question that dominated intellectual life at the close of the First World War and that had a special liveliness and visibility in the publishing and academic center that was New York City: After the great international upheaval, what were the polity and the culture to be like, and who was to make their terms?

Trilling not only found himself "bucking to be intelligent." Partly because the career of a novelist was as economically uncertain in the 1920s as it is now, but more because of the excitement and gratification in his undergraduate experience, he found himself wanting to teach literature. His was emphatically *not* the calling of the professional scholar, although he respected and admired scholarship. What he wanted was to perpetuate the spark-inducing discussions of General Honors and to extend, now as a professor rather than as a student, the consideration of those intellectual and moral values inherent in direct involvements with literature. He had found a congenial milieu that was taking seriously the humanistic tradition of personal magnanimity and social involvement, and he determined to remain a part of it.

He also had found, at first in an almost inarticulate form, his conception of criticism. In the ambience of Columbia College and in the talk in General Honors, he had discovered how the interpretation of the great works of the past could be both *interesting and cogent*[23] relative to the great and ongoing questions of contemporary society: What forms and consequences will characterize modern politics and modern culture? What will be the quality of modern life? How can those concerned with the imagination and with the life of the mind contribute to a more tolerable, a more generous world? These are not the questions with which formal scholarship typically deals, although formal scholarship is not irrelevant to them. They are, however, very much the questions which education must attend to, and Trilling's interest in education, begun then, continued as a strong one[24] and formed the basis of his seriousness and of the responsible enthusiasm that he invested in his role as a teacher.

In addition, his developing conception of criticism and his interest in education, probably interacting with his ambition to write fiction, led him to think of the most general audience possible for his own work. Unlike many who elect professorial careers, perhaps especially in the profession of English-teaching, Trilling from the beginning was less concerned with communicating with his academic peers and more with reaching the widest range available of people who respond to ideas and who participate in the life of the imaginative reason. To his last day in a classroom, teaching, particularly the teaching of undergraduates, significantly fulfilled that desire.

During this same period, Trilling had his first encounters with two powerful influences on his thought and outlook, Sigmund Freud and Karl Marx. To Freud, as a systematic thinker, he remained essentially committed, although he was never doctrinaire as a Freudian, and he certainly was not blind to some of Freud's deficiencies as an interpreter of literature.[25] Only for a short time did he consider himself a Marxist. Neither of these great figures provided him with a doctrinal authority so much as they forced upon him "the sense of the actuality and intimacy of history, of society, of culture" and made him feel "the necessity . . . of discovering the causative principles of these entities." What appealed to Trilling in both Freud and Marx was their convincing "programmatic rejection of the settled, institutionalized conception of reality and how it works . . . their discovery of principles of causation which lead to the conclusion that the settled, institutionalized reality is a falsehood, or . . . a mask. . . . They taught the intellectual classes that nothing was as it seemed, that the great work of intellect was to strike through the mask." They also, of course, "worked a revolution in the world-picture that was available to anyone who undertook to think at all," and for Trilling, Freud especially, but Marx too, "enforced a relationship to the past which was more comprehensive, more intimate, and more *active* than any that had existed before . . . they . . . intensified the relation of the individual to society, and to culture, and to the whole of mankind."[26]

In a number of ways, his familiarity with Freud increasingly shaped and gave a language to some of Trilling's most intimate experience and lent a distinctive color to some of his central values. With Marx, two quite different circumstances proved important. The first centers in the profound implication of Marx's thought in the Russian Revolution, only four years old when Trilling first enrolled at Columbia, and in the structure of the Soviet Union as the issue of the revolution. This state of affairs gave Marxian ideas an inevitable ideological cast; Marxian theory became thoroughly confounded with Soviet practice, and one could hardly read Marx without thinking of the revolution and its aftermath. The aftermath included intense and dramatic struggles inside the Soviet Communist Party. One of these battles pitted Leon Trotsky, intellectually a direct heir of Marx, and a revolutionary leader favored by V. I. Lenin as his successor as head of the new Union of Soviet Socialist Republics, against Josef Stalin, a highly capable administrator and astute politician, who commanded little of Trotsky's respect among the intellectuals as a Marxian theorist. When Lenin died in 1924, Stalin successfully ousted Trotsky and soon established himself as a powerful dictator. He violated a fundamental Marxian tenet—the ultimate "withering of the state"—in his policy of "consolidating socialism within one country" and in his strong and deliberate encouragement of nationalism. He reorganized the military along czarist disciplinary lines; he instituted highly conservative divorce and abortion laws, and he insisted on criteria of political "correctness" in the enterprises of education and the arts. Between 1934 and 1939, Stalin dealt with dissidence in the Soviet Union by means of a series of ruthless purges. Large numbers of once high-placed officials were executed; the total number of victims figured clearly in the millions, and the Soviet secret police, the instrument of the purges, became a symbol of terror. Before the world and in his own nation, Stalin always cited Marx as the almost scriptural authority for his actions. As a result, the confusion of Marxian theory with Soviet practice deepened into a confusion between Marx's ideas and Stalin's policies and techniques.

In the United States, a small and open Communist Party, which derived its political positions from Marx's theory, became difficult to distinguish from Stalin's sympathizers, who were primarily concerned with furthering the interests of the Soviet Union through secret organizations under direction by Russian agents. Although drawn to Marx's ideas, Trilling was revolted by totalitarian developments in the U.S.S.R. and even more outraged by manifestations of Stalinism, a thoroughly corrupt form of Marxism, in America. One of his most deeply felt and troubling preoccupations, until Stalin died in 1953, centered on the so-called fellow travelers—those Americans who were ordinarily better educated than most and liberal in their views and, though not Communist Party members, "went along" with Stalin, both in his domestic policies in Russia and in the functions of his underground apparatus in the United States, because of what they perceived as the importance, perhaps Utopian in its significance, of "the Soviet experiment."[27] The phenomena of the fellow traveler, Stalinism, and the authoritarian turn so quickly taken in the Soviet government complicated Marx's ideas almost as soon as Trilling became acquainted with them. They also deeply divided the liberal community, and Trilling's passionate antipathy to the complicating factors set him at odds with many members of that community with whom he otherwise could have made friendly common cause.

On the other hand, Marx gave Trilling a concept that enriched and broadened his experience, at *The Menorah Journal*, of grappling with "the idea of Jewishness." The concept was that of social class. His still rudimentary exposure to Marx made possible his perception that "One couldn't . . . think for very long about Jews without . . . using the category of social class. It was necessary not merely in order to think about Jews in their relation to the general society but in order to think about Jews as Jews, the class differences among them being so considerable and having so complex a relationship to the general concept of Jewishness that had at first claimed one's recognition and interest." The notion of social class as applied both to the idea of Jewishness and to the structure of the Jewish community acquired an energizing power. Trilling reports that it made society—that it made America—available to his imagination as it could not have been had he "tried to understand it with the categories offered by Mencken or Herbert Croly, or . . . Henry Adams." It connected his experience of Jewishness to an involvement in the Marxist intellectual radicalism of the thirties after the stock market crash of 1929. In the context of the radical movements of that time, he became familiar with the "moral urgency, the sense of crisis, and the concern with personal salvation that mark the existence of American intellectuals," and he discovered the realities that John Dos Passos forcefully documented in *The Big Money*. "Intellectuals who chose the life of liberty and enlightenment . . . [could be] destroyed by the cold actualities of this ideal existence . . . radicalism is not of its nature exempt from moral dangers."[28] As usual, complexity and difficulty, and the ambivalence that complexity and difficulty occasion, arose for Trilling out of his contemplation of human variousness and possibility. Ambivalence was the price of his growth and the basis for his freedom from the doctrinaire.

In 1925, Trilling was graduated from Columbia College. He remained at Columbia for another year to take his master's degree, and in 1926 went to the University of Wisconsin as a teaching assistant in Alexander Meiklejohn's Experimental College. That experience of the heartland widened his New Yorker's perspective on America; he was captivated by Madison as a university small town and by the countryside around Lake Mendota as a symbol of midwestern beauty, and he fully confirmed his decision to teach by his success and enjoyment in the classroom. But although genuinely drawn to Wisconsin and the academic life that he tasted there—they "would have given him a very sweet and gracious contentment"—he also feared something about the place and its culture. In "Notes on a Departure,"[29] a handsomely crafted and moving short story that he published in 1929, and that is clearly derived from this year in the Middle West, he speaks of the profound feeling "that the town was going to make him do things he must not do. It sought to include him in a life into which he must not go."

It seems reasonably clear that he was strongly tempted to forswear his Jewish identity, to assume the outward show of a gentile, as his name, appearance, accent, and manner made possible. To do so would have been the condition of full acceptance and a possible career at the University of Wisconsin and in the world that Madison represented. "To prevent this he . . . made use of a hitherto useless fact. He . . . said, 'I am a Jew,' and immediately he was free." Freedom, however, came only at a price: "if he embodied the sep-

arateness of his race . . . he found . . . too, that he had
assumed its antiquity. . . . 'If you will be as apart as a
Jew, be also as old as a Jew.' " Trilling's protagonist—
did not Trilling himself?—felt "old, wise, and empty . . .
a heavy senility seemed to touch him lightly all over."
The level of anguished conflict that he had reached reflects itself in his language. He was only twenty-four
when "Notes on a Departure" appeared, and it was
written out of an experience that occurred before he
was quite twenty-two. At one point, he

passionately denied all the logic he had used to strangle
what had been left of the green, irrelevant, unreal youth in
himself. For a little while, for another year, it might still
linger with him. Might it not? Ah, indeed, might it not?
He did not yet want the heavy weight, never to be
shaken off, of the real; he did not want the burden of the
good and peaceful things, of the necessary terrible things.
He wanted yet to spin out a world. He did not want the
burden and weight of good peace; he wanted to woo, in the
way of youth (at once sick and healthy), defeat and bitterness and high suffering, without the knowledge, fast creep-
ing in upon him, of what they truly were.

Trilling had passed through an ordeal of great intensity, and its stresses had at least two vital consequences for his character. First, he had made a choice
and established a basic point of honor: even if he
could, he would not forsake his Jewish origins. Second,
having made the choice, he laid down the bases for his
independence from the Jewish community. The echoes
of this Wisconsin experience reverberate some seventeen years later in Trilling's contribution in 1944 to a
symposium on the relationship of the Jew to American
society in the *Contemporary Jewish Record*.[30] His remarks hold special interest because they were made
toward the end of World War II, after he had published
his books on Matthew Arnold and on E. M. Forster,
and after his extended involvement with *The Menorah
Journal* and with Elliot Cohen.

After declaring that "I do not think of myself as a 'Jewish writer,'" Trilling says, "In what I might call my life as a citizen my being Jewish exists as a point of honor . . . the point of honor consists in feeling that I would not, even if I could, deny or escape being Jewish." And he quickly continues, "Surely it is at once clear how minimal such a position is—how much it hangs only upon a resistance (and even only a passive one) to the stupidity and brutality which make the Jewish situation so bad as it is." But having put himself on the record in this straightforward fashion, he charges the American Jewish community with "an impasse of sterility" and comes to a sharply critical, even a harsh conclusion:

As the Jewish community now exists, it can give no sustenance to the American artist or intellectual who is born a Jew. And so far as I am aware, it has not done so in the past. I know of writers who have used their Jewish experience as the subject of excellent work; I know of no writer in English who has added a micromillimetre to his stature by "realizing his Jewishness," although I know of some who have curtailed their promise by trying to heighten their Jewish consciousness.

On the road to this judgment, Trilling strikes a personal note, referring to his association with *The Menorah Journal*:

The effort of this journal . . . was . . . a generous one; but its results were sterile at best. I was deep in—and even contributed to—the literature of Jewish self-realization of which Ludwig Lewisohn was the best-known exponent. This was a literature which attacked the sin of "escaping" the Jewish heritage; its effect, it seems to me, was to make easier the sin of "adjustment" on a wholly neurotic basis. It fostered a willingness to accept exclusion and even to intensify it, a willingness to be provincial and parochial. It is in part accountable for the fact that the Jewish social group on its middle and wealthy levels—that is, where there is enough leisure to allow a conscious consideration of social

and spiritual problems—is now one of the most self-indulgent and self-admiring groups it is possible to imagine.

Trilling's writing in this brief statement has a tense
quality that appears almost nowhere else; and, although
his characteristic self-effacing and tone-softening devices—such as his acknowledging the "gracelessness"
of his position—reduce in some measure the tension, he
evinces a rare truculence. His point of honor aligns him
with a community that "does not *want* enough and is
nothing more than a resistance to an external force."
This state of affairs locks him in combat with those
who share his origins and the ethnic elements of his
identity. Trilling accepts this painful conflict with the
grim aggressiveness of a man who has been deeply
tested and who has emerged with his integrity intact.
Given the opportunity to escape his Jewish heritage,
he refused it as incompatible with honor. The election
to stand on the bedrock of his origins not only freed
him from temptation; it freed him from the self-
imposed exclusiveness of the "self-indulgent and self-
admiring" components of the Jewish community.

To understand this Wisconsin episode, its formative influence on Trilling, and its relationship to later
developments in his career as a "New York Jewish intellectual" is to understand some of his firmness of
character and something of the interplay between mind
and character in his personality. It also marks as mistaken, envious, or both, the portrayals of Trilling by
contemporaries like Alfred Kazin.[31] Respectful of
Trilling's subtlety and "the intense devotion behind the
wonderful book on Matthew Arnold," Kazin disparages
him for his "more than the usual literary connection to
things English," for "a self-protectiveness as elegant as
a fencer's," for his perceived consciousness "of social
position," for the "adopted finery in his conversation."
"No one," he charges, "could have been more discerning or less involved." Kazin's summary is that Trilling
"would always defend himself from the things that he

had left behind." What he supposedly had left behind, of course, was his status as an immigrant tailor's son, the background that should have disposed him toward a committed if intellectual radicalism, and—most of all —his Jewishness.

It seems quite clear that Trilling was leaving nothing behind. He was synthesizing his origins and his experience into a distinctive and independent selfhood. That process went on throughout his life, and the individuality that gave him value entailed his managing within himself the tensions and the contradictions of his culture. No matter how sympathetically or generously he might respond to a group, an idea, or an ideology, he reserved the room, which he felt he had earned, to search for its shortcomings and its perils. All human enterprises are subject to imperfections, often of a dangerous sort, and one of the tasks of criticism lies in the identification and the naming of the limitations and the hazards that attend creative effort in art, thought, and politics. Loyalty, Trilling had learned, frequently consists in simultaneously maintaining commitment and opposition, and selfhood always begins in defining oneself as "other," as different from even the groups in which one holds affectionate membership. Kazin and others, exuberantly finding their own identity in affiliation with an ideology or a subculture, have simply failed to recognize these elements in the human condition.

In 1927, however, Trilling had still a long developmental way to walk. When he returned to New York from Madison, he encountered an especially difficult time, alleviated only by his meeting with Diana Rubin, whom he married in 1929. She was beautiful. Her mind was quick and well-furnished, and her temperament both complemented and responded to his own. She developed her own career as critic and essayist, and their forty-six years together were deeply and warmly shared. Their first decade, however, as Mrs. Trilling has documented, was heavily shadowed and shot through with anxieties.

On a term-to-term arrangement, Trilling taught at Hunter College under the unfavorable and insecure conditions of the relationship the New York City colleges at that time had to the Tammany Hall system of patronage. Facing the necessity of a doctorate as the credential for full-fledged college teaching, he enrolled in the Graduate School at Columbia, and he increased his involvement at *The Menorah Journal*. For a long year, he worked as Elliot Cohen's assistant, apparently pleasing neither Cohen nor himself, although the personal relationship with Cohen remained intact. From 1930 through 1932, he taught evening classes at Hunter, earning slightly over $3 per hour for undergraduate and slightly over $5 per hour for graduate courses. Enrollment had to meet predetermined levels if the classes were to be given, so when insufficient graduate registration threatened, friends would sign up, recovering the fees of $15 from the Trillings out of the revenues from the course. When Trilling won a $1,800 fellowship at Columbia in 1931, he had to have special permission to continue his work at Hunter.

This was the period, of course, immediately following the stock-market crash of October, 1929, and the onset of the Great Depression. Diana's father lost everything in the market's failure; Lionel's father lost his fur business shortly thereafter. Shouldering the responsibility for his parents as well as themselves, the Trillings sustained a further blow when Diana developed a hyperthyroid condition that first made her dangerously ill and then required nearly ten years for her to regain her full strength and energy. In 1932, Ashley Thorndike, the chairman of the English department at Columbia, appointed Trilling to an instructorship. The action was as inexplicable as it was welcome; Thorndike had taken little notice of the obscure and harried graduate student who had not yet made significant progress toward his Ph.D. The post, however, paid $2,400 for teaching four courses concurrently with doctoral work. In addition, Trilling took any job he could wangle to meet the unremitting flow of debts: he reviewed books; for ten-dollar fees, he gave talks to women's clubs; he tutored needful students who could afford it; and he offered courses for private organizations like the Junior League.

His teaching seems to have suffered little under these strains, but his doctoral dissertation became a source of damaging frustration. It had been amorphously conceived as an intellectual biography of Matthew Arnold. Looking back, Trilling was "appalled" to "remember the state of ignorance and naivete I was in when I ventured upon this enterprise."[32] Ill-prepared himself, he found little support in the department of English for a project so big and so lacking in scholarly specificity. Accounting for Arnold's ideas seemed to entail a consideration of the entire intellectual history of the nineteenth century, and, even if one could somehow manage so formidable a task, there was little evidence that anyone else would care. Emery Neff, who directed Trilling's doctoral effort, was neither unfriendly nor unhelpful, but his own concerns with Arnold were essentially peripheral, and his student was, in fact, giving him little to encourage. Pressed for money, worried about his wife, and involved in an undertaking that proved always more difficult and more demanding than he had anticipated, Trilling was depressed, and his self-confidence was badly undermined. There were days when he set out for the library and wound up unseeingly at the movies, sitting through double features like a waif with nowhere else to go. Struggling against a disturbing although not total case of writer's block, he dully ground out uninspired chapters for presentation to Neff. Neff dealt with him gently, but repeatedly sent him back for another try.

Disaster fell after four years of this kind of grim

and fruitless round. The department notified him that his instructorship would not be renewed. The reason given was that the faculty understood that, "as a Freudian, a Marxist, and a Jew," he could not be happy at Columbia. When Trilling indicated that he *was* happy on Morningside Heights, the reply was that he clearly would be "more comfortable" elsewhere. There was undoubtedly an anti-Semitic element in the department's action, just as there was an anti-Marxist and an anti-Freudian cast to it. But Trilling at that time was also a frightened and heavily burdened graduate student who had not impressed his seniors, either with his intellectual competence or with the attractive facets of his temperament. His fortunes were at a depressingly low ebb; his self-esteem was tottering, and his relationships within the department were too distant for him to be known except by his unusual ethnic identity and his unorthodox interest in Marx and Freud.

A few days passed before Trilling responded directly to his notice of termination. During that period, he apparently brooded on his mother's high expectations for him and on his father's long intimacy with failure. When he finally took action, his behavior was out of character for both the thoroughly undistinguished graduate student he had been and the graciously urbane and deservedly honored professional he was to become. One by one, he called on the senior members of the department—Raymond Weaver, Mark Van Doren, Ashley Thorndike, Emery Neff, men of large authority as well as achieved eminence. He neither begged nor reasoned nor argued. Speaking with atypical forcefulness, he told each of them that they were making a serious error. They were dismissing the person who would bring distinction to the department and who would maintain and extend its prominence in the academic world; they would have to search long and hard to find any one else nearly so promising or so sure of success. It was not an act, played for the occasion;

Trilling meant what he said, and in an important sense he was making a promise—as much to himself as to the persons he addressed. Somehow, miraculously, he proved convincing. His instructorship was renewed for a year.

A dam had burst. The dispirited confusions about the Arnold project disappeared immediately. The depression lifted, and the case of writer's block cleared. In acting so decisively and at such great risk, Trilling had rediscovered his self-confidence, his self-discipline, and his wit. His instructorship was renewed thereafter by virtue of his performance and his new mode of self-presentation; and in two years he successfully submitted his dissertation for the Ph.D. degree.

Trilling himself was never sure of what had happened or of what were the sources of his acting in a fashion so foreign to his personality, and so unpredictable from his habits. He suspected that his previously mousy behavior had evoked the aggressive impulses of his senior professors: when one appears to beg so insistently for abuse, it is difficult not to oblige him. When, out of desperation, Trilling presented so different a self, they treated him as a man meriting respect and courtesy. It is also possible that his unexpected and forceful declaration of a profound self-confidence put a legitimate if tentative claim on their belief, and the faculty simply gave him the opportunity either to prove or to hang himself. Such dynamics may indeed have been the governing ones. Diana Trilling suggests a different explanation, not antithetical to these others, that finds its base in her husband's curious sense of self-worth, derived from the value that his parents had invested in him. Almost magical in its workings, possessed of strong affinities with the "sentiment of being" in Wordsworth, which later held so much fascination for him, this intuitive sense of his own worth is illustrated by an episode from his childhood. Returning home one day from school, he was set upon by a gang of boys who hurled snowballs, many of them containing stones, at him. Although frightened, he did not run. Continuing his course, he told himself that, like Balder, the Norse god of light, who could be harmed only by mistletoe, he was invulnerable. None of the snowballs reached its mark, and the street assault was not pressed. When driven to desperation's edge, when sufficiently *in extremis*, Trilling could somehow lay hold of that perception of his own being and find it in both the courage and the stimulus to his imagination to behave effectively. But his effectiveness was clearly *not*, as many have thought, the result of his being Fortune's darling, a stranger to hardship, insecurity, and self-doubt. It came through the stern cultivation of self-knowledge and integrity, and its cost may have had a great deal to do with the ghosts that always inhabited his eyes, even when they smiled.

Uncertainties still remained about his possible appointment to an assistant professorship. In 1938 and 1939, there were Jews at Columbia, but their numbers were remarkably small. They included Isadore Rabi, the Nobelist in physics, Meyer Schapiro, an art historian whose scholarly eminence was unsurpassed, and Irwin Edman and Felix Adler, philosophers whose intellectual achievements were reinforced by advantageous friendships in society and in the academic community. There were few, if any, others, and there certainly were none in the English department. Trilling had already ample evidence of the reluctance of his senior colleagues to break that barrier. Such, however, was his objective, and his drive toward the doctorate was, in his mind, simply preliminary to accomplishing it.

At that time, for the degree to be awarded, a dissertation had to be published. W. W. Norton agreed to take *Matthew Arnold* but only with a subsidy. The Trillings borrowed the necessary money, and the requirement was met. With the book just out, Trilling

Lionel Trilling: The Opposing Self   39

one day by chance encountered Irwin Edman. Edman, inquiring about his thesis, asked if he had sent a copy to Nicholas Murray Butler, the president of Columbia from 1902 to 1945. No, Trilling hadn't thought of doing so. But the president, Edman explained, *expected* his faculty to send him copies of their publications, and the procedure was well understood. First, using the campus mail, one wrote to the president, requesting permission to send him a copy of one's new work; two days later, without waiting for a reply that would not be forthcoming, one sent him the book, inscribed "To President Butler, Respectfully . . ." Protesting a bit vehemently, Trilling followed the protocol that Edman outlined.

Butler was an almost lengendary figure. When he first became Columbia's president, he acquired the leadership of a relatively small institution of modest reputation. In two decades, he had made it into a comprehensive university of genuine eminence in the academic world and set in motion the momentum that accounted in large part for its continued growth in both size and prominence. A close friend of financiers, politicians, and statesmen, he had aspirations to the presidency of the United States. In 1912, he was vice-presidential candidate on the unsuccessful Republican ticket. An internationalist and a strong advocate of world peace, he was instrumental in the founding of the Carnegie Endowment for International Peace, and in 1931 he shared with Jane Addams the Nobel Peace Prize. Butler despised Communism, and his dealings with suspected Communists and Communist sympathizers among Columbia's faculty and student body earned him the reputation of a repressive tyrant. That reputation may have been somewhat harsh, but it was quite consistent with his dominating administrative style. In a manner no longer possible in American universities, Butler in a very real sense *ruled* Columbia. However he may occasionally have abused it, Butler understood the uses of power and was an adept in power's exercise.

In the early spring of 1939, Butler, in response to *Matthew Arnold,* sent the Trillings one of his engraved invitations to dinner at the president's home. It obviously was something of a command performance. Trilling rented tails and a white tie; his wife bought long white gloves and a ball gown. On the appointed evening, they arrived at the presidential residence to find themselves simultaneously out of place in such illustrious company and the reason for its assemblage. Frank Fackenthaler, provost of the University, may have been present; Herbert Hawkes, dean of Columbia College, and Ernest Hunter Wright, newly appointed chairman of the English department, certainly were. After dinner, the ladies went with Mrs. Butler to her sitting room; the men joined the president for brandy and cigars in the library. Butler got quickly to his point. He had recently been in correspondence with the chancellor of the University of Berlin about an exchange of professors of philosophy. Columbia had proposed sending Felix Adler; the chancellor had written to indicate the unacceptability of a Jewish appointee. Looking with baleful firmness from Hawkes to Wright, Butler said, his tone making his purpose entirely clear, "I wrote back: 'At Columbia, sir, we recognize merit, not race.'" A few weeks later, in the summer, Butler, invoking his "summer powers," appointed Lionel Trilling an assistant professor of English, the first Jew to become a member of that department's faculty.

Trilling had found his intellectual home. He was promoted to an associate professorship in 1945 and became a full professor in 1948. In 1965, he was awarded the George Edward Woodberry Chair in Literature and Criticism, and he was named University Professor in 1970. When he retired in 1974, he continued to teach at Columbia on a part-time basis until

shortly before his death on November 5, 1975.
Through those years, from 1939 to 1975, he kept the
promise that he had made in 1936, when he staved off,
by his highly uncharacteristic act, his dismissal from an
instructorship.

In fulfilling that promise, Trilling persistently followed an unorthodox course. When he received his appointment from President Butler, Columbia ranked—as
it has continued to rank—among the most productive
universities in the United States on the score of research and scholarship. Its ethos was clearly that of
"publish or perish," and, if the literal rule of publication as a basis for professorial advancement was applied relatively loosely, the dominant spirit put a high
premium on the faculty's original contributions to the
disciplines that they represented. At the center of that
emphasis lay the assumption that each professor's work
would be addressed to his professional peers, that it
would appear in recognized scholarly journals, and that
the judgment of disciplinary peers, based on this kind
of technical and formal scholarly effort, defined the essential grounds on which decisions about such matters
as salary increases and promotions would be reached.
The central responsibility of a faculty member, in other
words, was to advance his discipline and to represent
his special field of interest within it in a distinctive
fashion. This conception of the professorial role led to
a tendency to look with some suspicion on creative
endeavors that could be regarded as "popular" or that
were intended for a general audience rather than for a
specialized and academic one, and it relegated teaching
to an important but secondary consideration. Within
the teaching function, the conducting of graduate seminars and the direction of research by graduate students
enjoyed greater prestige than the instruction of undergraduates. Even at the undergraduate level, giving
classes in one's own field was (and is) perceived as
more significant than participating in interdisciplinary

courses serving the ends of liberal or general education.

John Erskine's legacy had created a special situation at Columbia by virtue of his success with the General Honors program. The university had its share of great teachers who were also scholars of from adequate to outstanding reputation. But Erskine combined scholarly adequacy not only with brilliant teaching but with a career as a popular novelist and a popular commentator on American life. Although he was not the only American professor to transcend in his personal accomplishments the academic *Zeitgeist,* he was something of a rarity, and his influence on Trilling seems clearly facilitative and important. Trilling was undoubtedly correct in his judgment that "Erskine was not a person of the finest intellectual temper; he stood on the edge of flamboyance and at a distance from significant achievement in his undertakings as poet, novelist, musician, and critic."[33] But that evaluation overlooks the favorable conditions that Erskine had developed for Trilling's pursuing his own self-determined career path, and it must be understood in the context of Trilling's highly positive experience in General Honors during his own days as an undergraduate. General Honors, probably more than any other single influence, had formed his commitment, despite the chanciness entailed by his being a Jew, to a professorial life.

This background bears directly on his special way of keeping the promise to enhance the distinction of the English department that he had made to Thorndike and Neff, Van Doren and Weaver—and above all, to himself. He set himself at once to becoming not only an outstanding teacher, but an outstanding teacher of undergraduates. Few instructors could match him as a relaxed, clear, and witty lecturer. More importantly, he maintained throughout his career an eagerness to engage in the kinds of discussions with students that brought literature into intimate relation with their lives and that created for them windows on a larger world than they had previously known. His remarkable ability to *listen*, to understand empathically the concerns of undergraduates and the difficulties that they encountered in their reading, gave him special value and accounted for some of his popularity as a teacher. He quietly but relentlessly insisted on effort; he concentrated on the works that defined the content of his courses rather than on "student needs," and he was unsparing in his confronting the difficulty and the complexity of the ideas that the works both embodied and evoked. But he communicated, unmistakably, his own discriminating love of literature; he never failed to demonstrate effectively the ways in which literature is indeed, in Arnold's phrase, a criticism of life, and he made the consideration of literary materials a deeply and significantly human and personal experience. Nor did he forget Erskine's special stress on the element of "delight" as a condition for finding in literature the stimulus to intelligence and to a greater comprehension of culture and of one's own place and functions in society. Intellectual range, social cogency, and seriousness colored by gaiety were the hallmarks of Trilling's undergraduate classes for thirty-five years.

For him, they contrasted with his graduate seminars, which he ran with characteristic competence but with far less joy. The difference lay in the response and purposes of the students. His undergraduates shared with him in some degree his concern for the polity, for the character of the moral life, for the interplay between the individual and his culture. His graduate students, on the other hand, looked toward professional careers and were typically preoccupied with technical issues, with formal and biographical details, and with such immediate problems as identifying suitable topics for doctoral dissertations. Although sympathetic, helpful, and responsible in his relations with graduate students, Trilling found graduate instruction a not uninteresting but burdensome obligation. For him, it contained little of that warm opportunity for significant thought about manners and morals, about the quality of life in different cultural circumstances, about the nature of human experience and human destiny that characterized his work with undergraduates.

If, as a university faculty member, he invested himself as a teacher in an unusual way, he similarly followed a deviant road as a writer. Even in the dark and uncertain years in quest of his own doctorate, Trilling had "no wish to be a scholar," and his involvement with his dissertation on Matthew Arnold was animated by a "determination that the work should find its audience not among scholars but among the general public, that it was to be a work of criticism, not of scholarship." He enjoyed telling the story of how, at his final oral examination for his Ph.D., one of his examining professors leaned across the table toward him and remarked "severely that what I had presented was no doubt a good *book* but was by no means a good *dissertation.*"[34] Committed, despite the character of the academic climate, to that distinction between "books" and "dissertations," Trilling, after his inner-directed fashion, hewed exclusively to his own line. *Matthew Arnold*, which appeared in 1939, was followed in 1942 by *E. M. Forster*, a critical appraisal of Forster's novels and short stories. In 1947, he published *The Middle of the Journey*, his only novel. Meanwhile, during the decade of the forties, he wrote the essays that he collected in 1950 under the title of *The Liberal Imagination*. That book brought him immediate and widespread recognition. Established as a literary critic of the first rank and of distinctive range in the kinds of topics to which he addressed himself, and in the nature of his insights into the human condition, he found his career assured. For the next twenty-five years, with grace and an unassuming confidence, he walked the critic's path of his own choosing, a deeply respected and frequently honored figure in the intellectual world.

Yet in the music of Trilling's professional life between the ages of forty-five and seventy, there is a jangling discord, a puzzle in its harmony. Before he entered college, he had aspirations as a novelist, and the handful of short stories that he published between 1925 and 1945 showed both talent and a mastery of craft. Why was *The Middle of the Journey* the only novel by a man who was "always surprised [to] hear myself referred to as a critic"? "After some thirty years of having been called by that name, the role and the function it designates seem odd to me . . . being a critic was not, in Wordsworth's phrase, part of the plan that pleased my boyish thought, or my adolescent thought, or even my thought as a young man. The plan that did please my thought was certainly literary, but what it envisaged was the career of a novelist." Something moving, something that hints of a sense of failure in a person whom the world judged so successful, pervades a statement from the same source: "This isn't the occasion on which I might appropriately attempt to say why I did not pursue, or not beyond a certain point, the career of a writer of prose fiction, and perhaps such an occasion will not ever present itself."[35]

The mystery is deepened by two other observations. First, a story called "The Lesson and the Secret," which appeared in *Harper's Bazaar* in 1945, was conceived as a chapter for a novel that was never completed. Second, in an interview occasioned by the publication of *The Opposing Self* in 1955, Trilling remarked, "I think we have to let it stand that I am a critic, but it was kind of an accident." Surprisingly, when we recall his agonies over his doctoral work on Matthew Arnold, he continued, "In 1939 I did a critical dissertation on Matthew Arnold, and I found it was a good deal easier to write criticism than fiction." Then, putting his critical efforts in the past tense and making public his future plans, he said, "One essay led to another, but it was never actually a program—like writing fiction. From now on I plan to give a good deal of time to that. I'm writing a second novel at the moment."[36] He was nearing fifty. Few men exceeded him in self-knowledge, and, although he had achieved (*ad astra per aspera*) a considerable degree of self-esteem, he was never brash and never one to ignore commitments, including commitments made to himself. A jarring chord sounds in this disjunction between his comments here and the complete dearth of fiction from his pen after *The Liberal Imagination* brought him fame and security.

Perhaps a clue presents itself through Trilling's perception of the reactions evoked by *The Middle of the Journey*. In the introduction to the reissue of the book in 1975, he refers to it as an "obscure novel" and reports that it "was not warmly received upon its publication or widely read."[37] More revealingly, discussing his friendship with Robert Warshow, who had reviewed *The Middle of the Journey* in *Commentary*, he says, "I was uneasy about the book, being aware of all sorts of things that were wrong with it, and of course it was my uneasiness that made me especially sensitive to adverse criticism, but I thought that Warshow was captious and inaccurate in the particular objections he made—I still think so—and I took his review personally. My resentment apparently went quite deep."[38] Because this frank statement is the only one publicly available in which Trilling records his reactions to the reviews of his novel, and because Warshow's judgment of the book is both the harshest of those evaluations and quite representative of the doubts expressed by many, it is important to note his "particular objections."

In essence, he makes six charges.[39] First, *The Middle of the Journey* owes a debt to E. M. Forster, especially to *Howards End*, but Forster "has a complex sense of character and a richness of wit that Mr. Trilling lacks." Second, the book makes its major appeal to the intelligence; it is highly cerebral. As a consequence, Trilling as a novelist "is removed from experience *as*

experience; the problem of feeling—and thus the problem of art—is not faced." Third, in his treatment of the
character of Gifford Maxim, whose guilt-ridden conver-
sion from Stalinism to a kind of born-again Christianity
must be motored by powerful and deep-seated psychological drives, Trilling pays little attention to the matter
of motives. Indeed, "one of the underlying implications
of the book's thesis [is] that motivations do not really
'count.' But . . . such a thesis and such an approach to
character rest ultimately on the assumption that the
most fruitful way of dealing with experience is to pass
judgment on it—and this is not the assumption of a
novelist." Fourth, in the development of Duck Caldwell, a drunken and vicious representative of the lower
class, Trilling shows naiveté: "If it was a sentimental
error to credit the working class with a virtue and an
innocence that it never possessed, it is only another
kind of sentimentality to make too much of correcting
the error." Fifth, the author's clear identification with
John Laskell, the novel's protagonist, violates a fundamental novelistic rule—no character should obviously
define the writer's "mouthpiece." And finally, Trilling
reduces the experience of his characters to a conflict
between two orthodoxies, Stalinism and Christianity,
and the problem of how to discover the "right opinion"
that can be derived from them. In taking this reductive
approach to the people and the circumstances of his
book, Trilling fails "to detach himself from the cultural
atmosphere he seeks to transcend," thus displaying a
lack of that "Olympian disinterestedness (not neutrality) which enables Forster to encompass all the complexities and impurities of experience without strain or
shock." It also requires him to "convince his reader
that some characters are 'right' and others 'wrong' (although 'rightness' and 'wrongness' are qualities not of
human beings but only of ideas); whereas the true novelist tries only to make his characters and their behavior 'convincing,' which is something entirely differ-

ent." Warshow concludes not only that Trilling "is not a great novelist" but that he has "not yet solved the problem of being a novelist at all."

These strictures and the final judgment to which they lead are severe, and one can readily understand the sense of being wounded that an author might experience on reading them. Nor is their sting much moderated by Warshow's quite genuine acknowledgment of Trilling's "intelligence and honesty" and his warm tribute to his style: "Parts of this novel . . . are written with beauty, imagination, and intensity." But two considerations pose an important question. On the one hand, Warshow's concerns reflect typical reactions to *The Middle of the Journey* at the time of its first appearance. Richard Cordell, for instance, commented on how the "characters are more interesting than credible" and observed that, "To some readers the novel will be too chill and intellectual."[40] Similarly, the anonymous reviewer in *Time* for October 20, 1947, found Trilling to be "not yet a finished novelist," felt that he "mishandles the Dostoevskian character of Maxim," and charged that "A good deal of the book frays out in thin, earnest psychologizing." On the other hand, Warshow's condemnation stands quite alone in its intensity and in its almost unrelievedly negative tone. If the appraisals by Cordell and in *Time* were quite in keeping with the central negative features of the reviews, they also represent the positive emphasis that ran regularly through them. The piece in *Time* refers to the book as a "good and honest novel," in which Trilling "writes beautifully about children and sometimes with gently dazzling insight about their elders," and it indicates that he can 'rival E. M. Forster in the manipulation of surprise and anticlimax." Cordell calls *The Middle of the Journey* a "mature and intelligent novel . . . of ideas," marked by writing of "consistent excellence," and his final opinion is that "Trilling has chosen to write of the modern man whose dilemma is intellectual as well as emotional, and

has done so with acumen and compassionate understanding."

In short, the book may have been a good bit less
than a smashing success; but its critical reception—
Warshow's attack aside—was actually generous and respectful, with a fair share of praise outweighing the
expressed reservations. The reservations, however,
tended to be widely shared and to fall into the categories of Warshow's distinctive denunciation.

The question to which these two considerations
bring us is clear: Did Trilling respond in his hurt and
resentful manner *only* to Warshow's "captious and inaccurate objections"? Or was he disturbed by interaction between his own confessed awareness that "all
sorts of things were wrong" with *The Middle of the
Journey* and his perception of the consistency of the
negative comments about it? If the latter was the case,
then Warshow's dismissal of Trilling as a novelist may
have appeared as far more than a "captious and inaccurate" judgment. It may have sounded like an alarm
bell, warning him away from danger.

At age forty-two, Trilling had realized for the first
time his dream since boyhood of writing a novel. He
had his own doubts about it; and one reviewer, speaking with a special animosity but also speaking for most
other commentators on the book, sent him back for
another try. During four dark years, Emery Neff had
sent him back to try again as his dissertation chapters
failed to pass muster. Warshow, without Neff's spirit of
helpfulness, had touched a nerve still raw. Worse, his
objections probably seemed quite congruent to Trilling's own. Passionate as he was, he was devoted to
ideas and managed his life, both personally and profes-
sionally, by thought, by a rather severe reliance on cognitive and intellectual processes rather than by spontaneously translating his feelings into action. If his first
novel proved a highly cerebral form of art, it was what
one would expect, given its author's strong tendency to

live so fully through his brain. Was he *capable* of writing an extended work of fiction in which the visceral life, the life of feeling and emotion, could play a more central and authentic part? Moreover, his short stories all have an autobiographical cast. Their protagonists at least share striking resemblances to Trilling, if they are not straightforwardly his fictional doubles. ("The Other Margaret" may be an exception. Yet even here the similarities between central character and creator show straightforwardly. Elwin, for example, the story's protagonist, like Trilling, is too young to have served in the military during the first of the world wars and too old for service during the second.) This kind of identification makes for little doubt about which character speaks with the writer's voice. Was Trilling *able* to create a fictional world inhabited by convincing and authentic people, no one of whom was really himself? Involved as he was with ideas and principles, could he *novelistically* come to grips with the motives of his characters, capitalizing artistically on his interest in Freud and his rich comprehension of psychoanalysis? Or could he subdue, in an aesthetically appropriate fashion, his disposition to focus on tensions between ideas and world views rather than between persons? Was he, in short, characterologically fit to function as a novelist?

Such questions meshed all too closely with his intimate and protracted encounter, only ten years before, with failure—failure that had threatened his livelihood, his career, and his self-respect. Trilling's dismissal from his instructorship in 1936 had capped at least four years of unproductive wretchedness. He had not only drunk deeply of the gall of insecurity; he had experienced acute depression and, in his own eyes, had accomplished virtually nothing. He had had occasion to brood on the contrast between his mother's bright and hopeful aspirations for him and his father's lifelong sense of shame and of *being*, not merely experiencing, a failure, a sense essentially confirmed by his disastrously changing his occupation from that of a tailor to a furrier. When Trilling paid his startlingly uncharacteristic visits to the senior members of the English department, he had determined to avoid at all costs his father's unhappy destiny, and he had made a promise: If given the necessary opportunity, he would bring distinction to the department and add to its eminence.

If he had kept that promise in his own way, he had left no room to doubt the shining quality of his achievements. When *The Middle of the Journey* appeared in 1947, he was already known as a superb teacher. *Matthew Arnold* and *E. M. Forster* had won considerable praise, and a kind of respectful excitement had greeted eleven published essays that he was to collect with five others in 1950 as *The Liberal Imagination*. Criticism was proving a special and congenial *métier* for him. The short stories added a fillip and a dimension to both his intellectual contribution and to his image as a literary figure, but they were few in number and seemed peripheral to his primary commitments.

Against these rewarding developments, novels in which "all sorts of things were wrong" did not represent a fulfillment of his promise, nor were they in keeping with his anxiety-driven determination to avoid his father's immersion in failure. Indeed, the shift from successful critic and teacher to doubtfully regarded novelist may have seemed dimly but significantly akin to David Trilling's fateful shift from tailor to furrier. The recognition and admiration that teaching and criticism evoked were not only intrinsically pleasing. They discharged the debt that Trilling's promise imposed upon him; they vindicated the graduate student who had shown so little talent and who had so nearly failed to earn his doctorate, and they legitimized and justified the deep-seated but often beleaguered self-esteem on which he relied in crises. In contrast, his foray into novel-writing had engendered an "uneasiness" in him—

an uneasiness that began with his father, that was intensified by his experience as a Jew during the twenties and thirties in a heartlessly anti-Semitic America, and that had become intimately familiar between 1932 and 1936, when he had come perilously close to personal disaster. Warshow's uniquely damning review, given force by the much more mildly voiced but similar substance in other judgments of *The Middle of the Journey*, had raised the ghosts of the dark years between his return to New York from Wisconsin and his desperate confrontation of his departmental mentors in 1936.

Writing fiction after 1947, then, posed for Trilling an intense psychological threat. Even a person of his moral courage might well quail before the risks of failure that his experience with his first novel had unleashed. But his novelistic ambition had not only taken form early in his life, it was an "abiding" one.[41] As an abiding component of himself, it could be suppressed by the fears of failure associated with it, but it could not be completely dissipated. An understanding of this state of affairs may help in accounting for a secondary puzzle, a curiously fallow period in his productivity between 1956, when he declared in a public interview that he was busy with a second novel, and 1965, when *Beyond Culture* was published.

As we have seen, when his novel appeared in print, Trilling had completed eleven of the sixteen essays in *The Liberal Imagination*, which he published in 1950. That enthusiastically hailed book consolidated his critical reputation. Five years later, he published *The Opposing Self*, and in the following year, he brought out *A Gathering of Fugitives*, a charming compilation of seventeen relatively short pieces written between 1949 and 1956, eleven of them prepared originally for *The Griffin*, the magazine of the Readers' Subscription book club. Along with Jacques Barzun and Wystan Auden, he had served as an editor with the monthly task of selecting a book and reviewing it for the club's members. Some of these reviews combine a relaxed manner and a comfortable tone with a wit and a level of intellectual penetration that make them especially noteworthy. The present point, however, is that the time from the disturbance over *The Middle of the Journey* through *A Gathering of Fugitives* was richly productive. It was a time, too, when he became even more popular and in greater demand as a teacher. Part of his response to the anxiety that his novel's reception had elicited was to intensify his already impressive instructional and critical energies, and his doing so reassured him and restored his self-confidence.

But his next book, *Beyond Culture*, did not appear for almost a decade. Although a work of immense solidity and striking range, it contains only eight essays. Two of them are *pièces d'occasion*: the Freud Anniversary Lecture, delivered before the New York Psychoanalytic Society and the New York Psychoanalytic Institute in May of 1955; and the Henry Sidgwick Memorial Lecture, presented at Newnham College, Cambridge University, in February of 1965. It seems improbable that a man so intensely committed to his work should have done, by his own standards, so little in that nine-year span. The improbability is heightened by his having announced to the world in the interview of 1956 that he was occupied with a second novel. Because Trilling was hardly a man to renege on his commitments, it seems highly likely that he struggled for a considerable portion of that period with a fictional work that he longed to complete but could not bring himself to publish. The disappointments entangled with *The Middle of the Journey* had left him vulnerable, and the risks were simply too great even for him. In the light of his history, there can be little doubt that, beneath that splendid layer of public success, his private demons continued to harry him, and they at least played a major part in denying him the joyous satisfaction of realizing his long-dreamed-of career as a novelist.

That denial is intensified by a fateful irony. The American sales of *The Middle of the Journey* when it first appeared in 1947 approximated 5,000 copies. Nearly thirty years later, in 1975, it was reissued in paperback with Trilling's introduction, recounting the manner in which he had used Whittaker Chambers as the prototype for the novel's Gifford Maxim. Because Trilling died in November of that year, that piece may have been the last from his pen that he saw through the process of publication. In the five years following its author's death, *The Middle of the Journey* sold nearly 50,000 copies. Posthumously, Trilling achieved his boyhood ambition of becoming a successful writer of fiction, and his artistic aspirations won a significant degree of vindication.

Unaware, of course, of the vindicative but bitterly ironic destiny of his one novel, Trilling emerged, as he always did, a somewhat battered but authentic victor from his battles with his internal devils. After 1965, when he published *Beyond Culture* at the age of sixty, he edited the comprehensive anthologies, *The Experience of Literature* and *Literary Criticism,* the former with a remarkably insightful set of commentaries to accompany his selections. With his colleague Steven Marcus, he abridged Ernest Jones's three-volume *Life and Work of Sigmund Freud* into a more accessible one-volume edition. He served as coeditor of *The Oxford Anthology of English Literature* and as a member of the Planning Committee for the National Humanities Center. He received the first Thomas Jefferson Award from the National Endowment for the Humanities and gave the first Jefferson lecture, published as *Mind in the Modern World.*[42] In 1969 and 1970, he was Charles Eliot Norton Professor of Poetry at Harvard, and in 1972 and 1973, he was a Visiting Fellow at All Souls College at Oxford. Above all, he wrote what Irving Howe has called that "wonderful book,"[43] *Sincerity and Authenticity.* Even at the moment of his death, he remained in intellectual harness as the holder of a Guggenheim Fellowship.

Over the course of the precise half-century that elapsed between the publication of "Impediments" in *The Menorah Journal* in 1925 and his death, Trilling richly elaborated but never fundamentally altered his point of view or his preoccupation with four central human themes. His deepest and recurrent concerns centered on the struggle between the individual, striving for self-realization, and the culture that simultaneously nurtures him and ruthlessly bends him to its impersonal and corporate will; the precarious balance in our experience of freedom and necessity, the tension between personal will and the recognition of the world's intransigeance; the perils of Utopian dreams, of fanaticism, of the damage that can be done by decent people who have no doubts about their own ideas, their own ideals, or their own commitments; and the uses of the imagination in dealing with reality, especially social reality—the reality of politics and of our cultural experience. In making these concerns articulate in relation to a variety of specific topics and as a means of illuminating a wide range of literature, his achievement permits us to say of him what R. H. Super has said of Trilling's most important, except perhaps for Sigmund Freud, intellectual and spiritual model—Matthew Arnold:

in an age when the moral desperadoes might look to a past that could never be retrieved, when the liberals might lose sight of reality in claptrap and machinery, he perceived that . . . though the modern spirit was necessarily liberal, yet [that] liberalism was hopelessly inadequate to the demands of humanity. . . . By perceiving what elements of . . . liberalism gave promise for the [future], he became, not only what he called Emerson, "the friend and aider of those who would live in the spirit," but the best representative . . . of the modern spirit.[44]

2

ᚖᚖ

Civilization
and Its Discontents

No set of ideas so consistently, so dominantly, preoccupied Lionel Trilling throughout his career as those
formulated by Sigmund Freud in *Civilization and Its
Discontents*.[1] From the time of its first appearance in
English in 1930, Trilling frequently reread and pon-
dered this little book. He taught it often in his classes at
Columbia University, and it formed a significant and
fundamental component of the background of thought
out of which his lectures, essays, and judgments of literary and social affairs emerged. Our comprehension of
Trilling is enriched by an understanding of Freud's view
of how individuals develop in the cultures of which they
are inevitably a part.

Developed as a psychoanalytic theory of culture,
Freud's basic notions and primary thesis in *Civilization
and Its Discontents* are surprisingly independent of the
corpus of psychoanalytic thought.[2] One needn't be an
orthodox Freudian or belong to one of the derivative
but closely related psychological movements to find a
moving cogency in this reading of the human condition.
It begins with the observation that, from an evolutionary point of view, humankind has specialized in neither
strength nor speed nor adaptive camouflage. The grizzly
bear, the deer, and the chameleon are among our many
masters in these capacities. *Homo sapiens* survives and
thrives by virtue of being *homo faber*, the only member
of the animal kingdom who creates—who uses tools,

including weapons, who manipulates symbols and ideas, who *makes* the conditions that permit his living anywhere on earth, rather than being confined to a particular ecological niche. What enables our species to conceive of and to manufacture everything from surgical instruments to cyclotrons, from fur garments to air conditioning, from statutes and constitutions to songs and paintings, is essentially our complex nervous system, our big and highly convoluted brains.

That large and intricately folded brain of ours requires the birth of an extraordinarily incomplete organism. In contrast to kittens or puppies, or even to the offspring of monkeys and apes, all of which enjoy a reasonable chance of survival as independent organisms within a few short weeks after birth, the human baby enters the world much too soon. Yet the alternative, given the mammalian nature of the human species, would be mothers of gigantic size—much too large to function with necessary efficiency in a terrestrial environment, and quite lacking in earthly survival value. The open fontanels in the infant's skull are only one of the provisions in the evolutionary scheme for a nervous system that does not reach full maturity until about the eighteenth year of extrauterine life. The entailment of this peculiar neural specialization in the biological, evolutionary sense that gives humankind its distinctiveness is the uniquely long period that we know as infancy and childhood.

The price, then, of our remarkable nervous systems is an extended experience of virtually complete helplessness and dependency, during which our well-being and our very survival rest on the mediation of our needs by others. Perhaps even more importantly, all of us go through a stage of infantile omnipotence in which the world is simply an extension of ourselves, responding to our cries with food, warmth, tactile support, stroking and gentle stimulation, and similar ministrations. But, as we begin to recognize the external world as quite independent of us, we acquire the frightening knowledge that, far from being omnipotent, we are powerless—small, weak, ignorant, and quite literally dependent on adults over whom we can exercise no controls at all. Still later, as young children, as we begin in more autonomous ways to direct our energies and to interact with our environments, we learn to model our behavior on that of the adults whose presence remains indispensable to us and whose will, potency, and authority impress us as irresistible.

Simultaneously, however, the same evolutionary process that has made a long dependency and helplessness a part of our neural specialization has also endowed us with what Cannon[3] called "emergency reactions." These are the tendencies to flee or to do battle— the famous capacities for "fight or flight"—that become prepotent when we are threatened. These physiologically grounded propensities, which have a high survival value under primitive conditions but which have probably been untouched by evolutionary change for ten millennia or more,[4] prepare us for essentially violent activity and set up the internal conditions that we quickly learn to recognize as fear and anger, terror and hostility or hatred. Similarly, our biological endowment includes the raw sexual impulse that insures the continuation of the species but that, in itself, has little inherent connection to love, the qualities of intimacy in human relationships, or the experiences of affection that clothe survival with distinctively human value.

Quickly sketched, these circumstances set the stage on which the dramas of our individual lives must be played. On the one hand, we are clearly and definitely *cultural* beings. Inescapably, our initial survival and our later realization of at least some of the major potentials inherent in our nervous systems depend on our membership in a group and on our acceptance to some significant degree of the folkways and norms of that group. Even more critically, much of what we are

we learn from participating—first as a helpless dependent and later as a more or less full-fledged citizen—in
the affairs of the group. In short, we begin early to form
rudimentary concepts of right and wrong, good and
bad, desirable and undesirable, and to attach to these
dimly conceived ideas our feelings of security and acceptance by the people on whom we are dependent and
with whose destiny our own fate is somehow bound up.
This process defines the beginnings of our moral sense,
our perception of a moral order in the corporate life on
which we, willy-nilly, rely, regardless of how reluctantly, for our personal survival and growth. Out of
these beginnings develop both our awareness of the
moral bond that ties us to our society and our unconscious connection with the moral order that at once
protects and restrains us. If that involvement in the
moral dynamics of the culture is always tenuous, it
remains implacable, inevitable, and, to greater or lesser
degree, we incorporate into ourselves the norms and
values of our cultural context. On the other hand, we
are ineluctably *selves*. Inherently, we are self-protec-
tively drive-ridden animals, strongly inclined to take
what we desire, to destroy whatever frustrates us, and
to behave as amoral egoists under the control of biologically motored wishes.

Human life consists, then, in an endless encounter
between the impulse-dominated individual and the nay-
saying, regulatory culture. Without the supports of culture, we fail at even rudimentary levels to achieve the
attributes that we identify as distinctively those of *persons*, or to attain the security, the capacity for delight,
or the kinds of relationships that underlie our prizing of
life itself, and that permit us to behave in reasonably
rewarding and effective ways. But the culture exacts a
price: We may act on our impulses only under prescribed conditions; otherwise, the probability of punishment is high. In consequence, no matter how highly
socialized we may be, no matter how fully we have

interiorized the manners and morals of our society, we are not infrequently likely to feel trapped and thwarted by the network of regulations and commandments our society has woven around us, to experience alienation and loneliness by virtue of our "otherness" from that ruling social context in which we are inevitably imbedded, and to find all too familiar the pangs of conflict as we struggle to enhance our sense of selfhood against the constraints and restrictions of the culture in which we nevertheless live and move and have our being.

It is against this background that we can understand Trilling's insistence that the idea that "preoccupies . . . literature and is central to it" is the idea of the self. Although his reference here is to literary works of the nineteenth and twentieth centures, his incisive commentaries in *The Experience of Literature*, an anthology of fiction, drama, and poetry from Sophocles to Bernard Malamud and Robert Lowell, make it clear that he hardly regarded earlier works as discontinuous from later ones in this respect. What he perceived as distinctive about *modern* literature, however, was "its intense and adverse imagination of the culture" of which it is a part.[5] When Thomas Mann once indicated that all his work represented an effort to free himself from the middle class, he was articulating this yearning to realize self more fully by slipping the shackles of the determining culture. Trilling responded sympathetically and positively to that impulse toward selfhood, that assertion of individuality against the cabining influences of traditional values, that imagination of a socially unmediated commerce between the person and his distinctive experience.

But he also perceived that the longing to break the bonds of the middle class engaged a still deeper desire to escape society generally, to divorce the self from a culture conceived as alien and repressive. Without romanticizing it, Trilling would have found at once the moving significance in the story of Willy Wolfe.[6] Willy

began his life as the favored son of a well-to-do physician in Litchfield, Connecticut, one of New England's
most advantaged, beautiful, and tradition-steeped vil-
lages. He ended it at age twenty-three as Cujo the Unconquerable, the last guerrilla of the sordid Symbionese
Liberation Army, firing futilely at police and FBI
agents from the crawl space under a seedy little frame
house in Los Angeles, until the burning structure fell on
him. That journey from conventionally happy beginnings to a darkly nihilistic death symbolizes action in
obedience to the modern voices that tempt and lure
and urge beneath the surface and under the forms of
modern art. Although, obviously, Yeats and Eliot, Joyce
and Proust and Kafka, Lawrence, Mann, and Gide did
not directly incite Willy Wolfe to his frightening and
destructive quest, they embody and make articulate
some of the same drives, some of the same sensed discontent with the culture, to which Willy responded in so
fatal a fashion.

For Trilling, literature, which he took as the central diagnostic index of a society, always invites its
audience to new perceptions and new ideas, always re-
cruits readers to changed behavior and to changed styles
of living and of participating in the community. The
invitations and the recruiting efforts of the modern writers to whom he was most committed stem from an
enhancement of the self over culture, from a condemning analysis of the moral chaos and the often
brutal coerciveness of Western society, from the rejection of our inherited verities as deceptive and hypocriti-
cal, and from a critical questioning of the largely institutionalized values of our industrial age. The works
of the moderns emanating from these oppositional concerns are "manifestly contrived to be not static and
commemorative but mobile and aggressive, and one
does not describe a quinquereme or a howitzer or a
tank without estimating how much *damage* it can do."[7]
In the warfare between self and culture, the self may

prove the casualty. One doubts, for example, that Cujo the Unconquerable attained, even privately, a sufficient degree of self-actualization to warrant his wholesale, hostile, and finally self-defeating disavowal of his culture. And in that warfare, culture may lose much of its facilitative and developmental powers along with some of its nay-saying oppressiveness.

Recognizing this potential for damage aroused in Trilling a counter-sense of the human condition that conferred on Freud· and the Judaeo-Christian legacy a validity that the modern prophets, despite his sympathetic admiration of them, could not dissolve. For him, Freud's view of the nature of humanity preserved "something—much—of the stratum of hardness that runs through the Jewish and Christian traditions as they respond to the hardness of human destiny. Like the Book of Job, it propounds and accepts the mystery and the naturalness—the natural mystery, the mysterious naturalness—of suffering." In formulating his essentially austere vision, Freud "had the intention of sustaining the authenticity of human existence that formerly had been ratified by God."[8] Within himself, and therefore in his criticism and in his fiction, Trilling joined the issue. On the one hand, he found value in the massively liberating thrust of the moderns and supported their aggressive advocacy of a more richly realized self; on the other, he found in culture the very groundwork of humanity and defended it on historic principles. Although secular in conviction and outlook, he invested an informed seriousness in the moral traditions of both Jewish and Christian faith and theology. Although very much a modern, he adhered to classical ideals in his understanding of the antique maxims of "the middle way" and "nothing in excess" as entailing a measure of self-restraint[9] and often a personal and somewhat precarious balancing and management of unresolved and perhaps unresolvable tensions—like the tension between self and culture. And, although one of the least doctrinaire of men, he maintained a profound commitment to psychoanalytic ideas because he found compelling Freud's tragic view of the human condition.

This complex point of view—perhaps, more accurately, this complex and informed sensibility—found special nourishment in Trilling's encounter with Matthew Arnold. Concerned initially with Arnold as a poet "whose melancholy spoke to me in an especially personal way,"[10] Trilling's long immersion in the writer whom he came to identify as "the first literary intellectual in the English-speaking world" deepened and enriched his understanding of the modern era's special conflicts between self and culture. The experience of loneliness and the barriers to effective, durable, and mutually satisfying interpersonal relationships, the relationships of friendship and of love, came into clearer focus for him. His analysis of the well-known "Dover Beach" is illustrative. In that poem Arnold characterizes "the world"—that is, the human world, the culture —despite its seeming "To lie before us like a land of dreams, / So various, so beautiful, so new," as really affording

> neither joy, nor love, nor light,
> Nor certitude, nor peace, nor help for pain;
> And we are here as on a darkling plain
> Swept with confused alarms of struggle and flight,
> Where ignorant armies clash by night.

The reason for this disjunction between appearance and reality is that the "Sea of Faith," which once "round earth's shore / Lay like the folds of a bright girdle furl'd," now only howls

> Its melancholy, long, withdrawing roar,
> Retreating, to the breath
> Of the night-wind, down the vast edges drear
> And naked shingles of the world.

As an antidote to this state of sad and joyless uncertainty in the lot of humanity, the poet can only plead,

"Ah, love, let us be true / To one another!" He can only offer and ask for loyalty in intimacy—not pleasure, erotic excitement, a warm sharing of experience, a confidence in mutual understanding, but only loyalty. As Trilling notes,

perhaps never before in literature has a lover given a reason for love, and a reason, which, while asserting its necessity, denies its delight. It is believed by all lovers that love has the power not only of making the world various and beautiful and new, but also of maintaining it in variety, beauty, and novelty. But the lover of "Dover Beach" denies love's efficacy. . . .[11]

But there is more. Arnold comments that "Sophocles long ago" also heard the ocean's

> grating roar
> Of pebbles which the waves draw back, and fling,
> At their return, up the high strand,
> Begin, and cease, and then again begin,
> With tremulous cadence slow, and bring
> The eternal note of sadness in,

and his hearing this melancholy sound "brought / Into his mind the turbid ebb and flow / Of human misery." Although Arnold is responding in part to the ebbing of the sea of Christian faith under the impact of Darwin and the rising science of the latter half of the nineteenth century, his direct reference to Sophocles makes it clear that a waning Christianity fails to account by itself for his bleak reading of the human situation. Trilling makes two points. First, Arnold interpreted a lessening of religious faith as symptomatic of a general diminution in personal zest and vital self-confidence, in that delighted and essentially hopeful and optimistic involvement in life that William James called "animal faith." It is the erosion of that basic *feeling* that humanity enjoys a proud destiny that so deeply distresses him.

Second, Arnold almost certainly had in mind the third chorus of Sophocles's *Antigone*: "Blest are they whose days have not tasted of evil. For when a house hath once been shaken from heaven, there the curse fails nevermore, passing [from generation to generation] even as, when the surge is driven over the darkness of the deep by . . . Thracian sea-winds, it rolls up the black sand from the depths, and there is a sullen roar from the wind-vexed headlands that front the blows of the storm." Although the chorus speaks only of the dreadful and inescapable fate of the members of certain families under a curse, and not of human misery universally, "the generalization," as Trilling says, "can of course be made." Making it, we strongly suspect that Arnold thought further of the difference between this passage from the play and the tone of *Antigone's* second chorus, which opens "Wonders are many, and none is more wonderful than man," and then proceeds to sing of man's achievements and glories. The contrast underscores the vulnerability of both human pride and human security. Fate can deal harshly with that confident relish for life that lies at the heart of animal faith. When we perceive, in all their power, these harsh, uncaring, destructive forces in the universe, then we lose our rejuvenative wonder at the triumphant qualities of our species; the world seems suffused with uncertainties and dangers, and love is robbed of its joys and of its invigorating, revitalizing potentials.

This theme recurs often in Arnold, but if, in "Dover Beach," it reflects primarily a commentary on a disheartening, alienating culture, in the Marguerite poems, as Trilling observes, it cuts closer to the bone of personality itself. A love affair, as love affairs sometimes will, fails. Out of his heartache, and taking the ending of the relationship as the symbol of human separateness, the poet perceives that "in the sea of life enisled, / . . . We mortal millions live *alone*." Between person and person there surges an "unplumb'd, salt, estranging sea" that forces a grim recognition of a fundamental truth: "Thou hast been, shalt be, art, alone." If driven by loneliness, one asks, "And what heart knows another?" then the answer, simultaneously cold and touching, suggests itself at once: "Ah! who knows his own?" But if one turns from the world of culture to the world of nature, seeking both for self-knowledge and for the calm and composure that the sea and the stars seem to possess, the response tends to prove a bit Olympian for a member of the mortal millions. An "air-born voice" says, "Wouldst thou be as these are? Live as they." The forces of nature "demand not that the things without them / Yield them love, amusement, sympathy . . . /self-poised they live, nor pine with noting / All the fever of some differing soul." Although the poet hears in his heart an echoing and affirmative cry—"Resolve to be thyself; and know that he, / Who finds himself, loses his misery"—he cannot escape an awareness of the terrible entailments. If being oneself means absolute self-dependence, and if absolute self-dependence is the one means of escaping misery, then one remains forever cut off from the love, regard, and companionship of others. Of equal importance, it implies that one must achieve a complete indifference to others; one must be forever unmoved by their suffering, unattracted by their laughter or beauty. And we are back, as individuals, enisled within the unplumb'd, salt, estranging sea.

For Trilling (as for others), beyond the articulation here of the universal human vulnerability to loneliness, two ideas in this context have particular significance. One is Arnold's affirmation of the validity and centrality of *feeling* in human affairs. The fear of the loss of the power to feel defines one of the major and repeated themes of literature at least since the industrial revolution. D. H. Lawrence springs at once to mind, but Nietzsche, Kafka, and a host of others, including so current and so popular a writer as Philip Roth,[12] crowd close behind. For all his prizing of the intellect and of intellectual values, Arnold's concern with the desiccating effects of rationalism—the rationalism bound up with an increasingly scientific industrial and economic life—was profound. He saw this kind of rationalism as smothering the instinctual processes and narrowing the imaginative capacities of individuals, and Trilling, extending this view into the twentieth century, shared Arnold's alarm and with him looked largely to literature as a corrective. It is elements in the culture, not hardship or sorrow or old age, that threaten to dry up the wellsprings of emotion and imagination:

> we may suffer deeply, yet retain
> Power to be moved and soothed, for all our pain . . .
> No: 'tis the gradual furnace of the world,
> In whose hot air our spirits are upcurled
> Until they crumble, or else grow like steel—
> Which kills in us the bloom, the youth, the spring—
> Which leaves the fierce necessity to feel,
> But takes away the power . . .

The restricting, the hardening, the withering of the *power* to feel may be a function of a culture that sets a premium on a preeminent and narrow concept of reason. But what is the source of that *fierce necessity* that so obdurately remains? As much as did Freud, Arnold saw the self as taking shape under the molding influence of culture, as quite literally determined by it. But like Freud, he also thought of the self as in continuing opposition to the culture, as locked in a continuing struggle with it. Much of the energizing force, the motivating vigor, for that struggle stems from that fierce necessity to feel. If that emotional impetus lacks both direction and content until experience and reflection have colored it, it nevertheless operates as one of the inherent engines of human conduct and finds its seat not in the cultural surround but in the biology, the fundamental evolutionary nature, of humanity. Although this notion was deeply rooted in Arnold's thought, he never—Victorian literary intellectual that he was—discussed the biological groundwork of the idea. Freud, of course, made much of it. Trilling, steeped in Arnold, comments,

> . . . Freud may be right or he may be wrong in the place he gives to biology in human fate, but I think we must stop to consider whether this emphasis on biology, correct or incorrect, is not so far from being a reactionary idea that it is actually a liberating idea. It proposes to us that culture is not all-powerful. It suggests that there is a residue of human quality beyond the reach of cultural control, and that this residue of human quality, elemental as it may be, serves to bring culture itself under criticism and keeps it from being absolute . . . somewhere in the child, somewhere in the adult, there is a hard, irreducible, stubborn core of biological urgency, and biological necessity, and biological *reason*, that culture cannot reach and that reserves the right, which sooner or later it will exercise, to judge the culture and resist and revise it.[13]

To that form of reason and to that basis for the self's resistance to culture, Trilling unswervingly gave his allegiance. In significant part, his commitment to biologically grounded *feeling* as at least a fundamental datum in the human condition stemmed from Arnold's persuasiveness about the nature of emotion, of animal faith.

But Arnold's second idea carries rather different implications. If the gradual furnace of the world, the culture, burns away our power to feel, the cultivation of that power—the cultivation of the self in its distinctiveness—necessarily sets us increasingly apart from our fellows. The more richly we develop and diversify our private, inner lives, the more different we become from those from whom we expect love, amusement, and sympathy; and the greater that difference becomes, the more difficult and the more subject to misunderstanding the chancy process of communication grows:

> Are even lovers powerless to reveal
> To one another what indeed they feel?
> I knew the mass of men conceal'd

> Their thoughts, for fear that if reveal'd
> They would by other men be met
> With blank indifference, or with blame reproved;
> I knew they lived and moved
> Trick'd in disguises, alien to the rest
> Of men, and alien to themselves . . .
> But we, my love!—doth a like spell benumb
> Our hearts, our voices—must we too be dumb?

Arnold's answer is, in Trilling's phrase, an acknowledgment of "the general inability of human atoms to meet:"[14]

> Why each is striving, from of old,
> To love more deeply than he can?
> Still would be true, yet still grows cold?
> —Ask of the Powers that sport with man!
>
> They yok'd in him, for endless strife,
> A heart of ice, a soul of fire;
> And hurl'd him on the Field of Life,
> An aimless unallay'd Desire.

The result is an unwitting, frequent, damaging flaw in our relationships with one another—our relationships as friends, lovers, parents, and children. It was familiar to Freud; it was to Trilling. "No writer of his time," he says, "understood in terms as clear and straightforward as Arnold's this psychological phenomenon of the distortion of purpose and self and the assumption of a manner to meet the world."[15] The divorce between the reality of self and its appearance permeates our interpersonal transactions. In order to cope with the exigencies of the moment, to defend ourselves against some immediate threat or to serve some short-range objective, we play a role. While satisfying, through role-playing, the demands of these social impingements on our selfhood, we come to the rather bewildered and guilty realization that "what we say and do / Is eloquent, is well—but 'tis not true." Alienation from self may be intimately related to alienation from culture, but the two aspects of modern experience are far from identical.

For Trilling, it was Arnold the poet who made this distinction both humanly crucial and relevant to literature, that centrally important criticism of life that permits persons to keep alive their aspiration to be at once uniquely individual and corporately civilized. This insight of Arnold's, blending with Freud's perceptions, deeply affected Trilling. His understanding of it prevented his taking fashionable stands with those who account for all human ills on the grounds of oversimplified conceptions of cultural deficiencies and cultural oppression. It heightened his sense of complexity in human affairs while deepening his respect for the individual's limited but real capacity to influence his own destiny. And it provided him with a perspective from which he illuminated in a remarkably distinctive way much of the literature and many of the issues with which he so influentially concerned himself.

He exemplifies this perspective and its value in his treatment of Jane Austen. In agreement with F. R. Leavis that she is "the first truly modern novelist of England,"[16] Trilling speaks of her as requiring a reader "to make no mere literary judgment but a decision about his own character and personality, and about his relation to society and all of life." This kind of challenge most deeply commands his respect. It is the challenge of Yeats and Eliot, of Joyce and Proust and Kafka, of Lawrence, Mann, and Gide, who insistently ask "if we are content with ourselves, if we are saved or damned"; here is the radical criticism of life that excites his commitment, his fear, and his ambivalence.[17] Nowhere does Jane Austen throw down her gauntlet in a more complex or imperious fashion than in *Mansfield Park*.

Although its original publication evoked more admiration than any of the other five novels in her canon, Trilling notes that this book goes curiously against the modern grain. Austen's devotees, he says, find it an embarrassment; her detractors point to it as full justification for their animosity. Unlike the sprightly, responsive, and interestingly strong-minded heroines of the other stories, Fanny Price is sickly, priggish, and colorless. Worse, she is self-consciously virtuous and reaps, in an outlandish way, material benefits from her practice of self-righteousness. In contrast to the cosmic expansiveness and the generosity of spirit that pervade the other novels, *Mansfield Park* speaks as "no other work of genius has ever spoken . . . for cautiousness and constraint, even for dullness. No other great novel has so anxiously asserted the need to find security, to establish a refuge from the dangers of openness and chance." It seems to prefer stillness over action, withdrawal over involvement, in a manner that today strikes us initially as not only impracticable but irresponsible. And yet, Trilling argues, "it is a great novel, its greatness being commensurate with its power to offend."

One of the issues that preoccupies the characters in *Mansfield Park* has to do with whether Edmund Bertram shall become a clergyman—with, that is, the nature of his commitment to a profession. The idea of a profession had a peculiar importance for Jane Austen as it did for nineteenth-century England generally. As the earlier ideal of the gentleman lost its force, a considerable portion of its moral prestige descended on the professions. Daniel Doyce, the engineer in Dickens's *Little Dorritt*, and Dr. Lydgate, the physician in George Eliot's *Middlemarch*, illustrate the strongly emergent belief that one's moral life is deeply connected with one's devotion to the discipline of one's vocation. This belief, in turn, reflected a central concept in English ethical and spiritual life, the concept of duty. Edmund's consideration of the Anglican priesthood as a career was entirely consonant with this view of the professions. In 1814, when *Mansfield Park* first appeared, the church functioned in a fashion quite congruent to that of secular institutions: Its objective centered far less on salvation than on the performance of duty.

That notion of duty, for us on the eve of 1984, seems quaintly and even a bit harshly old-fashioned. Our contemporary locutions—"cooperation," "responsible action," "accepting group consensus," etc.—imply doing what one should do without subjecting the self to pain or even to serious inconvenience. Duty, on the other hand, suggests a self in which impulses and desires powerfully assert themselves but, by unremitting and uncomfortable effort, are offset by a willingness to subordinate them to some external and essentially abstract value. Matthew Arnold found it necessary to remind himself daily of his duty; he insisted that the impulses had to be "bridled" and "chained down," and he spoke eloquently of the "strain and labour and suffering" of the moral life. Trilling recounts a telling anecdote of F. W. H. Myers. He was walking one evening in Cambridge with George Eliot. Their talk turned on God, immortality, and duty; and she spoke of how inconceivable was the first, how unbelievable the second, "yet how peremptory and absolute the third." Myers continues, "Never, perhaps, have sterner accents affirmed the sovereignty of impersonal and unrecompensing Law. I listened, and night fell; her grave majestic countenance turned towards me like a sybil's in the gloom; it was as though she withdrew from my grasp, one by one, the two scrolls of promise, and left me the third scroll only, awful with inevitable fate."

Aware of the puzzlement that this psychological state of affairs characteristically evokes in readers verging on the twenty-first century, and knowing the unfamiliarity now attendant on this moral position, Trilling appeals to Wordsworth, as he often does, for a clarifying bridge across the years. He takes for granted some remembrance of the "Ode to Duty," in which that stern daughter of the voice of God is invoked as "a

light to guide," and as a power that "From vain temptations dost set free; / And calm'st the weary strife of frail
humanity." Personified (even deified to a degree), duty
is portrayed as having "saving arms" and a "smile upon
thy face," and as the giver of support and serenity. If
the discipline of duty proves severe, the rewards of
practicing it include serenity and a sure and uninterrupted sense of identity in which one can take a quiet
pride.

Against this background, we can understand the
use to which Trilling puts "Resolution and Independence." Wordsworth there poses the problem of how
the self can preserve itself from its own nature, how it
can protect itself from "the very sensibility and volatil-
ity that define it." Wordsworth is quite clear: "As high
as we have mounted in delight / In our dejection do we
sink as low"; and in the cultivation of self—of perceptiveness, of talent, of reputation, through aspiration
and achievement—we recognize an inherent potential
in ourselves (not in society or in circumstance, but in
ourselves) for anxiety and depression, for "despon-
dency and madness." An intercessor appears in the
person of a poor leech-gatherer ("The oldest man he
seemed that ever wore grey hairs"), a figure "not all
alive nor dead, / Nor all asleep." Although he obviously
"had many hardships to endure," the old man speaks
with a courteous gravity, and he is first seen "As a huge
stone is sometimes seen to lie / Couched on the bald top
of an eminence." Trilling characterizes the leech-gatherer as "rocklike in endurance, rocklike in insensibility,
annealed by a simple, rigorous religion, preserved in
life and in virtue by the 'anti-vital element' and trans-
figured by that element." The poet recognizes him as
what we would presently call a "model."[18] What he
embodies—and the point has the same validity today as
in 1802, when "Resolution and Independence" was
composed—is the perception "that the self may destroy the self by the very energies that define its being,

that the self may be preserved by the negation of its own energies. . . . Much of the nineteenth century pre-occupation with duty was not a love of law for its own sake, but rather a concern with the hygiene of the self."

This "hygiene of the self" constitutes the substance of *Mansfield Park*. A recognition of this conception is essential to our understanding of a seemingly absurd but central scene in the novel where a great and ostensibly pointless debate occurs over the amateur production of a play as a means of amusement in a relatively isolated country house. What is decisively at issue here is a rather primitive feeling about dramatic impersonation, a feeling that Jane Austen turns to pointed account. That feeling entails, as Trilling puts it, "the fear that the impersonation of a bad or inferior character will have a harmful effect upon the impersonator, that the impersonation of any other self will diminish the integrity of the real self."

The notion of role-playing, in which all of us as moderns are heavily and inescapably implicated, suddenly acquires a certain brittleness and confronts a surprising challenge. We hear here a resonant echo of Arnold's "what we say and do / Is eloquent, is well— but 'tis not true," and the contrast between Wordsworth's mercurial poet, troubled by anxieties and fearing madness, and the massively permanent and imperturbable identity of the leech-gatherer comes sharply into focus. In such context, the question of Edmund Bertram's choice of the clergy as a profession takes on new meaning. The election of a career can be primarily an assumption of a role, or it can be a commitment that contributes to a fixing of the nature of the self. Is the "impersonation" of a parson to be a permanent one that enlarges the true self and establishes Edmund's personal integrity, or is it to be a bit of role-playing that may serve momentarily to solve an external exigency but that carries him further from a sense of who, in a fundamental sense, he is? Is it, in other words, an act of sincerity?

Critical as it is for Edmund, the problem of sincerity takes crucial form—for the first time in the history of the novel in English—in the character of Mary Crawford. At first blush, Mary seems to be a kind of reprise on the engagingly attractive Elizabeth Bennet of *Pride and Prejudice*, an active and handsome woman of great charm, gaiety, and wit. As we become acquainted with her, however, we begin to realize a quality in her that is as disagreeable as it is familiar. She is not, as Trilling points out, a hypocrite; her intention is not to deceive the world. Rather, her aim—her necessity—is "to comfort herself; she impersonates the woman she thinks she ought to be. . . . In Mary Crawford we have the first brilliant example of a distinctively modern type, the person who cultivates the *style* of sensitivity, virtue, and intelligence. . . . Style, which expresses the innermost truth of any creation or action, can also hide the truth. . . . *Mansfield Park* proposes to us the possibility of this deception." In other words, Mary is a role-player, far from a true self. Disliking the clergy, for example, she justifies her aversion to Edmund by saying, "I speak what appears to me the general opinion; and when an opinion is general, it is usually correct." Although she looks upon marriage as a "maneuvering business" in which people are "taken in," she still recommends it wholesale: "I would have every body marry if they can do it properly; I do not like to have people throw themselves away; but every body should marry as soon as they can do it to advantage." When her brother involves himself in a loveless affair in London, Mary attaches no moral importance to it; as he himself says, "She saw it only as folly, and that folly stamped only by exposure." Trilling, knowing that Jane Austen was no prude, is quick with a clarification: It is not "sexuality that is being condemned, but precisely that form of asexuality that incurred D. H. Lawrence's greatest scorn . . . sexuality as a game, or as a drama, sexuality as an expression of mere will or mere personality, as a sign of power, or prestige, or autonomy; as, in short, an impersonation and an insincerity."

Lack of principle, the absence of a moral and psychological core—of *character*—creates no barrier to social respectability. Far from disrupting the social order, the busy, role-playing self can live harmoniously with virtually any society that requires only the outward and visible signs of conformity. In this sense, *Mansfield Park* is a brilliantly modern study of what David Riesman has called the other-directed personality.[19] As such, it insightfully contrasts character with personality and moral principle with moral style, and it documents the ways in which moral choice tends to be influenced not by the norm most applicable to the situation, but by the kind of selfhood that the moral agent wishes to "assume" or to "project." Painstakingly examining the operations of selfhood grounded neither in a viable tradition nor in explicit ideals of personal worth—with no leech-gatherer on the moral horizon—Jane Austen reveals to us the "ubiquitous anonymous judgment" that largely shapes the impersonations that make up much of our lives. To the extent that role-playing is a dominant motif in the dynamics of the contemporary self, we ironically learn from her, Trilling says, "what our lives should be and by what subtle and fierce criteria they will be judged, and how to pass upon the lives of our friends and fellows. Once we have comprehended her mode of judgment, the moral and spiritual lessons of contemporary literature are easy . . . Lawrence and Joyce, Yeats and Eliot, Proust and Gide, have but little to add save in the way of contemporary and abstruse examples." Simultaneously, however, she demonstrates, through Edmund, who finally makes a firm commitment to the clergy, and most of all through frail, quiet Fanny Price, that genuine heroine in spite of herself, that "the path to the wholeness of the self which is peace" lies not through adeptness in impersonation or the cultivation of personal style but through the sanctions of principle. Arnold's elegiac quest for the "best self" and Wordsworth's oddly sunny invocation of duty emerge as protectors of personhood.

But personhood stands always in need of protection, not least from the culture which, while giving individuals their very being, yet straitjackets them and forces them into molds. Arnold's reference to "the gradual furnace of the world" is developed in his thesis that "Most men in a brazen prison live," and Wordsworth's idea that "Shades of the prison-house begin to close / Upon the growing boy" reflects the spirit of Rousseau's "Man is born free, and everywhere he is in chains." These widespread feelings that culture imprisons, that it chains the human spirit and padlocks humanity's heart, define what Trilling called the "historic sense" of modern literature. That historic sense, he says, emerges from

a long *excess of civilization* [italics added] to which may be ascribed the bitterness and bloodshed both of the past and of the present and of which the peaceful aspects are to be thought of as mainly contemptible—its order achieved at the cost of extravagant personal repression, either that of coercion or that of acquiescence; its repose otiose; its tolerance either flaccid or capricious; its material comfort corrupt and corrupting; its taste a manifestation either of timidity or of pride; its rationality attained only at the price of energy and passion.[20]

Trilling's insistent emphasis here is the diagnosis, not the symptoms, however horrifying the catalogue of pathological indicators may be. As we read his statement (written in 1961) today, we think inevitably of events that range from the First World War through Hitler and Auschwitz to My Lai and the Iranian substitution for the Shah's repressive cruelty of the vengeful fanatacism of the Ayatollah Khomeini; of the repressive measures associated with the Red Raids of 1920, the fears that numbed the era of Senator Joe McCarthy, the feelings of threat and betrayal bound up with Watergate and its "list of enemies"; of the figures on deaths from starvation, on political imprisonings, on crimes against persons in the world's great cities; of the slow, reluctant, and sullen responsiveness of both corporations and institutions of the state to consumers and legitimate petitioners; of the number of people who hate their unrewarding jobs, who find their marriages joyless and their children sources of anxiety, who seek for surcease or for the semblance of delight in alcohol or other drugs; of the ways in which advertising and television capture, corrode, and corrupt our most creative talent. We are not bound—nor did Trilling intend for us to be bound—by the illustrative events about which he offered his commentary. His central point is that the appalling terror of whatever particulars that we contemplate pales before the judgment of modern literature: The disease lies in the nature of society itself, in an *excess of civilization*.

Although this diagnosis carries important political implications, it is not fundamentally a political matter. Reasonably well-educated persons of good will are consistently preoccupied with the elements of civilization's excess—with the issues that emerge from that root-deep malaise—and seek political redress for them. These preoccupations and meliorative efforts have clear virtue and specify the decencies of liberalism—that valuable but indefinable point of view that loosely comprises "a ready if mild suspiciousness of the profit motive, a belief in progress, science, social legislation, planning, and international cooperation" ("perhaps," Trilling added in 1940, "especially where Russia is in question"). What astonishes us is "that not a single first-rate writer has emerged to deal with these ideas, and the emotions that are consonant with them, in a great literary way." For Proust and Joyce and Lawrence, for Yeats and Pound and Eliot, for Mann and Gide (at least as novelists), and for Dostoevski, Rilke, and Kafka, "the liberal ideology has been at best a matter of indifference." They certainly have a commitment to justice and to a notion of a humanly fulfilling way of life, but "in not one of them does it take the form of a love of the ideas and emotions which liberal democracy, as known by our educated class, has declared respectable . . . no connection exists between . . . the political ideas of our educated class and the deep places of the imagination."[21] Some great writers, Trilling continues, "have in their work given utterance or credence to conservative and even reactionary ideas, and . . . some in their personal lives have maintained a settled indifference to all political issues, or a disdain of them. No reader is likely to derive political light from either the works or the table talk of a modern literary genius, and some readers (of weak mind) might even be led into bad political ways."[22]

Beyond politics, the passionate hostility to civilization in the foremost literature of almost two centuries focuses on society's basic nature, questioning not its particular forms and aspects but its very essence. To this depth and to this extremity, has literature, as a criticism of life, extended itself. Neither dismay nor regret, neither disbelief nor denial, constitutes a fruitful response to this massive cultural phenomenon. The serious puzzle consists in the extent to which this intensely held idea of an excess of civilization represents a sign of the decline and probable fall of the culture of the West, as against the extent to which it reflects the still critical energies of that culture—"the effort of society to identify in itself that which is but speciously good, the effort to understand afresh the nature of the life it is designed to foster."[23] The task of criticism may generate few specific resolutions to so large an issue, but its socially important functions are clear: to examine—sensitively, carefully, and unremittingly—

that fierce opposition to civilization for its human, personal significance, and to formulate the best judgments possible to help narrow the gap between our immediate political ideas and "the deep places of the imagination," to contribute to that informed struggle for a more widely distributed dignity that is the proper commitment of the liberal spirit.

In his own practice of the critic's responsibilities, Trilling's consideration of Dickens's *Little Dorritt* makes telling use of that image of the prison that haunts so much of modern literature. Its symbolic force derives from its prior actuality; the prison is the practical instrument by which society neutralizes and negates the individual will. As a result, Dickens's indictment of society as an overweening and cruel constraint on the personal variability and diversity that give both challenge and delight to individual life, and as a constraint on the range and depth of love and generosity as they can be expressed in a variety of human relationships, achieves power from the way that,

The story opens in a prison in Marseilles. It goes on to the Marshalsea, which in effect it never leaves. The second of the two parts of the novel begins in what we are urged to think of as a sort of prison, the monastery of the Great St. Bernard. The Circumlocution Office is the prison of the creative mind of England. Mr. Merdle is shown habitually holding himself by the wrist, taking himself into custody, and in a score of ways the theme of incarceration is carried out, persons and classes being imprisoned by their notions of their predestined fate or their religious duty, or by their occupations, their life schemes, their ideas of themselves, their very habits of language.[24]

Our comprehension of the richness and penetration of these metaphors and emblematic devices is deepened by Trilling's gloss on them. He recalls "a certain German picture of the time":

It represents a man lying in a medieval dungeon; he is asleep, his head pillowed on straw, and we know that he dreams of freedom because the bars on his window are shown being sawed by gnomes. This picture serves as the frontispiece of Freud's *Introductory Lectures on Psycho-analysis*—Freud used it to make plain one of the more elementary ideas of his psychology, the idea of the fulfill-ment in dream or fantasy of impulses of the will that can-not be fulfilled in actuality. His choice of this particular picture is not fortuitous . . . [his] general conception of the mind does indeed make the prison image peculiarly appro-priate . . . [Mind] is based upon the primacy of the will, and . . . the organization of the internal life is in the form, often fantastically parodic, of a criminal process in which the mind is at once the criminal, the victim, the police, the judge, and the executioner. And this is a fair description of Dickens' own view of the mind, as, having received the so-cial impress, it becomes in turn the matrix of society.[25]

Dickens's anticipation and social application of Freud's notion is central to *Little Dorrit*. The story turns essen-tially on Arthur Clennam's obsession with the thought that his family's fortune was amassed by virtue of an unjust injury to William Dorrit, who has been impris-oned for twenty years in the Marshalsea. He is correct in that his mother has indeed damaged a member of the Dorrit family, although Dorrit himself was locked up neither at the instigation nor under the wish of Mrs. Clennam. Arthur comes to his only partially right con-clusion by reflecting on his mother's years of inval-idism. While entirely active mentally, she has for a long time been confined through illness to a single room of her house, her movement completely restricted to ex-changing her bed for her chair. "A swift thought shot into [Arthur's] mind. In [Mr. Dorrit's] long impris-onment . . . and in her long confinement to her room, did his mother find a balance to be struck? I admit that I was accessory to that man's captivity. I have suffered it in kind. He has decayed in his prison; I in mine. I have paid the penalty."

Yet Dickens understands human complexity far too well to argue that prisons are merely instruments of social or psychological injustice. The character of Blandois represents the kind of depressing, frightening evil that our newspapers daily report. Blandois is among those, as Trilling phrases it, in whom "the social causes of their badness lie so far back that they can scarcely be reached, and in any case causation pales into irrelevance before the effects of their actions; our effort to 'understand' them becomes a mere *form* of thought." So long as a Blandois exists, prisons remain necessities. A kind of exemplar of the observation in *King Lear* that "The prince of darkness is a gentleman," Blandois is a forerunner of both Smerdyakov and the shabby-genteel devil of Dostoevski's *The Brothers Karamazov*, and he performs the same function for Dickens as his descendants do for the great Russian. As the man who acknowledges no social imperatives and seems quite without conscience, he owns no citizenship but is, in a vaguely cosmoplitan fashion, "French"—that is, Blandois behaves as a supreme rationalist and logically disdains all of society's protective and supportive regulations. He presents himself as "nature's gentleman dispossessed of his rightful place . . . the natural genius against whom the philistine world closes its dull ranks. And when the disguise, which deceives no one, is off, he makes use of the classic social rationalization: Society has made him what he is; he does in his own person only what society does in its corporate form and with its corporate self-justification." With Dickens, Trilling recognizes the hard actuality of the world's Blandoises; with Dickens, he insists, good Arnoldian that he is, on seeing the object as in itself it really is, and he refuses to be taken in by the typical Blandoisian self-justifications.

But if the sad and terrifying imperfections of humanity render prisons necessary, prisons still function as the great inhibitors of humanity positively realized. Part of the complex subtlety with which Dickens uses the prison metaphor reveals itself in his application of it to parenthood. At the very heart of *Little Dorritt* is Mrs. Clennam. A false mother in more ways than one, she does not deny love. She does, however, distort it and dull its effects by withholding the nourishment of love. She neither encourages liberty nor expresses tenderness; she shows no pleasure in companionship, and she provides no exposure to those arts that evoke and nurture the power to feel. Because of her harsh upbringing of her son, Arthur has reason to say of himself in his fortieth year, "I have no will." Trilling is prompt to point out that a person whose will is deficient and weak, who has no elements of selfhood that he is moved zestfully to assert in the arena of his relationships and in his commerce with the larger society, lives inevitably in a prison. Like Mary Crawford in *Mansfield Park*, he can only play roles dictated by others or by circumstance, or subject himself in a manner devoid of intrinsic rewards or enduring satisfactions to wills stronger than his own. "With Dickens as with Blake," Trilling says, "the perfect image of injustice is the unhappy child, and, like the historian Burckhardt, he connects the fate of nations with the treatment of children." Not least among the harms that prisons do is the stunting of childhood wills, leaving us as adults confined to a chamber of insecurities, a self-protective parochialism of outlook and imagination, and an inability to assert ourselves effectively in our interplay as persons with society. The best that remains is the futile stubbornness, to which Trilling often refers, of Melville's Bartleby the Scrivener: "I prefer not to."

Trilling persuasively argues that as it is with Dickens, so it is with Dostoevski, Gide, Joyce, and Eliot: Modern culture is a kind of prison. In opposition to it, the modern self seeks fulfillment through the experience of alienation. Alienation is a painful condition that entails the defining of one's society as "other," as a context hostilely foreign to the development of the person, and that commits the individual to strategies of avoidance, evasion, and subversion. The accompanying emotions are those of anger and anxiety, and the setting of oneself against one's culture represents a dangerous commitment against great odds. The story is told that Josef Stalin, when once told that the Pope had publicly disapproved of one of his actions, responded by asking, "How many divisions does the Pope command?" Against the alienated individual, society commands too many divisions for him to live without the heavy burdens of disruptive inconvenience, frustration, and fear. As a consequence, the dynamics of alienation characteristically include an element of ambivalence, an occasional wistful longing for a culture in which one's faith could find repose and from whose powers one could draw one's own strength. Although this component of alienation contributes to the pain of the experience, it also contains a kind of redeeming element. The great risk in alienation, according to Marx, especially the young Marx of the *Economic and Philosophical Manuscripts*, lies in the possibility of transforming the self into something not quite human. The person who would eject himself from his own civilization and maintain himself outside it must cope with this most serious of all hazards.[26]

For this reason, Joseph Conrad's *Heart of Darkness* troubles us in a peculiar and important fashion. For Trilling, this brilliant novella "contains in sum the whole of the radical critique of European civilization that has been made by literature in the years since its publication"[27] in 1899. It provides the template in relation to which the later moderns have shaped their ideas and their sensibilities.

The story significantly finds its base in what we would call today one of the nastiest racist imperialisms ever launched, the hegemony of Leopold II, the Belgian king, over the so-called Congo Free State. Begun in 1885, Leopold's rule concentrated on the lucrative extraction of African ivory through means that were ruthlessly exploitative and cruel. Nevertheless, the Belgian monarch readily convinced the Western world that he was shedding the light of Europe over those who had previously lived in darkness. When Marlow, Conrad's narrator, first lands in the Congo, he sees at once and experiences a deep revulsion over the contrast between these claims of humane benignity and the dreadful reality of oppression. On the other hand, Kurtz, the central character, who represents one of the great Belgian trading companies, works in the belief that he not only is promoting Africa economically, but advancing it culturally. Nowhere in the tale does he ever seem to realize the terrible discrepancy between Belgium's rationalizing claims and its ugly practices. Marlow first learns of Kurtz, however, as a gifted man whose perceptiveness and character inspire from other agents both respect and jealousy. He is astounded, as we are, to discover that Kurtz, who has gone alone to collect ivory up the far reaches of the Congo River, has established himself as the chief and essentially as the god of a local tribe. It becomes obvious that his command of the natives involves a cruelty remarkable even in the context of institutionalized Belgian heartlessness.

Kurtz harbors no illusions about the "noble savage."[28] Primitive life appalls him. In one of his high-minded reports on Congolese tribes that Marlow reads after his death, he has broken off his account to scrawl violently, "Exterminate all the brutes!" Comparably, Marlow can feel the fascination of tribal life and admire the virile grace of the natives, but he regards the culture that supports and impels them as sordid and revolting, as evil in its own fashion as the European culture that so demeaningly and harshly exploits it. Nor does Marlow believe that Kurtz, by electing the life of savagery, has achieved any sort of moral purification. He clearly has rid himself of none of the European vices, including personal greed. Yet, as Trilling points out, "By his regression to savagery, Kurtz has reached as far down beneath the constructs of civilization as it was possible to go, to the irreducible truth of man, the innermost core of his nature, his heart of darkness." From that complete rejection of the values of civilization comes a light

cast not only on the souls of the Belgian business agents, servants of what Marlow calls a "flabby, pretending, weak-eyed devil," but also on the soul of Kurtz's dedicated fiancée, who embodies all the self-cherishing, self-deceiving idealism of Europe . . . monumental in her bereavement, appalling to Marlow in her certitude that her lost lover had been the reproachless knight of altruism.[29]

But if, in the illumination shed by Kurtz's incredible career and death, Marlow understands civilization as fraudulent and shameful, he retains a passionate commitment to civilization—so long, as Trilling makes clear, that that civilization is English. Trilling characterizes the opening scene of *Heart of Darkness*, set on a yawl in the estuary of the Thames, as "a hymn . . . to the Englishness of the river," and he tellingly quotes Marlow:

The conquest of the earth, which mostly means the taking it away from those who have a different complexion or slightly flatter noses than ourselves, is not a pretty thing when you look at it too much. What redeems it is the idea only. An idea at the back of it; not a sentimental pretence but an idea; and an unselfish belief in the idea—something you can set up, and bow down before, and offer a sacrifice to.

"Marlow does not doubt," says Trilling, "that it is the English alone who have such an idea."

In Trilling's interpretation, then, Conrad's novella moves simultaneously toward quite opposite poles. On the one hand, it advances powerfully the idea that "civilization is of its nature so inauthentic that personal integrity can be wrested from it only by the inversion of all its avowed principles." On the other hand, it asserts that "civilization can and does fulfill its announced purposes, not universally, indeed, but at least in the significant instance of one particular nation."

Aside from noting it, we need not consider here Trilling's treatment of the ironies in Marlow's celebration of English society and its values that must strike any reader in the 1980s. What is important for our present purpose is his perception of the importance of a faith in *some* civilization, a belief that civilization *can* assume the institutional forms and embody the animating ideas that further human decency and that facilitate the positive potentials of humanity. That kind of animal faith, entirely compatible with a clear-eyed perception of the dark side and the failings of culture, provides a basis for investing hopeful energies in the improvement of civilization and in the quality of life lived in it. It also reduces the risks of alienation; the belief that, through some process of discovery or creation, an idea can be identified that "you can set up, and bow down before, and offer a sacrifice to" is a safeguard against the dehumanizing entailments of setting oneself outside society and in fundamental opposition to it.

That hazard compounds itself complexly when, in the interest of the self's greater autonomy of perception and judgment, the alienated come together to form, however loosely, a functional *adversary* culture. When an adversary culture, like that of artists, writers, and intellectuals in the West, becomes reasonably well-established, it "shares something of the character of the larger culture to which it was—to which it still is— adversary, and . . . it generates its own assumptions and preconceptions, and contrives its own sanctions to protect them."[30] No matter how radical its origins, no matter how antagonistically it may criticize and struggle against the traditional society, the established adversary culture transmutes itself, willy-nilly, into a constraint on the individuals who adhere to it and into an environmental force that the autonomy-seeking self must

resist. Even in a climate of radical opposition to tradition and convention, the old struggle between the assertive self and a nay-saying world takes its ineluctable
and uneasy course.

For these reasons, and because of his concern with
these complexities, Trilling took his stand, gravely, a
little grimly, and a bit unfashionably, with the Freud
whose most encompassing vision found expression in
Civilization and Its Discontents. In that small but enduringly insightful book, Freud

puts to us the question of whether or not we want to *accept*
civilization . . . [not as] a divagation from a state of innocence. Freud had no illusions about primitive innocence . . .
[but] with all its contradictions, with all its pains. . . . He
had his own answer to the question—his tragic, or stoic,
sense of life dictated it: We do well to accept it, although
we also do well to cast a cold eye on the fate that makes it
our better part to accept it.[31]

But that cold-eyed acceptance hardly does justice
to the zest that it releases. Helped by Matthew Arnold,
Trilling discovered early what fortunate men and
women repeatedly and beneficially discover: "it is the
strange power of art that it can give Joy through sadness." Although art in general and literature in particular "can settle no questions, give no directives . . . it
can . . . cultivate what is best in the reader—his moral
poise," and it can bring "relief to the reader's own
moments of philosophic despair, naming and ordering
his own incoherent emotions, taking them beyond the
special misery of privacy."[32] That shared and public
sense of humanity's struggle, the quality of moral poise,
and—most of all—a pervasive tone of joy are not the
least of the gifts that Trilling's ambivalent (which can
be a synonym for "balanced") self has bestowed on
modern culture.

3

Freedom vs. Necessity

From the point of view that Lionel Trilling distinctively crafted out of the ideas of Sigmund Freud and Matthew Arnold, the egoistically assertive self, which is the "subject" of literature, engages the culture that both nurtures it and constricts it in a lifelong battle. This inevitable struggle between self and society is the stuff of tragedy and inevitably raises the question of whether we as persons want to accept the civilization that provides our human matrix. With Freud and with Arnold, Trilling concluded that "we do well to accept it."

For all the price that the acceptance of civilization exacts, what makes it our better part is the larger range of choices that civilized life presents to individuals. The power of persons to avail themselves of those options that civilization makes possible is what defines freedom, and the functions of the liberal imagination are to envision the "variousness and possibility" that increase the scope of choice, and to give voice to the sentiments and yearnings that energize the great human quest for freedom. Because, as Charles Péguy put it, *"Tout commence en mystique et finit en politique,"* the liberal outlook entails a political posture and an involvement in political affairs. That posture and that involvement, however, although they must direct themselves toward some organizational and corporate end, concern themselves most fundamentally with "the modification of sentiments, which is to say, the quality of human life."[1] For this reason, art and literature are deeply bound up with political considerations, especially those political considerations that bear on the autonomy of the self in relation to the growing network of social controls—the politics of freedom. Since the late eighteenth century, Trilling notes,

Of the writers . . . who command our continuing attention, the very large majority have in one way or another turned their passions, their adverse, critical, and very intense passions, upon the condition of the polity. The preoccupation with the research into the self that has marked this literature, and the revival of the concepts of religion that has marked a notable part of it, do not controvert but rather support the statement about its essential commitment to politics.[2]

Three considerations become central here to an understanding of Trilling's perceptions and of his position.

First, politics as a literary motif—at times, and in some great writers, a literary compulsion—only occasionally entails the politics of party or of ideology. As we have seen, the widespread judgment, powerfully registered by Lawrence, Yeats, Mann, and others, that modern life suffers from an "excess of civilization" lies beyond politics in its typical forms, but it certainly is not without political implications. Trilling illustrates the point by Lear's agonized reflections during the violent storm in Shakespeare's play. Reviewing his own record as a ruler (and pressing us to review our experience generally of the state and of political authority), the king cries out,

> Poor naked wretches, whereso'er you are,
> That bide the pelting of this pitiless storm,
> How shall your houseless heads and unfed sides,
> Your loop'd and window'd raggedness, defend you
> From seasons such as this? O, I have ta'en
> Too little care of this: Take physic, pomp;
> Expose thyself to feel what wretches feel,

> That thou mayst shake the superflux to them,
> And show the heavens more just.

If there is little here that translates easily into parties, doctrines, and the electoral process, there is, Trilling insists,[3] much that bears on the moral basis for a humane politics—a new consciousness of justice and a sense of *caritas*, a concern or caring for the well-being of the individuals whom society comprises. Indeed, the play underscores this crucial idea, Trilling says, by the very act out of which the terrors of *King Lear* arise, Lear's division of his kingdom among his daughters. His taking this step violates the unity of the state, the organic relationships among the parts of a polity; to portion out a realm, to deal with it as if it were less than a whole and living thing, not only marks a failure in prudence but a transgression of a moral norm fundamental to both political decency and political effectiveness. Despite the despairing references to the gods ("As flies to wanton boys, are we to the gods,/They kill us for their sport"), the horrors and misfortunes here do not issue from a divinely engineered fate. They are the consequences of willful acts by men and women, rich in political significance despite their apparent remoteness from the next election.

Second, Trilling took with great seriousness the political propositions of literature, whether of the implicative type that *Lear* illustrates or of the more direct kind exemplified in Robert Lowell's "For the Union Dead"[4] or Virgil Gheorghiu's *The Twenty-Fifth Hour*.[5] For him, art always functions under motives that are more than aesthetic and demands responses from those who attend to it. Art, like ideas, has consequences, including political consequences, and Trilling never failed to communicate his conviction, often to share it compellingly, that, because of their consequences, the writers and the issues that he discussed are *important*, that they figure among the things that matter most. He frequently commented, in his classroom and over luncheon tables, on the influential power of art generally and of literature in particular, and on how political dictators understood this kind of potency that arises from the imaginative reason. From their point of view, they are quite correct in looking to censorship and to the control or banishment of poets as among the safeguards of their authoritarian regimes. In Trilling's eyes, politics is a means of coping with the endless tension between the individual's yearning for unconditioned freedom and the nay-saying culture's insistence on order as one of the necessities of social life. As a focus of literary concern, in either what we are here calling its implicative or its direct mode, politics becomes the evaluation of that tension by the powers of mind and imagination.

Third, conceiving in this fashion of politics as an intrinsic literary concern, Trilling confronted the paradox of the freedom-affirming liberalism to which he was drawn. The liberal spirit puts a special premium on human emotions, witness the way in which a notion of happiness occupies the center of its thought. The liberal mission is essentially to envision the "variousness and possibility" with which such affects as joy, love, curiosity and interest, and positive excitement can be more firmly established and given wider play in our experience as persons. When John Stuart Mill, despite his massive and sharp disagreement with Coleridge, exhorted his liberal confreres in the nineteenth century to become acquainted with Coleridge's powerful conservative mind, he did so for two reasons. He hoped that Coleridge's intellectual and imaginative pressure would force liberals to examine their own position for its weaknesses, and he hoped that the poetic vision within which Coleridge cast his political and metaphysical views would stimulate and buttress the liberal commitment to a freer emotional life. For, in spite of liberalism's premium on the emotions, the politicizing of the liberal spirit seems to chill its conception of humanity and to yield what Mill called a "prosaic" formulation of its purposes. This transformation occurs partly because the political impulse necessarily expresses itself through organization, and, as Trilling puts it, organization

means delegation, and agencies, and bureaus, and technicians, and that the ideas that can survive delegation, that can be passed on to agencies and bureaus and technicians, incline to be ideas of a certain kind and of a certain simplicity; they give up something of their largeness and modulation and complexity in order to survive. The lively sense of contingency and possibility, and of those exceptions to the rule which may be the beginning of the end of the rule—this sense does not suit well with the impulse to organization . . . we have to expect that there will be a discrepancy between what I have called the primal imagination of liberalism and its . . . particular manifestations.[6]

The dream of freedom, in other words, collides with reality's necessities. The liberal spirit encounters the mundane but ineluctable requirements of organizational life. The self faces its own dependency on the culture. The quest for an unlimited range of choices must contend with the intractable elements in our own nature, in the external world, and in our social and corporate experience of one another. If literature is the activity that takes most richly into account variousness and possibility, it also, at its finest and most serious, attends with comparable vigor to complexity and difficulty; and if the job of criticism is to recall liberalism "to its first essential imagination of variousness and possibility," that task inherently implies an awareness of the complexity and difficulty that lie always before it. Perceived in such terms, the zestfully carried burden of complexity and difficulty rode on Trilling's shoulders throughout his career.

That burden is managed with a firm delicacy in one of his best short stories, "The Other Margaret," published in 1945.[7] Its dramatis personae includes

Lucy and Stephen Elwin and their thirteen-year-old daughter, Margaret, the members of a decent, affectionate, comfortable middle-class family; the title character, who has the same name as the Elwins' daughter, is a maid of disagreeable temper, contemptuous manner, and a penchant for "accidentally" breaking valuable objects like pieces of the Elwins' china. The first complexity, the first difficulty, stems from the fact that "the other Margaret" is black.

Presiding over the relationships among these four people is a portrait, a print of Rouault's king, holding a spray of flowers, that Elwin has just bought and brought home. "A person looking at it for the first time might find it repellent, even brutal or cruel. . . . The king, blackbearded and crowned . . . had a fierce quality that had modulated, but not softened, to authority . . . He had passed beyond ordinary matters of personality and was worthy of the crown. . . . Yet he was human and tragic." While buying the picture, Elwin meets a young and newly commissioned second lieutenant who, he learns, has "said he did not want to miss sharing the experience of his generation"—which is, of course, the Second World War. Elwin never hears this commonplace comment of the time without a twinge of envy and a touch of guilt. In this instance, in the presence of Rouault's king, he is comforted by the notion "that this man with the black beard and the flowers had done his fighting without any remarks about experience and generations." The portrait projects a "tragic authority" that rests on its more fundamental projection of a capacity for *being*. The king seems to know who he is and what he is, and out of that knowledge he can both do what must be done and refrain from doing what must not be done quite independent of fashion, public opinion, or sheer considerations of role.

This preoccupation with being, with questions of personal identity, was pervasive in Trilling's thought. It is peculiarly fitting in a critic who regards the self as the central subject matter of literature, and it is still more fitting in a man who explicitly strove to make his work accessible to a general public and not just to a community of literary scholars.[8] It accounts for his rare invocation of Walt Whitman: "There is, in sanest hours, a consciousness, a thought that rises, independent, lifted out from all else, calm, like the stars, shining eternal. This is the thought of identity—yours for you, whoever you are, as mine for me. Miracle of miracles, beyond statement, most spiritual and vaguest of earth's dreams, yet hardest basic fact and only entrance to all facts." This passage appealed to Trilling because it is "boldly explicit" about "the sentiment of being," and because Whitman "goes on to speak of this 'hardest basic fact' as a political fact, as the basis, and the criterion, of democracy."[9]

Most of all, the preoccupation with the nature of personal identity accounts for Trilling's admiration of Wordsworth, one of the very few poets to whom he repeatedly devoted his critical attention.[10] And the Wordsworth he frequently appealed to is the reflective artist and observer of the human condition who was "contented" only when

> I felt the sentiment of Being spread
> O'er all that moves and all that seemeth still;
> O'er all that, lost beyond the reach of thought
> And human knowledge, to the human eye
> Invisible, yet liveth to the heart.

That weighty "sentiment of Being" has intimate connections with the will, with aspiration, with the energies of selfhood. Responding to the beauty and the ruggedness of the Alps, Wordsworth avows that

> Whether we be young or old,
> Our destiny, our being's heart and home,
> Is with infinitude, and only there;
> With hope it is, hope that can never die,

> Effort, and expectation, and desire,
> And something evermore about to be.

But that affirmation of the will takes a sudden and distinctive turn:

> Under such banners militant, the soul
> Seeks for no trophies, struggles for no spoils
> That may attest her prowess, blest in thoughts
> That are their own perfection and reward,
> Strong in herself and in beatitude . . .

The energies of the self serve properly only to enlarge the self and to refine its perceptiveness, not to assert the self's dominion over others or to engage in conquest. When fully conscious of the sentiment of being, the self is "unsubdued . . . by the regular action of the world." It can be "Rebellious, acting in a devious mood," and constitute "A local spirit of its own, at war / With general tendency," but by its welcome and beneficent discipline, it remains "Subservient strictly to external things" with which it communes. What Trilling calls this "unassailable intuition" represents, for him, our "entrance [to] . . . social and political life—it is through our conscious certitude of our personal selfhood that we reach our knowledge of others."[11] In this notion of how we construct social reality, Trilling echoes William James.

> The world of living realities as contrasted with unrealities is . . . anchored in the Ego, considered as an active and emotional term. That is the hook from which the rest dangles, the absolute support . . . *Whatever things have intimate and continuous connection with my life are things of whose reality I cannot doubt.* Whatever things fail to establish this connection are things which are practically no better for me than if they existed not at all. (Italics in original.)[12]

It is against this background that we can best understand the Elwins in relation to "The Other Margaret" as their little drama unfolds under the shadow of Rouault's king.

Margaret, the daughter, has absorbed from a much adored teacher at a modern progressive school the feeling and the principle that black people cannot be blamed for what they do; they are the victims of a cruel and prejudicial society. Hearing her parents comment in irritated and condemnatory ways about the other Margaret, the perpetually angry black maid, she can hardly bear it. She reminds them that the maid "has a handicap. . . . She has to struggle so hard—against prejudice. It's so *hard* for her." She seeks refuge in "her own world of sure right reason. In that world one knew where one was, one knew that to say things about Jews was bad and that working men were good. And *therefore*." Are not these the "obvious" imperatives under which civilized people live? Victims cannot be justly held accountable; they can only be compassionately understood.

Her father also shares the civilized imperatives, but Elwin, by the explicit effort of thought, brings himself to transcend the reflex pieties of liberalism. Black or otherwise, he reflects, the other Margaret probably is, as his wife Lucy has characterized her, "a nasty, mean person." She also is a genuine victim of a culture riddled with prejudice. But she remains responsible; she is inherently responsible for what she does, including the deliberate breaking of the Elwins' Wedgwood. Who, however, has the authority to hold her responsible, to require her, for example, to pay for the smashed valuables? If the will cannot resist an ineluctable fact when it presents itself to a reasonably responsive intelligence, neither can the will attack an ineluctable reality in the service of a principle that the reality refuses to acknowledge. Dealing with Margaret illustrates the burden of actual living in the contemporary world. She exemplifies an all-too-familiar kind of personality that baffles almost daily our interpersonal understanding. She is a prototype of that often-encountered figure who defeats our hopes, frustrates our best and most sincerely held intentions, and mocks our ideals of warmth and sympathy. For Trilling, Margaret sums up a frequently experienced form of social reality in the presence of which we lose faith in our capacity to translate concepts of decency and humane aspirations into effective concrete action. She cherishes her anger and claims her desire for revenge as a right. In doing so, she establishes a link—she defines a downright and frightening similarity—between victims and aggressors in the reality of our corporate life.

Unlike Elwin, daughter Margaret, unable to realize the import of these sad and alarming reflections, explains away the maid's breakage as accidents: "She didn't mean to." But at the end of the story, the other Margaret knocks off a table a ceramic lamb that the little girl has made and given that afternoon to her mother as an early birthday present. Her creative investment in fashioning the clay piece had been considerable, and she had enjoyed enormously her mother's delighted reception of the gift. Seeing the lamb in fragments, the daughter's liberal sentiments dissolve in copious tears, and she sobs repeatedly, "She *meant* to do it." Her parents, knowing what a "foolish and weak thing" it is to say, can only murmur, "It's all right, Margaret. Don't worry . . . it just happened." But beyond the impotence there is insight. As his child weeps passionately on the sofa—"She meant to. She didn't like me. She hated me."—Elwin becomes aware that "it was not because the other Margaret hated her that his Margaret wept, but because she had with her own eyes seen the actual possibility of what she herself might do, the insupportable fact of her own moral life." The connections between victim and aggressor, between hatred and self-pity, between envy and guilt, between fear and vengefulness, have all come full circle. Trying to comfort his shattered daughter, Elwin's eyes fall on Rouault's king; "at the moment he seemed only quaint, extravagant and beside the point."

The theme of "The Other Margaret," then, is the world's intractability. It is not absolute, not completely impervious to meliorative effort, but the complexity and obstinacy of social reality repeatedly defeat consciousness and good will. The translation of knowledgable awareness into effective action meets the fate of frustration a good deal of the time, largely because of what Trilling calls "the inextricable tangle of good and evil." For this reason, he praises E. M. Forster for his clear-eyed concern with "moral realism, which is not the awareness of morality itself but of the contradictions, paradoxes and dangers of living the moral life," and he quotes from Milton's *Areopagitica*, "one of the charter-documents of liberalism":

Good and evil we know in the field of this world grow up together almost inseparably; and the knowledge of good is so involved and interwoven with the knowledge of evil, and in so many cunning resemblances hardly to be discerned, that those confused seeds which were imposed upon Psyche as an incessant labor to cull out, and sort asunder, were not more intermixed. It was from out the rind of one apple tasted, that the knowledge of good and evil, as two twins cleaving together, leaped forth into the world. And perhaps this is that doom which Adam fell into of knowing good and evil, that is to say, of knowing good by evil.[13]

The "mystery of the twins" inevitably conditions the quest for freedom in the world of the real—that is, in the world, the only world that we know, inhabited by "other Margarets." The freedom that matters is likely to be found through cultivating the sentiment of being, which may be ". . . at times Rebellious . . . / A local spirit of his own, at war / With general tendency, but for the most, / Subservient strictly to external things." When we cope with the world's intractability, as we inevitably must, we are not likely to enjoy sufficient

success sufficiently often to feel proudly satisfied. Rouault's king is "human and tragic," because he knows,
out of his fiercely won authority, what he must refrain
from doing as well as what he must do, and that knowledge derives from his keen sense of his own being. Yet
clarity about one's own identity implies clarity about
one's own limitations, especially the limits on one's
capacity to turn perception and comprehension into social action. It is not so much illegitimate as futile for
the soul to seek for trophies or to struggle for spoils
that may attest her prowess.

The function of that necessity defined by the
"mystery of the twins" and apprehended by what
Forster identified as "not the knowledge of good and
evil, but the knowledge of good-and-evil" occupies
Trilling in his analysis of William Morris's News from
Nowhere.[14] When Morris died in 1896 at the age of
sixty-two, one of his physicians diagnosed his illness as
"simply being William Morris and having done more
work than most men."[15] Poet and writer of prose ro-
mances, first-rate businessman and outstanding printer,
translator of Icelandic legends, and the most influential
designer and theorist of design in his time, Morris was a
passionate socialist, strongly responsive to Marx, and a
devoted and energetic participant in the radical politics
of Victorian England. In the generation following his
own, both William Butler Yeats and George Bernard
Shaw, profoundly dissimilar though they were, acknowledged his massive impact on their thought and on their
imagination of possibility. As Trilling points out, "The
young Yeats was encouraged in his dreams of an authentic existence by Morris's celebrations of the old
cultures of Northern Europe. In the socialism which
was the central concern of Morris's later years, Shaw
found confirmation of his own vision of a society that
would be the perfection of rational order and peace."
Here was a man cut to generous scale, and uncom-
monly joyous in his fulfillment of it. As Trilling ob-

serves, "His thought was large, was ultimate; its informing idea was the goodness of life, and its end in
view was nothing less than making that goodness universally apparent and universally accessible."

Nowhere is a Utopia in which both private property and factory-based industry have been abolished. In
Trilling's summary, the natural environment, which
meant a great deal to Morris, is clean, lush, and lovely.
Money has disappeared; because there is plenty of
everything, distribution follows the principle of to each
according to not just his needs but his desires and even
his whims, which can be counted on not to run counter
to the corporate good. With economic necessity no
longer either a driving force or a grinding condition in
experience, people display a relaxed beauty and a cooperative friendliness that make easy the love of one's
neighbor. Because the future entails no anxieties, the
present fully occupies individual consciousness, and
consciousness focuses primarily on two sources of rich
satisfaction—an awareness of one's own adequacy of
being and of one's own innocent appetites and their
gratification, and an awareness of one's fellows, a sense
of community and a high confidence in the positive
regard of others. Work in *Nowhere* provides particular
satisfactions. "Everyone does some sort of physical
work; no one does work he does not like; hopelessly
unpleasant and dehumanizing work is relegated to a
certain few highly sophisticated machines which have a
kind of secret existence, and there is no residual necessary work that someone does not find pleasure in
doing." Harvesting the fields and building roads illustrate a category of "easy-hard" work that is looked
upon in much the way that we regard athletics. Erotic
love involves the only complexity. Essentially uninhibited, it entails intense emotions; when love goes un-
requited, it is one of the few sources of deep and painful disappointment and frustration in *Nowhere*. In Trilling's phrase, "in the general felicity it is the only source

of pain." It is also the only source of aggression. When a jealous man kills a rival in love, as infrequently but occasionally happens, the social response is one of comprehending grief, as great for the murderer as for the victim and his surviving family and friends. There is no retaliation, because the perpetrator of the murderous act, as we would call it, will surely be moved to shattering remorse for the rest of his days and never behave again with such disruptive violence.

Nowhere, then, is, for Trilling, a world in which

The state having withered away, there are no politics with their inevitable implications of present aggressivity. Such questions of policy as do exist—for instance, where a bridge shall be built—may arouse debate, but never a passionate commitment to one's own views. Although conversation is not in short supply, there is no intellectual activity as we would define it; the world is an aesthetic object to be delighted in and not speculated about or investigated; the nature and destiny of man raise no questions, being now wholly manifest . . . the judgment having once been made that grandiosity in art is not conformable with happiness and that Sir Christopher Wren has exemplified radical error in designing St. Paul's, the race has settled upon a style for all its artifacts that is simple and modestly elegant, and no one undertakes to surprise or shock or impress by stylistic invention.

Felicity in Nowhere, while entirely genuine, entails, in short, the expense of high art, of science, of philosophy —indeed, of all that we would subsume under the name of achievement. The poignant element in this state of affairs emerges quietly in a remark by one of Morris's characters: "I wish that we were interesting enough to be written about or painted about."

This rather touching observation lies close to the heart of the point that Trilling underscores. If felicity in Nowhere is won at the cost of achievement, of being interesting, then it finds its foundations in the virtual extinction of all aggressive impulses. War, imperialistic ambitions, interpersonal hostility (except in the noted rare cases of sexual frustration), and such self-destructive behavior as suicide not only do not occur, they neither tempt nor threaten, because they have been literally uprooted through the massive and systematic reinforcement of contrary tendencies. The term *reinforcement* suggests affinities between *News from Nowhere* and B. F. Skinner's notions of human engineering and social control, as expressed in his *Beyond Freedom and Dignity* and in his own earlier Utopian novel, *Walden Two*. Trilling had these affinities clearly in mind—witness his skeptical and critical reference at the end of his essay to *Beyond Freedom and Dignity* as evidence for the probability of "a new and clandestine mode of aggression," rather than a "regenerate peaceableness" as the outcome of deliberate efforts to fashion a culture unmarked and unmarred by aggressivity. His main business, however, lay elsewhere.

First, Trilling is at pains to demonstrate that Morris knew explicitly what he was doing in bringing us the *News*. What Morris says of his Utopian dispensation is that it is the regaining of childhood and the epoch of man's rest. "Not maturity and activity but childhood and rest are represented as making the ideal condition of man." This conception not only repudiates the ethos of capitalism but the entire humanistic tradition of what constitutes self-esteem; it jettisons, Trilling points out, the fundamental assumption in Western culture that

man's nature and destiny are fulfilled not through his success in achieving pleasure but through setting himself goals which are beyond pleasure—though not, of course, beyond gratification—and pursuing them with unremitting energy, with ceaseless devotion in the face of defeat and frustration. It is from this "effort and expectation and desire"—the phrase is Wordsworth's—that man's highest value to himself is commonly thought to derive, that is to say, his sense of his largeness of spirit, his dignity, his transcendent significance. . . . Morris's social creed . . . is overtly hostile to conceptions of largeness and dignity. It rejects the line of thought which connects transcendence with the putting forth of superlative effort and with the risk of defeat and frustration. . . . Its conception of man's nature and destiny is informed by . . . a calculated modesty.

Trilling is not arguing Pollyanna's case for the blessings of adversity. He is calling attention to the intractable *fact* of adversity in all known human experience and to the moral implications of our response to it. He is also at least raising a question about an important distinction. In the humanistic tradition, he says, the aggressive energies, "even when they are defeated, constitute the ground of man's . . . projection of himself into the permanence of the future, into what he calls 'immortality' and 'glory' or at least 'dignity,' which is to say 'worth.' " He couples a quotation from Keats with his favorite, and much invoked, one from William James. "Though a quarrel in the streets," reads a passage in one of Keats's letters, "is a thing to be hated, the energies displayed in it are fine; the commonest Man shows a grace in his quarrel. . . . This is the very thing in which consists poetry." And James declares himself, "If this life be not a real fight in which something is eternally gained for the universe by success, it is no better than a game of private theatricals from which one may withdraw at will. But it *feels* like a fight."

The reference to James, whose search for a moral equivalent of war commanded much admiration but little following, underscores the distinction with which Trilling concerns himself. In our own time, on the eve of 1984, a deep animus has established itself in our culture and in our selves against the humanistic values of disciplined persistence in the pursuit of prized ends, of the uncomplaining sacrifice of one good in order to attain another, of the maintenance of effort in the face of failure and frustration. Trilling draws the parallel:

"By something of the same logic that moved Morris,"
he says,

hostile aggression, the aggression of one man against his
fellow, has been assimilated (perhaps not without reason)
to that manifestation of aggression which presumably goes
into creative achievement. . . . That special kind of fighting
in which, as Keats puts it, consists poetry—in which consists high art in general—is now looked at with a skeptical
eye; the preeminent genius is less likely to be thought of
as having gained something for the universe and is now
open to the charge of having sequestered for his own purposes the creative forces of the race, of being an illicitly
dominating figure . . . there is . . . a tendency to identify
with the aggression imputed to nationalism and capitalism
that element of "fighting" which, in the cultural tradition
of the West, has been thought essential to the artistic life,
the intellectual life, and the moral life, and thus to repro-
bate and reject it.

Here is vintage Trilling. While a clear moral passion warms his words, his courtesy never flags; his
sense of complexity and difficulty never falters. The
parenthesis indicates his acceptance of the possibility
that hostile aggression and creative aggression are separated, if they are separated at all, by too thin a mem-
brane to make the distinction that he seeks a persuasive
one. Although his liberal disposition aligns him with the
judgment that nationalism, capitalism, and imperialism
entail hostilities that are destructive of selves—that
limit the individual's sentiment of being—he uses the
term "imputed," acknowledging a complicated matter
that cannot be dealt with adequately in a line or a
paragraph and about which there is always room for
honest debate. Despite his own yearning for "regenerate peaceableness," he puts himself clearly on record:
The price is high art, serious intellectual achievement,
and—perhaps most of all—moral commitments of a
kind tested by a long and distinguished tradition. He

will not pay it; but while he makes his argument with the full force of his mind and with genuine emotional intensity, he attempts only to raise the issue for others of whether the outcome merits the expense. The echo of Paul Elmer More's "law of costingness"[16] lends iron to Trilling's formulation and specifies a necessity that human experience cannot escape.

This position entails a dislike and a mistrust of Utopian literature, Utopian thought, and Utopian politics. The long line of ideal societies, from Plato's *Republic* through Sir Thomas More's *Utopia* to Edward Bellamy's *Looking Backward* and Aldous Huxley's *Island*, do indeed represent the envisionings of human variousness and possibility that Trilling prized. But, with rare exceptions, they also express that fundamental and tragically self-defeating human desire to get something for nothing, to enjoy an enhanced freedom without regard for necessity, for the intractability of the world, which refuses to disappear merely because it is unrecognized.

The redeeming contrast lies with More, who treats his ideal society with skeptical irony. It was Sir Thomas who invented the term Utopia, as a pun on two Greek words meaning "good place" and "no place," and it seems clear that he believed that the good place that was no place could exist nowhere else. In his book, which was first published in 1516, he gives the description of the ideal society under consideration to a character named Hythloday, the Greek word for "babbler," and against Hythloday's enthusiastic recommendations that England at once adopt the forms and procedures of Utopia, he opposes careful arguments for introducing such social and political novelties gradually, with adequate determinations of their suitability for the English people. The English people, after all, do not exist "no place" but in a realm that is concrete and definite not only in its geography but in its culture, its history, and its distinctive range of personal temperaments. Like

Lear's kingdom, it constitutes an organic whole, constantly changing but equally constantly unitary. Just as dividing it arbitrarily—as in Shakespeare's play—sets in train a series of fatal disruptions and disasters, so imposing upon it the dreams of political idealists risks a comparable chaos through its reckless denial of the world's intractability, of the tenuousness of the ties between social reality and the sentiment of being. Utopian dreams have their genuine uses; but their usefulness depends heavily on the degree to which those who dream and those who respond to dreams realize, in Yeats's phrase, that "in dreams begin responsibilities."

His mistrust of Utopias and his heeding of the Yeatsian warning underlie Trilling's insightful evaluations of writers as poles apart as Rudyard Kipling and Scott Fitzgerald. Because he admires Fitzgerald,[17] he presses a bold, even a startling, comparison and makes it hold: "between Goethe, at twenty-four the author of *Werther*, and Fitzgerald, at twenty-four the author of *This Side of Paradise*, there is not really so entire a difference as piety and textbooks might make us think; both the young men so handsome, both winning immediate and notorious success, both rather more interested in life than in art, each the spokesman and symbol of his own restless generation." This involvement of Fitzgerald with one of the greatest names in Western culture takes fully into account Fitzgerald's lack of prudence, his having been, in his own language, "only a mediocre caretaker . . . of my talent," his too frequent carelessness of style. Its justification rests, for Trilling, on two characteristics of his fiction and the stance that it reflects.

The first of these qualities Trilling calls "the delicate tension" that Fitzgerald "maintained between his idea of personal free will and his idea of circumstance," the seriousness with which he took the responsibility that begins in dreams. Quite aware of the multitude of ways in which society is flawed and at fault, he knew that social realities define the field of personal tragedy, but his novels never make the case that his heroes (whom he called his "brothers" in his meticulously kept notebooks) suffer tragic destinies by virtue of the world's imposition, and he never presented himself as the victim of the social order. This sense of a personal directorship over one's own fate contrasts, as Trilling notes, with the fashion of the 'twenties and 'thirties (as of now) to lay all personal difficulties at the door of the culture. It also lies at the root of Fitzgerald's moral outlook and of his politics. As we cannot feel of all moralists, we feel of him, in Trilling's words, that "he did not attach himself to the good because this attachment would sanction his fierceness toward the bad—his first impulse was to love the good . . . " He was not, as was the case with so many of the splintered peace movements during the war in Vietnam, seeking moral sanctions for drubbing the villains and assaulting the varmints of the social world; his moral goals were positive, loving without sentimentality. Free of self-righteousness, he was also free of rancorous hostility and hatred. This complex of factors gives a "tone and pitch to [his] sentences which suggest his warmth and tenderness, and, what is rare nowadays and not likely to be admired, his gentleness without softness."

Fitzgerald's moral position is related to the second of the qualities in his work that Trilling valued. His books combine a detailed and accurate representation of contemporary manners—his novels provide a remarkable sociological record of the mores of the jazz age—with an awareness of how any given historical moment embodies enduring human concerns. *The Great Gatsby*, for example, can be read not only as a documentary of the 1920s; as a literary work, it remains "as fresh as when it first appeared; it has even gained in weight and relevance, which can be said of very few American books of its time." This achievement results basically from the conception of Gatsby as its hero. Although he remains largely undeveloped, growing only in the understanding of the narrator, Gatsby acquires enormous significance. Trilling perceives him, "divided between power and dream," as "coming to represent America itself . . . the only nation that prides itself upon a dream and gives its name to one, 'the American dream.'" He continues, "To the world it is anomalous in America, just as in the novel it is anomalous in Gatsby, that so much raw power should be haunted by envisioned romance. Yet in that anomaly lies, for good or bad, much of the truth of our national life."

In other words, Gatsby as a personality and Gatsby's society are deeply examined in the light of an active and serious sense of the past and of the demands that the past levies on the present. That clear awareness of a complex human continuity gives authenticity to Fitzgerald's voice:

I became aware of the old island here that flowered once for Dutch sailors' eyes—a fresh green breast of the new world. Its vanished trees, the trees that had made way for Gatsby's house, had once pandered in whispers to the last and greatest of all human dreams; for a transitory and enchanted moment man must have held his breath in the presence of this continent, compelled into an aesthetic contemplation he neither understood nor desired, face to face for the last time in history with something commensurate to his capacity for wonder.

Trilling speaks of this well-known passage as illustrating "the habitual music of Fitzgerald's seriousness." That habitual music of seriousness, together with his dream-born sense of personal responsibility, earns for Fitzgerald, despite the grief and humiliation of his last years, the "exemplary role" of a tragic hero among the writers who have contributed most to our understanding of the American experience. More successful

than many, he ranks in Trilling's eyes among the few
who have attempted to bridge the dangerous chasm between liberal politics and the liberal imagination.

With Kipling,[18] the poet of the white man's
burden, of prototypical imperialism, and of a concept
of nation contaminated by "swagger and swank . . .
bullying ruthlessness, and self-righteousness," Trilling
deals with a much more complicated nest of issues. T.
S. Eliot has argued that Kipling was not a fascist but
simply a Tory. While Trilling agrees that Kipling was
not a fascist, he balks at ordering him to a class that
includes Dr. Johnson, Edmund Burke, and Walter
Scott. The complications of judgment arise from primarily three sources: Kipling's considerable assets as
both poet and novelist, his almost paradoxical "anthropological" point of view, and his massive influence
as the perceived spokesman for British imperial ambitions and the "callousness, arrogance, and brutality"
attached to them.

Kipling's literary capabilities, Trilling acknowledges, remain undeniable if short of greatness. Few
treatments of animal life have been more exquisitely
imagined than *The Jungle Book*. Beyond "the marvelous but credible abilities of Mowgli," it embodies "a
whole council of strength and wisdom which was as benign as it was dangerous" and communicates a comfortable sense of the integrity and "benignity of the
feral world." The Pack and its Law encompass a highly
generalized idea of society, deeply in tune with the processes of socialization that every viable culture must
rely upon for its continuity.[19] The Law is persuasively
presented as "mysterious, firm, certain, noble, in every
way admirable." Kipling's admiration of craft and special competence, his keen ear for speech and his attentiveness to dialects and accents, and his powers as an
observer of terrain and atmosphere and behavior are
illustrated richly in the poetry and in such fiction as
Plain Tales from the Hills, The Light that Failed,

Stalky & Co., and *Kim,* his best book. Only when his enthusiasms are insufficiently restrained does he become vulgar or silly. If he seldom fully involves an adult reader, he just as seldom bores or wearies him, and he is often informative and sometimes movingly admirable.

Moreover, in what Trilling perceptively identifies as his "anthropological view," Kipling clearly and strongly holds to the "perception that another man's idea of virtue and honor may be different from one's own, but quite to be respected." The dominant emotions in *Kim,* despite the dislike it has always evoked in India, "are love and respect for the aspects of Indian life that the ethos of the West does not usually regard even with leniency." And *Kim,* like much of the verse and many of the stories, suggests a merit in "the rank, greasy, over-rich things, the life that was valuable outside the notions of orderliness, success and gentility." Kipling shows genuine sympathy toward not only a wide variety of ways of life, but also toward a wide vairety of modes of thought, and it is essential that we "remember this when we condemn his mindless imperialism."

Yet his mindless imperialism remains, and it has a context. Kipling continues to occupy, although with diminishing force, the odd status of a popular villain. His writings originally commanded a wide audience, and his influence seems somehow to maintain itself in significant measure through the conservative, expansionist, somewhat jingoistic spirit that he so wholeheartedly represented. It is not too much to say that he hated liberal intellectuals, and liberal intellectuals "responded by hating everything that Kipling loved, even when it had its element of virtue and enlightenment." For this reason, Trilling calls him "one of liberalism's major intellectual misfortunes." Mill urged his fellow liberals to study Coleridge as an "enemy who would make us worthy of ourselves." Kipling, says Trilling, was "an enemy who had the opposite effect. He tempted liberals to be content with easy victories of right feeling and with moral self-congratulation." On two issues, this "opposite effect" proved crucially important.

First, one of the great divisions between conservatives and liberals has centered in the conservative's reliance on administration and executive authority, as opposed to the liberal's faith in legislation. Kipling constantly supported the administrator, and just as constantly viewed the legislator with an almost paranoid suspicion. After observing that one of the weaknesses of liberalism is "a fogginess about administration (or, when the fog clears away a little, a fancy and absolute notion of administration such as Wells and Shaw gave way to)," Trilling commits himself. "This [attitude of Kipling's] is foolish, but . . . it is a prejudice which, in the hands of an intelligent man, say a man like Walter Bagehot or like Fitzjames Stephen, might make clear to the man of principled theory, to the liberal, what the difficulties not merely of government but of *governing* really are." Such seems to have been Kipling's original intention, but he so colored his effort with ill temper, with contempt and caste feeling, with an impatient dismissal of intellect, "that he simply could not be listened to or believed, he could only be reacted against." In that capacity to elicit reactions nearly as mindless as his own positions lay his strangely great influence, and it sealed his fate as an artist. Trilling's judgment embodies both his values and his sublety of perception: Kipling's work, for all its considered virtues, "is unloved and unlovable not by reason of his beliefs but by reason of the temperament that gave them literary expression."

Second, Kipling, Trilling charges, "did more than any writer of our time to bring the national idea into discredit." People tend less and less to give their loyalty to their country or to find the concept of their nation intellectually or emotionally compelling. The exceptions are those countries where at least the forms of patriotism are enforced by powerful tyrannies, or those where nationalism of a kind finds nourishment in active threats from other governments or in actual domination by a foreign authority. Otherwise, men and women increasingly tie their interests and their affiliative longings "to their class, or to the idea of a social organization more comprehensive than that of the nation, or to a cultural ideal or a spiritual fatherland.[20] True enough, a part of this disposition appears associated with "the modern impulse to say that politics is not really a proper human activity at all; the reluctance to give loyalty to any social organization which falls short of some ideal organization of the future may imply a disgust not so much with the merely national life as with civic life itself." Such ideas, which are partially descendants of the unthinking reactions that Kipling evoked, are anathema to Trilling. Politics, for all its imperfections and the vices to which it is susceptible, is the properly limited means for a people's dealing corporately with the world's intractability; and Trilling directs his sharpest scorn against those who seek for apolitical ways of coping with the inherent tensions in society. When, for example, Virgil Gheorghiu argues, in *The Twenty-Fifth Hour*, "the total rejection of the political life in favor of the individual life of the spirit," he draws this reply:

Mr. Gheorghiu is not checked in his triumphant exposition of this dull and inaccurate idea by any historical recollection, although a native of Rumania, a nation whose history is peculiarly marked by cruelty, should have recalled that, say, Vlad the Impaler reigned in an age of faith . . . when, by the bloodiest means, the masses of Rumanian people were kept in the most extreme subjection. Yet in the face of such obvious considerations, Mr. Gheorghiu goes on to tell us that modern men have sunk to the level of *citizens,* and the citizen, we are told, is "the most dangerous wild beast" that has appeared on the face of the earth since the cross be-

tween man and the mechanical slave." Political ideas as
feeble as these . . .[21]

appeal not at all to the imaginative reason but only
to thoughtless despair.

It is the feebleness, far more than the content, of
Kipling's political ideas that evokes Trilling's final
harsh assessment. Reluctantly, he accepts Eliot's notion
of Kipling as a Tory rather than a fascist, but the contrast with Samuel Johnson and Johnson's tradition
mocks the classification. Kipling had nothing of Johnson's comprehension of nationhood in Shakespearean
terms—as an organic unity with its serious limitations
and its considerable dangers, but with the potential for
drawing people together in their loneliness and for providing them with the mechanism for recognizing and for
resolving their shared problems, and for identifying and
attaining their shared aspirations. He had nothing of
Johnson's respect for citizenship as the condition of the
"individualism [that is] morally prepotent and [of] the
freedom of the individual [that] is the first criterion of
social good."[22] He lacked Johnson's generosity and
displayed none of his largeness of mind. Quite unlike
Johnson's, Kipling's toryism was too often marked by
"a lower-middle-class snarl of defeated gentility," and
his mindless imperialism offends and is self-defeating
less because of its imperial commitments than because
of its thoughtless ignoring of their costs and consequences in the contexts of modern social reality.

Trilling's judgment of Kipling, contrasting so
sharply with his evaluation of Fitzgerald, explains in
large part his obdurate opposition to "the degraded version of Marxism known as Stalinism."[23] During the
1930s and 1940s, a large segment of the intelligentsia
of the West became persuaded that the Soviet Union
"had resolved all social and political contradictions and
was well on the way toward realizing the highest possibilities of human life." For Trilling, this persuasion

did not represent a political position at all; rather, it reflected "a settled disgust with politics, or at least with what politics entails of contingency, vigilance, and effort." Stalinist intellectuals perceived in an imposed and monolithic state "the promise of rest from the particular acts of will which are needed to meet the many, often clashing requirements of democratic society . . . they cherished the idea of revolution as the final, all-embracing act of will which would forever end the exertions of our individual wills." Impatient with politics, they rejected the responsibilities that their dreams of freedom demanded.

For Trilling, this Utopian animus against individual wills in conflict leads to a devaluing of thought and feeling, of art, and of "all such energies of the human spirit as are marked by spontaneity, complexity, and variety." When human variousness and human possibilities rank among the highest human values, absolutism in any form is their dangerous enemy; and their price is an honest grappling with the complexities and difficulties that are inherently a part of the world's intractability. To subject oneself to an absolute or to deny that cost amounts to stunting growth in the sentiment of being that is the essence of selfhood and of personal freedom.

Trilling's battle with the Stalinist mentality obviously did not end with the death of the Russian dictator from whom its identity was derived. The China of Mao Tse-tung and the Cuba of Fidel Castro became for many the symbols of political arrangements that rendered unnecessary that unremitting engagement of the will in social experience. Even the regime of North Vietnam was invested with virtue that it did not possess, as an expression of the longing for relief from the exigencies of the human condition.[24] In the hippie movements and the counterculture of the 1960s, "hostility, authoritarianism, perversity, and mindless paranoia"[25] clearly dominated freedom of choice and left little room

for even the costly felicity of Morris's *News from Nowhere*. While condemning the violence of the war in
Indochina and of police oppression, the counterculture
admired third-world revolutionaries, Black Panthers,
and motorcycle gangs like Hell's Angels. While de-
ploring the materialism of contemporary civilization, it
devoted itself to motorcycles, stereo sets, and electronic
guitars. Although an extreme example, the "family" of
Charles Manson illustrates in a particularly ugly and
sypmtomatic fashion the persistence and the pervasive-
ness of Stalinism in guises quite different from its original form. Its essence consists always in the substitution
of apolitical processes for that engagement—known as
politics—of the imaginative reason, powered by will, in
the endless human effort to resolve the issues of corporate life in ways that maximize freedom while taking
account of necessity.

If freedom, which is another word for human
variousness and possibility, consists in a wide range of
choices, then each choice entails an expense, demands a
negation. In education, in the election of a career, in
the establishment of a family, Trilling reminds us,

If you set yourself to shaping a self, a life, you limit yourself
to that self and that life. You preclude any other kind of
selfhood remaining available to you. . . . Such limitation,
once acceptable, now goes against the cultural grain—it is
almost as if the fluidity of the contemporary world demands
an analogous limitlessness in our personal perspective. Any
doctrine, that of the family, religion, the school, that does
not sustain this increasingly felt need for a multiplicity of
options and instead offers an ideal of a shaped life, a formed
life, has the sign on it of a retrograde and depriving authority, which, it is felt, must be resisted.[26]

The politics of such a resistance is not a liberal politics, a politics of the extended choices that constitute
freedom; it is a politics of Utopia, of *Nowhere*, of the
resignation of the individual will that is no-choice.

To be significant, both for the development of

self and for the development of a more humane culture, choice must entail commitment and a coming to terms with the law of costingness, with necessity. When Joseph Frank charges Trilling with conceiving his task as "to defend not freedom but the virtues of acknowledging necessity,"[27] he is only partially correct; given our modern circumstances, the "charge" implies more than a measure of homage, and what Frank fails to understand is that the acknowledgement of necessity is a *condition* of freedom.

4

Decent People
Who Have No Doubts

The dominant focus in Lionel Trilling's thought lies in his strong tendency "to see literary situations as cultural situations, and cultural situations as great elaborate fights about moral issues, and moral issues as having something to do with . . . images of personal being, and images of personal being as having something to do with literary style."[1] In the often embattled interplay between the struggles of the self and conceptions of the moral life, between literary values and the quality of the larger culture, Trilling found the basic stuff of modern human experience. Characteristically, his insistence on complexity and difficulty led him to the contradictions and the conflicts in that experience.

Central among those contradictions and conflicts is the frequent and soul-rending gap between our "good impulses" and the outcome of our actions. In the mirror held up to life by books as different as E. M. Forster's *The Longest Journey* and Henry James's *The Princess Casamassima*, richly developed characters passionately and articulately concern themselves with social injustice; their taking up arms in such a cause has the ring of rightness and even nobility about it, and their valiant, well-intentioned efforts, rather than solving social problems, generate new ones of peculiar complication and intensity. The moral outcome, in an all-too-familiar fashion, lacks congruence to the manifest moral intention.[2]

Trilling introduces his argument gently. He quotes from a publicity release from a publisher:

Blank & Company reports that the current interest in horror stories has attracted a great number of readers to John Dash's novel . . . because of its depiction of Nazi brutality. Critics and readers alike have commented on the stark realism of Dash's handling of the torture scenes in the book. The publishers, who originally envisaged a woman's market because of the love story, now find men reading the book because of the other angle . . . I cite the example only to suggest that something may indeed lie behind our sober intelligent interest in moral politics. In this instance the pleasure in the cruelty is licensed by moral indignation. In other instances moral indignation . . . may be in itself an exquisite pleasure. To understand this does not invalidate moral indignation but only sets up the conditions on which it ought to be entertained, only says when it is legitimate and when not.[3]

But the gentle, amusing approach pulls us into a daring enterprise—the examination of the seamy side of the laudable drive, inherent to the liberal spirit, to create an atmosphere in which injustice finds it harder to flourish. Trilling anticipates his opposition: "Life presses us so hard, time is so short, the suffering of the world is so huge, simple, unendurable—anything that complicates our moral fervor in dealing with reality as we immediately see it and wish to drive headlong upon it must be regarded with some impatience."[4] But if the power of the moral passions, the welling up of self-righteousness, at least matches the urgent potency of the self-seeking drives, "All history is at one in telling us that their tendency is to be not only liberating but also restrictive." The conclusion cuts close to the bone of both our individual and collective experience:

Some paradox of our nature leads us, when once we have made our fellow men the objects of our enlightened interest . . . to make them the objects of our pity, then of our wisdom, ultimately of our coercion. It is to prevent this corruption, the most ironic and tragic that man knows, that we stand in need of the moral realism which is the product of the free play of the moral imagination.[5]

This eloquently phrased observation not only reminds us of our personal experience of well-intentioned people "who live for others": You can tell the "others" by the hunted look in their eyes. It takes us to the heart of the Inquisition, of the terror that followed the French Revolution, of the purges and liquidations in Stalin's Russia and Mao's China. It carries disturbing echoes of the impulses on which Kipling played with his urgent admonition to "take up the white man's burden," and it anticipates the continuation of torture and summary executions in Iran after the overthrow of the Shah in the name of justice and equity.

A Richard Sennett has aptly noted,[6] Trilling perceived that "the most destructive acts are committed by decent people who have no doubts," by those whose ideas, ideals, and moral commitments are "presided over by an impassioned longing to believe."[7] The positions that we take, and from which we act, are not patterned abstractions, susceptible only to the criteria of pure reason; they implicate us as needful, striving, willing (and willful) selves. If we fail to take this circumstance into account, then our formulated intentions overlook, at best, determinative components in our actual aims, and our moral objections, distorted and partially hidden, can only be linked in a tenuous way with the often disappointing and distressing surprises that are the outcomes of our conduct.

This concern focuses on what, in old-fashioned terms, we would call the roots of evil. Preoccupied with it throughout his career, although never heavy-handedly, Trilling examined it in special detail and with special penetration in two books. One is his novel, *The Middle of the Journey*, published in 1947; the other is *Sincerity and Authenticity*, which appeared in 1972.

For all its author's doubts about it, and despite his

painful overreaction to what he regarded as its reception,[8] *The Middle of the Journey* is a firmly conceived and handsomely written piece of fiction that may most fully represent the general cast of Trilling's mind. Set in the 1930s, when Stalinist Communism was central to the intellectual *Zeitgeist*, the novel brings together five principal characters, each distinctly individual, but exemplifying different tendencies within the liberal community of informed and thoughtful people.

The protagonist is John Laskell, "a fortunate young man of the middle class," for whom the world "might perhaps have absorbing doubts but certainly not any fears." His recently published *Theories of Housing* has established him as an expert on urban affairs; he is untroubled by economic adversity, and his outlook is that of a generous and sensible man, who shares the dreams of a more just and decent world, while still discriminating between the aspirations of dreams and the demands of reality. Mature and skeptical, Laskell has been shaken by two brushes with death. His fiancee has recently died, and he himself, when the story opens, is convalescent from an illness that has nearly proved fatal. At thirty-three, he finds himself particularly alert to the press of fate against the contours of his self and at that point at which *The Divine Comedy* begins—*nel mezzo del cammin*—where crucial orientations must be developed.

Laskell's most deeply loved friends are Nancy and Arthur Croom, with whom he spends a few weeks recovering from his illness, at their summer place in Connecticut. Arthur, a professor of economics, has just won considerable recognition by a book on business cycles and anticipates a call to Washington to serve the New Deal. He also writes occasionally for liberal magazines, and he and Nancy live more or less on the fringe of radical politics. Pregnant with her second child, Nancy has charm and warmth and shares with her husband a "passionate expectation of the future" as a time when justice will be more generously distributed and when reason will prevail in the large affairs of the nation and the world. As bright, industrious, good-hearted people, the Crooms occupy a place in Laskell's heart as something of a "justification of human existence."

Kermit Simpson, a relatively minor but necessary figure, enjoys a friendship with both Laskell and the Crooms. A man of inherited wealth, Simpson has a genuine interest in liberal causes, but he also is rather touchingly driven by a need to prove his personal worth in the face of the great advantages that the luck of his birth has conferred upon him. He publishes, at his own expense, *The New Era*, "a rather sad liberal monthly," that provides a forum for leftist ideas and programs.

Finally, there is Gifford Maxim, known to both the Crooms and to Laskell. He has long worked as an underground agent for the Communists, and his ascetic devotion to realizing the Marxist vision of a good society has marked him for Laskell as "a man of the far future, the bloody, moral, apocalyptic future that was sure to come." In Laskell's and the Crooms' eyes, Maxim's dedication, self-sacrifice, and the willingness to take major personal risks make him the measure—by which they are consistently a bit embarrassed—of their own more prudent, less hazardous, and more conventional political involvements and loyalties. This special status that Maxim occupies deeply influences the nature of the relationships involved. Although friendly, Maxim and Laskell, for example, are not quite friends:

Laskell saw him flanked by two great watching figures. They were abstracted and motionless, having the air that figures in a mural have. . . . On one side of Maxim stood the figure of the huge, sad, stern morality of all the suffering and exploited men in the world, all of them, without distinction of color or creed. On the other side of Maxim stood the figure of power, noble, fierce, indomitable. . . . The face of the one was old and tragic, the face of the other was young and proud. Yet both had that brooding blind look that is given by men to the abstractions they admire, in the belief that a lack of personal being is the mark of all great and admirable things. Behind Maxim and his two great flanking figures were the infinite dim vistas of History, which was not the past but the future.

If Maxim is very much a person, he is also a symbol and a moral force. If his presence is always compelling, he rarely seems likeable, and he is seldom available for those shared intimacies that are one of the foundations on which friendship rests.

Although the matter has little bearing on the quality of *The Middle of the Journey* as a work of art, at least one aspect of the novel's significance, its realistic connection with history, gains clarity through the realization that the prototype for Gifford Maxim was Whittaker Chambers.[9] Chambers won his minor but visible part on the American public record by instigating and serving as chief witness in the case of Alger Hiss, an official in the Department of State, whom he charged with transmitting government documents to the Soviet Union. Accused of treason, Hiss was found guilty in 1950 of perjury and served a five-year prison term, always and consistently protesting his innocence. At least three elements of the litigation make it memorable. First, it established the reputation of a member of the House of Representatives who functioned as an avid prosecutor. In 1952, Richard Nixon became Dwight D. Eisenhower's vice-president, largely on the strength of the impression he made in the Hiss case, and, in 1968, he was elected to the presidency of the United States. Second, Hiss's protracted and bitter hearings and his trial carried the dramatic freight of intense moral issues, as well as of the politics of national security. Chambers and Hiss had once been fast friends, and the betrayal of that relationship put Chambers as much on trial as the man whom he had brought to the bar. And the revelations by persons who had once belonged either to the American Communist Party or to the Soviet espionage apparatus in the United States—the two were far from synonymous—both alarmed and divided the country. Prior to that time, there had been little public awareness of the extent of the Russian underground in America, and the notion of its reaching to the high post that Hiss had held, and to people as distinguished and as trusted as he had been, shook national confidence.

At the same time, the whole legal process seemed to many to be overblown and contrived, an effort to promote political support for anti-Communists more than a serious investigation of treason. The lack of convincing evidence that Hiss had indeed given government documents to the Soviets, and the settlement of the case by a conviction for perjury, struck large numbers as a demonstration of the rigged nature of the affair. For others, however—also in large numbers—that outcome appeared a miscarriage of justice, the punishment of a profound violation of American security by little more than a slap on the wrist. Finally, the Hiss case conferred a kind of legitimacy and prominence on Communists who had recanted; in generating widespread public interest and sympathy for their accounts of life in the subterranean reaches of Russian intelligence, it did much to usher in the age of suspicion and witch-hunting associated with the name of Senator Joseph McCarthy.

Among the recanting Communists, Chambers found himself most sharply in the limelight. He had joined the Party in 1925. In 1932, he was drafted from the editorship of the *New Masses* to serve in the Soviet underground. By 1936, he had become disenchanted with Communism as a theory of government and with the Russian translation of that theory into practices that included overseas political infiltration and espionage. Searching for a way out of his secret involvements, he confronted the crucial distinction. To break with the American Communist Party—legally constituted, the publisher of low-subscription periodicals like the *Daily Worker* and *New Masses*, the parent of large numbers of more or less impotent committees, and the distributor of petitions—meant little more than outrage from one's associates and a period of condemnation in the Communist press. But to break with the secret organization that ultimately took its orders from Moscow entailed the risk of one's life. To protect himself, he enlisted his acquaintances in establishing for himself a socially recognized identity and public existence marked by routines and by formalized and steady relationships with others. If he could regularly be seen by people who could testify that he had been alive on a given day, then he would enjoy some measure of safety from the reprisals that his defection would evoke.

In a remote fashion, Trilling was acquainted with Chambers when they both were undergraduates at Columbia College. They were never friends, although, if there was something about Chambers that repelled, there was also something that commanded interest and respect. Solemn and seeming never to have been young, Chambers exercised a moral authority rare among students, enjoyed a degree of prestige because of his talent as a writer, and made his commitment to radical politics the controlling core of his personal being. With a number of his friends, Trilling had been tenuously involved with the Communist Party in 1932 and 1933. After Hitler came to power in the latter year, that involvement deteriorated rapidly and became mistrustful and hostile.

Trilling knew of Chambers's going underground; and in a peripheral way, he was among those who, in 1936, helped him to a degree of security when he left the espionage apparatus. When one of Hiss's attorneys in 1948, well after the publication of *The Middle of the Journey*, asked that he speak against Chambers in court, Trilling refused. "Whittaker Chambers had been engaged in espionage against his own country; when a change of heart and principle led to his defecting from his apparatus, he had eventually not only confessed his own treason but named the comrades who shared it, including one whom for a time he had cherished as a friend. I hold that when this has been said of him, it is still possible to say that he was a man of honor."[10] One of the questions that *The Middle of the Journey* poses bears on the extent to which honor protects a person from that disjunction between his good impulses and the outcome of his acting on them, which is the "most ironic and tragic" experience of corruption that we know. Another asks about the character of the functional differences between extreme moral and political points of view; like his prototype Chambers, Maxim adopts an essentially dialectical version of Christianity when he defects from Communism.

The novel opens in the quiet heat of late summer. Laskell, having escaped death by a narrow margin from a raging febrile illness is closing his apartment in New York to spend a few weeks of convalescence with his friends the Crooms in the Connecticut countryside. A frightened Maxim appears, announcing his break with the Party. To lessen the likelihood of assassination, he asks Laskell to persuade Kermit Simpson to give him a job on the staff of *The New Era*; neither the nature of the work nor the pay matters, but the appearance of his name on the masthead and his having an office to go to every day are crucial. Shocked by Maxim's political turnabout, Laskell reluctantly telephones Simpson and wins from him an agreement to talk with Maxim the next day at his Westport summer house. At Maxim's instigation, which, despite his distaste, Laskell is still too weak to resist, the two men arrange to take the train together as far as Westport. The next morning, Maxim presents himself in need of a bath and a shave; for the sake of his safety, he has spent the night on Laskell's roof. The two depart, Maxim's fear of being murdered for political reasons serving as a counterpoint to Laskell's intense but objectless anxiety, born of his recent intimacy with death, about the short trip by rail from New York to the Crooms' country place.

Although experiencing something like horrified disgust at Maxim's forsaking his political ideals, Laskell finds himself in a similar situation; he also must take new bearings and find new directions. During his long illness, one of his nurses commented on the "great love affair" that he was having with a tawny pink rose on his bedside table. Recalling his fascination with the beautiful flower, he is startled by the realization that its evanescent perfection symbolized the peace of eternity and that in becoming preoccupied with it, he was accepting his own death. The episode strikes him as momentous, but once with the Crooms, settled with a nearby family in whose house they have arranged for him to stay, he discovers that he cannot discuss the event with his friends. Deeply concerned about him and warmly welcoming, they simply refuse to admit serious illness and death into their optimistic and rational world of thought and discourse. Indeed, they look upon death, with its implied denial of a bright, reasonable, and egalitarian future, to be achieved through political effort, as a reactionary idea. Though they treat him with affectionate tenderness, whenever Laskell tries to talk about what it was like to be seriously ill and to come so close to dying, the Crooms disengage themselves "in a polite, intelligent, concerted way . . . as if they were the parents of a little boy and were following the line of giving no heed to the obscenities their son picked up on the street and insisted on bringing to the dinner table. . . . They simply, in a sensible modern way, paid no attention at all."

This refusal to recognize the importance of Laskell's experience is joined in a complex but comprehensible manner with the Crooms' perception of Duck Caldwell, their handyman. Duck drinks too much, cannot be relied on, is a womanizer of the coarsest sort, and escapes indigence by unwillingly taking odd jobs in the town. The support he provides for his wife and daughter barely exceeds subsistence; and while he hardly represents a large-scale source of evil, he dully and irritatingly exemplifies "the pure will of nothingness."

Emily, his wife, however, seems cut from quite a different cloth. On the one hand, she behaves in a mildly absurd way that is sometimes touching, sometimes embarrassing. She affects a bohemianism that is a bit out of date; her intellectual pretensions leave her looking foolish, as when she talks about "doom" resounding through Spengler's *Decline of the West*, which she has borrowed from the Crooms, and "vague gentilities" mark her speech, her dress, and her manner. But as the sensitive and responsible mother of her vivacious little girl, Susan, in "her worry about Susan's education, in her function as a housekeeper with her little prides in the midst of poverty, in her not at all striking talk about ordinary things," she has, Laskell learns, "a womanly dignity that (does) . . . not depend on intellect—a kind of biological intelligence."

Because the Crooms' attitude toward the lower class is determined essentially by political principle and not by familiarity, because their benevolence is abstract and not a matter of immediate sympathy, Nancy and Arthur perceive the Caldwells not as distinctive persons but as examples of their kind. Emily's ingrained integrity and fundamental common sense levies less on their generosity than Duck's shiftlessness and untrustworthy habits. They consequently respond with malice to Emily's awkwardness and sometimes silly ideas and comportment. On the other hand, they refer often and romantically to Duck as "a high manifestation of ordinary life," as a kind of noble savage. Duck, Arthur rather admiringly tells Laskell, "has his own way of doing things and . . . can't be hurried." Laskell reacts to this characteristic observation by wondering why his

progressive friends, so eager to hurry other reconstruc-
tions of reality, extend an exemption to their unsavory
handyman while subjecting his wife to a kind of courteous scorn.

Dimly perceiving the association between the
Crooms' judgment of his experience of intimacy with
death as somehow politically reactionary and their peculiarly principled exclusion from their consciousness
of the ugly actuality that Duck presents, Laskell puts
off telling Nancy and Arthur about Maxim's break with
the Party. Finally, knowing that they will regard his
withholding of this news as a sort of betrayal, he recounts for them the story of Maxim's visit in New
York, his declaration of his defection, his overwhelming fears of being murdered in reprisal, and his plea for
a job with Kermit Simpson as a means of establishing a
protective public identity. Predictably, the Crooms
react with angry shock. Maxim has abdicated the heroic
role of the radical activist in which they had cast him;
he has proved disloyal to the basic tenets of radical
politics, and he cannot, in their view, be justified in his
fear of retaliation, which impresses them as paranoid.
Furiously, they pronounce him mad, and they express
displeasure with Laskell for his failure to dissuade
Maxim from his unforgivably insane course.

A few days later, the latest issue of *The New Era*
arrives in the mail. Maxim's name occupies a place on
its masthead, and an article under his by-line makes
evident that he has not only rejected Communism but
that he has embraced a relatively extreme form of
Christian theology. Entitled "Spirit and Law," Maxim's
piece analyzes Melville's *Billy Budd*. The argument
holds that the character of Claggart represents Evil in
the world and that Billy, while not absolutely pure,
stands for Spirit. Captain Vere embodies the principle
of Law or of Necessity in human affairs. Because Claggart or Evil exists, Vere or Law must rule to insure the
safety and orderliness on which bearable social inter-

actions depend. Vere's judgment against Billy Budd,
Maxim writes, is therefore both ineluctably correct and
quite incomprehensible to modern liberals. Insisting
that "Spirit should find its complete expression at once,"
liberals find Captain Vere culpable because of his refusal to acquit Billy in defiance of Law. Melville's perception, the essay continues, is quite different. So long
as Evil inhabits the world, Law rather than Spirit must
dominate, and Vere's tragic choice as judge is that of
"God the Father, who must condemn his own Son,"
although the condemnation represents "not the familiar
transaction of . . . a sacrifice and an atonement" but
must be enforced "for the sake of the Son himself, for
the sake of Spirit in humanity."

Maxim is quite right. His meditation on the problem of evil, for which *Billy Budd* is the point of departure, both offends and lies beyond the comprehension
of the Crooms. This new creed of an ex-Communist
appears to them as reactionary and disgustingly ob-
scurantist. Even for Laskell, it carries no meaning beyond "the odor of corruption." But the intellectual and
ideological stage has been set. With all the moral force
and personal dedication that he once gave to Communism, Maxim has been established as the proponent
of conventional law and societal necessity, sanctified by
religious considerations. Nancy and Arthur Croom,
energized by angry disappointment and their aroused
need for a radical hero, become his antagonists, the
spokesmen for the thesis that he once so largely stood
for and to which he now opposes an antithesis.

Into this tense air, Maxim emerges. He and Simpson have formed a surprisingly easy relationship, and in
Simpson's shiny new camper-trailer, the two of them
are taking a brief holiday through New England that
includes a visit for a few days with the Crooms and
Laskell. The visit coincides with the village's annual
church bazaar. This event traditionally concludes with

an entertainment involving both local residents and the "summer people." As a part of the entertainment, Susan, Emily and Duck Caldwell's daughter, is to give a recitation of Blake's "Jerusalem." Laskell, feeling considerable affection for the little girl and having won her trust, has been hearing her practice. To his not entirely comfortable amusement, she declaims the poem in an old-fashioned elocutionary manner, stamping her foot in passionate refusal at the line, "I will *not* cease from mental fight." He gently recommends that the stresses might better be evenly distributed: *"I will not cease . . ."* Her readiness to be persuaded gives him some qualms, but the presentation does become less ludicrous when she makes the suggested modification. On the afternoon of the performance, however, she unthinkingly reads the line after her original fashion, stamping her foot. Her dismay at her mistake leaves her unable to continue, until Laskell, seated near the stage, softly supplies her with the necessary words. Her little girl's poise recovered, Susan winds up with a gallant flourish and wins a friendly and approving ovation from the spectators.

But during her recitation, Duck, freshly shaved for the occasion but dead drunk, has come into the church. As his daughter leaves the stage in triumph, he stumbles toward her, saying, "A fine one you are. A disgrace." He slaps her twice. She falls, and when she is picked up, she is dead; her heart has failed. Laskell has earlier learned from Emily that she has never told her husband of Susan's serious cardiac disorder for fear that, in his arrogant virility, he would not "respect" their child. Although no question of murder arises, a winsome little girl has still died as a consequence of her father's insensitive and careless brutishness.

This devastating and grief-producing event becomes the background for the inevitable confrontation between Maxim and the Crooms. Sitting before the fireplace on a day when the weather has turned rainy and cold, the five principals of *The Middle of the Journey*, all of them deeply touched by the sadness of Susan's death and its mindless manner, try to sort out what requires resolution and judgment. The Crooms do not hold Duck responsible. When Nancy insists passionately that "It's not his fault," Arthur explains, a little professorially, that "social causes, environment, education or lack of education, economic pressure, the character-pattern imposed by society, in this case a disorganized society, all . . . account for any given individual's actions." Nancy agrees fully but imposes a distressed condition: "We can't say he's to blame personally, individually. But I can't stand the idea of having him around me. Not that I'd be afraid, but I'd always be thinking that this man killed his child."

At this point, Maxim states the issue from his newfound Christian perspective:

Nancy's dilemma is an inevitable one. She refuses to say that Caldwell has any responsibility, any blame or guilt. And then she refuses to allow him to come near her . . . I reverse your whole process. I believe that Duck Caldwell—like you or me or any of us—is wholly responsible for his acts. Wholly. And for eternity, for everlasting. That is what gives him value in my eyes—his eternal, everlasting responsibility. . . . Yet in my system there is one thing that yours lacks. In my system, although there is never-ending responsibility, there is such a thing as mercy. . . . Duck can be forgiven. I can personally forgive him because I believe that God can forgive him. . . . I think his will is a bad one, but not much worse, not different in kind, from other wills. And so you and I stand opposed. For you—no responsibility for the individual, but no forgiveness. For me—ultimate, absolute responsibility for the individual, but mercy. Absolute responsibility: it is the only way that men can keep their value, can be thought of as other than mere *things* . . . social causes, environment, education—do you think they really make a difference between one human soul and another? In the eyes of God are such differences of any meaning at all?

In the silence that ensues, Simpson turns to Laskell to ask, "John, what is your feeling about this?" Trilling's interposed comment is wryly important: "To Kermit a difference of opinion was a difference of opinion and showed that liberalism still flourished." Laskell, called upon, has a response: "An absolute freedom from responsibility—that much of a child none of us can be. An absolute responsibility—that much of a divine or metaphysical essence none of us is." And he explains: "I cannot absolve the world or society or God or my parents or nature from all blame from what I am or do. I didn't make myself and I don't dare cut my connection with all the things in the world that made me. I cannot hold myself free of these things. I will blame them when they injure and reduce me, as they do every moment of the day. And for that matter, I cannot avoid my gratitude to them."

Both Maxim and the Crooms react with anger to Laskell's position. "Neither beast nor angel!" Maxim sneers, "Pascal said it long ago." Nancy snaps, "Certainly there's a good deal of shilly-shally in what you've just said, John." And Arthur adds, "And a good deal of name-calling and motive-attributing." Trilling's commentary is explicit. Laskell

knew why they were angry at him. It was the anger of the masked will at the appearance of an idea in modulation. The open will does not show that anger, only the will masked in virtue shows it. His idea . . . had affronted them. They were staring at him as silently as the great mural figures that once had flanked Gifford Maxim when he talked of politics and the future.

Maxim reveals something of the nature of "the masked will" by an invasion of Laskell's privacy, and he forcefully poses the great issue that is the novel's central business. Perceptive observer that he is, Maxim has correctly inferred that Laskell has had an affair with Emily Caldwell. Their sexual union, and the man-

ner of Emily's participation in it, has contributed to
Laskell's return to life after his intense encounter with
illness and death. Without loving her, feeling "no community of passion with her," he nevertheless realizes
that "in that moment, in all the empty world, she was
the one person who existed for him in love." Not long
before the interchanges that have just culminated in
Laskell's becoming the object of anger from both the
Crooms and Maxim, Laskell and Emily have met for
the last time. With great dignity and simple honesty,
making no demands, Emily tells him, against his pro-
tests, "you have been very good"—to Susan, to her,
even to Duck, and she lightly kisses his cheek in goodbye. Maxim has seen the episode and uses it both as a
weapon and to make a point.

"You spoke," he says, "as a forgiven man, because of what happened on the road this afternoon
between you and Emily Caldwell." He drives on:

"You spoke with courage and the intelligence of courage
because you felt forgiven. It was a frightening thing to be,
wasn't it? . . . What a blow—to be kissed on the cheek and
forgiven! . . . You were freed from guilt—from the immediate guilt of not having loved Emily Caldwell, though
you had made love to her, for having valued her low,
though you liked her and got pleasure and help from her.
And from the general guilt of other people's sins, or of
their suffering, or of their death. Perhaps you were freed
from your guilt of your own death. . . . I think we do not
fear extinction, not extinction of our whole being but the
part of our being that keeps everything else in check. As if
we feared the death of conscience in ourselves, or the death
of the State, or as if we were killing our parents—whatever
it is that keeps in check every filthy impulse in our selves
that would overwhelm us . . . this afternoon poor Emily
Caldwell gave you what you think was forgiveness, and
now you feel that being human is permissible. That's why
you spoke out of the old knowledge of what the human
fate is. . . . It is too late for that . . . the day for being
human in the way you feel now is over. Gone. Done for.

Finished. Maybe it will come again. But . . . not until the Crooms and I have won and established ourselves against the anarchy of the world. . . . [The Crooms] will preach the law for the masses. I will preach the law for the leaders. For the masses, rights and the freedom from blame. For the leaders, duties and nothing but blame, from without and from within. We will hate each other and we will make the new world."

Kermit Simpson reacts to Maxim's speech by exclaiming, "Giff, I swear I think you're crazy," and Nancy says, "He is crazy. He's insane." But Laskell responds, "No, he's not." And Maxim leaps, almost gaily, for the kill: "Remember it! . . . The supreme act of the humanistic critical intelligence—it perceives the cogency of the argument and acquiesces in the fact of its own extinction." Holding to his conception of "the human being in maturity, at once responsible and conditioned," Laskell replies, "I do not acquiesce."

To digest *The Middle of the Journey* in this fashion violates the book's carefully constructed architecture, its subtlety, and its insights into the interplay of character and ideological commitments. Explicitly conceived as a novel of ideas, it may have limited appeal, but few works of fiction from the 1940s retain the cogency, the provocative power, or the perceptiveness into the contemporary human heart that this one does. It embodies three major themes.

First, Trilling himself, commenting on the "polemical" element in his story, indicates that his aim was to illuminate "the clandestine negation of the political life which Stalinist Communism had fostered among the intellectuals of the West. This negation was one aspect of an ever more imperious and bitter refusal to consent to the conditioned nature of human existence."[11] When that consent is withheld, then absolutism and its twin, the conviction that ends justify means, become dominant. Both inhibit the ability of the imaginative reason to conceive of human variousness and possibility in novel ways and to explore the means of facilitating their attainment. Licensed by good intentions and given the dream of a successful method by ideology, human beings aspire to the status of angels, simultaneously just, loving, and rational in a world to be achieved. In pursuit of that achievement, they risk becoming beasts. With only minor regrets, both the Maxims and the Crooms willingly liquidate the John Laskells—the "humanistic critical intelligence"—to usher in a social order presided over by rational authority and marked somehow by both equality and excellence. If the appeal of Stalinism to Western intellectuals in the 1930s illustrates this kind of corruption of the liberal spirit, its significance lies more in the susceptibility of intellectuals to this kind of corrosion than in Stalinism as the specific corrosive. In the years since *The Middle of the Journey's* first publication, readers have needed only to substitute the names of different ideologies and to perceive the striking similarities among different concrete circumstances to find the book a penetrating gloss on widely shared human tendencies and on the vulnerability of the civilized self to "the dangers which lie in our most generous wishes."[12]

The second theme illuminates the first. Its vehicle is Nancy Croom, whose brightness, warmth, and personal decency lie beyond doubt. Her politics, which includes a fellow traveler's commitment to Communism, expresses a personal demand that the world fulfill "the promises" that have been made to "the well-loved child" of modern, middle-class society. Beneath her liberal rhetoric, she has transformed a deeply felt insecurity of her own into a sense of destiny, projecting her own wish and will in political form onto the future. In consequence, she is capable of striking cruelty. The flippant symbol of her destructiveness is her order to Laskell when he inadvertently steps into her flowerbed: "Step out of the cosmos, John." The lighthearted pun only emphasizes by contrast Nancy's willingness to remove from the larger cosmos virtually anyone who seems to stand in the way of her realizing the politicized actualization of her inner longings. When, for example, Laskell tells her and her husband about Maxim's defection, she attacks him as a "romantic" who cannot grow beyond old-fashioned ideas and who has allowed himself to become a little addled by the death of his fiancee. Shocked, Laskell becomes aware that whether Maxim is or is not in the danger that he has claimed, it is clear that emotions at least compatible with political murder are easily aroused among Communists and Communist sympathizers. Profoundly invested in Communism as an idea, Nancy has no appreciation for the need to modulate that idea in relation to the passions associated with it or to the actions that it instigates. For all her pleasant ways and her capacity for tenderness, Nancy is dangerous because she lives in what Wordsworth called that "Tempting region . . . / For Zeal to enter and refresh herself, / Where passions had the privilege to work / Without ever hearing the sound of their own names." What Trilling calls "the masked will" involves, in part, the exclusion from awareness of the feelings, the personal impulses, and the private wishes that cling like barnacles to political concepts and political commitments. Zeal suffers no hindrance from the healthy doubts that only self-knowledge provides.

Finally, there is the theme of John Laskell's reaffirming return to life. In the course of his near-mortal illness, he had "taken a fancy" to an experienced state "just short of extinction. It was the removal of all the adverse conditions of the self, the personality living in nothing but delight in itself." From this intimate intimation of mortality, he derives the insight to oppose a quiet knowledge against Nancy Croom's insistence that "History shows that man is dialectically developing and improving himself all the time." Suffering cannot be "improved." An immunity to death cannot be "developed." The ultimate finiteness of human beings can confront anyone at any time. In the middle of his journey, Laskell has learned from his close encounter with death that ripeness indeed is all, that "maturity" brings the future and present together, "that you lived your life *now* instead of preparing and committing yourself to some better day to come." This awareness derives not at all from self-indulgence or immediate gratification. Rather, it has its roots in Pascal:

. . . the present is generally painful to us. We conceal it from our sight, because it troubles us; and if it be delightful to us, we regret to see it pass away. We try to sustain it by the future, and think of arranging matters which are not in our power, for a time which we have no certainty of reaching. . . . The present is never our end. The past and the present are our means, the future alone is our end. So we never live, but we hope to live; and, as we are always preparing to be happy, it is inevitable we should never be so.[13]

But to live, to achieve some semblance of happiness, entails three requirements. One is the cultivation of the sentiment of being, self-knowledge that includes "the adverse conditions of . . . the personality" as well as the bases for self-esteem. The second is a willingness to acknowledge and grapple with exigency and contingency as inherent components of the world and of culture. Because, as imperfect beings, we always imperfectly perceive our environment, our experience is necessarily colored by surprises, not all of them pleasant. And third, there is the discrimination between wish and world, between the character and direction of our will and wish, and the character of the external world, including the external world of other persons. Not as adages or imposed prescriptions, but as qualities of his perception and his personhood, these comprehensions have been achieved by Laskell as a consequence of his confrontation first with death and then with the Crooms and Maxim during his convalescence. It is a tribute to Trilling's novelistic powers that *The Middle of the Journey* displays this kind of human growth with a min-

imum of sheer conceptualization and with no preaching. Very much a novel of ideas, it makes its intellectual point through the interplay of circumstance and
character.

Twenty-five years later, with still greater firmness,
Trilling was again dealing with similar themes. *Sincerity
and Authenticity*, although far from a study in politics,
concentrates on the bases for stability and an appropriately conditioned quality in our political intelligence.
Significantly, except for *Matthew Arnold*, it is Trilling's
only critical book conceived as a whole and prepared as
a self-contained unit. All his other volumes are collections of essays, unified by the concerns that focused his
thought and engaged his sensibility as he responded to
the shifting patterns of culture at particular periods in
his life. Developed originally as the Charles Eliot Norton Lectures at Harvard in 1971, *Sincerity and Authenticity* incorporates Trilling's experience of the 1960s.
True to his Arnoldian distinction between the realm of
ideas and ideals and the realm of practical politics, he
does not deal with the specfic issues of that harried
decade in American history. Rather, he reviews nearly
400 years of cultural changes to provide a perspective for
those issues. In the course of his analysis, Trilling ex-
amines the sea-changes that beset human purposes, as
they move from intention and impulse to actual consequences both in society and in the formation of the
self.

That examination demonstrates that, repeatedly,
in the interplay between persons and their culture, the
corruption of goodwill emerges as a danger against
which eternal vigilance remains the tenuous but only
available protection. Trilling perceived the sixties as an
era that began in great goodwill. Through a failure of
vigilance, of exigent self-monitoring, goodwill soured
into egocentricity and nihilism. What he saw as the
hallmarks of the decade—ugliness, violence, incivility,
self-indulgence—amounted to the expressions of a de-

generate egocentricity and nihilism turned pointless and
self-defeating. The central issues of the time were those
of civil rights and the war in Vietnam. Neither, in Trilling's judgment, was resolved or meliorated through the
actions that emerged from the dynamics of egocentricity and nihilism, the dynamics of the masked will. As
was *The Middle of the Journey*, *Sincerity and Authenticity* is, in a very real sense, a lament over the
human tendency to corrupt goodwill as it moves into
practical action. The self-centered rejection of compromise, the refusal to accept the conditioned nature of
striving humankind, replaces benign intentions with
destructive combat that loses sight of generous purposes. Such was the pattern, as Trilling understood it,
of the 1960s.

But it is also a human pattern that has displayed
itself before. Continuing his faith in the power of people to rearrange their patterns of life if they will look
honestly into the mirror of their cultural and personal
histories, Trilling holds up that mirror, in *Sincerity and
Authenticity*, for our not always comfortable examination. He begins by indicating that, as a central element
in the moral life, the notion of sincerity rose to prominence in the sixteenth century. We can hardly discuss
the patriarch Abraham in terms of his sincerity, and the
extent to which Achilles or Beowulf were sincere is a
clear irrelevancy. But when Polonius says to Laertes,

> This above all: to thine own self be true
> And it doth follow, as the night the day,
> Thou canst not then be false to any man,

we face something novel. We cannot even accommodate the lines to our perception of Polonius as a near-
senile, bumbling self-server, such is their "lucid moral
lyricism."

The central idea of sincerity involves two components, both touched on in Polonius's speech. One has

to do with the degree of congruence between avowal and actual feeling (to thine own self be true); the other stresses the social consequences of that congruence (thou canst not then be false to any man). If sincerity demands a kind of private classical practice of the examined life—a considerable measure of self-knowledge —it also requires a public pattern of accurate self-disclosure, of not representing oneself socially as one is not, of honesty not only about events but about the self.

The difficulties here, however, seem predictable. Trilling resorts to one of his principal teachers, Matthew Arnold ("The poets," Freud remarked, "not I, discovered the unconscious"), to make them manifest:

Below the surface-stream, shallow and light,
Of what we say we feel—below the stream,
As light, of what we *think* we feel—there flows
With noiseless current strong, obscure, and deep,
The central stream of what we feel indeed.

Locating the "own self," to which we can and must be true, is and remains far from a simple matter. "And yet at a certain point in history certain men and classes of men conceived that the making of [the] effort [to do so] was of supreme importance in the moral life, and the value they attached to the enterprise of sincerity became a salient, perhaps definitive, characteristic of Western culture for some four hundred years."

Despite that saliency, the difficulties of being sincere have always included, of course, discrepancies between the intentions clustered about the effort at sincerity and the social consequences engendered by the effort. Trilling finds in Molière's *Le Misanthrope* a fitting example. The character of Alceste persuasively claims that "My chief talent is to be frank and sincere"; his chief pride derives from his sincerity, from his remorseless dedication to truth. But, as Trilling observes,

"The obsessiveness and obduracy of his sincerity amount to *hubris,* that state of being in which truth is obscured through the ascendancy of self-regarding will over intelligence. It is to his will and not, as he persuades himself, to truth that Alceste gives his stern allegiance." Although Moliere handles Alceste's absolutism gently, by questioning it and teasing it, he makes it contrast sharply with quite a different idea of right conduct. That idea, so much more difficult to live by and to realize in a life-style, requires the testing of behavior by the touchstones of good sense and realism, by judgments of the quality of inevitable compromises between idealized conceptions of the truth and both one's own internal inconsistencies and the outright defects of the society in which persons always hold membership. For Alceste, however, his experience of disappointment, disillusion, and despair arises not from the fact

that first one and then another of the members of his immediate circle, and then still another and at last almost all of them, out of vanity or for material advantage, make avowals which are not in accord with what they feel or believe, but rather that the life of man in a developed community must inevitably be a corruption of truth. When in the end Alceste vows himself to solitude, it is not out of mere personal disappointment in the entrancing Celimene but out of disgust with society, an entity whose nature is not to be exactly defined by the nature of the individuals who constitute it.

Unclear about the character of his "own self," Alceste has projected onto abstract society (after the fashion of Nancy Croom) the requirement that it conform to those qualities in himself to which his pride is most intimately attached and from which the strivings of his will take their direction. As is typical when societies are conceived as abstractions and not as complicated patterns of individual wills contending together under culturally established rules, Alceste really cares not a fig for his commitment to truth. In reality, his commitment is to the imposition of his will on others. As a result, he produces effects far different from those that he intends, and he himself suffers pain, helplessness, and impotent anger as an outcome of this incongruity that he cannot understand.

In many ways, Trilling's treatment of sincerity both as a state of being and as a social virtue amounts to an elaboration of a comment in his "Of This Time, Of That Place," a short story that he published in 1943. At the opening of an academic year, the protagonist, Dr. Howe, a college professor of literature and a published poet, finds pleasure in "a busy and official day of cards and sheets, arrangements and small decisions. Even when it was time to attend the first of the weekly Convocations he felt the charm of the beginning of things, when intention is still innocent and uncorrupted by effort."[14] Whatever other impediments that it may encounter, does sincerity depend in some measure on the "innocence" associated with "the beginning of things"? And to what extent is sincerity inherently eroded by the corruptions of effort—that is, by the entailment of working with very different others toward goals that, because of those very differences, can only be partially shared, partially held in common? The raising of these movingly central questions echoes the concern in *The Liberal Imagination*—the way in which opportunities for the realization in society of liberal ideas and liberal ideals confer "value and necessity" on the organizational impulse of liberalism, but the organizational impulse "means delegation, and agencies, and bureaus . . . and . . . the ideas that can survive delegation . . . give up something of their largeness and modulation and complexity in order to survive."[15]

In what Trilling calls an "old and merely fanciful etymology," the word "sincere" stems from *sine cera*, without wax; it implies an object that has not been patched up, that is not passed off as sound when it has been broken and cunningly repaired. In that sense, pure

ideas become necessarily less sincere when they un-
dergo the effort demanded by their translation into reality, when they are exposed to the contending and quite
different wills that compose society and the social process, when they are acted on by the organizational impulse. In a way that may be paradoxical, and in a
manner that may occasion deeply felt regret, their becoming less sincere seems to become a condition of
their effectiveness.[16]

If this observation is anathema to the absolutist,
an outrageous disappointment to the passionate idealist, it reflects once again Trilling's insistence on human
limitation, on the acknowledgment of necessity, on consenting to the conditioned nature of human life. This
insistence, which lies at the base of his humanism,
undergirds his liberal position, gives him flexibility in
coping with particular issues, and permits his breadth
and generosity of perspective. Grounding himself in his
fundamental views and capitalizing on the powers that
they make possible, he achieves a special sharpness and
a rare intensity in his analysis of authenticity as a modern idea that has superceded sincerity as a moral quality and that has become chic, a kind of modish if
self-destructive instrument in the warfare of self with
culture. From these same moral emplacements, he
directs his heaviest fire against those who argue that
"madness" represents a legitimate and even desirable
route to authenticity in a culture that is corruptly and
decadently inauthentic or phony.

Trilling accepts authenticity as "suggesting a more
strenuous moral experience than 'sincerity' does, a
more exigent conception of the self and of what being
true to it consists in, a wider reference to the universe
and man's place in it, and a less acceptant and genial
view of the social circumstances of life." As the concept of authenticity has come to supplant that of sincerity, many cultural attributes—traditional and conven-

tional belief systems and institutions, the structures of interpersonal courtesy, the dominant mores—have lost much of their value. They appear increasingly as fantasies, empty rituals, or sheer shams. On the other hand, much that the culture has directly disapproved or outlawed has seemed to acquire a peculiar moral authority by virtue of the authenticity, somehow, sometimes mysteriously, invested in it—cultivated disorder in dress and conduct, destructive violence against both property and persons, the elevation (not infrequently with the help of various drugs) of the instinctual, the intuitive, and the emotional over the rational.

With his lasting concern for the power to feel, with his intimate knowledge of the inevitability of relationships that sorely try the individual spirit, Trilling does not lack appreciation for this tendency. Among other things, he notes that although authenticity can deny art, it can also figure prominently as the "dark source" of art. He quotes Yeats, writing at the moment "when all his performances seemed to him of no account and he had to discover how to devise new ones":

> Those masterful images because complete
> Grew in pure mind, but out of what began?
> A mound of refuse or the sweepings of a street,
> Old kettles, old bottles, and a broken can,
> Old iron, old bones, old rags, that raving slut
> Who kept the till. Now that my ladder's gone
> I must lie down where all the ladders start,
> In the foul rag-and-bone shop of the heart.

Moved as he is by Yeats's clear-eyed fusion of desperation and determination, Trilling still recalls, in contrast, Sir Philip Sidney's admonition through the Muse to poets: "Look in thy heart and write!" And his dryly impassioned comment is, "There is no foul rag-and-bone shop in *that* heart."

Diderot's *Rameau's Nephew* provides Trilling with

the vehicle for demonstrating the breakdown in the eighteenth century of the social values of sincerity before the rising allure of authenticity's private and internal attractions. Diderot's novel articulated a strengthening sense that the "own self" to which one's being true permitted one to relate to others in socially approved ways was, at bottom, merely a role. Who and what one *really* is cannot be communicated through social forms. It becomes lost in the tissue of cultural expectancies, and it loses its validity when burdened by the normative requirements of one's neighborhood, class, or nation. Because society demands "impersonations," obedient role-playing, dancing in minutely choreographed patterns, it crushes personal integrity and deprives individuals of the dignity that resides in their selfhood. The moral judgment that the perceptive person must make of society, therefore, is one of condemnation—absolute, unremitting, and implacably hostile, even when the tactics of opposition entail a superficial and entirely cynical conformity.

But Trilling emphasizes a second element in *Rameau's Nephew*. Rather gaily, that element suggests that the moral categories of society are "not ultimate, that man's nature and destiny are not wholly comprehended within the narrow space between virtue and vice." Whatever must be said about the reprehensible character of culture, the Nephew transcends society's restrictions and the adverse judgments that they generate. Regarding himself "as an aspect of humanity . . . as the liberty that we wish to believe is inherent in the human spirit, in its energy of effort, expectation, and desire, in its consciousness of itself and its limitless contradictions," the Nephew invokes the moral categories at the same time that he violates and exposes them. This second component in Diderot's work gives it a lasting charm and worth. It stands as one of the great studies in the delicate balance between self and culture that is not only one of the dominant and persistent themes of literature but the condition of reasonable serenity and decent competence in life. But, through the history of ideas, this aspect of *Rameau's Nephew* has consistently lost ground to the first, the exhibition of socially expressed forms of selfhood as merely imposed social roles. Through Rousseau and others, this idea gave impetus to the exponents of authenticity who look upon "madness" as an appropriate and even commendable means of negating an unendurable culture.

In our own day, these exponents comprise a not inconsiderable group—Herbert Marcuse, Norman O. Brown, Michel Foucault, R. D. Laing, and David Cooper. Marcuse evokes from Trilling an assault tempered by a cordial and discriminating understanding. Although he casts himself as the prophet of "the virtual end of necessity," Marcuse "discovers in it a perverse beneficence—upon its harsh imperatives depends the authenticity of the individual and his experience." Besides, Trilling observes in a vein of sly geniality, Marcuse "*likes* people to have 'character,' cost what it may in frustration. He holds fast to the belief that the right quality of human life, its intensity, its creativity, its felt actuality, its weightiness, requires the stimulus of exigence." Because he acknowledges the intransigeance of much of our social experience, because he honors the concept of character as a component of selfhood that is derived from the culture, Marcuse enjoys a degree of gentle respect that is a bit surprising; his radical outlook embraces a number of features that Trilling strongly objected to.[17] With the others, however, Trilling permitted himself a measure of severity to which he rarely gave public voice.

In general, the position occupied by Brown and Foucault, Laing and Cooper, holds that "madness," insanity, is a state of human existence that commands esteem and admiration for two basic reasons. First, it is a "direct and appropriate response to the coercive inauthenticity of society." It is not only a condition en-

gendered by the culture, passively but somewhat heroically endured; it is also an effort to meet and to
overcome the immoral coercion that figures centrally in
the etiology of psychosis. Further, madness is a critical
act: It makes public the nature of society, exposing it
as the heartless and demeaning force that it is. Second,
madness denies the general limitations on human nature. It provides a form of existence in which "power is
assured by self-sufficiency," and it represents a distinctive and profound way of knowing, of penetrating in
perception to the outermost fringes of human capability
and potential.

Having accurately summarized in this fashion the
posture of his opponents, Trilling first restates the humane passion that energized his entire career:

Who that has had experience of our social reality will doubt
its alienated condition? And who that has thought of his
experience in the light of certain momentous speculations
made over the last two centuries . . . will not be disposed to
find some seed of cogency in a view that proposes an anti-
nomian reversal of all accepted values, of all received
realities?

But once he has established his comprehension of the
proponents of madness, and once he has reminded us of
his bases for responding to them sympathetically, he
has work to do.

To deal with these formulations by analytic argument, he says, would be "supererogatory":

This is the intellectual mode that once went under the
name of cant. The disappearance of the word from the modern vocabulary is worth remarking. In characterizing the
position as I do it is not my purpose to minimize its cultural
significance, which, in fact, I take to be momentous.

It was . . . not quite cant that Norman O. Brown ut-
tered when . . . he spoke of the "blessing" and the "super-
natural powers" which he desired to attain and which . . .
come only with madness . . . Fully achieved cant is to be

seen in David Cooper . . . "Madness," he says . . . "is a way of seizing *in extremis* the racinating groundwork of the truth that underlies our more specific realization of what we are about. . . . Madness is a form of vision that destroys itself by its own choice of oblivion in the face of existing forms of social tactics and strategy. . . . [It] is a matter of voicing the realization that I am (or you are) Christ." . . . Laing [contends that] "transcendental experiences . . . break through in psychosis [and that] true sanity entails in one way or another the dissolution of the normal ego, that false self completely adjusted to our alienated social reality."

Cant neither merits analysis nor can be refuted by it. Instead, Trilling resorts to two majestically phrased questions that he asks us to consider as intimately and as profoundly as we can. They are questions that invoke the terrors of loneliness and the degree to which the very humanity of each of us as persons depends on social connectedness—on love, on shared work, on the mutual stimulation of friendly discourse and communication about common concerns, and even on the experience of finding our will locked in conflict with the will of another. First, "Who that has spoken, or tried to speak, with a psychotic friend will consent to betray the masked pain of his bewilderment and solitude by making it the paradigm of liberation from the imprisoning falsehoods of an alienated social reality?" And then, "Who that finds intelligible the sentences that describe madness (to use the word that cant prefers) in terms of transcendence and charisma will fail to penetrate to the great refusal of human connection that they express, the appalling belief that human existence is made authentic by the possession of a power, or the persuasion of its possession, which is not to be qualified or restricted by the coordinate existence of any fellow man?"

Trilling's sharpest and most trenchant criticism of our contemporary cultural experience rests on his obviously implied answer to these poignant and fundamental questions. We are endangered, he says, by the extent to which "many among us find it gratifying . . . that alienation is to be overcome only by the completeness of alienation, and that alienation completed is not a deprivation . . . but a potency." After analytically summarizing the most important reflections over four centuries on the clash between the personal sentiment of being and the exigent demands of social organization, he concludes, "no expression of disaffection from the social existence was ever so desperate as this eagerness to say that authenticity of personal being is achieved through an ultimate isolateness and through the power that this is presumed to bring." Not in his most uninhibited imaginings did the Diderot of *Rameau's Nephew* anticipate so self-defeatingly nihilistic an outcome to his criticisms of culture or so self-destructive an extension of his meliorative intent.

Yet for all the fervor that he atypically allows himself here, and despite his leveling the charge of cant against the advocates of madness, Trilling does not build his case *ad hominem*. Marcuse and Brown, Foucault and Laing and Cooper occupy him only because they serve so well as the spokesmen of a trend all too similar to the trends represented by Gifford Maxim and by Nancy and Arthur Croom. Buffeted by their own perceptive awareness of the ancient enemies of selfhood —poverty and deprivation, alienation and exclusion, oppression and its internalized equivalent of repression —decent people are sorely tempted to overreact, to politicize their compassion, and to attempt to write their goodwilled impulses into prevailing social attitudes, into social policy, and into a mandated form of social reality. When a sense of urgency, no matter how humane its intentions may be, engenders that "impassioned longing to believe," our best impulses lose the modulation and the regulation by an informed perception of complexity that an acceptance of the conditioned nature of human existence confers. Under these circumstances, ends come to justify means, and decent people who have no doubts think destructive thoughts, exercise destructive influences, and commit destructive acts. For Trilling, the most pernicious threats to human serenity, harmony, and creativity operate under this dissembling mantle of good intentions. To expose the weapons concealed beneath this garment was the unifying purpose of his career.

5

ᘈᘈᘈᘈᘈᘈᘈᘈᘈᘈᘈᘈᘈᘈᘈᘈᘈᘈᘈᘈᘈᘈᘈᘈᘈᘈᘈᘈᘈᘈᘈᘈᘈᘈᘈᘈᘈᘈᘈ

Imagination
and Reality

The Matthew Arnold who "engaged my first interest," Lionel Trilling writes, "was . . . the melancholy poet, the passive sufferer from the stresses and tendencies of his culture. When the book [*Matthew Arnold*] was finished my concern was with the man who had pitted himself against the culture, who had tried to understand the culture for the purpose of shaping it—with the critic."[1] What Trilling brought to his encounter with Arnold and what, as a result of it, established Arnold as his lifelong mentor go far toward accounting for one of the major themes in his work. If Arnold's conception of criticism provided the bases for Trilling's own ideas of the proper task of the critic, and if Arnold's frequent preoccupation with extraliterary issues and problems legitimized Trilling's primary focus on moral and cultural matters, Arnold's most crucial legacy to Trilling was an approach to the question of how society changes and of how it *ought* to change.

Trilling came to his study of Arnold under at least four powerful influences. First, he was a sensitive, intellectually disposed, and reflective child of his time. Caught up in the radical idealism that followed the First World War and swept painfully over the threshold of the Great Depression, he deeply shared the impression, confirmed by his exposure to Yeats and Eliot, Proust, Mann, and Kafka, "that the culture of humanism was at a point of crisis . . . That the society

which had sustained this culture was in dire straits . . ."[2]
Second, he had responded in a distinctive fashion to the
ideas of Marx and Freud. To Freud, of course, he maintained an increasingly sophisticated commitment. To
Marx, although Trilling had a brief experience in 1932
and 1933 as a Communist fellow traveler, he never fully
gave his allegiance. But his admiration for both rested
less on the specifics of doctrine than on the sense that
they gave him of the intimacy and the actuality of society, of culture, and of history as forces impinging on
personalities and as social processes, massive in their
dynamics but yet subject to some measure of human
direction and control.

Third, Trilling's novelistic ambitions cannot be
overestimated. Profoundly responsive from boyhood to
the genre in which he wanted to establish his own career, he derived "primarily from novelists" his conceptions and his convictions of "what is interesting and
problematical in life, of what reality consists in and
what makes for illusion, of what must be held to and
what let go."[3] Finding a fertile soil in his creative
aspirations, fiction early and permanently embedded itself in his consciousness as the criticism of life that
Arnold said it is, and works of the imagination furnished him with both the touchstones by which he
judged reality and the visions of possibility on which he
based his values. And finally, Trilling's disposition
toward ambivalence, his taste for subtlety, and his willingness to wrestle with complexity found warm and
productive nurturance in Arnold's similar qualities—
his insistence on seeing the object as in itself it really is,
including its contradictions, his concern for the intertwined Hellenistic and Hebraic tendencies in the intellectual and the moral life, his concurrent emphases on
politics and the great current issues of society and on
personal inwardness and the cultivation of the individual spirit.

Equipped in this manner, Trilling found in Arnold

the articulate assumptions and the general directions
that, despite his resolution to avoid becoming "an Arnold man" among English professors, significantly
guided him for the rest of his days. To hold, for example, as Arnold did, that literature is a criticism of life
is to affirm the power of thought in the governing of
humanity. It leads directly to Arnold's contention, so
fundamentally congenial to Trilling, that democracy is
characterized by its response to ideas and that it can
advance only by the discovery and maintenance of the
best of them. In the light of this notion, criticism becomes the instrument for the discovery and the evaluation of those ideas that matter most to the polity and to
the quality of life experienced by the persons whom it
comprises.

From this formulation, it follows that the "literature" that is itself a criticism of life and that provides
the stuff on which the critic works is not exclusively
literary. Of Arnold's principal critical essays between
1863 and 1865, "only four deal primarily with the literary life," Trilling notes a little triumphantly. "But
six," he continues, "deal, directly or indirectly, with
religion . . . one of the discoveries of Arnold's criticism
was that intellect was not enough, that it could not be
the guide to a multitude of matters for the multitude of
mankind . . . his criticism is the reconciliation of the
two traditions whose warfare had so disturbed his
youth—rationalism and faith." Written in 1938, this
characterization of Arnold becomes, in hindsight, something of a prescient anticipation of Trilling's own efforts. Arnold's criticism, he says, "is an attempt to bring
this synthesis to bear on all the aspects of modern life.
He steers a course both by compass and by stars; reason, but not the cold and formal reason that makes the
mind a machine; faith, but not the escape from earth-
binding facts." And then the sentence from Arnold that
expresses the animating principle in nearly all of Trilling's work: "The main element of the modern spirit's

life is neither the senses and understanding, nor the heart and imagination; it is the imaginative reason."[4]

The exercise of the imaginative reason entails two major principles—*disinterestedness*, and what Arnold, always with an upper-case letter, somewhat ambiguously referred to as *Joy*. Trilling, laboring conscientiously to understand them in Arnold, incorporated both of these conceptions not only into his intellectual apparatus but into his style of perception and his processes of judgment.

Arnold develops his argument for disinterestedness in his great essay on "The Function of Criticism at the Present Time." Disinterestedness rests on curiosity. Curiosity "obeys an instinct prompting it to try to know the best that is known and thought in the world, irrespectively of practice, politics, and everything of the kind; and to value knowledge and thought as they approach this best, without the intrusion of any other considerations whatever." In order "to produce fruit for the future," criticism finds in "flutterings of curiosity" its fundamental rule. That rule

may be summed up in one word,—*disinterestedness*. And how is criticism to show disinterestedness? By keeping aloof from what is called "the practical view of things"; by resolutely following the law of its own nature, which is to be a free play of the mind on all subjects which it touches. By steadily refusing to lend itself to any of those ulterior, political, practical considerations about ideas, which plenty of people will be sure to attach to them, which perhaps ought to be attached to them, which in this country at any rate are certain to be attached to them quite sufficiently, but which criticism has really nothing to do with. The business is . . . simply to know the best that is known and thought in the world, and by in its turn making this known, to create a current of true and fresh ideas. Its business is to do this with inflexible honesty, with due ability; but its business is to do no more, and to leave alone all questions of practical consequences and applications, questions which will never fail to have due prominence given to them.

As Trilling observes, Arnold insists on this total independence of criticism from the practical spirit for a particular reason. For him, the French Revolution had proved far less the fulfillment of the ideas of the great eighteenth-century philosophers of France than their large-scale betrayal. That betrayal, evidenced by the Reign of Terror and by the events that quickly brought Napoleon into authoritarian power, was the direct result of the impatient (and uncritical) desire of human beings to give "an immediate and practical application to all these fine ideas of the reason." Trilling does not make the parallel explicit, but it is difficult to imagine him—hardly twenty years after the Russian Revolution, with the Soviet purges and Stalin's pact with Hitler fresh in his consciousness, and with the agonies of the Great Depression still dominant in his experience—not responding strongly to this warning about the gulf that yawns between ideas and their too-prompt translation into political policy and social reality. Conceivably, that gulf could be narrowed, and the narrowing could save a great deal of human wretchedness, if the consequences of ideas could first be more extensively explored. One route of exploration lies through those thoughtful dreams called fictions, of which only men and women are capable; another route lies through disinterested criticism, as Arnold defined it.

In this light, Trilling's gloss carries a special intensity. "The spirit of criticism," he says, ". . . measures the actual and the practical by the ideal. It never relinquishes its vision of what *might be*." But on the other hand, it "never says that what *can be* is perfect merely because it is better than what *is*."[5] Above all, it strives to maintain that difficult but crucial discrimination between what is reasonable and beneficent in imagination but disruptive or corrupt in realization, and what may, in some way, serve beneficent practical ends but entail spiritual shortcomings.

In Arnold's case, Trilling takes pains to point out that

He welcomed the new democracy but he suspected it. He welcomed rationalism but feared its effects. He was far from being at one with established religion yet he feared the void which its disappearance would leave. He saw old institutions crumbling and was glad, but he was uneasy lest their fall bring down more than themselves. He wanted progress but he feared the "acridity" which would characterize the forward movement. Consequently, he found it necessary to formulate a point of view which, while it affirmed the modern spirit . . . would still allow him to defend the passing order.[6]

For Arnold, the social and intellectual ideas of the French Revolution deserved full-scale support, but he could supply that support only if the moral tone of the Revolution were supplanted by something more humane. Intelligence and energy were in themselves insufficient; they required melding with "moral balance" and "nobleness of soul and character," with love.[7] Trilling, who could have been a Marxist were it not for its ready corruption into Stalinism, who had looked through Freud's lens at the ways in which human hostility self-deceptively finds justification in the ideologies of decency, and who knew both from his direct experience and from remarkably wide reading about the imperfections of the human animal and the anxieties to which it is subject, understood. As centrally important as the intellect is, it does not encompass human wholeness, and it cannot provide the motive for morality. He set himself to comprehend what Arnold meant by "Joy."

What he learned was that Joy begins in the misty but critical region of personhood, where sincerity is rooted—in not only *knowing* oneself but in *being* oneself. "Resolve to be thyself: and know, that he/Who finds himself, loses his misery." Not only relief from misery, however, depends on being oneself; creativity and a functional moral sense operate only from a base in personal integration, personal wholeness. The chief threat to wholeness comes from a rationalistic society that blunts the power to feel, that reinforces an evasion of the emotional side of one's nature, and that prizes practical and logical thought above the affects and the imagination. At the same time, it is obvious that Arnold was far from anti-intellectual in either his outlook or his practice. Neither, just as obviously, was Trilling. Trilling carefully points out that, for Arnold, as for himself, "the antithesis to the head is not the heart but the *whole being*," and he underscores the point by quoting Coleridge's comment that creative powers remain unknown to "the sensual and the proud."[8]

Creative expression, then, cannot issue from "a restless effort of the will"; it reflects "a precipitation of the whole personality . . . a distillation of the complete being." It is *not* a matter of simply releasing the emotions or of giving free play to the impulses. If the imagination and the intellect often war with each other within the person, a creatively productive settlement does not consist in the establishment of one over the other. In that direction lie only the alternatives of a sentimentality that borders on the maudlin or a chilly and sterile didacticism. Only when thought and feeling *fuse*, when the integration of the personality reaches wholeness, does art result. There is no exaltation of the artist as the prototype of happiness entailed by this conception of creativity as a function of Joy, of the exercise of the imaginative reason. Trilling quotes Coleridge again: Creative potency derives from "not mirth or high spirits, or even happiness, but a consciousness of entire and therefore well being, when the emotional and intellectual faculties are in equipoise."[9] Joy serves as both a condition and a concomitant of the ripening and disciplined expression of the creative impulse; it is neither a safeguard against the pains of life nor a panacea for the vulnerabilities and the cruelties to which human beings are subject.

A similar notion obtains in the moral sphere. For Arnold, "the real problem of conduct was not to know the rules," Trilling says: "these are easy to know and everybody knows them: the real problem was to put the rules into practice, an enormously difficult task." Morality is not a matter of reason alone but of the emotions as well. Arnold solved the problem to his own satisfaction by a reinterpretation of Pauline Christianity, in which the concept of "righteousness" plays a central role. In order to give "a fuller idea of righteousness, to reapply emotion to it, and thus by reapplying emotion, to disperse the feeling of being amiss and helpless, to give the sense of being right and effective," he defined religion as "not simply *morality*, but *morality touched by emotion.*" Trilling points out that the solution is a psychological one. It is not inappropriate because "religion's basis and method are psychological." But he also notes that Arnold's psychological approach deliberately cut away from Protestant Christianity virtually all of its usually associated metaphysics, its theology, its structure of beliefs about the nature of God and the destiny of the human world.

What remained was the model of Paul's "passionate attachment to Jesus by which he received strength for righteousness." Arnold justified the model of the love of Jesus as the foundation of morality by arguing simply that "everyone knows how being in love changes for the time a man's spiritual atmosphere and makes animation and buoyancy where before there was flatness and dullness." The idea of faith sheds its usual implication of commitment to dogma and becomes entirely a matter of relationship, of fidelity, which Arnold defined as a "holding fast to an unseen power of goodness." Through fidelity in the love of Jesus, one comes into possession of the method and the "secret" of this reconceived form of Pauline religion. The method is repentance, "the setting up a great unceasing inward movement of attention and verification" in matters of conduct; the secret is that repentance, cultivated in the context of fidelity, yields "joy and peace, missed on every other line . . . reached on this."[10]

Skeptical, Jewish, and heir of an unreligious age, Trilling cannot follow where Arnold would lead him. But he recognizes, honors, and builds into himself Arnold's *sense*, his human agenda, his perceptively formulated goals. The sincerity based on *knowing* oneself and the authenticity grounded in *being* oneself are fundamental values of both personhood and the inescapable social life to which human beings are bound. Their psychological and cultural importance cannot be overstated. Each, however, can generate destructive excesses. Sincerity may develop into sheer egocentricity, ranging from preening self-display to wallowing disruptively and unproductively in one's own misery. Authenticity may eventuate in anarchy, a wanton disregard of the feelings, the welfare, and the legitimate objectives of others. As a corrective, they require the simultaneous constraint and support of a sense of unity, a validation of one's own being by its participation in a palpitant world greater than itself. That greater world is both generally cosmic—there seems to be no better word—and explicitly political. Only when the discipline and the sustaining quality of unity are actively *sought* does Joy result. Joy comes only to the person who maintains himself as at once apart and *engagé*. Dogma, neither the dogma of religion nor the dogma of social theory, never suffices. "Whatever of sense and reason Benthamism and Communism might bring," Trilling writes, "they [do] not . . . bring the sense of Joy, of wonder, of pleasure at being alive, of a world illuminated and bursting to tell a secret."[11]

Politically, Trilling found in Arnold the foundation of the liberal imagination. His experience, his education, his omnivorous reading had certainly prepared him for this discovery. But Arnold furnished the conception, and it was in the context of Arnold's reflections and style that he made it his own. Once he had done so, he wrote little that did not either press for a fuller understanding and a fuller realization of Arnold's vision, or that did not call attention to defections and departures from it. Arnold had, he said,

the democratic insight that a human value exists in the degree that it is shared, that a truth may exist but be un-alive until it receives assent, that a good may have meaning but no reality until it is participated in. The very rewards which society bestows for virtue have their full reality only when bestowed by equals, and only the ungenerous mind finds satisfaction in receiving honor from inferiors. The artist has in a certain sense, failed, though through no fault of his own, when his intention is not understood by reason of the inferior capabilities of his fellows and his very artistic existence depends on the nature of his society. The en-lightened man must require a general development of his fellow-men as an effort of self-salvation.[12]

It was on this basis that "Arnold had formed his entire religious theory to supply the lacks of the French Revolution and he had to continue his fight against the Revolution's moral and psychological assumptions even while he fought for its social principles." The idea of faith, meaning fidelity in the love of Jesus, as Arnold developed it, "does not apply only to the individual man's relations with Christ. It implies the ideal of the State, the cooperative ideal. . . . It is with this concep-tion of unity in Christ that Arnold finds his way to solve the dilemma of community and assent in politics. For each man may discover the Socrates in his own breast by the religious act of . . . dissolving his lower nature in . . . finding accord with his fellows in Christ."[13] If the genuinely liberal imagination discriminates between the things that are Caesar's and the things that are God's, it also descries and takes seriously the connectedness be-tween matters of state and matters of spirit.

But Arnold's attempt to revise and revitalize the teachings of St. Paul also drew Trilling into a closer

relationship to Wordsworth, whose conception of the
sentiment of being came unfettered by Anglican, Protestant, or even Christian theological entailments.
Wordsworth's Christianity was, of course, incontest-
able, but it was not a necessary condition of the experience that he describes in Book Two of *The Prelude*:

> Contented, when with bliss ineffable
> I felt the sentiment of Being spread
> O'er all that moves and all that seemeth still;
> O'er all that, lost beyond the reach of thought
> And human knowledge, to the human eye
> Invisible, yet liveth in the heart;
>   . . . Wonder not
> If high the transport, great the joy I felt,
> Communing in this sort through earth and heaven . . .
> One song they sang, and it was audible,
> Most audible, then, when the fleshly ear,
> O'ercome by humblest prelude of that strain,
> Forgot her functions, and slept undisturbed.
>   . . . I am content
> With my own modest pleasures . . .
>   . . . in these times of fear,
> The melancholy waste of hopes o'erthrown,
> . . . 'mid indifference and apathy,
> And wicked exultation when good men
> On every side fall off, we know not how,
> To selfishness, disguised in gentle names
> Of peace and quiet and domestic love,
> Yet mingled not unwillingly with sneers
> Of visionary minds; . . . in this time
> Of dereliction and dismay, I yet
> Despair not of our nature, but retain
> A more than Roman confidence, a faith
> That fails not . . .
>   . . . I find
> A never-failing principle of joy
> And purest passion.

Wordsworth's sentiment of being may well comprise a mystical, pantheistic element. But Trilling is
undoubtedly correct when he identifies it as consisting

essentially and fundamentally of four components: (a) an intense pleasure (b) in the validation of his own identity (c) through a sense of unity with the world (d) without a need to exercise the will.[14] He likens the sentiment of being to Hegel's definition of *Gemüt*, a personal state which has "no particular aims, such as riches, honors, and the like; in fact, it does not concern itself with any w rldly condition of wealth, prestige, etc., but with the entire condition of the soul—a general sense of enjoyment." Without the imposition of one's will on an object, a task, or another person, the sentiment of being evokes Joy simply through the intimate experience of existing selfhood confirmed by the perception of its unity with something larger than itself. Unique and actual, one's individual being presents itself as an integral part of the world, and that ontological fact gives rise to both delight and significance.

Understood in this fashion, the sentiment of being as the basis for Joy returns us, by two avenues, to that other component of the imaginative reason, disinterestedness. For Arnold, Trilling observes, himself sharing the principle involved, "the first premise of democracy . . . is that each individual has the capability—actual or potential—of interpreting the world for himself and of choosing his own course. Democracy is based on the intellect; it can progress only by the intellect, by the circulation of sound ideas so clear and distinct as to win general agreement."[15] If such is the case, then the ideas relevant to a democratic polity must take account of its members as persons with distinctive identities and with the potential for "expanding" their selfhood in rewarding ways.[16] Wordsworth's preoccupation with being carries, in other words, political implications.

Commenting on "The Old Cumberland Beggar," Trilling points out two of them. One Wordsworth makes explicitly: The old beggar cannot in good conscience be condemned to a workhouse because he serves a useful social function; his presence evokes an "habitual charity" and thus creates "a kind of communal institution, a communal bond."

> Where'er the aged Beggar takes his rounds,
> The mild necessity of use compels
> To acts of love . . .

But the implicit political proposition is still more important. The old beggar simply *is*; as a person who still finds pleasure in his own identity, he cannot justly be considered "a mere social unit." A good society, stimulating what Arnold called "the best selves" of its members, will include him willingly and gladly within the political unity.

> . . . man is dear to man; the poorest poor
> Long for some moments in a weary life
> When they can know and feel that they have been,
> Themselves, the fathers and the dealers-out
> Of some small blessings, have been kind to such
> As needed kindness, for this single cause,
> That we have all of us one human heart.

The liberal imagination, accepting the obligation of evaluating the real against the ideal, undertakes to explore the circumstances—personal, institutional, societal, and cultural—that may indeed make man dear to man and that will bring closer to realization the sense that we have all of us one human heart.

The other link between Joy and disinterestedness affects the critic himself, the practitioner of the imaginative reason. In order to learn "the best that is known and thought in the world, and by . . . making this known, to create a current of true and fresh ideas," the critic suspends in a significant degree and manner his own will. At the very least, it is incumbent on him to examine seriously and to curb his most basic and cherished preconceptions and prejudices and to make explicit any role that they may play in his critical effort. His obligation is not to take a firm position with respect to any particular issue until he has responsibly explored the implications and possibilities of alternative positions and the complex contexts in which important issues always are embedded. Most of all, he refuses to align himself with contending forces in the arenas of power. The critic's task is not to make his will prevail, either alone or in concert with some party; it is to "create a current of true and fresh ideas."

At the same time, the imaginative reason certainly does not imply indifference. Its exercise leads typically to passionate convictions and to the wish that the convictions should prevail. The fundamental distinction, however, must be maintained: Although the realm of ideas and the realm of politics and practice are intimately related, their confusion imperils both the soul and the society. The realm of ideas encompasses thoughts, ideals, sentiments, and feelings; the realm of politics and practice operates under the mandate of will and the might that will can summon. When a bill is to be passed or defeated, a legislated act to be administered in this way or that, a suit to be settled through the adversarial processes of the courts, then ideas, principles, fundamental values, and sensibilities occupy only a peripheral place and command little attention. Mobilized force, focused on the immediacies of winning or losing, does not define the atmosphere in which the intellect most brilliantly blooms or in which the ideals that the imagination can conceive most usefully acquire form and articulateness.

Trilling learned from Arnold that "the grand error of the French Revolution" was its "quitting of the intellectual sphere and rushing furiously into the political sphere," with the result that it evoked "no such intellectual fruit as the movement of ideas in the Renascence" and created a disfiguring and reactionary "opposition to itself."[17] The effective "criticism of life" that is the function of literature, and the "current of true and fresh ideas" that it is the critic's job to circulate, aim at creating a climate of "sweetness and light" in public opinion; as that more enlightened "movement of ideas" expands and takes hold, then, without "acridity," outmoded and inhumane institutions are dissolved and new social forms and political processes emerge to advance the humanization of man in society, which is the meaning of civilization.

Trilling's conception of the imagination and its proper uses derives directly from this Arnoldian base. Two observations seem especially important. The first and more obvious bears on his carefully maintained distinction between liberalism as "a large tendency" and liberalism as an effort to organize "the elements of life in a rational way." The other deals with that less explicit but pervasive and perhaps more fundamental component of his work, his concern for "character" as an aspect of selfhood, for a large-scaled but unsentimental sympathy in estimating the quality of life made possible by particular social and cultural circumstances, and for the nature of the individual's emotional experience—his access to Joy.

The first can be quickly disposed of. It is Arnold, fully integrated into Trilling as a man and a mind of the twentieth century, who stands firmly behind the statement,

when we approach liberalism in a critical spirit, we shall fail in critical completeness if we do not take into account the value and necessity of its organizational impulse. But at the same time we must understand that organization means delegation, and agencies, and bureaus, and technicians, and that the ideas that can survive delegation, that can be passed on to agencies and bureaus and technicians, incline to be ideas of a certain kind and of a certain simplicity: they give up something of their largeness and modulation and complexity in order to survive. The lively sense of contingency and possibility, and of those exceptions to the rule which may be the beginning of the end of the rule—this sense does not suit well with the impulse to organization . . . we have to expect that there will be a discrepancy between what I have called the primal imagination of liberalism and its present particular manifestations.[18]

Trilling could just as well have mentioned legisla-
tures and adminstrative officers. He is discussing the
fate of the liberal tendency when it quits the sphere of
intellect and art and rushes into the arenas of political
struggle. What transforms Arnold's insights and makes
them contemporary is Trilling's sense of necessity and
his perception of the conditioned nature of human effort. The politicizing of the liberal spirit is necessary for
its actualization, but the entry of the liberal imagination
into the realm of politics and practice lies under the law
of costingness; liberal ideas and liberal values become
conditioned by the reality of controversy and antagonism, compromise and contending forces. As in the
inevitable warfare between self and culture, a tension
that is at once delicate and grim must be maintained to
elude disaster and to produce results that enlarge, in
some measure and in some humane fashion, the zestful
experience of human "variousness and possibility." The
task of the artist and the task of the critic are to make
that tension articulate and publicly available, to keep
fresh the imagined outcomes of the liberal spirit at
work in the world, and to make explicit the price that
must be paid for its translation at any given moment
into reality.

The second issue is more subtle, less immediately
connected with Arnold, and complicated by the almost
embarrassingly old-fashioned connotations of Joy. Yet
Joy provides both the fortitude and the enthusiastic
commitment necessary for the critical enterprise, the
practice of the imaginative reason, if one engages in it
responsibly, fully, and faithfully. What Trilling says of
Arnold can be readily generalized: "Perhaps no man
has ever formulated—though some have practised—so
difficult an intellectual course . . . only the man of
perfect equipoise and great spiritual strength may
undertake it, the man utterly sure of the beneficent goal
toward which he is striving."[19] And Trilling's comment
is deeply informed by an awareness, acquired from

Freud, of the readiness by which surety about beneficent goals can serve self-deceptively as a mask for the
personal will. The critic of our time not only runs a
difficult intellectual course; he does so guarding himself
against the intrusions of self-deception to which he has
learned that he is susceptible. With reduced access to
"A presence that disturbs me with the joy / Of elevated
thoughts; a sense sublime / Of something far more
deeply interfused," and largely incapable of fidelity in
the love of Jesus, how does the critic of our troubled
and secular age find the sustaining and animating motive appropriate to the pursuit of the imaginative reason? What now are the grounds for discovering an intense pleasure in the affirmation of self through the
sense of something larger than oneself when the personal will is in suspension?

Although he never dealt with them in a head-on
fashion, Trilling obviously took such questions seriously. His concern for the self, which he gave a central
place by calling it the subject matter of literature, his
attentiveness to Wordsworth's sentiment of being,
which amounted to a lasting preoccupation, and his
unremitting focus on the embattled relationship between self and culture, which made psychoanalysis so
important to him, all testify significantly, if a bit indirectly, to the persistence of this theme. He appears to
have searched productively for his answers along two
routes.

First, Trilling was sharply aware of the intimate
interplay between ideas and emotions, especially in the
formation of those convictions that influence one's personal life and that enter into politics and public policy.
"Goethe says somewhere," Trilling writes, "that there
is no such thing as a liberal idea, that there are only
liberal sentiments." He continues,

This is true. Yet it is also true that certain sentiments con-
sort only with certain ideas and not with others. What is
more, sentiments become ideas by a natural and impercepti-

ble process. "Our continued influxes of feeling" said Wordsworth, "are modified and directed by our thoughts, which
are indeed the representatives of all our past feelings." The
converse is also true: just as sentiments become ideas, ideas
eventually establish themselves as sentiments.[20]

This insistent recognition that thought and sentiment interact continuously in vigorous and complex
ways carries at least three vital implications. First, the
imagination is "properly the joint possession of the
emotions and the intellect." Without the spur and nourishment of the emotions, the imagination grows torpid
and inactive; and without the imagination, the intellect
itself "withers and dies . . . the mind cannot work and
cannot properly conceive itself." Second, among the
affects that influence ideas, those that are unconscious
play determinative roles. The roles may be constructive
or ominous, insightful or self-deceiving, but they are
deeply at work. For this reason, Freud rather more
fully than most creators of literature provides us with
"the sense of the human mystery, of tragedy truly conceived in the great terms of free will, necessity, and
hope." And finally, what is "properly called an idea"
emerges when "two contradictory emotions are made to
confront each other and are required to have a relationship with each other." Ideas also spring from "the opposition of ideals and in the felt awareness of the impact of new circumstances upon old forms of feeling
and estimation, in the response to the conflict between
new exigencies and old pieties." The cogency of such
ideas depends on the "degree that the confronting emotions go deep, or in the degree that the old pieties are
firmly held and the new exigencies strongly apprehended."

Here is Arnold again, actively promoting the ideas
of the French Revolution but carefully defending the
passing order, finding in that deliberately sustained conflict a morally poised and zestful sense of self. In literary terms, the cogent imagination—in the best of

Hemingway and Faulkner, for example, among Americans—conveys "a sense that the amount and intensity of [its] activity are in a satisfying proportion to the recalcitrance of the material," which is precisely the fully apprehended conflicts that arise from the complex interlacing of sentiments and concepts, the clash between old pieties and new exigencies. Neither great works of literature nor great works of criticism pretend to say the last word about matters of such human depth and difficulty, but they are relentlessly active in their efforts to comprehend them. Comprehension, however, does not rest on the notion of ideas as "pellets of intellection . . . precise and completed, and defined by their coherence and their procedural recommendations." Rather, it bases itself in an awareness of "ideas as living things, inescapably connected with our wills and desires, as susceptible of growth and development by their very nature, as showing their life by their tendency to change, as being liable, by this very tendency, to deteriorate and become corrupt and to work harm."[21] In personal terms, this not entirely comfortable realization and a welcoming response to it, an eager willingness to cope with the oppositions and contradictions within one's deepest perceptions, and the use of the imagination in the unremitting but endless search for effective resolutions furnish the foundations for the sentiment of being, for the Joy that a sense of firm and active selfhood brings.

The other avenue of Trilling's effort here is suggested by a curious and characteristic meditation of his on Freud's notions of the relationship between the individual and his culture. A bit abruptly, he introduces the findings in 1954 of the Committee on Social Issues of the Group for the Advancement of Psychiatry. This body had considered the developmental effects of loyalty oaths, the requirement that people in positions of public importance swear a special allegiance to the United States and submit to governmental investigations of their ideas, their attitudes, and their previous personal associations.[22] In addition to reporting that a climate of surveillance and repression has a generally negative influence on public mental health, the psychiatrists found that if powerful interdicts by society interfere with the exploration of the world of objects (which includes persons and ideas), and if restrictions are placed on the impulse to adventure, then the growth of the ego is impaired. Similarly, the development of the superego suffers damage because "a mature superego can optimally develop only in a free and democratic society." Trilling fully assents: "If you enslave a man, he will develop the psychology of a slave. If you exclude a man from free access to the benefits of society, his human quality will be diminished." But he then asks, "What, to take a relevant example, was the cultural and political situation in which Freud's thought developed, and his ego and his superego too?" While Freud did not live under conditions of direct and actual oppression, the Vienna of his time was "anything but a free and democratic society . . . and Freud was not an enfranchised citizen of it until his middle years." His experience of Viennese society and politics may go far "to explain why some of his views are tragic or skeptical, and very far toward explaining why he conceived of the self as standing in opposition to the general culture. But the cultural circumstance in which he was reared did not, so far as I can make out, impair the functioning of his ego or superego."

The catalogue that Trilling enumerates in answer to the question of why it did not merits reproducing. There was, for instance, his family. If the family certainly serves as a conduit for the transmission of cultural values, it also provides a bulwark against cultural impingements; like individuals, families are distinctive, and one of their realms of distinctiveness has to do with the manner in which they modulate, screen, and soften particular cultural influences while enthusiastically enhancing and enforcing others. There was also Freud's ethnic situation. "He was a Jew; and enough of the Jewish sub-culture reached him to make a countervailing force against the general culture." Nor can the worth here of Freud's education be minimized. Who can say "what part in his self-respect, in his ability to move to a point beyond the reach of the surrounding dominant culture, was played by the old classical education, with its image of *the other culture*, the ideal culture, that wonderful imagined culture of the ancient world . . . ? The schoolboy who kept his diary in Greek, as Freud did, was not submitting his ego or his super-ego to the debilitating influences of a restrictive society." In addition, Freud's love of England, generated early, furnished still another defense in the form of a contrasting model of social organization and individual expression. He became deeply involved with science and with the requirement of intellectual freedom that science levies, and, in his imagination, Freud reflected on what his own culture, given its very real strengths, could have been and could be. And then there was his sense of himself as a biological fact, unduplicated and unduplicable, his "naive belief that there is a human *given* in all persons."

What Trilling is saying is straightforward and important. The validation of selfhood through a sense of unity with something larger than itself, which brings such intense pleasure that it qualifies as Joy, can derive from many sources. Wordsworth's extolling of an upper-case Nature is entirely appropriate but not at all restrictive. The sentiment of being emerges from the supports of the family and of enduring and reciprocated love generally. It is facilitated by commitments to large-scale enterprises like science. Most of all, it gains strength from identifications, which are partially acts of the imagination—identification with an ethnic tradition, identification with an idealized culture of antiquity, identification with an adopted culture like Freud's England, and, although Trilling does not mention it explicitly in this context, identification with the worlds revealed in great fiction. Running through all these processes is the power of the imagination to create ideals out of conflicting emotions, out of oppositions between received pieties and new exigencies. Those ideals, those visions of possibility, approximate what Arnold called "a power not ourselves" which, when suitably wedded to disinterestedness, makes if not for "righteousness," then for the quest for righteousness, meaning a full engagement with the complexities and difficulties in clarifying cogent ideas and in exploring the potentials and the perils of translating them into dynamisms of social and cultural change. This quest is the quest of criticism, the quest of the imaginative reason in the twentieth century.

Out of this quest comes Trilling's conception of politics and of the relation of imaginative literature to politics:

. . . our fate, for better or worse, is political. It is therefore not a happy fate, even if it has an heroic sound, but there is no escape from it, and the only possibility of enduring it is to force into our definition of politics every human activity and every subtlety of every human activity. There are manifest dangers in doing this, but greater dangers in not doing it. Unless we insist that politics is imagination and mind, we will learn that imagination and mind are politics, and of a kind that we will not like.[23]

Within this political context, the question of power inevitably arises, and one aspect of this question bears on the power of writers and of the literature that they create. For Trilling, the appropriate power of the imagination takes its form and energy from the conditions of a democratic culture.

From the democratic point of view, we must say that . . . nothing should be done *for* the people. The writer who defines his audience by its limitations is indulging in the

unforgivable arrogance. The writer must define his audience
by its abilities, by its perfections, so far as he is gifted to
conceive them. . . . The writer serves his daemon and his
subject. And the democracy that does not know that the
daemon and the subject must be served is not, in any ideal
sense of the word, a democracy at all.[24]

In other words, the power of ideas and ideals, the
rightful realm of literature as a criticism of life, must be
protected first from underestimation and then from "the
temptations of grossness and crudeness" which appear
whenever the question of power is raised. If, as Trilling
insists, the activity of politics is to be "united with the
imagination under the aspect of mind," then poets,
novelists, and critics fall under the obligation of maintaining their focus on the judgment of social reality by
a vision of the humane ideal that can be generated
through the mating of reason and the sentiment of
being, of thought and a full awareness of the demanding, self-related, extrarational elements that are integral
to human experience.

Pervading this notion of politics is a disciplined
faith to which Trilling remained steadfast, although the
momentous events of his lifetime often severely shook
him in it. That faith holds that the success of liberal
democracy, if its success is attainable at all, depends on
three vital processes. Each is closely intertwined with
the others.

The first of these processes entails an ever sharper
discrimination by increasingly large numbers of people
between the realm of ideas and ideals and the realm of
practical politics. Obviously, this discrimination includes greater and greater clarity in the perception of
the interplay between the two domains. If the world of
ideas and ideals furnishes the function of evaluation
and critical judgment essential to a democratic polity,
then the world of practical politics supplies the approximations in actual society to those human goals and
aspirations that begin in dreams—or, if not in dreams,

in exigent experience that has been deeply reflected upon. Such a relationship has no end; it simply identifies the ongoing interaction between imagination and reality that makes viable the "large tendency" that is liberalism. In the light of this state of affairs, citizenship imposes the requirement of a respectful comprehension of these two quite different but actively interrelated elements in political life. One is the role of art and criticism, keeping themselves free from the immediate demands and the hurly-burly of practical politics. The other is the inevitably approximate nature of achievements in legislation and public policy, won through the inescapable climate of conflict and compromise that permeates institutional deliberative bodies and bureaucratic agencies.

Fastening on this basic discrimination and the respectful understanding bound up with it, Trilling judged such overly engaged works as the proletarian novels of the 1930s—the writing of, for example, Upton Sinclair and Albert Maltz—as a form of what Arnold had called philistinism. They were essentially propagandistic efforts that inappropriately and self-defeatingly subordinated the realm of ideas and ideals to the realm of practical politics. Consequently, while they articulated a "code of excited humanitarianism," they did little to facilitate the movement of imaginative reason that enriches the culture and that brings a somewhat greater degree of wisdom to political decisions. Such a literature finally amounts to little more than a kind of "flattery by which the progressive middle-class reader is cockered up with a sense of his own virtue and made to feel that he lives in a world of perfect certainties in which critical thought or self-critical feeling are the only dangers."[25] If we come close once more to the notion of rendering unto Caesar the things that are Caesar's, so that we can render unto God the things that are God's, we also hear echoes of the Socratic observation that the unexamined life is not worth living. Trilling remains entirely consistent in his stress on crucial distinctions and in his insistence on grappling with modern life's complexities.

Second, this insightful appreciation of art and criticism in our overarching political fate implies a slowing down in the implementation through legislation and executive action of those programmatic concepts that reason, *without* its imaginative component, tends to produce in the realm of practical politics as responses to the press and urgency of societal realities. Two considerations operate to lend centrality to this plank in Trilling's platform of faith. One grows obviously and directly from Arnold's conviction, hardly subject to serious challenge, that the French Revolution destroyed —by its violence, by its rapid deterioration into authoritarianism, and by its arousal of implacable resistances against itself—the creative ideas and ideals of a more generously distributed decency that originally gave it its impetus. That destruction of the humane spirit of the revolution occurred because of a premature rush from the domain of ideas into the domain of practical politics. The result was not the approximations, those acceptable if imperfect translations into reality of the visions shaped by the imaginative reason, that citizens may properly expect; it was cruelty, corruption, and the frustration of hopes. As it was with the French Revolution, so it is typically when thoughts and principles are too hurriedly transformed into law and social programs and into self-interested agencies of implementation. For a polity to realize democratic purposes, the pace of implementation must be reduced and the tests of disinterestedness applied more fully to explore possibilities and implications.

The other consideration here stems from an observation of Freud's to which Trilling repeatedly gave his attention. Genuinely concerned with social reform, Freud saw political relief as limited not by defects in governmental systems or political procedures, but by inherent factors. As he put it in *Civilization and Its Discontents,*

> In rightly finding fault . . . with our present state of civilization for so inadequately providing us with what we require to make us happy in life, and for the amount of suffering of a probably avoidable nature it lays us open to—in doing our utmost to lay bare the roots of its deficiencies by our unsparing criticisms, we are undoubtedly exercising our just rights and not showing ourselves enemies of culture. We may expect that in the course of time changes will be carried out in our civilization so that it becomes more satisfying to our needs and no longer open to the reproaches we have made against it. But perhaps we shall also accustom ourselves to the idea that there are certain difficulties inherent in the very nature of culture which will not yield to any efforts at reform. Over and above the obligations of putting restrictions upon our instincts, which we see to be inevitable, we are imminently threatened with the dangers of a state one may call *"la misère psychologique"* of groups. This danger is most menacing where the social forces of cohesion consist predominantly of identifications of the individuals in the group with one another, whilst leading personalities fail to acquire the significance that should fall to them in the process of group-formation.[26]

Two themes, both of great significance for Trilling, are stated here. Both comment trenchantly on the tragic quality in the human condition. The first focuses on the civil war within the personality of the socialized individual, the eternal conflict, sometimes violently and agonizingly disruptive, between what Trilling calls "the hidden and the visible" elements in human nature.[27] The parties to that civil war are our innate motivational and emotional equipment on the one side, and on the other, the executive and self-regulatory capabilities and habits, themselves not always in a comfortable alliance, that we acquire from our experience as members of a culture. And yet, because none of us can realize in any sense or in any degree our potentials as human beings without that socializing discipline, without the nay-saying that the culture—that all cultures—subject us to, we have no alternative to the internal battles that incorporate into our individual identities the opposition between self and society that Trilling, a committed student of Freud, so fully and poignantly documents.[28] This struggle with the inevitable "restrictions upon our instincts" limits reform through political processes and must condition our expectancies. Such contentment as we may achieve rests on our learning to enjoy approximations to our dreams and our ideals, on our neither asking too much of politics nor permitting politics to override the satisfactions afforded by mind and imagination.

The second theme in Freud's statement has to do with the problem of democracy and leadership. The issue is an old one. Arnold did not solve it; neither have political scientists before or since *Culture and Anarchy* was published. Not surprisingly, Trilling did no better. Recalling in 1971 his concerns in the 1930s, he reports his perception of a "kind of self-deception" in the prevailing intellectual-political climate—"an impulse toward moral aggrandizement through the taking of extreme and apocalyptic positions which, while they *seemed* political, actually expressed a desire to transcend the political condition—which, as I saw things, and still do, meant an eventual acquiescence in tyranny." We have previously noted[29] this side of Trilling's meditations on politics, his well-grounded fear of substituting a kind of "final solution" for the endless clash of individual wills in the open political marketplace. But, he continues, this "impulse toward moral aggrandizement" could mean the covert but imperious desire to exercise raw power:

I account as one of the most significant moments of my intellectual life an encounter that I had in my late twenties with a Russian emigre, an aging man of impressive mien, a Menshevik who had spent years in the Czar's prisons and in Siberia, who had fled his native land after the defeat of the revolutionary programs of his party by the Bolsheviks. In the course of conversation he said that what motivated intellectuals was the desire for *power*. He did not mean merely that they wished to make their ideas prevail, believing them to be good for mankind—he meant that behind the ideals there lay the desire for power in itself. He meant that the intellectual, however disinterested he claimed to be, was not *innocent* . . . Power blinds us to the object; to the work of art, to the complexity.[30]

When Freud speaks of *la misère psychologique* of groups, including states and societies, he refers to the condition under which individuals, identifying with each other rather than with a unifying leader, grow hungry for power. Their tendency is to extend an appropriate effort to prevent, to escape, or to overthrow *authoritarian* controls to an inappropriate refusal to acknowledge *authority*. Anarchy then threatens through the rise of a revolutionary spirit that acquires potency but that embodies a dangerous self-deception. Characteristically, rebellion against authority (*not* a totalitarian regime or authoritarian rule, but authority) claims its legitimacy and license from some ideology of decency. Marxism is a clear modern example. That ideological justification is the "visible" element. The dominant dynamics of rebellion, however, lie in the "hidden" components of human motivation. They consist in precisely that imperious yearning to impose one's will on others that Trilling's Menshevik mentioned. They include the energies of frustration undirected by the humane imagination, accumulated resentments unmodulated by rational considerations, the aggressions that are inherent in human nature, and raw wishes for immediate self-gratification. Because they are so seldom under the direction of conditioned and ripened ideas and so frequently motored by these hidden components of our humanity, revolutions typically leave histories of either brutal and bloody failure or, as in the case of the French and Russian revolutions, a quick

corruption and destructive betrayal of their presumably
animating ideals. The first of these themes, the limited
nature of politics and the appropriate relationship between politics and the life of the mind and the imagination, commanded a central place in Trilling's thought
when he published *The Liberal Imagination* in 1950.
The second theme, the tendency, by virtue of *la misère
psychologique*, of the revolutionary impulse to betray
and pervert itself, proved paramount when he wrote
Sincerity and Authenticity in 1972. The continuity and
integrity of his outlook remained quite of a piece; his
emphases differed because of the different conditions of
American life and American culture.

Finally, the third article of Trilling's faith turned
on the cultivation of the sentiment of being. For him,
self-knowledge is fundamental, and self-knowledge implies a sense of the self as distinctive, existent, *real*.
Alienation and opposition define that sense of self. The
groundwork of our recognizable and recognized identity
takes form from our realization of our separateness
from others and from society and from our perduring
conflict with the demands of our culture. The "very
principle of society," Trilling writes, "is the individual's
abnegation of personal autonomy in order to win the
forebearance and esteem of others." Consequently, "society, though necessary for survival, corrupts the life it
fosters."[31] Imperfectly and with difficulty, personhood
emerges from the endless struggle by the individual to
conduct simultaneously two contradictory ventures.
One entails maintaining a relationship with society that
maximizes survival; the other involves the virtually deliberate development of anomie, an active and often
hostile divorcing of the self from culture. Once again
we confront the issue with which Trilling was unremittingly preoccupied. As human beings, we are social
animals who need the love, the approval, and the support of our kind, but as human beings, we are also

individuals who need to feel ourselves in some measure autonomous, unique, and self-contained—whole in ourselves.

In his conception of the sentiment of being, Trilling reminds us that it is a synonym for "that 'strength' which, Schiller tells us, 'man brought with him from the state of savagery' and which he finds it so difficult to preserve in a highly developed culture. The sentiment of being is the sentiment of being strong." But being strong is *not* synonymous with being powerful. It is not concerned "with energy directed outward upon the world in aggression and dominance, but, rather, with such energy as contrives that the centre shall hold, that the circumference of the self keep unbroken, that the person be an integer, impenetrable, perdurable, and autonomous in being if not in action."[32] To avoid the confusion of strength with power—the power that "blinds us to the object," that prevents our seeing the object as in itself it really is—two conditions, as we have seen, are necessary. One is the person's identification with something larger than himself; the other is the capacity on crucial occasions to suspend the individual will.

Trilling insists on the importance of these requirements in the cultivation of the sentiment of being, even when he sympathetically acknowledges the "violence" that may be demanded in the face of particular cultural circumstances to make possible the cultivation of selfhood. In speaking of the position taken in the nineteenth century by writers like Schiller, Wilde, and Nietzsche, and of the later works of Gide, Mann, and Kafka, he observes,

Sometimes we are a little puzzled to understand why this art was greeted upon its first appearance with so violent a resistance, forgetting how much violence there was in its creative will, how ruthless an act was required to assert autonomy in a culture schooled in duty and in obedience to peremptory and absolute law, and how extreme an exercise of personal will was needed to overcome the sentiment of non-being.[33]

Among his illustrations of non-being are Melville's Bartleby and Flaubert's Frederic Moreau. In *Bartleby the Scrivener*, the protagonist finds the social world so deficient in authenticity that he "prefers not to" exert any effort at survival but literally to die in his preferred isolation. In *The Sentimental Education*, Moreau experiences only duplicity and hollowness in every human venture—love, friendship, art, politics. The world is perceived as providing only preconceived roles to play; there is no room for an authentic self, for the delight and strength that the sentiment of being furnishes. To overcome such cultural impingements and limitations on personhood, a degree of violence is justified, but Trilling conceives of that justified violence as occurring primarily in the imagination, in the envisioning of possibilities and the routes by which they may be attained, by "dealing with the universe in the peculiarly human spirit of play. In that spirit the universe might be taken apart and put together in a new way."[34]

This tripartite faith—in firmly maintaining the distinction between the realm of ideas and ideals and the realm of practical politics, in the slowing down of the processes of implementing political concepts, and in the cultivation of the sentiment of being—specifies the implicit undergirding of almost all of Trilling's work. Because Trilling, like Arnold, held systems in a kind of hostile mistrust, he never systematically articulated these principles. Strategically, his permitting them to operate without explicit statement gave him his flexibility, his ability to deal with the always shifting character of social and aesthetic circumstance and with the always changing configurations of the culture. Twice, however, in his treatments of Keats and of Joyce, and both treatments, interestingly, dealt with those authors' presentations of themselves through their letters—he came close to making manifest this loosely held but functional credo of how the imagination is best related to reality.

Keats's primary (although far from his sole) appeal for Trilling resides in his gracefully embodying an ideal of character. That ideal "implies a direct relationship to the world of external reality, which by activity, it seeks to understand, or to master, or to come to honorable terms with; and it implies fortitude, and responsibility for both one's duties and one's fate, and intention, and an insistence upon one's personal value and honor." Consistent with that characterological ideal, Keats was acutely attuned to what Freud called the reality principle. "Was it ever by anyone more starkly asserted," Trilling asks, "than in the phrase he used to Fanny Brawne: 'I would mention that there are impossibilities in this world' "? And yet Keats's capacity for uninhibited pleasure—in his fundamental appetites, in his creative processes, in what he called "the continual drinking of Knowledge"—richly balanced his intimate familiarity with despair, with conflict, and with the world's intractability. The balance that he achieved reflects what Trilling calls his "dialectical view of any large question,"[35] a disposition to respond fearlessly and unhurriedly when confronted by contradictions and oppositions, either within himself, in his environment, or in his relationship to society and the universe.

Out of this dialectical view, Keats formulated his notion of Negative Capability, which he described as "when a man is capable of being in uncertainties, mysteries, doubts, without any irritable reaching after fact and reason." In clarification of the famous conception, Trilling carefully points out that Negative Capability is not appropriate to problems like those of science. But it *is* appropriate to large and significant human problems, including "nothing less than the problem of evil." Developing his argument, he quotes Keats further: "The excellence of every art is its *intensity* (italics added), capable of making all disagreeables evaporate, from their being in close relation with Beauty and Truth . . . with a great poet the sense of Beauty overcomes every other consideration, or rather obliterates all consideration."[36] Understanding the objections and misunderstandings to which this formulation is subject, Trilling explains that Beauty was neither a term of aesthetic judgment for Keats nor a concept through which he could evade issues. Keats knew full well the extent to which human experience includes ugliness, heartache, and pain; he comprehended evil as integral to reality. For this reason, as Trilling points out, he believed that "to see life truly; that is, as it must be seen if we are to endure to live it," one must see it tragically. The "matter of tragedy is ugly or painful truth seen as beauty," and the tragic poet, confronting "the terrible truth of . . . evil . . . sees it so intensely that it becomes an element of the beauty which is created by his act of perception." The beauty achieved through intensity (and the courage that this kind of perceptual intensity requires) links, Trilling says, two kinds of truth: "through the mediation of beauty, truth of fact becomes truth of affirmation, truth of life." Although his reading of Keats describes the response to evil that tragedy, in the literary sense, both reflects and encourages, Trilling's focus characteristically centers on more than literary concerns. What we must understand about Keats, he insists, is "that he sought strenuously to discover the reason why we should live, and that he called those things good, or beautiful, or true, which induced us to live or which conduced to our health."[37] Keats's mode of perceiving life is certainly that of the great poet, the poet of Shakespeare's caliber, but what gives it force and high importance is that it is profoundly moral.

That moral vision, characterized by the intensity that engenders beauty, depends on at least two factors.

First, "doctrinal utterances about the nature of life, about life's goodness or badness or perfectibility" must be avoided. Resting in available ideologies blocks the intensity that full moral perception requires. Protection against this temptation derives from Negative Capability, the ability to remain in uncertainty and doubt without grasping at the straws of conventional wisdom or of ready-to-hand systems. What psychologists call "tolerance of ambiguity" is a condition and facilitator of those moral insights that conduce to our health. But the second factor is even more significant. "Negative Capability, the faculty of not having to make up one's mind about everything, depends upon the sense of one's personal identity and is the sign of personal identity. Only the self that is certain of its existence, of its identity, can do without the armor of systematic certainties." The essential truth with which Keats is concerned, Trilling says, speaking as much for himself as for the poet, is "that truth which is to be discovered between love and death, between the sense of personal identity and the certainty of pain and extinction."[38] That truth, attained by an intense exercise of the imagination, accords entirely with the reality principle. Politically, Keats was an active partisan of socially liberal, meliorative ideas and programs. But "he had no hope whatever that life could be ordered in such a way that its condition might be anything but tragic."

Twinned, however, with that clear-eyed ability to face the fact of evil was Keats's self-knowledge and his affirmation of "the creativity of the self that opposes circumstance, the self that is imagination and desire, that . . . assigns names and values to things, and that can realize what it envisions." Unlike most of us, who "suppose that what is grim and cruel is more real than what is pleasant," Keats, although never deceiving himself that "the power of the imagination is sovereign," found the experience of selfhood—the sentiment of being and the intense pleasure that it makes possible—

just as real as the evil that destroys it. He "brought his two knowledges face to face, the knowledge of the world of circumstance, of death and cancer, and the knowledge of the world of self, of spirit and creation, and the delight in them. Each seems a whole knowledge considered alone; each is but a half-knowledge when taken with the other; both together constitute a truth."[39]

The positive, affirmative nature of that truth, made accessible through Negative Capability, means much to Trilling—as well it might. Keats concludes that human life, at even its most remotely imaginable best, can only prove tragic. Nature's very components, it seems to him, are hostile to humanity, and human nature itself is hardly conducive to happiness. Having made as extreme a case as he can for the inevitability of misery, frustration, and wretchedness as inherent to the fate of humankind, he "breaks out," Trilling admiringly comments, "with a sudden contempt for those who call the world a vale of tears." Trilling quotes Keats's words as an impassioned and lyrical articulation of his own thoughts:

What a little circumscribed straightened notion! Call the world if you please "The vale of Soul-making!"—I say *Soul making*—Soul as distinguished from Intelligence— There may be intelligences or sparks of the divinity in millions—but they are not Souls until they acquire identities, till each one is personally itself. . . . Do you not see how necessary a World of Pains and troubles is to school an Intelligence and make it a Soul? A place where the heart must feel and suffer in a thousand ways! . . . the Heart . . . is the Minds Bible, it is the Minds experience, it is the teat from which the Mind or intelligence sucks its identity.[40]

Trilling gives his unstinting admiration to "the idea . . . of souls creating themselves in their confrontation of circumstance" and to "the implicit and explicit commitment to the self even in the moment of its extinction." Keats's vision of human wholeness, his zestful acceptance of struggle, his rejection of political or psychological resolutions of life's problems simply because they are available and conventionally approved, his refusal to be rushed—to be forced into reaching irritably after fact and reason when in doubt, when uncertain, when anxious—all inspire a degree of exhortation not typical of Trilling. We "cannot now attain" Keats's "spiritual and moral health" merely by "wishing for it. But we cannot attain it without wishing for it and clearly *imagining* it" (italics added). And he gives the last word properly to Keats himself. "The imagination may be compared to Adam's dream—he awoke and found it truth."[41]

Trilling puts us in his debt by demonstrating in a writer as different from Keats as James Joyce the same positive affirmation, achieved through an intensity that is at once vigorous and almost infinitely patient in the confronting of circumstance. Joyce, too, was a soul-maker. In 1935, he ended a letter to his son, "Here I conclude. My eyes are tired. For over half a century they have gazed into nullity, where they have found a lovely nothing."[42] Joyce, Trilling says, "can be understood to say that human existence is nullity right enough, yet if it is looked into with a vision such as his, the nothing that can be perceived really *is* lovely, though the maintenance of the vision is fatiguing work." Once again, the rigorous use of the imagination reveals that "Beauty is truth, truth beauty." In Joyce's case, the cost of the energy necessary to attain this insight proved high. There was much that was unattractive in Joyce's personality; and in his later years, "the personal life seems to have been burned out, calcined." But there remained a strange serenity, a rare courage, and an eye that, however weary, continued to see the world *sub specie aeternitatis*, even when there are no longer "any indications of an interplay between the self and the life around it." In the making of his own soul, Trilling observes, Joyce achieves a view in which "a thousand years are as but a day, or the other way around, and the fall of the sparrow does not go unnoticed. The round of birth, copulation, and death receives his sanction . . . in the awful silence of the infinite spaces, and his inscrutable but on the whole affectionate irony is directed upon all that men contrive in their cities for their survival, with a somewhat wryer glance toward what they contrive for their delight."

But, if Joyce alienated himself from the usual involvement with life and society to a degree that Trilling finds "chilling," he also celebrates "human existence even in the pain, defeat, and humiliation that make up so large a part of its substance." He "consciously intended Molly Bloom's ultimate 'Yes' as a doctrinal statement, a judgment in life's favor," and he fashioned "a rich poetry out of the humble and sordid, the sad repeated round of the commonplace, laying a significant emphasis on the little, nameless, unremembered acts of kindness and of love." He could speak in what Trilling calls a "thrilling archaic phrase" of "the fair courts of life" even as he responded only with apathy to society's developments and culture's elaborations.

Obviously, a fierce ambivalence is at work here. Trilling regards as unparalleled and perhaps unmatchable the "focus [of] this much power of love and hate into so sustained a rage of effectual intention as Joyce was capable of, so ferocious an ambition, so nearly absolute a commitment of himself to himself." Toward his Ireland, Joyce's "hatred was as relentless as the love was unfailing." He looked upon *Dubliners* as an effort to construct a conscience for his "wretched race," and he referred to himself on occasion as a "socialist artist"; but he contemptuously avoided political activity and associations. Overtly interested in subverting existing society, he was preoccupied with his own social status, with being a "gentleman," and looked upon his family's crest as his most treasured possession. Sexually, his passions had a powerfully polymorphous-perverse quality, but he cherished an authentic part of his personality as "austere, almost priestly propriety."

Under the steel sway of his imagination, that ambivalence provided what Trilling characterizes as "the controlling tendency of Joyce's genius—to move through the fullest realization of the human, the all-too-human, to that which transcends and denies the human." In Trilling's eyes, Joyce does not contradict the principle that the fulfilled self is marked by the nature of the alienation that it achieves. He simply creates an existence for himself on the far side of all the carefully sampled, experienced, and evaluated fulfillments that human life has to offer. Unhurried, steadily confronting circumstance, after a long period in uncertainties, mysteries, doubts—with never any irritable reaching after fact and reason—Joyce arrived at his summing up. As Trilling puts it,

The fair courts of life still beckoned invitation and seemed to await his entrance. He was to conclude that their walls and gates enclosed nothing. His genius is defined by his having concluded this rather than taking it for granted, as many of the generations that came after him have found it possible to do.[43]

What is important here for Trilling is not just Joyce's "discovery" that "the world is a cheat, its social arrangements a sham, its rewards a sell." The point is that, in the light of that discovery, the fair courts of life continue to beckon, and the "nothing" within them is "lovely." Entirely aware of the vital affirmation of the "Here Comes Everybody" theme in *Finnegans Wake* and the buoyancy and genuine gaiety in the "funferall" that Joyce puts in progress in his great last work, Trilling praises Joyce for his Keatsian intensity and Negative Capability that lie at the base of the moral courage necessary for looking long and deep into nullity and finally finding it beautiful. By keeping the realm of ideas and ideals distinct from the realm of practicality, Joyce taught us perhaps more than anyone else that although "as getters and spenders we take (the world) to be actual and there," a reality with which some accommodation must be reached, "as persons of moral sensibility, we *know* that the values of the world do not deserve our interest," that it is "at most . . . an absurdity."[44] By refusing to participate in the urgencies of Ireland's politics, Joyce contributed to the development of the Irish national conscience and to the value of its culture. And above all, by making the prodigious empathic effort necessary, Joyce identified himself with the human "nothing" that he perceived as so "lovely." In doing so, his personal will suspended despite the energies of his creative will, he affirmed humanity through making manifest his own sentiment of being.

When Trilling emerged from his long initial encounter with Matthew Arnold, his concern had shifted from the melancholy poet to the man who "had tried to understand the culture for the purpose of shaping it." What Trilling acquired from Arnold and truly possessed as his own was the sense that humanly positive changes in culture occur most frequently from the consequences of energetic and persistent efforts of the imagination. As a thoroughly modern man, profoundly educated and almost painfully perceptive, Trilling could not share Arnold's goal of "human perfection." But in fashioning Arnold's insights and method into intellectual processes distinctively his own, Trilling believed that the cultural changes that "induce us to live or conduce to our health," that improve in some measure the quality of life as we experience it in this vale of soulmaking, depend on the manner in which the imagination, interacting with rational disinterestedness, can transform reality as we perceive it, and therefore alter in humane ways our relationship to it. Throughout his career, he held to this faith without sentimentality and, like Freud, Keats, and Joyce, without winking at the tragic nature of human destiny.

6

∿∿

The Honest Place "Between"

Reacting to Lionel Trilling's insistent examination of all aspects of an issue, to his characteristic acknowledgment of the merits of quite contrary cases, Richard Sennett once accused him, "You have no position; you are always in between." Trilling's reply poignantly illustrates his fundamental critical stance. "Between," he said, "is the only honest place to be."[1]

Trilling fashioned "between," the honest place within which he conducted his quiet but intensely dramatic dialectic, from two basic materials. One was his deep and enduring sense of human existence as a continuous struggle, of culture itself as "not a free creation but a continuous bargaining with life."[2] The other was his conviction that the quality of personal experience results less from the outcomes of that struggle than from the comprehensiveness, the subtlety, and the energies of mind and imagination with which it is managed. These persuasions gave the distinctive color to his work as critic and as writer of fiction.

Because he invested the utmost seriousness in Matthew Arnold's conception of literature as a criticism of life, and because his consistent focus was on the destiny of the individual self in its often painful relationship to civilization, Trilling's consistent effort revolved around two poles: One was the honest, open exploration of the "variousness and possibilities" with which the inevitable and conflict-filled encounter be-

tween person and culture can be conceived. The other
was an examination of the criteria by which the forms
of variousness and possibility may appropriately be
judged. Although a man of finely honed tastes with a
disposition toward elegance, his aesthetic concerns always remained secondary. His fundamental interests
were moral and therefore psychological and sociopolitical. Like the Arnold that he so richly understood and
admired, he disliked and mistrusted systematic theories
of literature as overly rarified and as essentially irrelevant to the complexly related and central problems of
how personal integrity may be achieved and how corporate life can be humanely arranged. More than that,
he regarded these issues as inevitably recurrent. They
cannot be resolved; they reject systemization. They can
only be dealt with—*struggled* with—in the mind and
imagination and then in the political marketplace,
where individual wills contend with one another under
social rules.

Trilling early claimed the honest place "between"
and rarely left the position that he established there. It
was apparent in *Matthew Arnold*, his first book, in his
advocacy of the Arnold who sought so unremittingly
for ways to support the social principles of the French
Revolution, but who simultaneously extolled the benefits and virtues of the passing order and attempted to
ground the political notions of liberty, equality, and
fraternity in a firmer and nobler psychological and
moral base. It found expression four years later, in
1943, in Trilling's admiration of E. M. Forster's moral
realism, of what he perceived in Forster as "not the
knowledge of good and evil, but the knowledge of good-
and-evil." In his treatment of Vernon Parrington, one
of Trilling's few explicit acts of intellectual demolition,
his assault on *Main Currents in American Thought*
arose not from revulsion at Parrington's favorable comparison of James Branch Cabell with Herman Melville
or from dissent against Parrington's disapproving judg-

ment of Hawthorne. Trilling concentrated his artillery
on what he disdained as Parrington's "limited sense of
what constitutes a difficulty," and he found weak and
offensive Parrington's belief in "a thing called *reality*; it
is one and immutable, it is wholly external, it is irreducible. Men's minds may waver, but reality is always
reliable, always the same, always easily to be known.
And the artist's relation to reality . . . [is] a simple
one." Out of these fundamental shortcomings, Trilling
charges, grows Parrington's tendency to meet "evidence
of imagination and creativeness with a settled hostility
the expression of which suggests that he regards them
as the natural enemies of democracy." The foundations
have been laid for Trilling's ultimate verdict:

Parrington's characteristic weakness as a historian is suggested by his title, for the culture of a nation is not truly
figured in the image of the current. A culture is not a flow,
nor even a confluence; the form of its existence is struggle
. . . it is nothing if not a dialectic. And in any culture there
are likely to be certain artists who contain a large part of
the dialectic within themselves, their meaning and power
lying in their contradictions; they contain within themselves . . . the very essence of the culture, and the sign of
this is that they do not submit to serve the ends of any one
ideological group or tendency. . . . Parrington . . . expresses
the chronic American belief that there exists an opposition
between reality and mind and that one must enlist oneself
in the party of reality.[3]

Two of the major entailments of occupying that
honest place "between" strongly manifest themselves
here. One is the emphasis on the dialectical struggle
inherent in human experience; the other is the possibility of transforming reality—meaning always, for Trilling, social reality, the reality of culture—by the power
of the imagination.

The heart of that struggle beats with the active and
unremitting warfare between the individual self and the
civilization that simultaneously gives it its life and its

central character and yet restricts, cabins, and imprisons it. In Trilling's eyes, as in Freud's, selfhood requires
and depends on alienation. To be a person demands not
only an active declaration of difference from the dominant tendencies of culture but a stubborn and combative resistance to culture's rules, to culture's nay-saying.
As it is in life, so it is in serious literature:

> In its essence literature is concerned with the self; and the
> particular concern of the literature of the last two centuries
> has been with the self in its standing quarrel with culture.
> We cannot mention the name of any great writer of the
> modern period whose work has not in some way, and usually
> in a passionate and explicit way, insisted on this quarrel,
> who has not expressed the bitterness of his discontent with
> civilization, who has not said that the self made greater
> legitimate demands than any culture could hope to satisfy.
> This intense conviction of the existence of the self apart
> from culture is, as culture well knows, its noblest and most
> generous achievement.[4]

In the phrase of William James that Trilling so often
found useful, the life of the individual consistently
"feels like a fight." What gives art, especially literature,
its importance is the way that it articulately reflects and
illuminates the subtleties, the complexities, and the intensities of that inescapable battle for selfhood that persons must wage with the civilization that is at once the
powerful opponent and the basic groundwork of their
being.

But if Trilling consistently sided with the self in its
unceasing strife with civilization, he remained clear-
eyed about culture's furnishing the foundations of personal being. Beside his conviction that the self makes
greater legitimate demands than any civilization can
satisfy, he maintained, beyond that of any other modern critic, a focused awareness on the cultural *nature* of
human beings; the notion of a feral humanity was for
him a flat contradiction in terms. With Freud, he knew
that the alleged freedom of primitive life was a roman-

tic illusion, and he found no opposition between finding extensive fault with contemporary sociocultural forms and, with Arnold, committing himself to the humanization of man-in-society. That commitment, Trilling believed, defines the quest that lies at the core of an enlightened politics. Without society, without culture, *Homo sapiens* can claim neither humanity nor selfhood.

In consequence, Trilling could respond with a tenderness that never became sentimental to social institutions like the family. Perceptive about the way in which Dickens, for example, "specializes in the depiction of inadequate parents and no one knew better than he how truly the Victorian family could be . . . a hell," he is impressed by how, "if we now look back over the great literary enterprises of our time, we cannot but be struck by how deeply preoccupied these are with the family idea." Given all the stress on alienation, the force and persuasiveness of its images derive "from the sense of the violation of . . . childhood peace and familial security." And after noting that "Lawrence, Proust, Joyce, Faulkner give to the family a place in their vision of life which is no less fundamental than that of Dickens," Trilling observes that Dickens is one of the strongest articulators of "the great modern theme of 'little boy lost,' of the child's elemental emotions and familial trust being violated by the ideas and institutions of modern life."[5] The trust, the experience of love, the security that a good childhood may provide lay down the foundations for character, for one's sentiment of being, and for the interpersonal sensitivity upon which both a proud selfhood and a viable society depend.

This point of view and these values underlie Trilling's reaction to the first Kinsey Report, *Sexual Behavior in the Human Male*. That reaction, incidentally, illustrates how the honest place "between" was not at all a home for indifference or neutrality; it frequently proved the breeding ground and the platform for strongly held convictions. In the case of Kinsey, Trilling quotes a key sentence from the discussion of premature ejaculation: "It would be difficult to find another situation in which an individual who was quick and intense in his responses was labeled anything but superior, and that in most instances is exactly what the rapidly ejaculating male probably is, however inconvenient and unfortunate his qualities may be from the standpoint of the wife in the relationship." The response reveals much about Trilling's style, his eye for details, his concern for relationships and for the decencies and decorum that make corporate life fruitful as well as inevitable. Most of all, it encapsulates his conception of humanity. "But by such reasoning," he writes, in answer to Kinsey,

the human male who is quick and intense in his leap to the lifeboat is natural and superior, however inconvenient his speed and intensity may be to the wife he leaves standing on the deck, as is also the man who makes a snap judgment, who bites his dentist's finger, who kicks the child who annoys him, who bolts his—or another's—food, who is incontinent of his feces. Surely the problem of the natural in the human was solved four centuries ago by Rabelais, and in the simplest naturalistic terms; and it is sad to have the issue all confused again by the naiveté of men of science. Rabelais' solution lay in the simple perception of the *natural* ability and tendency of man to grow in the direction of organization and control. The young Gargantua in his natural infancy had all the quick and intense responses just enumerated; had his teachers confused the traits of his natural infancy with those of his natural manhood, he would not have been the more natural but the less; he would have been a monster.[6]

Growth in personal organizations, in self-regulation, and in respect for others may seem old-fashioned virtues. Similarly, the idea of a natural adulthood that differs markedly from the self-indulgences appropriate to a natural childhood may hold little appeal for an age that worships youth if not infancy and that puts a premium on self-expression through acting uninhibitedly on impulse. For Trilling, they were basic features of an authentically human life. His insightful affection for children, demonstrated in his treatment of Susan Caldwell in *The Middle of the Journey* and of the daughter in "The Other Margaret," reflects this view of human development no less than does his admiration of Keats, of Jane Austen, and of Arnold as models of adult maturity.

That same moral vision of the basic features of a human life embraces Trilling's concern for order, for civil peace. Order in society, however, must be organic; the parts of a polity must enjoy an intimate connection with each other, created by processes of historical development. His long hostility to Stalinism in all its forms attests to Trilling's unshakable rejection of what he regarded as the pseudo order achieved through authoritarian rule. Order conducive to civilization can only be achieved; it cannot be imposed. Yet the achievement, like all achievements as he conceived them, is precarious. Social order always entails an expense of the self, a bending of the individual to conform to the contours of the community, a surrendering of some portion of personal autonomy to corporate authority.

The proper response of the individual to such pressures is opposition; the authentic self is an opposing self. Yet selfhood depends on relationships, on a sense of belonging to a group and to history, on the status of being a protected citizen in some kind of organized association of human beings. Once again we encounter the motif of struggle, the embattled state that relates self to culture, even when the conditions of social order are genuinely achieved and not tyrannically imposed. The complexities and ramifications of this motif of struggle give literature its high importance. On the one hand, "the idea that preoccupies . . . literature and is central to it . . . [is] the idea of the self."[7] On the other hand, "what constitutes the matter of literature is the discordant and destructive reality that threatens the peace which makes literature possible"[8]—that is, that makes possible the contemplation and development of selfhood under the aegis of the imaginative reason.

Literature and life for Trilling are clearly not distant cousins or related only through the intellectual tracing of common lineages, like the anthropological demonstration of a primitive kinship system. They are inseparable. This insistence on the *cogency* of literature informed his work as a critic and accounts for his skeptical view of art as a self-justifying venture. Art "does not always tell the truth or the best kind of truth and does not always point out the right way . . . it can even generate falsehood and habituate us to it."[9] Literature has consequences, and those consequences can be dangerous. The dangers are greatest when literature flirts with the cultish, when it becomes organized, however loosely, into an "adversary culture" that threatens individual autonomy by virtue of its taking on those organizational characteristics that always entail costs to selfhood. Fashionable art, whether it reflects the qualities and aims of the dominant or the adversary culture, does not do and cannot be the work of artists who contain within themselves the dialectic of their place and time, who derive their meaning and power from their internal contradictions, and who do not "submit to serve the ends of any one ideological group or tendency." It was on this basis that Trilling in the 1930s could find little merit in writers like James T. Farrell and George Sklar, whose doctrinal positions he found congenial. On the same basis, in the sixties and seventies, he reacted negatively to Beckett, Burroughs, and Sartre, whose ideas struck him as both wrongheaded and perilous. In both instances, he characteristically condemned the lack of that dialectic quality that emerges from experience examined by the imaginative reason.

Trilling acquired the idea of the imaginative reason from Arnold and transformed it into a concept all his own. It combines three elements: a rather severe and broadly informed rationality, a deliberate and habitual envisioning of alternatives (again the characteristic emphasis on "variousness and possibility"), and an insistence on *feeling*, on the integral relationship of emotion and will to ideas. This last factor has seldom been understood as essential to Trilling's approach and method. Passion is part of the atmosphere of the honest place "between." But it is passion controlled, made to motor thought but not to dominate it.

The sources of the deliberate control of emotion bear on Trilling's substance as well as on his critical style. To begin with, there is his notion of courtesy as a component of morality. Good manners are more than mere forms. They are at once the interpersonal mucilage that holds society, always subject to the centrifugal force of individual selves and individual wills, together and the means by which we minimize our tendency to hurt each other. Trilling had no compunction about combat or about giving or receiving wounds as entailments of battle. But for him, the distinction was crucial between principled and justified hostilities as against indulging the aggressive impulse, acting vindictively, or salving one's own ego by damaging another person.

Second, he deeply believed that "objectivity" of judgment depends on "a programmatic prejudice in favor of the work or author being studied"; "sympathy and even admiration"[10] serve as routes to insight and as the bases for critical appraisals of genuine value. Aversion and dislike rarely promote acuity in either perception or evaluation.

When Trilling occasionally broke this self-imposed discipline—as in his treatments of Parrington and Dreiser,[11] of Gheorghiu's *The Twenty-Fifth Hour*,[12] of C. P. Snow and F. R. Leavis for their roles in the so-called two-cultures controversy,[13] and of R. D. Laing and comparable psychoanalytic revisionists[14]—he did so only because his sympathy and admiration and commitment to explicit principles, which he saw as seriously contravened by those whom he defined as his opponents, required it. Positive passion, the passion of dedication and enthusiasm, enjoyed free rein as the energizer of creative and critical powers; negative passion, the passion of hostility and hatred, Trilling kept closely curbed.

Finally, there is just a hint of the omnipresent Wordsworth. Like poetry, criticism flowers most brightly and most enduringly when powerful emotions are recollected in tranquillity—that is, when the critic, although quite in tune with his own strongest feelings, places them in perspective and fully comprehends their meanings rather than accepting them at their manifest values. The critic as an opposing self works under the obligation of self-knowledge and of the self-restraints demanded by his mission of cultural change.

Cultural change, of course, is precisely the function of the imaginative reason and was just as precisely what Trilling sought and hoped for. The ways in which he bridled his passion in his exercise of the imaginative reason provide clues to the directions that for him specified desirable modifications in our common life. Trilling saw both creativity and a democratic civil experience as necessarily entailing "aggression" in the sense of persistence in the face of frequent frustration, a full-scale investment of the will, consciously directed and determinedly sustained energies—the doctrine, once again, of *ad astra per aspera.* He worked consistently to distinguish this kind of human aggressiveness from hostility, bigotry, and authoritarianism, the aggressions of person against person, the aggressions of the imperial self and of the imperial nation.

Trilling perceived alienation as an essential condition of selfhood, and he understood the manner in which opposition and difference become definitive of one's sense of personal being. But he also felt and articulated the functions of group membership, of personal relationships, and of identification with others in the forging of personhood. Together with the promotion of individuality—his preoccupation with human variousness and possibility—Trilling pressed for the recognition of human commonalities, of the unheroic but genuine worth of what Eliot called "the common routine"[15] and even of the dutiful, dull, thoughtless "morality of inertia"[16] embodied in Willa Cather's *Ethan Frome*. He understood William James's characterization of habit as "the enormous fly-wheel of society, its most precious conservative agent,"[17] and Alfred North Whitehead's similar observation that "Civilization advances by extending the number of important operations which we can perform without thinking about them."[18]

For Trilling, caring so deeply about the stability and peacefulness of society and about the quality of civilization led directly to his concerns with the requirements of civility and with the dynamics of character formation. The interaction between a society's standards of decency and the processes of character development deeply influences two major components of selfhood. One is the contours of the individual's sentiment of being, the shape and central tendency of one's identity. The other is the quality and tone of the judgments that each person makes about himself. The peculiar mix of contentment and despair, of esteem and doubt, of pride and self-loathing with which we evaluate ourselves derives primarily from the interplay between the moral norms of one's culture and the form and furnishings of one's own character. Similarly, when the rules of civility command respect and the attributes of character elicit honor, then our social experience enjoys a reduction in the abrasiveness, the untrustworthiness, and the crass getting-and-spending elements that otherwise permeate our corporate life. Both good manners and morality, in this sense, matter as much by virtue of their political implications as through their being the outward manifestations of inward graces.

Because he held the point of view as inherent to the topography of the honest place "between," Trilling, when he identified himself as a liberal, did not—any more than Arnold did—mean that he supported the received ideology of practical liberal politics. Nor did he endorse by reflex action the catchwords and slogans of progressive opinion at any particular moment. At times, when he publicly aligned himself on some special issue, he assumed the characteristic liberal stance. For example, along with a large number of his Columbia colleagues, he signed a strong statement, which appeared in *The New York Times* (October 16, 1952), in support of the presidential candidacy of Governor Adlai Stevenson in his first campaign against General Dwight D. Eisenhower, then serving as Columbia's president. Late in 1953, in the heyday of Senator Joseph McCarthy's witch-hunts and investigations of "subversives," Trilling was vigorous and active in his defense of intellectual and academic freedom.

During that difficult period on college and university campuses, he led the Columbia faculty in registering its opposition to a proposed inquiry into Communist sympathies and influences among university professors. Chairing a drafting committee that comprised Polycarp Kusch, a Nobel laureate in physics, David B. Truman, a distinguished political scientist, and Harold E. Lowe, the director of admissions, Trilling argued that such attempts to impose criteria of political acceptability on education and on artists and scholars are beside the point and work harm. They are unnecessary because only a handful of faculty members have had even remote associations with Communism; they work harm by creating a climate of "apprehension and distrust that jeopardize(s) the cause of free inquiry and the right to dissent, which is the foundation of civil liberties in a free society." Trilling and his committee held that, although membership in Communist organizations suggests "submission to an intellectual control which is entirely at variance with the principles of academic competence," issues of academic capability must be resolved within the academic community and not by governmental intervention; "professional competence and personal integrity" are and must remain the only proper tests of fitness for university teaching, and only academic scholars and educators hold the qualifications to apply these tests in an appropriate fashion.

But these and other acts were undertaken simply as a responsible citizen, voicing his will in contention with others in the arena of practical politics. As a writer and critic, Trilling's point of view toward sociopolitical change emphasized quite different efforts. The Arnoldian trend in those efforts found a voice in his discussion of John Dos Passos as early as 1938.[19] One of the considerable virtues that Trilling identifies in U.S.A., John Dos Passos's great trilogy of the 1930s, is its subordination of politics to morality; the criterion of political action for those who participate in it and live under its consequences is the quality of moral experience that it promotes. If "Dos Passos is a social historian . . . he is that in order to be a more complete moralist. It is of the greatest significance that for him the barometer of social breakdown is not suffering through economic deprivation but always moral degradation through moral choice." Trilling consistently used the same barometer, regarding it as peculiarly sensitive to modern moral and political weather.

In a time that combines intense self-consciousness with high and anxious uncertainty about social directions and a breakdown in the persuasiveness of traditional codes of conduct, moral choice turns on the probable consequences of action for the personality. When the ends and outcomes of one's decisions appear dim, inconclusive, or unpredictable, the central question becomes one of how choice will affect the character of the chooser. The issue is less one of what he should *do* than one of what he will *become* as a result of his choosing, of how his choice will influence the quality of his selfhood, of his sentiment of being. This moral criterion, which Trilling salutes Dos Passos for applying in *U.S.A.* with insight and a compassionate but wide-ranging rigor, derives from John Dewey, who put the case in this fashion:

What shall the (moral) agent *be*? What sort of a character shall he assume? . . . The distinctively moral situation is . . . one in which elements of value and control are bound up with the processes of deliberation and desire; and are bound up in a peculiar way: *viz.*, they decide what kind of a character shall control further desires and deliberations. When ends are genuinely incompatible, no common denominator can be found except by deciding what sort of character is most highly prized and shall be given supremacy.[20]

But if this view derives from Dewey, it also illustrates the process of soul-making that Trilling so deeply admired in Keats and in Joyce's creation of "loveliness" out of the "nullity" that he regarded as human life. And it is very much of a piece with Arnold's emphasis on "culture"—by which he means reading, observing, and reflecting—as a means to transcend the "ordinary self" by achieving one's "best self" and therefore to infuse the realm of practical politics and social change with some of the beauty and intelligence ("sweetness and light") that depend on the disinterestedness and Joy that mark the realm of ideas and ideals.

In other words, the moral growth and transformation of persons lay at the root of Trilling's notion of social change in a democratic polity. Personal moral growth and transformation depend in significant measure on a rich flow of fruitful ideas clothed in the emotions that are integral to the human estate. The central task of the intellectual, the artist, and the critic is to maintain that stream of ideas touched with feeling. Without discounting the importance of economics, Trilling understood the limitations and the contradictions in economic solutions to problems arising from cultural and psychological sources. He was aware, for example, of the mounting tension between capitalism and democracy, despite the popular view that they complement each other. Capitalism depends on risk-taking initiative, and democracy provides the freedom for that kind of boldness to succeed. But the same sort of freedom also defines the condition under which heart-rending, destructive, and socially disruptive failures occur with a punishing frequency. Political redress for economic inequities and governmental protection against at least the most grinding forms of failure become humanly necessary.

As a result, conflicts arise, and impediments to the processes of both capitalism and democracy begin to operate. Politicians in a democratic state preserve public confidence in both themselves and society's institutions through responsiveness to their constituencies. Yet their responsiveness may strain the system with a load of obligations and rising expectations that it cannot safely carry. In an effort to extend equality and to broaden the base of economic security, high taxes and restrictive regulations may sap capitalism of its vitality and deprive citizens of their self-reliance, their independence, and their privacy. Industrious and clever strivers lose their economic rewards; those who have encountered failure in their experience must wear its label on their personhood. Neither economic performance nor democratic satisfactions are enhanced.

Perceiving these complexities, Trilling invested no faith in economic wizardry. Rather, he looked to political leadership responding to a people affected by the imaginative reason. His goals included a redefinition of the responsibilities of the state, of both profit and non-profit private enterprise, and the individual. That re-definition entailed the restoration and preservation of trust in government, of strength in private effort, and of dignity in persons. Overwhelmingly, the achievement of these objectives and purposes rested, in Trilling's eyes, on raising the level of moral awareness and elevating the plane of moral meaning throughout the nation. For him, that moral function was the chief (though never the sole) justification for the efforts of intellectuals and artists, especially of novelists. Those efforts supply, however imperfectly—and the prime task of the critic is to assess their effectiveness—the models and the stimuli out of which individuals at least partially fashion their own moral selves, what Arnold called their "best selves" in contrast to their "ordinary selves." When those moral selves set their distinctive wills in political con-tention, subject to the procedural regulations of democ-racy, the quality of legislation and of executive leader-ship and executive responsiveness tends to transcend the otherwise dominant considerations of party solidar-ity, discipline, and expedience. The tone and substance of the dialectic, of the inherent and unremitting human struggle, become a bit more elevated. Sympathies grow more comprehensive; expressed interests are less in-tensely parochial and therefore less divisive, and the im-mediate outcomes are more tempered by realism. "In the long run," Trilling asks, "is not the political choice fundamentally a choice of personal quality?"[21]

The question stands, of course, as entirely rhetori-cal. Trilling's affirmative answer constitutes one of the blocks out of which the honest place "between" is con-structed. From that vantage point flow some of his representative judgments. He liked Ignazio Silone's *Bread and Wine*, for example, because of its depiction of how membership in a revolutionary party, whatever its values may be, clearly fails to solve in itself the personal, moral, and even the political problems that beset modern men and women. In the "heartbreak" of Bernard Shaw's *Heartbreak House*, he found "the beginning of new courage, and I can think of no more useful *political* job for the literary man today than, by the representation of despair, to cauterize the exposed soft tissue of too-easy hope."[22] He rejects the Utopian element in Herbert Marcuse's politics, as he rejects Utopian political thought generally, on the grounds that it promotes "a character-structure and a culture . . . as deficient in grace as in authenticity."[23] And he energetically reverses the verdict on Dos Passos's trilogy, rendered by T. K. Whipple and Malcom Cowley, as expressing a political despair that is "negative to the point of being politically harmful." Despair that abandons illusion, Trilling argues, "is very different from despair which generates tender new cynicism." *U.S.A.*'s achievement lies in its presentation of the intimately personal as well as the political consequences of moral choice: "If it is made on the wrong (the safe) side, the loss of human quality, so that instead of a man we have a Success and instead of two lovers a Statue and a Bust in the public square."[24]

These illustrative judgments reflect a personality *engagé* but far from orthodoxly partisan, a mind and a character discriminating between the sphere of ideas and ideals and the sphere of practical politics but understanding the connections between them, an intellect passionately concerned with the quality of quotidian life for the *persons* caught up in the endless conflict between selfhood and civilization. They also reflect a rejection of the chic and the currently approved in assessments of literature and contemporary life, in favor of a commitment to the complexity and the necessity for some effective balance among the contending drives, interests, and perilous contingencies of the contemporary world. This commitment, so integral to the honest place "between," has enraged not a few. Roger Sale, by no means an ungenerous critic, represents those who have responded to Trilling's disinterestedness with explosive frustration.

Sale, a proponent of "our own voice, our ignorant voice, our American voice," characterizes Trilling as "a voice that one could not expect to adapt itself easily to the sixties," and charges—the word is used advisedly—that he "wanted to be Matthew Arnold." Sale concludes, in a final dismissal of Trilling, that "we had best be done with models, that we can keep the past alive not by imitating or emulating it but by reading its words aloud and by answering them in whatever authentic voice we have, wildly, loudly, or in hushed tones."[25] Saul Bellow, whom Sale much admires, disagrees. "What one sees on Broadway while bound for the bus," muses the wise old title character of *Mr. Sammler's Planet*:

All human types reproduced, the barbarian, redskin, or Fiji, the dandy, the buffalo hunter, the desperado, the queer, the sexual fantasist, the squaw, bluestocking, princess, poet, painter, prospector, troubadour, guerrilla, Che Guevara, the new Thomas à Becket. Not imitated are the businessman, the soldier, the priest, and the square. . . . They sought originality. They obviously were derivative. And of what—of Paiutes, of Fidel Castro? No, of Hollywood extras. Acting mythic. Casting themselves into chaos, hoping to adhere to higher consciousness, to be washed up on the shores of truth. Better, thought Sammler, to accept the inevitability of imitation and then to imitate good things. The ancients had this right. Greatness without models? Inconceivable. One could not be the thing itself—Reality. One must be satisfied with the symbols. Make it the object of imitation to reach and release the high qualities. Make peace therefore with intermediacy and representation. But choose higher representations. Otherwise the individual must be the failure he now sees and knows himself to be.

And there is Bellow's comment on the sixties, the *Zeitgeist* of which, according to Sale, lay beyond Trill-

ing's powers of "adaptation." Asked to address a semi-
nar at Columbia University, Mr. Sammler has had his
lecture broken up under the vulgar leadership of a presumed student "in Levi's, thick-bearded but possibly
young, a figure of compact distortion." Out of the
amphitheater, Sammler

was not so much personally offended by the event as struck
by the will to offend. What a passion to be *real*. But *real*
was also brutal. And the acceptance of excrement as a
standard? How extraordinary! Youth? Together with the
idea of sexual potency? All this confused sex-excrement-
militancy, explosiveness, abusiveness, tooth-showing. Bar-
bary ape howling. Or like the spider monkeys in the trees,
as Sammler once had read, defecating into their hands, and
shrieking, pelting the explorers below.[26]

Although there is nothing simian in Roger Sale's
informed and intelligent appraisals, when he speaks so
ardently of "our own voice, our ignorant voice, our
American voice . . . whatever authentic voice we have,"
he illustrates precisely the defects of authenticity that
Trilling took pains to document. Three points seem
worth making. First, in contrast to the rule of sincerity,
which requires that public statements be congruent to
private thoughts and feelings, the rule of authenticity
demands self-disclosure, especially the disclosure of one's
affects and feelings. Exercised judiciously, authenticity
carries the twinned values of being oneself and of enhancing the self through a courteous and courageous
outspokenness. Without the element of judiciousness, it
degenerates quickly into an obliteration of the bound-
ary between the private and the public realms; the result destroys relationships and sunders the community.
The principle of sincerity remains intact, for example,
if, in order to avoid hurting another person needlessly,
one withholds from him a damaging feeling or judgment. When authenticity becomes warped and overblown, such a consideration loses all significance, and
the notion of interpersonal or social decency undergoes

a degree of erosion. The virtue of respect and the potential for learning from someone else, from a tradition,
or from an imperfect but functioning society are undermined.

Second, authenticity unconstrained makes self-
disclosure into a kind of fundamental measure of credibility and truth. Only when I am telling you what I feel
do I have a sense of meaningfully expressing myself,
and the precondition of this kind of expression is a
central concentration on my own raw affects. Psychologists have long known this state of affairs as narcissism.
Although he chooses not to use the term, Trilling has
sharply exposed this narcissistic tendency in authenticity, especially in his analysis of Sartre.[27] Narcissism
denies the degree to which the self grows organically
out of the culture in which it is embedded, and it makes
subjectivity an end in itself, entailing a focus on the
nature of private feeling to the neglect of what is objec-
tively felt. Under these conditions of self-absorption,
expression tends to lose its force, turning, at best, eccentric and crotchety rather than original, and the process of self-disclosure itself becomes amorphous and
recedes from any real communicative enterprise among
persons.

Finally, the notion of authenticity, as it acquired
meaning and force during the decade of the 1960s,
represents what Trilling calls "something like a muta-
tion in human nature." Emerging as a response to the
hypocrisies and dark violence of the war in Vietnam, its
intensity grimly follows Sainte-Beuve's observation that
"nothing resembles a hollow so much as a hill." Confronted by horror, the devotee of authenticity copes
with it by merging with it, by becoming a part of it.
Trilling's brilliantly chosen example is Conrad's Kurtz in
Heart of Darkness. Kurtz does not, like most Belgians
and other whites in the Congo, look away from the
savagery that exists there, essentially denying it. But
neither does he face it, attempt to understand it, and

make an effort to master it. Instead, he incorporates it and exploits it, and his famous judgment, "The horror, the horror," amounts to an evaluation of himself as well as of the culture that he has joined. Authenticity at the extreme, as in Kurtz, undoes the nay-saying that civilization imposes on the self; the result is the primitivation of the personality, the feralizing of the self, rather than the humanization of man-in-society.

These considerations anxiously preoccupied Trilling during the latter part of the 1960s and run like the threads of the Fates through the pages of *Sincerity and Authenticity*. The same considerations lie at the base of Bellow-Sammler's reflections on the brutality of being "real" and on the importance of good models and their imitation. The humanization of man-in-society requires traditions and the inheritance of moral distinctions between what is humane and what is destructive of humanity. The importance and desirability of changes in those traditions and moral legacies cannot be doubted, and change, it must be remembered, was Trilling's foremost goal. But change, if it is to support and enhance the fragile potentials of humanity, cannot occur too abruptly or without an adequate moral base, and certainly not through the process of joining horror in its essence if not in its particular forms.

Trilling's unflagging opposition to Stalinism had its roots in precisely this concern. The justification for the Russian Revolution was to end the horrors of the Czarist regime and to replace that brutal totalitarianism with a more just and egalitarian culture. In actuality, internal dissensions within the Communist Party led to Stalin's purges, which grimly outdid the repressive acts of the Czars, to social control through terror in a fashion that made the aftermath of the French Revolution seem pale, and to a despotism that at least matched that of the Romanoffs in its reality if it differed in its appearance. Like Conrad's Kurtz, the Communists—or at least their leadership—had fused with the horror,

becoming one with it, instead of combatting it or containing it. This perception of the central core of Stalinism underlay Trilling's response to the upsets and disruptions of the 1960s. Interviewed in the spring of
1968, when Columbia was beset by a student uprising
of a kind then epidemic in American universities, Trilling characterized the issues posed by the student dis-
senters as "gratuitous," "factitious," "symbolic."[28]

The resulting misunderstandings have proved
startling. William Chace illustrates the point when he
claims that Trilling's "attitudes were akin to those of
William Butler Yeats when he said of the First World
War that 'We should not attribute a very high degree of
reality to the Great War.'"[29] Few comments could
stand farther from accuracy. Trilling meant precisely
what he said: The *issues* presented during the Columbia
crisis were symbolic and adventitious, and the gratuitous quality of the *issues* flowed from what worried
Trilling most deeply and impressed him as the heart of
the student revolt—its Stalinist style. As he saw things,
the issues served as a rhetorical mask behind which
destructive impulses, the wish for power for sheer power's sake, and the narcissistic indulgence and exhibition
of the ego were given unbridled play. The horror of the
American involvement in Indochina and of American
race relations had not been faced, understood, and attacked; the horror had been joined and participated in
after the manner of the Communists emulating the bru-
talities of the Czars. License the beast within one's own
bosom by pointing to the beasts in other hearts. When
Roger Sale talks, then, of Trilling's inability to "adapt
. . . easily to the sixties," he simply fails to comprehend
Trilling's steadfast position. Trilling had no wish to
"adapt" to the spirit of that time. He deplored it, opposed it, and suffered real anxieties about its probable
consequences.

One illustration should suffice. Trilling quotes a
comment by Archibald Cox, the author of the *Report*

of the Fact-Finding Commission to Investigate the Disturbances at Columbia University in April and May 1968: "The present generation of young people in our universities are the best informed, the most intelligent, and the most idealistic this country has ever known." With this somewhat bewildering assertion on the record, Trilling points out that through television and radio, mass journalism, and other cultural agencies, "there is unceasingly borne in upon us the consciousness that we live in circumstances of an unprecedented sort." These circumstances entail unprecedented difficulties, but, according to the messages of the communications media, we are entitled to believe "not only that we can properly identify the difficulties . . . but also that we can cope with them . . . and that . . . our consciousness of difficulties to be coped with gives us moral distinction." In the light of this situation, what Cox celebrates "as knowledge and intelligence . . . is merely a congeries of 'advanced' public attitudes." Superficiality and fashion have been misinterpreted as information and idealism. But Cox's deference to students seems less significant than another implication of his statement in the report—its acceptance of "another of the master traits of our contemporary culture; its willingness—its eagerness—to forgo the particularization of conduct. Recognizing the great store now placed on selfhood and the energies of the self, Professor Cox met and matched the culture in its principled indifference to the intellectual and moral forms in which the self chooses to be presented."[30]

Trilling perceived the primary choice exercised during the Columbia disturbances as a Stalinist one. The strong presence at Columbia of the Weathermen, a terrorist group formed out of the original Students for a Democratic Society, makes it at least unlikely that he was entirely wrong, and crude posters reading, "Wanted: Dead or Alive—Lionel Trilling," appear hardly irrelevant to his judgment. Sale and Chace are certainly entitled to different readings of that turbulent period, but their remarks about Trilling seem badly mistaken on two important counts. They fail to note the courageous consistency with which Trilling maintained a lifelong stance against *all* forms of authoritarianism, against merging with the horror, and they charge him with not adapting or with being intellectually distant from events in which he was actually heavily implicated, about which he was profoundly and articulately concerned, and toward which he took a definite and clear position.

That position characteristically found its locus, however, in the honest place "between." Although *Sincerity and Authenticity* carries a tincture of nostalgia for the "moral lyricism" of the old culture of sincerity, it welcomes and affirms the strenuousness, the exigence, and the combative siding with self against culture that inhere in the style of authenticity. What else would one expect from a thoughtful man who sees struggle as the root metaphor of human life, whose work has always reflected "the idea that society, though necessary for survival, corrupts the life it fosters," for whom the Latin tag of *ad astra per aspera* has consistently held such rich meaning? But, like the Arnold who wholeheartedly supported the ideas of the French Revolution but simultaneously sought to defend what was humane in the passing order, Trilling at once hails authenticity and warns of its vulnerability to serious pathology.

Human beings remain culture-made animals; to deny culture, to make the goal of the self's autonomy into an absolute unrelated to society, to accord moral authority to the "authenticity" of disorder, violence, and unreason, are to destroy the peace on which creativity depends and to put beyond the pale the wholeness on which personhood rests. The state becomes ungovernable and therefore dangerous to individuals and to individuality; the idea of community loses all significance, and history suggests that a repressive backlash, led by a Napoleon, a Stalin, a Hitler, will not be far behind.

Meanwhile, "The falsities of an alienated social reality are rejected in favour of an upward psychopathic mobility to the point of divinity, each one of us a Christ—but with none of the inconveniences of undertaking to intercede, of being a sacrifice, of reasoning with rabbis, or making sermons, of having disciples, of going to weddings and to funerals, of beginning something and at a certain point remarking that it is finished."[31] The notion that "alienation is to be overcome only by the completeness of alienation, and that alienation completed is not a deprivation or deficiency but a potency" is a mindless one. It may reflect a desperation that warrants wholesale trembling for the precariousness of civilization, but it also reflects an ominous and sad failure to understand that no man is an island, that the life of each person remains forever conditioned and qualified but also enriched by the interdependent lives of others. Narcissism is not autonomy, and susceptibility to blatant narcissism is the inherent defect of authenticity. The pathology is not inevitable, but it must be guarded against.

In Trilling's simultaneous welcoming of authenticity and his warning of its narcissistic pathology, as in other instances where his dual-mindedness has been characteristic, two components of the honest place "between" reveal themselves. One consists in Trilling's sense of the tragic quality in human experience. The other reflects his adaptation of Keats's principle of negative capability, the capacity to sustain doubt and uncertainties and to forgo easy or doctrinaire resolutions. Both undergird the wide sweep of his work, providing it with the quality of combined solidity and ambivalence that has puzzled many in relation to the variety and range of the works, the writers, and the issues that Trilling addressed.

Roger Sale again represents the failure of compre-

hension that often greeted efforts that somehow commanded admiration at the same time that their lack of
system, or declared theory, proved baffling. Symptomat-
ically, Sale writes that "the whole idea of being plumply
judicious about subjects of concern is one which has
seen better days," and he couples this derogating comment with the quite accurate observation that Trilling
"is a thinker, he is generous, but he is no theoretician."
Trilling was quite clear about his stubborn but reasoned
and explicitly deliberate resistance to theory, to system,
and, if one charitably ignores that snide adverb
"plumply," one can ask a serious and too frequently
ignored question. Not only what is wrong with being
judicious about subjects of concern, but what better—
what more humane—approach is there to subjects of
concern? Trilling's judiciousness grounded itself in his
angle of regard, and that angle of regard comprised his
tragic view of human life and the utility that he found,
following Keats, in the requirements of negative capability.

The notion of tragedy lends itself to at least two
quite different conceptions, not at all antithetical to
each other. One takes its definition from the great tragic
literature of the Greeks, Shakespeare and the Eliza-
bethans, Racine and Corneille, Melville and Hardy and
Dostoevski. It entails a figure of heroic proportions engaged in an action of extraordinary painfulness and difficulty that pits the self against some implacable force—
its own fatal flaws, the unyielding power of circumstance, or the dictates of destiny whether fate rests on
the decrees of the gods or on the interplay of character
and the conditions of the world. In this essentially classic sense, tragedy has a monumental quality; it invades
and disturbs our minds and hearts with the impact of
myth and through the transfiguring conceptions that
myths embody.

But another idea of tragedy, far less grand and
mythic but more pervasive, immediate, and intimate,

enjoys its own validity. As Paul Elmer More phrased it, all men and women live under "the law of costingness,"[32] the rule that one pays for what one gets, and one gets what one pays for. The universal temptation to evade the expense of what one has received or to obtain more than one has paid for defines the bedrock of moral experience. That temptation complicates the process of our living as human beings, and it endows virtually all our exercises of choice with tragic potentials.

To select one object or course means the foregoing of another. That foregoing of other options has consequences that we cannot fully predict; it may demand a price that we ultimately find exorbitant, and we not infrequently encounter situations where we cannot meet the cost of what we most want—one of the conditions that arouses and lends force to that universal temptation to deny, to escape, or somehow to override the ineluctable law of costingness.

Thoreau had something of this pattern in mind when he movingly observed that "most men lead lives of quiet desperation." And Whitehead's somber comment on the implications of modern science goes to the heart of the same matter: "The essence of . . . tragedy is not unhappiness. It resides in the solemnity of the remorseless working of things. This inevitableness of destiny can only be illustrated in terms of human life by incidents which in fact involve unhappiness. For it is only by them that the futility of escape can be made evident."[33] Destiny cannot be discounted; although we may be captains of our fate, our captaincy remains subject to the remorseless working of things and to the law of costingness.

When Trilling refers to the "conditioned" nature of human existence, as he does insistently, he reflects the tragic vision in this second sense. From "Impediments," the short story published when he was twenty, through "Whitaker Chambers' Journey," the introduction to the reissue of *The Middle of the Journey* in the last year of his life, and the posthumous "Why We Read Jane Austen,"[34] this conception of tragedy functions as a powerful undercurrent to his perceptions and his sensibility. It explains why, in spite of his frequent invocation of the idea of tragedy, Trilling so seldom dealt directly with any of the great literary expressions that spring to mind when that idea is given voice. Only in his commentaries on *Oedipus Rex* and *Lear* in his anthology, *The Experience of Literature*, does he address himself in any comprehensive fashion to works of this sort. His main interests lay elsewhere—with the problems of life faced not by the extraordinary heroes of Sophocles and Shakespeare but by relatively common folk with no more than a reasonable sensitivity to the nature of their efforts to cope with reality.

This concern and his special conception of the tragic as a widespread and crucial aspect of personal experience stand in flat contradiction of the charge of "mandarin exclusiveness"[35] sometimes brought against him. Deeply conscious of the tragic threads that run through most lives, Trilling cared, and his caring emerged from and was intertwined with his sharp awareness of the futility that frequently besets human endeavor, of the pain that attends the struggle for a moral identity, and of the hard-won and often deficient quality of self-respect when its bases are directly and honestly examined. He knew a good deal about the secret grades that people give themselves when they confront themselves in those hours that at once are darkest and present the most undeniable forms of self-knowledge. Those who avoid that kind of confrontation, those who mask their wills even from themselves, refusing to acknowledge the tragic—the conditioned—nature of the human estate excited his impatience and probably his fear. His distinctive sense of tragedy accounts in many ways for his opposition not only to

Stalinism but to the Stalinist personality in all its varia-
tions.

Trilling's most direct statement of his view of
tragedy takes a fictional form. "Of This Time, Of That
Place,"[36] remarkably successful in its evocation of
academic life, enmeshes its protagonist, Dr. Joseph
Howe—a poet, who, like many poets, earns his livelihood by conscientiously teaching literature—with two
students. Ferdinand Tertan exudes a genuine brilliance
and, as Howe writes in his endorsement of Tertan for
membership in the college literary society, "is marked
by his intense devotion to letters and by his exceptional
love of all things of the mind." He also proves to
be diagnosably and, presumably, incurably psychotic.
Theodore Blackburn, on the other hand, walks as an
undergraduate the road of professional sycophancy.
Energetically self-serving, he holds the vice-presidency
of the student council, manages the debating team,
serves as secretary of the literary society, and has never
received a grade lower than B—. But he can write an
examination in which he characterizes the world of
Coleridge's "The Ancient Mariner" as a "warm and
honey-sweet land of charming dreams" where "we can
relax and enjoy ourselves."

The story's context involves a stunning gallery of
representative students and a series of people and
scenes that capture the essence of college life. De Witt
appears, exhibiting a "beautiful and clear, if still arrogant, mind." Johnson displays a "stolid mediocrity."
Stettenhoven, a football player who could have served
as a model for Phidias, responds to discussions of Ib-
sen's *Ghosts* with an irritated boredom that clearly
arises from his bafflement. Casebeer combines flawless
coherence with marginal understanding and unfailing
dullness. The college dean is a thoughtful man, large-
hearted and incisive, who still embodies that quality of
distance from the front lines of instruction and scholar-

ship that marks most academic administrators. Familiar as they are, none of these figures degenerates into stereotype; each is individual, convincing, and obedient to the distinctive laws of his own character. Similarly, the details of classroom and campus life have a firmness and a credibility that pay homage to Trilling's eye and to his ability to create precisely the right image, to describe exactly the relevant action, which evoke assent from anyone who has spent time in an academic environment. And the dialogue, though colored by the vanished courtesies of 1945, continues to ring true for all its lack of four-letter words.

Within this framework, Dr. Howe develops a "various and warm" relationship with Tertan, the shambling, passionately intellectual freshman who opens his theme on the conventional topic of "Who I am and why I came to Dwight College" in an arresting fashion: "Existence without alloy," he writes, "is the question presented . . . Tertan I am, but what is Tertan? Of this time, of that place, of some parentage, what does it matter?" As the academic year wears on, Howe discovers Tertan's power to "hit, deviously and eventually, the literary point of almost everything," but he also recognizes that that power is vitiated by the young man's wild verbosity that consistently obscures insight with meaninglessness. "Their conferences had been frequent and long but had done nothing to reduce to order the splendid confusion of the boy's ideas. Yet, impossible though its expression was, Tertan's incandescent mind could always strike for a moment into some dark corner of thought." Forced to the realization, Howe acknowledges finally that Tertan is probably insane—technically, certifiably mad.

That acknowledgment requires Howe to think of his student as a "case" to be put before the dean. Yet he hesitates. Tertan has been very much a person—interesting, touching, authentically literary, and intellectual in a way that most undergraduates are not—and

Howe has felt a real affection for this strange youngster. That affection lifts a barrier against "official" solutions, against the necessity of obtaining a psychiatric final answer to the question, "What is Tertan?" Howe "alone could keep it still a question. Some sure instinct told him that he must not surrender the question to a clean official desk in a clear official light to be dealt with, settled and closed." In spite of that "sure instinct," he suddenly hears himself asking a secretary, "Is the Dean busy at the moment? I'd like to see him."

Later, when he reviewed the events . . . [of] that year, it was over this moment . . . that he paused longest. It was frequently to be with fear and never without a certainty of its meaning in his own knowledge of himself that he would recall this simple, routine request and the feeling of shame and freedom it gave him as he sent everything down the official chute. In the end, of course, no matter what he did to "protect" Tertan, he would have had to make the same request and lay the matter on the Dean's clean desk. But it would always be a landmark of his life that, at the very moment when he was rejecting the official way, he had been, without will or intention, so gladly drawn to it.

The situation becomes still more complicated by a letter that Tertan has sent to the dean: ". . . certain are chosen out of the human race to be the consoler of some other. Of these, for example, is Joseph Baker Howe. . . . Of intellects not the first yet of true intellect and lambent instructions . . . what is judged by him is of the heart and not the head. . . . To him more than another I give my gratitude. . . ." Howe acknowledges the statement for what it is. "This was love. There was no escape from it. Try as Howe might to remember that Tertan was mad and all his emotions invalidated, he could not destroy the effect upon him of his student's stern, affectionate regard."

The conclusion cannot be avoided. Howe had diminished himself in dismissing Tertan from the status of complex and unique personhood to that of a "case," a generalized and simply factual instance of psychosis. "He had betrayed not only a power of mind but a power of love." The betrayal cannot be undone by invoking the necessity, the inevitability of Tertan's psychiatric referral through the dean. Such an effort leads only to the remorseless working of things, which defines the central point. The remorseless working of things *entails* the betrayal of a power of mind and a power of love. In doing what is necessary and even what is just— for as Tertan's madness worsened, his presence at Dwight College would have become corporately intolerable—we violate the personhood of others, including others who command our interest, our loyalty, and our affection.

But if this powerful implication of Trilling's quiet little microcosm represents the essence of his conception of tragedy, he presses home an intensifying observation. On a midterm examination, Howe fails Blackburn, the other student with whom he is entangled, for his discussion of the "honey-sweet world where all is rich and strange" as the atmosphere of "The Ancient Mariner." In their conference, although Blackburn is furious and exhibits little understanding of his teacher's explanations of the F, Howe suggests that the student "really prepare" and take another examination in two weeks. "We'll forget this one and count the other." On this second try, Blackburn does no better. Howe gives him a C—, "carefully and consciously committing a cowardice." Telling himself that the overly generous grade results from wanting no more to do with a youngster whom he dislikes, he cannot still the awareness that he fears Blackburn. Blackburn spurns the grade, and this time he threatens to complain to the dean about Howe's arbitrary imposition of his own opinions and about Howe's having recommended Tertan to the college literary society—"a student who is crazy, who threw the meeting into an uproar." Howe takes the bluebook, strikes out the C—

and writes an F. "Now you may take the paper to the Dean," he says. "Tell him that after reconsidering it, I lowered the grade." Blackburn comes apart, changes his approach from bullying threats to abject pleading, and goes down on his knees in supplication. Howe, thinking "The boy is mad," rises abruptly and orders him out of the office.

On the college's commencement day, Howe and Blackburn have two more encounters. Blackburn, a graduating senior, expresses satisfaction at having finally met Howe's standards. Howe blazes, "You didn't pass my course. I passed you out of my course. I passed you without even reading your paper. I wanted to be sure the college would be rid of you. And, when all the grades were in and I did read your paper, I saw I was right not to have read it first." In the teacher's recollections, "The paper had been fantastic. The paper had been, if he wished to see it so, mad." At this point, the dean comes upon them and takes their arms, "linking Howe and Blackburn," and comments warmly that Blackburn already has a job, "the first man of his class to be placed." The story ends as Howe "hurried off to join the processional."

Howe has behaved toward Blackburn as virtually any self-respecting college professor would, and, although the relationship has hardly tested his mettle in any stringent sense, he has shown both fairness and a degree of courage. Yet his passing Blackburn out of his course to insure the college's being quit of him has contributed to the boy's receiving his baccalaureate degree and therefore to his obtaining a job, "the first man of his class to be placed." The contrast to the consequences for Tertan are a bit overwhelming. Tertan's academic career and probably far more than that are coming to an unhappy termination, whereas Blackburn, equally mad but in quite a different way, seems embarked on a life of success. If there are some forms of madness that society abhors and will not tolerate, there are others that it rewards. Howe, although doing the defensible "right thing" in both instances, has allied himself with society, connecting himself through officialdom and ceremony—the dean's arms linking him to Blackburn and his hurrying to join the academic processional on graduation day—to the remorseless working of things. His selfhood has been twice defeated, twice diminished—by his betrayal of Tertan and, ironically, by his calling of Blackburn's bluff—and on both occasions by his necessarily folding himself into the contours of ineluctable cultural demands.

Robert Boyers, a sympathetic and sensitive critic, denies the tragic element in "Of This Time, Of That Place," although he admires its fictional success.[37] His error derives from two sources. One is the common tendency to conceive of tragedy only in the first, classical, and almost exclusively literary sense and to judge it in terms of literary conventions like harmony, reconciliation, catharsis, and transfiguration. The other is the failure to realize that Trilling's deepest concerns were only secondarily literary. His focus was on "moral questions . . . the questions raised by the experience of quotidian life and by the experience of culture and history." He was consistently "a little skeptical of literature, impatient with it, or at least with the claims of literature to be an autonomous, self-justifying activity."[38] To read him, either as a critic or as a writer of fiction, without an understanding of that quietly passionate connection that Trilling always made between literature and life is to miss what is essential in him. At one with Freud's, Trilling's tragic vision encompassed Everyman, noting with an unsentimental empathy the diminutions of self that each of us suffers in his encounters with the law of costingness and the remorseless working of things, especially that expense to the self demanded by its inescapable engagements with the remorseless working of technically civilized society.

Speaking of his career as an undergraduate and of

his frustrated but lifelong yearning to be a novelist, Trilling once remarked, "I did not count myself among those who were intelligent . . . intelligence . . . did not seem a quality that a novelist needed to have, only a quick eye for behavior and motive and a feeling heart."[39] Intelligence he accumulated in abundance; it became the trait by which he was best known. But the feeling heart remained central in virtually all of his work, expressed most richly in his perception of the tragic destiny of the Toms, Dicks, and Harriets of this world. Those who overlook this dimension of both his criticism and his fiction overlook one of the defining characteristics of his mind and his character.

A comparable component of Trilling's human angle of regard—of that honest place "between," from which he examined experience—derived from Keats's conception of Negative Capability. In his well known letter to his brothers, Keats referred to Negative Capability as "when a man is capable of being in uncertainties, mysteries, doubts, without any irritable reaching after fact and reason." For Trilling, that idea amounted, in some measure, to a rationale for his often remarked ambivalence, an ingrained element of his cognitive style if not of his temperament. More importantly, it specified an aspect of the *struggle* that he perceived as inherent to the human quest, an entailment of the dialectic appropriate to any large issue that presents itself to the imaginative reason.[40] The power to sustain over time an intense and open-minded consideration of contradictory and conflicting ideas and values becomes the condition of sound judgment and significant artistry. Trilling's praise of Dos Passos's *U.S.A.* contrasts with his disappointment in the later work, beginning with *Number One*, less because of Dos Passos's rapid slide toward the political right than because of his loss of dialectical tension, of Negative Capability. He no longer embodied within himself the contradictions of America, forcing their deeper understanding through his novelistic gifts; he had submitted "to serve the ends of . . . one ideological group or tendency," and, in doing so, he foreswore the coping with complexity, the dealing with reality's contrarieties, that mark writers of genuine distinction and critics of the first rank.

But Negative Capability cuts still more deeply. "Man is neither angel nor brute," observes Pascal,[41] adding, "and the unfortunate thing is that he who would act the angel acts the brute." And in another of the *Pensées*, he reflects,

It is dangerous to make man see too clearly his equality with the brutes without showing him his greatness. It is also dangerous to make him see his greatness too clearly, apart from his vileness. It is still more dangerous to leave him in ignorance of both. But it is very advantageous to show him both. Man must not think that he is on a level either with the brutes or with the angels, nor must he be ignorant of both sides of his nature; but he must know both.

From these two meditations, a third follows: "Man does not know in what rank to place himself. He has plainly gone astray, and fallen from his true place without being able to find it again. He seeks anxiously and unsuccessfully everywhere in impenetrable darkness."

Pascal represents one of the subterranean foundation stones of Trilling's thought. There are five references to him in *Matthew Arnold*; his perceptions figure prominently in *The Middle of the Journey*, and the pivotal role assigned in *Sincerity and Authenticity* to *Rameau's Nephew* is precisely a function of the way in which "Diderot's dialogue continues and further particularizes Pascal's sense of the human contradiction of man as the opposite of himself." The passage cited from Pascal as the text for Trilling's discussion of Diderot's novel is the famous one: "What a chimera then is man! What a novelty! What a monster, what a chaos, what a contradiction, what a prodigy! Judge of all things, imbecile worm of the earth; depository of truth, a sink of uncertainty and error; the pride and refuse of the universe!" With none of Pascal's religious faith, Trilling responded with profound seriousness to his intense sense of humanity's contradictory nature and to the insoluble ambiguity of the notion of human beings as *neither* beasts *nor* angels.

That ambiguity lies at the base of the appeal that Negative Capability held for Trilling; it accounts for the parallels between his affirmations of life and his dark warnings of its inherent hazards. Unable—and *unwilling*—to resolve the issue of humankind as the pride and refuse of the universe by resorting to religion, he found in the *Pensées* much of the groundwork of his twinned convictions: that struggle defines the proper and telling metaphor for personal existence and for cultural experience, and that the style with which the struggle is managed specifies the substance of character. An ideal entailment of that style is the perception of human contradictions without demanding that they be reconciled. Moral insight depends on the intensity of the perception, not on solutions that can only prove expedient or spurious.

Conceived in this fashion, the high value of Negative Capability is the high value that Trilling finds in Hawthorne despite (or perhaps because of) his being "not gratifying."[42] Like Kafka's, Hawthorne's main concern revolves around "man's dark odyssey in an alien world," and, like Kafka's, Hawthorne's "fiction does not make a very determined reference to the concrete substantialities of life." Society as Hawthorne conceives it is "thinly composed," thereby facilitating his "representation of the world as . . . susceptible to penetration and suffusion by agencies not material and mundane." Because of that thin composition of culture, "the autonomy of the spirit is the more easily imagined." But "if it is indeed true that Hawthorne's world is thinly composed . . . whatever its composition lacks in thickness is supplied by an iron hardness . . .

for Hawthorne the world is always and ineluctably *there* and in a very stubborn and uncompromising way." The intractability of life-in-society holds sway through all of Hawthorne's works, even though he consistently displays "the moral life as existing beyond the merely pragmatic . . . as a mystery, as being hidden, dark, and dangerous, and as having some part of its existence in a world which is not that of our ordinary knowledge. This other world . . . interpenetrates the world of material circumstance, and . . . provides . . . [it] with its most intense significances." At his best, Hawthorne has an instructive and "quick response to the non-rational," a "lively awareness of the primitive and chthonic, of the dark roots of life," but these qualities never "deflect the naturalistic and humanistic tendency of his mind . . . however successfully he may project illusion, he must point beyond it to the irrefrangible solidity."

Yet over this hard and funereal conception of the self in its relation to culture, Hawthorne's imagination literally *plays*: "He takes," Trilling says, "somber moral principles and makes them into toys." But through the playfulness, elements of ambivalence and ambiguity operate. Unlike the ambivalence and ambiguity that also characterize Kafka, whom Hawthorne so much resembles, these attributes lead not to Kafka's "mute, riddling power." Rather, in Trilling's judgment, they provide an avenue by which he approaches Montaigne's *Que sais-je?*—"the ironic childlike question, the question which conscious or calculated modesty asks, out of which all the questions come. It is *questions* which Hawthorne leaves us with" (italics added).

For Trilling, a crucial test of mature personhood is the ability to live with questions—critical and profound questions—without an irritable, or an anxious, grasping for fact or reason to achieve a reassuring but bogus answer. Humanity remains neither beast nor angel, and the determination of what humankind *is* becomes the object of the often frightening quest of the self in its alien world. As was the case in the great quests of antiquity—the quest for the Grail, for example—what matters in this one is less the location of its object than the style, the seriousness, the courage, the intelligence, and the grace of its pursuit.

Boyers, in his genial, receptive, and informed fashion, sees Trilling's commitment to Negative Capability as a jusifying rationale for a "wisdom of avoidance," for a disposition to stand above the battles of both politics and intimate and immediate interpersonal relationships.[43] In his perception, he approximates the judgment of Joseph Frank.[44] Frank charges Trilling with a preference for "stability and stasis" that underestimates and derogates the individual will. In one sense, Frank says, Trilling's position amounts to little more than an effort to reincarnate Irving Babbitt's notion of the "inner check" (the *frein vital* in contrast to the *élan vital*). In another, it entails a substitution of "contemplation for an active grappling with social reality" and an effort to cloak "social passivity and quietism" with an undeserved and quite false dignity. Trilling, Frank argues, is simply a rhetorically elegant reactionary.

Boyers errs, once again, because of his overstrict attention to literary matters. We have had repeated occasion to note that the honest place "between" was no neutral eremite's retreat. It was consistently the locus of frequently passionate convictions, but convictions emerging from an insistent concern for complexity, for difficulty, and for avoiding the relatively easy but regularly misleading solutions that ideology provides. For Trilling, ideology was perhaps the prototypical form of an irritable grasping for fact or reason as a way of escaping from serious and complicated questions. And the issues confronted from the honest place "between" were only secondarily literary. Those issues were, however, conceived and dealt with under the aegis of the

Arnoldian distinction between the sphere of ideas and
ideals and the sphere of practical politics. That distinction makes Frank's evaluation of Trilling into something of a curiosity.

When an intellectual (and Frank's bona fides here
lie beyond dispute) disparages "contemplation" in
favor of "an active grappling with social reality," one
wonders what is afoot. Such a contention comes close
to denying that the imaginative reason has anything to
do with the achievement of political wisdom and that
mind has any relevance to the problems that "social
reality" presents. Similarly, when Frank talks about
Trilling's depreciation of the will and, in the same
breath, his attempt to reinstate Babbitt's "inner check,"
he makes two flat mistakes. First, Trilling summarizes
and recapitulates the case he made over his entire career when he writes, "The issue, which I believe must
occupy the consciousness of our culture for a long time
to come, is whether life is the better or the worse for
putting a high valuation on the will. It is my position
that it is the better."[45] Nothing could be plainer. Further, Babbitt's *frein vital* requires precisely an act of
volition and finds its base in that spiritual strenuousness
that the New Humanists most prized.[46] If more linkages exist between Babbitt and Trilling than the latter
may have been aware of, they do not and cannot consist of either a disparagement of the will or a taste for
quietism.

Finally, the notion of Trilling as a reactionary
holds meaning to almost exactly the same extent that
the notion of Arnold as a reactionary would hold meaning. If the critical attempt to conserve what is humane
and functional from a passing order amounts to reaction, if the investment of a degree of skepticism in virtually any radical politics amounts to reaction, if a
measure of mistrust in absolutist commitments of almost any sort and especially in ideological fanaticisms
amounts to reaction, then Trilling, like Arnold, is a

reactionary. Meanwhile, such an inference must cope with Trilling's awareness that much of the evil of the world is accomplished by decent people who have no doubts, and one has room to wonder if such a consciousness, such an insistent effort to deal with complexity, dwells even in the neighborhood of either reaction or "social passivity." In any event, Trilling's reflections on Morris's *News from Nowhere*,[47] where he once yet again asserts the doctrine of *ad astra per aspera*, stands as a straightforward answer to Frank's rather astonishing evaluation.

Trilling's treatment of Henry James's *The Princess Casamassima*[48] also provides an answer to Frank in the capaciousness, depth, and subtlety of the attitudes that it both displays and advocates and in the warmth and novelty of the understanding that it exhibits. Trilling begins with one of James's self-characterizations to which he was peculiarly resonant: "I have the imagination of disaster," James wrote in a letter of 1896, "and see life as ferocious and sinister." Set in a context of anarchist terrorism, *The Princess Casamassima* certainly fulfills in two respects expectations of ferocity and danger: in the detailed evocation of an anarchist organization in which assassination is coldly conceived as an ethical instrument of politics, and in the fate of Hyacinth Robinson, the novel's protagonist. Hyacinth elects to commit suicide when he finds that he can neither betray the anarchist cause with which he has aligned himself nor execute the order that he has received from the organization to murder the duke. Trilling trenchantly summarizes the reasons for this decision: "Sometimes society offers an opposition of motives in which the antagonists are in such a balance of authority and appeal that a man who so wholly perceives them as to embody them in his very being cannot choose between them and is therefore destroyed. This is known as tragedy."

Hyacinth's tragedy, however, is that of a very

human hero who dies not innocently but under a burden of guilt. Hyacinth recognizes, Trilling points out, "what very few people wish to admit, that civilization has a price, and a high one . . . all civilizations . . . renounce something for something else." In general, the civilized ideal of widespread security works against the equally civilized ideal of high and distinctive achievement and of nobility of artistic expression. The first reflects the emphasis and spirit of radical democracy; the second embodies the aristocratic aspiration of individual distinction. Hyacinth, caught up in the egalitarian desire to increase and broaden the experience of both justice and security by destroying the dominance of the ruling class, also has become aware that "the monuments of art and learning and taste have been reared upon coercive power." As Hazlitt once noted, Trilling reminds us, "poetry has an affinity with political power in its autocratic and aristocratic form and . . . is not a friend of the democratic virtues." Committed to anarchy as a political principle, Hyacinth is also "of the company of Rabelais, Shakespeare, Scott, Dickens, Balzac, and Lawrence, men who saw the lordliness and establishment of the aristocrat and the gentleman as the proper condition for the spirit of man, and who, most of them, demanded it for themselves."

Hyacinth's conflict, then, entails a double guilt. He has discovered something of what typically lies behind abstract radical ideals: envy, the impulse to revenge, the desire for personal dominance, narcissism. But he has also discovered that a "passion for life at its richest and noblest" entails consenting to the coercive power of the established order. Hyacinth's tragedy is a genuine and moving one, because "he dares to do more than civilization does: embodying two ideals at once, he takes upon himself, in full consciousness, the guilt of each. . . . By his death," Trilling says, "he instructs us in the nature of civilized life and by his consciousness he transcends it."

Here is the kind of moral realism that Trilling first identified and discussed in E. M. Forster, a clear-eyed knowledge not of good and evil but of good-and-evil. But he adds a dimension here, in an essay first published in 1948, that, although he seldom refers to it explicitly, he carries with him as moral equipment for the remaining twenty-seven years of his life. Calling it "the imagination of love," Trilling either discovers it or creates it from James's handling of the characters in *The Princess Casamassima*. If we think, he says, of

a father of many children who truly loves them all, we may suppose that he will see very vividly their differences from one another, for he has no wish to impose upon them a similarity which would be himself; and he will be quite willing to see their faults, for his affection leaves him free to love them, not because they are faultless but because they are they; yet while he sees their faults he will be able, from long connection and because there is no reason to avoid the truth, to perceive the many reasons for their actions. The discriminations and modifications of such a man would be enormous, yet the moral realism they would constitute would not arise from an analytical intelligence as we usually conceive it but from love.

Trilling concretizes his perception through a series of vignettes from James's book. Rosy Muniment is crippled, sharp-tongued, courageous, quaint, and unkind. James "forces us to admire her courage, pride, and intellect and seems to forbid us to take account of her cruelty because she directs it against able-bodied or aristocratic people." Only at the end of the novel do we discover that Hyacinth doesn't like Rosy "and that we don't have to." That insight provides "an emotional relief and a moral enlightenment." But, although James explicitly permits us to dislike Rosy, he himself "does not avail himself of the same privilege. In the family of the novel Rosy's status has not changed."

Millicent Henning has a "strength, affectionateness, and warm sensuality" that James depicts with un-

bridled admiration. At the same time, he clarifies un-
sparingly "not only . . . her desire to pull down what is
above her but also . . . her desire to imitate and conform to it and to despise what she herself is." In Paul
Muniment, genuine idealism couples with a secret desire for personal power. Radiating charisma and a gift
for leadership, he illustrates at once the authenticity
of humane dreams and some characteristic modern
ironies. To a moral realist, those ironies include "the
liberal exhausting the scrupulosity which made him
deprecate all power and becoming extravagantly toler-
ant of what he had once denounced, and the idealist
who takes license from his ideals for the unrestrained
exercise of power." Yet Paul is consistently an attractive and admirable if highly complex and not entirely
trustworthy man.

As for the Princess herself, she is the Christina
Light of James's earlier *Roderick Hudson*. As one of
the other characters, Madame Grandoni, says of her,
"she sold herself for a title and a fortune. She regards
her doing so as such a terrible piece of frivolity that she
can never for the rest of her days be serious enough to
make up for it." Trilling's comment is that "Seriousness
has become her ruling passion, and . . . it is her fatal
sin, for seriousness is not exempt from the tendency
of ruling passions to lead to error. And yet it has an
aspect of heroism, this hunt of hers for reality, for a
strong and final basis of life." In the Princess, Trilling
finds "the very embodiment of the modern will which
masks itself in virtue, making itself appear harmless,
the will that hates itself and finds its manifestations
guilty and is able to exist only if it operates in the name
of virtue, that despises the variety and modulations of
the human story and longs for an absolute humanity,
which is but another way of saying a nothingness."
But the Princess continues to command our compassion.

Trilling's assessment of *The Princess Casamas-*

sima is that it is "an incomparable representation of the spiritual circumstances of civilization." That assessment, however, enjoys less importance than Trilling's insight into moral realism as the basis for James's undeniable achievement:

. . . the novelist can tell the truth about Paul and the Princess only if, while he represents them in their ambiguity and error, he also allows them to exist in their pride and beauty: the moral realism that shows the ambiguity and error cannot refrain from showing the pride and beauty. Its power to tell the truth arises from its power of love. James had the imagination of disaster and that is why he is immediately relevant to us; but together with the imagination of disaster he had what the imagination of disaster often destroys and in our time is daily destroying, the imagination of love.

If his literary perceptions were notably acute, Trilling's focus in his treatment of James's novel centered, as always, on the moral ideas of which the literary work gives rise, and on the connections between those moral ideas and the quality of our corporate—our political—life.

A distinctive sense of tragedy as an inherent component of daily experience, a feeling for the intellectual and moral power of negative capability as a means of coping with complexity, and a concept of moral realism humanized by the imagination of love, then, are the tools with which Trilling worked on the authors, the works, and above all, the issues that struck him as important in the ongoing struggle between the self and its at once nurturing and imprisoning culture. They also define the primary avenues by which he enters our moral consciousness. Gracefully and accurately, William Chace has caught his essence: "Rather than historian, philosopher, or theorist, Lionel Trilling was a sensibility who patiently cultivated thinking in order to subsume it to the rhythms of his search for wisdom."[49]

It is hard to conceive of a more humane model of self-aware and socially responsible personhood.

Chace's accuracy slips a little when he characterizes Trilling's career as revolving around two major themes, "the power of death and the corruption of doctrinaire politics."[50] The statement, while true enough, lacks trenchancy. Four brief comments may sharpen the point of Chace's perception.

First, at the root of anything that may be called the tragic sense of life lies the distinctive human awareness of mortality, of finitude, of death. Like all who share that tragic sense, Trilling invested a suitable seriousness in the fact of death and in our awareness that, whatever our state of being at any given moment, we cannot live forever. His main concern, however, focused on the moral and political implications of the various attitudinal forms that that awareness may assume. In *The Middle of the Journey*, for example, he examined the tendency of American liberals to regard death as a taboo topic because of its "reactionary" denial of progressive trends and of human perfectibility through the restructuring of society. Trilling found this tendency disturbing because it entails a winking at an ultimate reality, a wishful rejection of the final "conditioned" state to which all human beings are subject, a major failure to see the object as in itself it really is. But his disturbance grew far more richly out of the conception of life that these faults involve than out of any special concentration on the ineluctable fact of death.

Second, although Trilling was indeed preoccupied with "the corruption of doctrinaire politics," his stern and committed opposition to Stalinism extended beyond political corruption and doctrinaire positions. Ideologies, panaceas, Utopias, all impressed him as inappropriately and dangerously easy solutions to society's profoundly complex problems and as violations of the advantage and virtues of negative capability. In his Arnoldian way, he fought them unremittingly. More immediately, he stood always embattled against all forms of authoritarianism, whether of the polity or of the personality. If anything, the authoritarian style, the incorporation into the self of a disposition to subordinate the wills of others to one's own and to curtail arbitrarily and through might alone the freedom of others, struck him as more damaging and frightening than authoritarian governments.

Third, as central as politics—conceived typically in the domain of ideas and ideals rather than in the realm of current practicalities—was for Trilling, he looked upon politics as a component of culture. The larger sweep of the culture, of which politics was only a part, and the quality of life that that cultural movement promoted, commanded his first interest. That interest occupied itself most diligently with society's moral climate, the network of ideas and sentiments that influence our relationships with one another, that determine our feelings about social responsibility and the ways in which we can properly come to terms with the corporate dimension of our lives, and that shape our imaginations of how we can and should conduct our interactions on both intimate and societal levels. In a sense, his concerns with death and Stalinism found their fullest meaning only within this always shifting moral matrix of civilization as it impinges on individual consciousness.

Finally, Trilling's curiosity, patient but passionate, fastened most avidly on questions of personal development, of the contours of the sentiment of being, of the nature and dynamics of character. Issues of individual identity and integrity appeared in his eyes as axiomatically fundamental. Experience as a self and of the self is the quintessence of the human condition.

His finding in literature a criticism of life so broadly and so deeply conceived constitutes Trilling's tribute to the literary enterprise and forms the basis of his vigorous seriousness as both a critic and a writer of fiction. In the latter role, he produced two short stories, "The Other Margaret" and "Of This Time, Of That Place," that merit the status of minor masterpieces, beautifully crafted, fully persuasive in their characterizations, and complexly significant and essentially timeless in their themes. "Notes on a Departure" stands not far behind in richness of conception and quality of execution. *The Middle of the Journey*, so disappointingly received when it first was issued and so ironically successful after its author's death, patently serves a dialectical purpose and has a logical sequence and structure perhaps more suitable to argument than to art. Nevertheless, when this point has been made, the novel still achieves a high economy of episode, builds the tensions relevant to its subject matter and its characters with a convincing inevitability, and explores with a brilliant cogency the interplay of private passions and public ideologies in contemporary experience. Nowhere else in American fiction since the end of World War II has the relationship of personality to politics found so subtly perceptive a student.

As a critic, Trilling continues, in a fashion finely tuned to the crises, turbulences, and stridencies of the twentieth century, the great humanistic tradition that takes its course from Dr. Johnson through Hazlitt and Arnold. As an heir—one is tempted to say *the* heir—of that tradition, Trilling is the child of both the Enlightenment with its realistic empiricism and its emphasis on decorum, and Romanticism, with its idealistic expansiveness and its insistence on individuality.

His range and professional seriousness invite comparison with Edmund Wilson, the magisterial dean of modern literary critics. Wilson certainly covered more critical ground, demonstrated a weightier and more catholic learning, and was sharper, more forthright, and more challengingly quirky in his opinions. Both Wilson and Trilling regarded life, including political life, as more important than art, but both found in literature a window on the world that enlarged and lent perspective to their perceptions of life. Both mistrusted systematic literary theories as breakers of the connection between literary art and the common human experience, and neither depended to any significant degree for his critical judgments on either the apparatus or the fruits of formal literary scholarship, although both were somewhat distantly respectful of the scholarly profession.

Trilling, working consistently at the problem of the relationship of the self to the character of culture, probed more deeply than Wilson did into the actualities of living, and he was more successful in using literary materials for the exploration of the moral problems that the struggle between the individual, striving for autonomy, and civilization, insisting on homogeneity and order, complexly poses. In achieving that success, he fulfilled, in a greater measure than Wilson, one of the requirements of the humanistic tradition. He demonstrated both the positive importance and the hazards of literature as a moral force in society.

Most of all, Trilling built the honest place "between." Never a home for evasive neutrality, it was a kind of debaters' hall where, in conscious and articulate forms, the conflicting, contradictory trends in a contemporary culture could contend with each other, each assured of a carefully attended hearing and a just and accurate interpreter. The careful attention and the just and accurate interpretation took precedence over any service to a particular point of view or party. As a result, Trilling's formulations from the honest place "between" had a richness of both texture and implication that only fully apprehended complexity can confer, and his ideas enjoyed a moral cogency that can only be attained through enduring the often painful tension that is entailed by incorporating within oneself the clashing contradictories of one's civilization. By sustaining that tension within himself for precisely half a century, Trilling, as both a discerning mind and an exemplary character, taught us much about ourselves and the civilization that is both our groundwork and our albatross. Fortunately for all of us, his works embody both the mind and the character, and they remain.

Notes

1. LIONEL TRILLING: THE OPPOSING SELF

Detailed biographical information about Lionel Trilling is scarce. This chapter is heavily indebted to Diana Trilling, both for generous conversations about her husband and for her extremely useful "Lionel Trilling, A Jew at Columbia" in *Commentary*, 1979 (March), Vol. 67 (No. 3), pp. 40–46. This essay has been reprinted as an appendix (pp. 411–429) to *Speaking of Literature and Society*, the final volume in the Uniform Edition of the Works of Lionel Trilling. Mrs. Trilling carries no responsibility, of course, for the inferences, interpretations, and speculations here; but her helpfulness, her kindness, and the centrality of her contribution should be thoroughly understood. In addition, the material in this section derives from personal acquaintance between 1950 and 1965, from correspondence from 1965 until Trilling's death ten years later, and from a number of conversations (rather than formal interviews) with Trilling's colleagues and students.

1. *E. M. Forster*, p. 37.
2. *The Liberal Imagination*, pp. 206–207, xv.
3. *A Gathering of Fugitives*, p. 90.
4. *Sincerity and Authenticity*, p. 120.
5. *The Liberal Imagination*, pp. 3–22.
6. *Beyond Culture*, pp. 145–178.
7. *Sincerity and Authenticity*, pp. 167–172.
8. *A Gathering of Fugitives*, p. 114.
9. *A Gathering of Fugitives*, p. 87.
10. *The Last Decade*, p. 158.
11. *A Gathering of Fugitives*, p. 55.
12. *A Gathering of Fugitives*, p. 65.
13. *The Opposing Self*, pp. 118–150.

14. *Of This Time, Of That Place, and Other Stories,* pp. 3–10.
15. Lionel Trilling, "Introduction" to Robert Warshow, *The Immediate Experience* (Garden City, N.Y.: Doubleday, 1962), p. 15.
16. "Introduction," pp. 14–15.
17. Since the Second World War, the circumstances of Jews in the United States have improved dramatically, and, despite the memories of Hitler and the Holocaust, it is difficult for the postwar generations to understand the extent and the effects of American anti-Semitism in the 1920s and 1930s. Nevertheless, anti-Semitism still has its measure of virulence, and, while it represents a distinctive form of prejudice, it is closely related to other forms of racism, including the massive variety that takes blacks as its object. The literature, of course, is huge. One of the best vehicles for developing a sense of the Jewish immigrant community in New York City in the early decades of the twentieth century is Henry Roth's novel, *Call It Sleep,* first published in 1934 and reissued thirty years later in a paperback edition by Avon Books. A great deal of information is available in the comprehensive volume edited by Louis Finkelstein, *The Jews* (New York: Harper, 1960). On the dynamics of prejudice, see the still richly seminal book by Leonard Doob, *et al., Frustration and Aggression* (New Haven: Yale University Press, 1939); Gordon Allport, *The Nature of Prejudice* (Cambridge, Mass.: Addison-Wesley Press, 1954); and Kenneth Gould, *They Got the Blame: The Story of Scapegoats in History* (New York: Association Press, 1942). More recent work concentrates much more on black-white relations than on anti-Semitism and its consequences, but it remains highly relevant psychologically. Excellent sources are Charles V. Willie, Bernard M. Kramer, and Bertram S. Brown, eds., *Racism and Mental Health* (Pittsburgh: University of Pittsburgh Press, 1973); Louis L. Knowles and Kenneth Prewitt, eds., *Institutional Racism in America* (Englewood Cliffs, N.J.: Prentice-Hall, 1969); Joel Kovel, *White Racism: A Psychohistory* (New York: Vintage Books, 1971)·

and Pierre L. van den Berge, *Race and Racism* (New York: Wiley, 1967).

18. *The Last Decade*, pp. 11–12.

19. *A Gathering of Fugitives*, pp. 58–59.

20. The best and most available brief account of the General Honors program and its rationale is John Erskine's *My Life as a Teacher* (Philadelphia: Lippincott, 1948), pp. 165–175 *et passim*. See also his *The Moral Obligation to Be Intelligent* (New York: Bobbs-Merrill, 1921), especially the title essay, pp. 3–32. Quotations here are taken from *My Life as a Teacher*.

21. *The Last Decade*, p. 231.

22. *The Last Decade*, p. 234.

23. *A Gathering of Fugitives*, pp. 135–136.

24. For Trilling on education, see "Preface" in *Beyond Culture*, pp. ix–xviii, and the essays "On the Teaching of Modern Literature," pp. 3–30, and "The Two Environments: Reflections on the Study of English, pp. 209–234. In *The Last Decade*, "Mind in the Modern World," his Jefferson Humanities Lecture, pp. 100–128, "The Uncertain Future of the Humanistic Educational Ideal," pp. 160–176, and "Why We Read Jane Austen," pp. 204–225, all exemplify his concern with teaching, learning, and the importance of educational institutions. Throughout his writings, Trilling sprinkles observations and reflections on education, the significance of some of his interactions with students, and the ways in which education does or should provide a liberating, developmental experience for persons both young and old.

25. *The Liberal Imagination*, pp. 34–37.

26. *The Last Decade*, pp. 236–237.

27. The peculiar and complex role of Communism in the United States between the Russian Revolution and the Second World War, especially its appeal to intellectuals and its importance in shaping the American *Zeitgeist*, was an extensive one. See Christopher Lasch, *The American Liberals and the Russian Revolution* (New York: McGraw-Hill, 1972); Theodore Draper, *The Roots of American Communism* (New York: Viking Press, 1957) and his *American Communism and Soviet Russia* (New York: Macmillan,

1960); Daniel Aaron, *Writers on the Left* (New York: Harcourt, Brace and World, 1961); and—perhaps best of all for its special subject—David Caute, *The Fellow Travellers* (New York: Macmillan, 1972).

28. *The Last Decade*, pp. 14–16.

29. *Of This Time, Of That Place, and Other Stories*, pp. 38–57.

30. This statement of Trilling's is most accessible in Theodore L. Gross, ed., *The Literature of American Jews* (New York: Free Press, 1973), pp. 358–360. It is reprinted from the *Contemporary Jewish Record* for February, 1944.

31. Alfred Kazin, *New York Jew* (New York: Knopf, 1978). Quotations here are taken from the Vintage Books edition of 1979, pp. 64–70. See also pp. 292–298 and p. 391.

32. *The Last Decade*, p. 238.

33. *The Last Decade*, p. 164.

34. *The Last Decade*, pp. 238–239.

35. *The Last Decade*, p. 227.

36. Bernard Kalb, "The Author," *Saturday Review*, 12 February, 1955, p. 11.

37. Lionel Trilling, "Introduction" to the reissue in 1975 by Avon Books of *The Middle of the Journey*. The essay is reprinted in *The Last Decade* under the title of Whittaker Chambers' Journey," pp. 185–203.

38. "Introduction," *The Immediate Experience*, pp. 14–15.

39. Warshow, pp. 42–48. The review appeared originally in *Commentary* for December, 1947.

40. Richard Cordell, "Clash of Ideas," *Saturday Review*, 11 October, 1947, p. 25.

41. *The Last Decade*, p. 227.

42. Lionel Trilling, *Mind in the Modern World* (New York: Viking Press, 1972). The Jefferson Memorial Lecture is reprinted under the same title, "Mind in the Modern World," in *The Last Decade*, pp. 100–128.

43. Irving Howe, *Celebrations and Attacks* (New York: Horizon Press, 1979), p. 214. Howe's discussion of

Trilling's *Sincerity and Authenticity* first appeared in *Commentary*, February, 1973.

44. R. H. Super, *The Time-Spirit of Matthew Arnold* (Ann Arbor: University of Michigan Press, 1970), pp. 90–91.

2. CIVILIZATION AND ITS DISCONTENTS

1. Sigmund Freud, *Civilization and Its Discontents.* (London: Hogarth Press, 1930). In translations by either Joan Riviere or James Strachey, paperback editions are widely available.

2. Much of this introductory statement draws heavily on two papers: E. J. Shoben, Jr., "The Tragic Nature of Human Destiny," *American Journal of Orthopsychiatry*, 1979 (October), Vol. 49 (No. 4), pp. 564–570; and E. J. Shoben, Jr., "Tragedy as Moral Concept and as Moral Problem," a keynote address to the Eighth Annual Conference on Piagetian Theory and the Helping Professions in Los Angeles, February, 1978.

3. Walter Cannon, *The Wisdom of the Body* (New York: Norton, 1932). See also Carroll E. Izard, *Human Emotions* (New York: Plenum Press, 1977), and Howard S. Liddell, *Emotional Hazards in Animals and Man* (Springfield, Ill.: Charles C. Thomas, 1956).

4. A large literature documents this point. Among the best and most readable references are C. Judson Herrick, *The Evolution of Human Nature* (Austin: University of Texas Press, 1956); Albert Szent-Gyorgyi, *The Crazy Ape* (New York: Philosophical Library, 1970); and Bernard Campbell, *Human Evolution* (Chicago: Aldine Press, 1974).

5. *The Opposing Self*, xiii.

6. Jean Kinney, *An American Journey: The Short Life of Willy Wolfe* (New York: Simon and Shuster, 1979).

7. *Beyond Culture*, p. 13.

8. *Sincerity and Authenticity*, p. 156.

9. Trilling's insistent attention to moral issues and his emphasis on judgment, restraint, and a framework of articulate values in the conduct of life suggest linkages between his ideas and those of the New Humanists—Irving Babbitt, Paul Elmer More, Stuart Pratt Sherman, and Norman Foerster. Similarities, such as the congruence of Trilling's stress on self-control as a personal virtue to Babbitt's concept of the *frein vital* (as opposed to the romantic or Bergsonian *élan vital*) or "inner check," do appear and seem significant. Trilling's only direct references to Babbitt and More, however, occur in *Matthew Arnold*. For the most part, they simply acknowledge Arnold's considerable influence on the New Humanists. In one instance, with noticeable asperity, he "disposes," not with one weapon but with two, of one of Babbitt's condemnations of the romantic melancholy that colors Arnold's poetry. He first documents Arnold's awareness that melancholy is "always bad" and his persistent and deliberate cultivation of *Tüchtigkeit*, a kind of cheerful inner peace. He then refers to a bit of scholarship, published some dozen years after Babbitt's attack, demonstrating that the lines from "The Scholar Gypsy" that Babbitt had submitted as damning evidence referred not at all to Arnold himself but to Goethe. (See *Matthew Arnold*, p. 140.) Nevertheless, if the New Humanists did not directly impress themselves on Trilling or become a part of his conscious intellectual and moral equipment, they and he derive from common traditions—witness their mutual admiration of Arnold as critic if not as poet—and Trilling's affinity for their ideas may have been greater than he himself thought. That likely affinity is often remarked by those who charge Trilling with "conservatism." Joseph Frank exemplifies this disposition in *The Widening Gyre* (New Brunswick, N.J.: Rutgers University Press, 1963), pp. 253–254, 257.

10. *The Last Decade*, p. 238.

11. *The Experience of Literature*, pp. 900–901.

12. Although his inclusion in this list may jar, Philip

Roth's popularity should obscure neither his crafts-
manship nor his subtlety. He certainly must rank
among the best of our contemporary stylists. More
importantly, his bumptiousness of manner and his
taste for the outrageous mask a curious and serious
concern for precisely the power to feel that is under
discussion here. Even in *Portnoy's Complaint*, wit
serves as a kind of substitute for the power to feel,
and the undercurrent of this theme accounts for much
of the touching quality of the novel. In *My Life as a
Man*, the inhibition of feeling through the deterioration of a relationship, and the generalizing of that
inhibition to all relationships and to the power to
feel itself, are what the book is essentially "about."
The Professor of Desire is essentially an explicit study
in the mutability and evanescence of feeling, and
The Ghost Writer involves the substitution of
fantasy for feeling in a manner that is reminiscent,
despite a quite different matter, of *Portnoy's* examination of wit as a shadowy alternative to genuine
feeling. What makes many of Roth's characters
interesting for us is their clear retention of the
"fierce necessity" as against their loss of "the power"
to feel.

13.   *Beyond Culture*, pp. 113, 115.
14.   *Matthew Arnold*, p. 124.
15.   *Matthew Arnold*, p. 136.
16.   Trilling refers frequently to Jane Austen, and on at
       least three occasions he devoted rich essays to her
       work. His consideration of *Mansfield Park* is in *The
       Opposing Self*, pp. 206–230. He deals with "Emma
       and the Legend of Jane Austen," in *Beyond Culture*,
       pp. 31–56; and *The Last Decade* includes his post-
       humous and unfinished treatment of "Why We Read
       Jane Austen," pp. 204–225. From the last piece, it
       is clear that his appreciation of her stemmed in large
       part from the trenchancy with which she portrayed
       society at the very beginning of the modern period
       and from the prescience of her psychological insights
       into the ways that changes in that society were to im-
       pose additional burdens on selfhood.
17.   *Beyond Culture*, pp. 8, 13.

18. Basically, the psychological concept of "modeling" refers simply to our learning new forms of behavior by observing their performance in other people. At more complex levels, it has to do with deliberate emulation, the acceptance of another person, in limited or comprehensive ways, as a kind of master. In its most developed form, modeling entails one's guiding one's own behavior in problematic situations by asking, in effect, the question, "What would my model do, how would he respond, were he in my shoes at this moment?" A counterpart of this process involves the use of the model's probable behavior—including his attitudes, his feelings, and his values—as a touchstone for judging one's own conduct and in directing one's own will. The idea has clear connections with that of indentification, the incorporation into the essential structure of the self of attributes of another. Sentiments of liking and admiration tend to be associated with the choice of a model, but fear and helplessness can sometimes also promote the selection of models. The latter phenomenon was first clearly recognized and studied in the curiously positive responses of some inmates of Nazi concentration camps to their guards; it plays a major role in the reactions of some hostages to contemporary terrorists. See T. W. Adorno, *et al.*, *The Authoritarian Personality* (New York: Harper, 1950); and Albert Bandura, *Aggression: A Social Learning Analysis* (Englewood Cliffs, N.J.: Prentice-Hall, 1973). More familiarly, modeling functions importantly in both the socialization of children and the processes of psychotherapy. In the present case of Wordsworth and the leech-gatherer, the analogue to the latter is a striking one. The best general reference is probably Albert Bandura's *Social Learning Theory* (Englewood Cliffs, N.J.: Prentice-Hall, 1977).

19. David Riesman, *The Lonely Crowd* (New Haven: Yale University Press, 1950). See also Riesman's *Individualism Reconsidered* (Glencoe, Ill.: The Free Press, 1954). Trilling, enthusiastically and at some length, reviews both books in A *Gathering of Fugitives*, pp. 85–100.

20. *Beyond Culture*, pp. 16–17. For detailed and current documentations of the charges that Trilling abstractly summarizes, see Kurt Glaser and Stefan Posony, *Victims of Politics* (New York: Columbia University Press, 1979).
21. *The Liberal Imagination*, pp. 98–99. In the same passage, Trilling speaks of "the tendency of our educated liberal class to reject the tough, complex psychology of Freud for the easy rationalistic optimism of Horney and Fromm." He may have erred in regarding Horney and Fromm as peas from the same pod, but he was certainly correct in his contrasting of Freud and Fromm. It is impossible to imagine Freud, with his painstakingly and often unwillingly developed tragic reading of the human condition, bypassing character for technique and artfulness in so sentimental a fashion as Fromm does in his *The Art of Loving* (London: George Allen and Unwin, 1957).
22. *Beyond Culture*, p. 167.
23. *Beyond Culture*, p. 169.
24. *Beyond Culture*, p. 52.
25. *Beyond Culture*, pp. 53–54.
26. Alienation as a concept came into general use through Marx's use of the term in *Das Kapital* to describe the remoteness of the worker from the end products of his labor and the resulting dissatisfaction and emptiness associated with assembly-line jobs and other highly specialized operations in industry. It has since been variously defined and is closely linked to the sociological notion of anomie. See Robert K. Merton, *Social Theory and Social Structure*. (Glencoe, Ill.: The Free Press, 1957). Trilling's frequent use of the term tends to be a trifle hazy, and it is touched with cloudiness in the present context (*Sincerity and Authenticity*, pp. 122–125). He concisely distinguishes the early Marx's meaning of alienation from Hegel's; but we cannot be sure of the precision with which he is identifying similarities among the ideas of Marx, Arnold, Wilde, and Ruskin. In his *Economic and Philosophical Manuscripts*, written when he was only twenty-six but not published until as late as 1932, Marx was somewhat clearer than Trilling suggests

about the meaning of that remarkable but rather gnomic statement, "Let us assume *man* to be *man*, and his relation to the world a human one." See Karl Marx, *Early Writings* (New York: McGraw-Hill, 1964).

27. *Sincerity and Authenticity*, p. 106.

28. The idea of the "noble savage" has great mythic appeal. As Trilling uses it in his consideration of *Heart of Darkness*, it refers to a frequent component of the romantic faith—the belief that human beings are intrinsically good, that their "natural" dignity and integrity are ruined only by the imposition of the conventions and requirements of civilized society, and that primitives embody a capacity for nobility of conduct that has been stripped away from Euro-Americans by the dehumanizing constrictions of "advanced" culture. The instinctual life enjoys high honor in this view, and childhood takes on the aura of a primitive innocence out of which a strange and wonderful wisdom can emerge. The idea cuts, however, in two other directions. One deals with the notion of the internal wild man, the primitive within ourselves; it poses the question of the degree to which life will be enhanced or damaged by the degree to which we control or unleash the primitive tendencies that are an inherent part of human nature. The other has to do with the operation of primitive as against civilized forces in society. The great portrayal of this conception is *The Tempest*, where Shakespeare pits Prospero against Caliban in a dramatic tension that remains unresolved at the play's ending. Cervantes also develops this theme, at about the same time as Shakespeare, in his character of Cardenio. This young nobleman, under crisis, disintegrates into a wild man, but, with the help of Don Quixote, reconstitutes his civilized humanity on a broader and more generous basis. Shakespeare, a little like the Greek tragedians, conceives of humankind as caught forever in an unresolvable conflict between demonic forces and the gods; Cervantes, while hardly optimistic, has the redemptive view that the person can find both God and himself on his life's quest. One can only regret that

Trilling never dealt directly with this pervasive theme of humanity's conception of itself and of its cultures. The standard work on this interesting topic remains Hoxie Neale Fairchild's *The Noble Savage* (New York: Columbia University Press, 1928. Also useful and stimulating are the essays collected under the editorship of Edward Dudley and Maximillian E. Novak, *The Wild Man Within* (Pittsburgh: University of Pittsburgh Press, 1972).

29. *Sincerity and Authenticity*, p. 108.
30. *Beyond Culture*, p. xvi.
31. *Beyond Culture*, p. 23.
32. *Matthew Arnold*, pp. 150, 153.

3. FREEDOM VS. NECESSITY

1. *The Liberal Imagination*, p. xi.
2. *The Liberal Imagination*, p. xii.
3. *The Experience of Literature*, pp. 131–132.
4. *The Experience of Literature*, pp. 960–964.
5. *A Gathering of Fugitives*, pp. 79–84.
6. *The Liberal Imagination*, p. xii.
7. *Of This Time, of That Place, and Other Stories*, pp. 11–37.
8. *The Last Decade*, pp. 238–239.
9. *The Opposing Self*, p. 137.
10. Although Trilling's love for poetry was obvious, he seems oddly to have been uncomfortable with it in his role as critic. Surprisingly little of his work focused on poets. Even Matthew Arnold, one of his chief mentors, whose verse he dealt with extensively and competently in *Matthew Arnold*, is treated in Trilling's introductory essay "Matthew Arnold, Poet," in *Major British Writers* (New York: Harcourt Brace & World, 1954) as primarily a man of ideas whose poetry represents essentially an early expression of the concepts later developed in his literary criticism, his social thought, and his writings on religion. His extensive admiration for Keats is founded far more in Keats's personal character and in the insightfulness of his letters than in his poetry. In his commentaries on

poems in *The Experience of Literature,* Trilling appears sympathetically workmanlike and professional rather than deeply involved. The contrast with his commentaries on fiction in the same anthology is striking, although the difference must be understood as one of tone and not of intellectual penetration.

With one exception, the only poet to whom he devotes an entire essay is Robert Graves, and his romping, joyous "A Ramble on Graves" (*A Gathering of Fugitives,* pp. 20–30) takes its color from Graves's Englishness of style and diction, which appealed to Trilling's acknowledged Anglophilia, and from Graves's uninhibited "passion for pleasure, for love, for sexuality, for masculinity, for femininity, for activity, for rest . . . a passion for integrity of the self—and a passion for civilization."

The one exception is Wordsworth. In *The Liberal Imagination* there is an affectionate, strongly positive reading of "The Immortality Ode." In *The Opposing Self* "Wordsworth and the Rabbis" is an engaging and subtle *jeu d'esprit* concerned with the sentiment of being, and in *Sincerity and Authenticity* Wordsworth is cited much more frequently than any other poet except Shakespeare and is used more systematically than any other including Shakespeare. What appears to give Wordsworth so much centrality for Trilling is the variousness and subtlety with which the poet explores the ways in which the personal will finds "its own affirmation by its rejection of the aims which the world sets before it and by turning its energies upon itself in self-realization" (*The Opposing Self,* p. 150). The quotations used here are from Book Two, lines 401–405, and Book Six, lines 603–613, of *The Prelude.*

11. *Sincerity and Authenticity,* p. 92.
12. William James, *Principles of Psychology* (New York: Henry Holt, 1890), vol. II, pp. 297–298.
13. *E. M. Forster,* pp. 12–14.
14. *The Last Decade,* pp. 148–159.
15. Asa Briggs, "Introduction," *William Morris: Selected Writings and Designs* (Baltimore: Penguin Books, 1963).

16. Paul Elmer More, *The Catholic Faith* (Princeton, N.J.: Princeton University Press, 1931).
17. *The Liberal Imagination*, pp. 243–254.
18. *The Liberal Imagination*, pp. 118–128.
19. In order to perpetuate itself and to preserve its core identity through the processes of change, every society, regardless of how simple and primitive or how complex and industrialized, must deal with the problem of transforming its children into citizens. While a human baby is by no means a tabula rasa, the character that it acquires and the kind of adult that it becomes are largely the result of the social influences that play over it. Without exception, all cultures vigorously attempt to mold the plastic material of the infant into those forms—and only those forms— of personality that are believed to be contributory to the survival and to the welfare of the group. Many of the functions of such core institutions as the family and the school derive their legitimacy from participating in this process of influencing, of deliberately shaping, the young in socially acceptable directions.

   Known to psychologists and other social scientists as *socialization*, the training of children in the manners, the morals, the valued skills, and the likes and dislikes of society is a key to cultural stability. For the most part, it goes on more through informal channels and through the weight of tradition and convention than through explicit and articulately directed efforts. In the United States (and pretty much throughout the Western world), however, public concern for the last forty years with child-rearing practices and options attests to the degree to which socialization has become an increasingly conscious and rather anxiety-laden matter. Its complexity is, of course, very great, and it is the essence of that lifelong conflict between the individual and his culture that Freud discussed with tragic sensitivity in *Civilization and Its Discontents*.

   To sample the voluminous and fascinating technical literature on socialization, see, for example, John Whiting and Irvin Child, *Child Training and Personality* (New Haven: Yale University Press, 1953);

Erik Erikson, *Childhood and Society* (New York: Norton, 1950); and Louis Breger, *From Instinct to Identity* (Englewood Cliffs, N.J.: Prentice-Hall, 1974). All children's literature in some fundamental sense has implications for socialization, as, for that matter, have all children's television programs. In the case of *The Jungle Book*, Kipling's alluringly presented conception of the Pack and the Law represents in a feral world the conditions that young wolves (and by logical extension all young, including children) must meet in order to enjoy the benefits of truly "belonging" to their society, the all-powerful Pack.

20. This statement was published in 1950, when perceptions of social class membership, ideas of a world state or of a United Nations Organization that would genuinely constitute a "parliament of man," and conceptions of a Good Society, perhaps like that of "the great experiment" being conducted in the Soviet Union, all enjoyed a more positive and more hopeful ambience than they do now. The point, however, remains unchanged. In "the culture of narcissism," where privatistic goals predominate, self-aggrandizement and self-gratification take clear precedence over any sort of commitment to the nation, and sentiments of patriotism typically seem hollow, false, or jingoistic. See Christopher Lasch, *The Culture of Narcissism* (New York: Norton, 1978).

21. *A Gathering of Fugitives*, p. 82.
22. *A Gathering of Fugitives*, p. 98.
23. *The Last Decade*, p. 140.
24. Strenuous opposition to the American involvement in Indochina had ample legitimacy without this romanticizing of the North Vietnamese government and without the deification, remarkable figure that he was, of Ho Chi Minh. Indeed, the dressing of North Vietnam's regime in the clothing of righteousness may have, in some significant degree, diverted attention from the real issue—the moral errors and the serious mistakes in international politics that marked from the first the actions of the United States in Southeast Asia. The literature here remains of high importance, despite the understandable desire to forget that sullied

Notes

decade between 1963 and 1973. See especially Paul Mus, *Vietnam: Sociologie d'une Guerre* (Paris: Editions du Seuil, 1952); Jean Lacouture, *Ho Chi Minh* (New York: Random House, 1968); Frances Fitzgerald, *Fire in the Lake* (Boston: Little, Brown and Co., 1972); and Alexander Kendrick, *The Wound Within* (Boston: Little, Brown & Co., 1974).

25. William L. O'Neill, *Coming Apart: An Informal History of America in the 1960s* (Chicago: Quadrangle Books, 1971), pp. 263–265 *et passim;* and Milton Viorst, *Fire in the Streets* (New York: Simon and Shuster, 1979). See also the anthology edited by Edward Quinn and Paul J. Dolan, *The Sense of the 60s* (New York: The Free Press, 1968); and the second volume of William Manchester's *The Glory and the Dream* (Boston: Little, Brown & Co., 1974).

26. *The Last Decade*, p. 175.

27. Joseph Frank, *The Widening Gyre* (New Brunswick, N.J.: Rutgers University Press, 1963), p. 268.

4. DECENT PEOPLE WHO HAVE NO DOUBTS

1. *Beyond Culture*, p. 13.
2. *The Liberal Imagination*, pp. 218–219.
3. *The Liberal Imagination*, p. 220.
4. *The Liberal Imagination*, p. 221.
5. *The Liberal Imagination*, pp. 221–222.
6. Richard Sennett, "Lionel Trilling," *The New Yorker*, 5 November, 1979, p. 204.
7. *The Last Decade*, p. 198.
8. See ch. 1, pp. 36–45.
9. *The Last Decade*, pp. 185–203.
10. *The Last Decade*, p. 200.
11. *The Last Decade*, p. 200.
12. *The Liberal Imagination*, p. 221.
13. T. S. Eliot, ed., *Pascal's Pensées* (New York: E. P. Dutton, 1958), pp. 49–50 (*Pensée* 182).
14. *Of This Time, Of That Place and Other Stories*, p. 78.
15. *The Liberal Imagination*, pp. xiv–xv.
16. There are some interesting parallels between Trilling's ideas on this score and the notions of Robert Penn Warren. See "Pure and Impure Poetry" in Warren's

Selected Essays (New York: Vintage Books, 1966), pp. 3–31.

17.   The effort by Herbert Marcuse, an authority on Hegel, to "radicalize" Freud has a special importance by virtue of both its sophistication and its intent. Marcuse knows psychoanalysis intimately; his purpose in attempting to revise it is to specify the psychodynamic conditions of human development that will produce a society marked by peace, freedom, and pleasure. His argument, although far too complex to summarize without doing violence to it, concentrates on the lessened need for a harsh superego by virtue of technological and economic changes. As these environmental conditions continue to alter, what he calls "surplus repression" and the "performance principle" will lose their force within the personality; competition among persons will markedly decline, and neither the inhibitions nor the frustrations associated with sexuality will interfere with intrapsychic serenity or interpersonal relatedness.

Marcuse's vision entails an uncompromising attack on Freud's famous criteria of individual mental health, the ability to work and the capacity for love. For work to prove satisfying, the worker must contend with difficulty and challenge and must respond to at least the threat of failure with persistence and discipline. For love to occur on what Freud regarded as the fully genital level, earlier modes of gratification—for example, the "polymorphous perverse" patterns of childhood—must be renounced. What Marcuse seeks is a culture in which human beings can develop without acquiring strong achievement needs and without guilt.

In the course of sketching the lineaments of such a society, he abrogates civil liberties in favor of his conception of civil rights; he bypasses the inherent conflict between egalitarian values and the values of excellence that undergird the technological advances on which the lessened influence of the superego depends; and, although his touchstones of appropriateness are less than precise, he legitimizes violence when it reflects resistance to a repressive established order.

Trilling's objections to such a view are clearly predictable. Perhaps the best entries into Marcuse's thought
are *Eros and Civilization* (Boston: Beacon Press,
1969) and his essay on "Repressive Tolerance" in *A
Critique of Pure Tolerance*, written with Robert Paul
Wolff and Barrington Moore, Jr. (Boston: Beacon
Press, 1965).

5.   IMAGINATION AND REALITY

1. *The Last Decade*, p. 239.
2. *The Last Decade*, p. 235.
3. *The Last Decade*, pp. 227–228.
4. *Matthew Arnold*, pp. 192–194. The sentence from
    Arnold occurs in "Pagan and Medieval Religious
    Sentiment" in *Essays in Criticism*, First Series.
5. *Matthew Arnold*, p. 205.
6. *Matthew Arnold*, p. 206.
7. *Matthew Arnold*, p. 208. Arnold's concern with
    "acridity" and its dangers is expressed in his essay on
    Heinrich Heine, in *Essays in Criticism*, First Series.
8. *Matthew Arnold*, pp. 24–25. Coleridge's observation
    occurs in "Dejection: An Ode." The conception of
    creativity formulated here is entirely consonant with
    the formulations of modern psychology. See Frank
    Barron, *Creativity and Psychological Health* (New
    York: Van Nostrand, 1963); Arthur Koestler, *The
    Act of Creation* (New York: Macmillan, 1964); Sil-
    vano Arieti, *Creativity: The Magic Synthesis* (Berke-
    ley, Calif.: University of California Press, 1952). Of
    special interest is Brewster Ghislin's *The Creative
    Process* (Berkeley, Calif.: University of California
    Press, 1952), a collection of accounts of their own
    creative processes by people as various as Albert Ein-
    stein, Carl Jung, D. H. Lawrence, Vincent Van Gogh,
    Amy Lowell, Wolfgang Amadeus Mozart, Jean Coc-
    teau, and many others.
9. *Matthew Arnold*, p. 26.
10. *Mathew Arnold*, pp. 339, 349, 336. Arnold's rationale
    for the love of Jesus as morally transformative comes
    from his *St. Paul and Protestantism* (1870).

11. *Matthew Arnold*, p. 352.

12. *Matthew Arnold*, pp. 269–270.

13. *Matthew Arnold*, pp. 370, 351.

14. *The Opposing Self*, pp. 141–145. Trilling also speaks here of Wordsworth's "conception of the world as being semantic." This phrase is one of the extremely rare instances in which he uses language that, if it is not completely meaningless, seems quite without communicative effectiveness.

15. *Matthew Arnold*, pp. 161–162.

16. For Trilling's summary and commentary on Arnold's notion that "Civilization is the humanization of man in society" and his concept of "expansion" as a means of achieving this end, see *Matthew Arnold*, pp. 381–388. The primary source in Arnold is the preface and the essays on "Democracy," "Equality," and "George Sand" in *Mixed Essays*, originally issued in London in 1879.

17. See Arnold's "The Function of Criticism at the Present Time" in *Essays in Criticism*, First Series, first published in London in 1865, and *Matthew Arnold*, pp. 204–208 and pp. 216–218.

18. *The Liberal Imagination*, pp. xiv–xv.

19. *Matthew Arnold*, p. 205.

20. *The Liberal Imagination*, p. xi. This passage is redolent of William James's "The Sentiment of Rationality," first published in *The Will to Believe and Other Essays* (New York: Holt, 1912). It also echoes much in John Dewey's *How We Think* (New York: D. C. Heath, 1910). Trilling was familiar with both works, admired them, and acknowledged them as part of his formative intellectual background.

21. *The Liberal Imagination*, pp. 298–303.

22. *Beyond Culture*, pp. 108–113. See the report of the Committee on Social Issues, *Considerations Regarding the Loyalty Oath as a Manifestation of Current Social Tension and Anxiety* (Topeka, Kans.: Group for the Advancement of Psychiatry, 1954).

23. *The Liberal Imagination*, p. 100.

24. *The Liberal Imagination*, pp. 101–102.

25. "The Situation in American Writing," *Partisan Review*, 1939 (Fall), Vol. 6 (No. 5), p. 109.

26. Sigmund Freud, *Civilization and Its Discontents*, Joan Riviere trans. (London: Hogarth Press, 1930), pp. 92–93. The closing portion of this passage, for all of Irving Babbitt's dislike of psychoanalysis, has striking affinities to themes developed in his *Democracy and Leadership* (Boston: Houghton Mifflin, 1924).

27. *The Liberal Imagination*, p. 36.

28. See Chapter 2.

29. See Chapter 3, especially pp. 112–117.

30. *The Last Decade*, pp. 240–241.

31. *Sincerity and Authenticity*, p. 60.

32. *Sincerity and Authenticity*, p. 99.

33. *Sincerity and Authenticity*, pp. 131–132.

34. *Sincerity and Authenticity*, p. 31.

35. *The Opposing Self*, pp. 24, 31.

36. *The Opposing Self*, pp. 34–35.

37. *The Opposing Self*, pp. 36–37.

38. *The Opposing Self*, p. 37.

39. *The Opposing Self*, pp. 40–42.

40. *The Opposing Self*, p. 44. Keats's statement occurs in the long letter, begun on February 14, 1819, and completed on the following May 3, to his brother George and his sister-in-law, Georgiana Wylie Keats. See Trilling's edition of *The Selected Letters of John Keats* (New York: Farrar, Straus and Young, 1951), pp. 203–217, especially pp. 215–216.

41. *The Opposing Self*, pp. 45, 48–49.

42. *The Last Decade*, p. 25. Joyce always wrote to his children in Italian. The original reads as follows: "*Adesso termino. Ho gli occhi stanchi. Da più di mezzo seculo scrutano nel nulla dove hanno trovato un bellisimo niente.*" See the third volume, edited by Richard Ellmann, of *The Letters of James Joyce* (New York: Viking Press, 1966).

43. *The Last Decade*, p. 56.

44. *The Last Decade*, p. 30.

6. THE HONEST PLACE "BETWEEN"

1. Richard Sennett, "On Lionel Trilling." *The New Yorker*, November 5, 1979, p. 209.

2. *A Gathering of Fugitives*, p. 65.
3. *The Liberal Imagination*, pp. 1–10.
4. *Beyond Culture*, p. 118.
5. *A Gathering of Fugitives*, pp. 43–44.
6. *The Liberal Imagination*, pp. 236–237.
7. *The Opposing Self*, p. ix.
8. *A Gathering of Fugitives*, p. 55.
9. *Beyond Culture*, p. xvii.
10. *The Last Decade*, pp. 226–227.
11. *The Liberal Imagination*, pp. 3–21.
12. *A Gathering of Fugitives*, pp. 79–84.
13. *Beyond Culture*, pp. 145–178.
14. *Sincerity and Authenticity*, pp. 167–172.
15. *The Opposing Self*, pp. 145–148.
16. *A Gathering of Fugitives*, pp. 31–40.
17. William James, *Principles of Psychology* (New York: Henry Holt, 1890), vol. I, p. 121.
18. Alfred North Whitehead, *An Introduction to Mathematics* (New York: Oxford University Press, 1948), p. 42.
19. Lionel Trilling, "The America of John Dos Passos," in Andrew Hook, ed., *Dos Passos: A Collection of Critical Essays* (Englewood Cliffs, N.J.: Prentice-Hall, 1974), pp. 93–100. First published in *Partisan Review*, 1938 (April), Vol. 4 (No. 5), pp. 26–32.
20. John Dewey and J. H. Tufts, *Ethics* (New York: Henry Holt, 1908), p. 210.
21. "The America of John Dos Passos," p. 100.
22. "The America of John Dos Passos," p. 96.
23. *Sincerity and Authenticity*, p. 167.
24. "The America of John Dos Passos," pp. 97, 100. The assessments of Dos Passos by Cowley and Whipple are available in Hook's *Dos Passos: A Collection of Critical Essays*, pp. 76–86 and 87–92.
25. Roger Sale, *On Not Being Good Enough* (New York: Oxford University Press, 1979), pp. 148–157.
26. Saul Bellow, *Mr. Sammler's Planet* (New York: Penguin Books, 1979), pp. 135–137, 42–43. (Originally published by Viking Press in 1970).
27. *Sincerity and Authenticity*, pp. 100–105, 144–149.
28. Stephen Donadio, "Columbia: Seven Interviews,"

Partisan Review, 1968 (Summer), Vol. 35 (No. 3), pp. 386–387.

29. William Chace, *Lionel Trilling: Criticism and Politics* (Stanford, Calif.: Stanford University Press, 1980), p. 150.

30. *The Last Decade*, pp. 173–174.

31. *Sincerity and Authenticity*, pp. 171–172.

32. Paul Elmer More, *The Catholic Faith* (Princeton, N.J.: Princeton University Press, 1931).

33. Alfred North Whitehead, *Science and the Modern World* (New York: Macmillan, 1928), pp. 15–16.

34. *The Last Decade*, pp. 204–225.

35. See, for example, Mark L. Krupnick, "Lionel Trilling: Criticism and Illusion." *Modern Occasions*, 1971 (Winter), Vol. 1 (No. 2), 282–287. Krupnick, in a quite contradictory fashion, combines his accusation of "mandarin exclusiveness" and an "overripe aestheticism" with an image of Trilling's "straining after the quotidian." Written in the spirit of the 1960s, Krupnick's essay reflects the yearnings and the temper of that period, including the faith that personal problems will somehow be solved by identification with a radical movement of some sort. Trilling had been repeatedly clear about his position on such an issue, notably (but not exclusively) in his treatments of Dos Passos and Fitzgerald and in his introduction to Tess Schlessinger's *The Unpossessed*. Disagreement would be one thing; rather sullen name-calling, based on a central misunderstanding, seems quite another.

36. *Of This Time, Of That Place, and Other Stories*, pp. 72–116.

37. Robert Boyers, *Lionel Trilling: Negative Capability and the Wisdom of Avoidance* (Columbia, Mo.: University of Missouri Press, 1977), pp. 4–19.

38. *The Last Decade*, p. 228.

39. *The Last Decade*, p. 231.

40. See the discussion of Trilling on Keats and Joyce, especially the former, in chapter 5. In Trilling's essay on Keats in *The Opposing Self* (pp. 3–49), Negative Capability is the central subject of pp. 32–45.

41. T. S. Eliot, ed., *Pascal's Pensées* (New York: E. P.

Dutton, 1958). The *Pensées* were originally published in 1669, seven years after Pascal's death. The *pensées* quoted in this paragraph are No. 358 (p. 99), No. 418 (p. 111), and No. 427 (p. 114). The one in the following paragraph, cited by Trilling on pp. 29–30 of *Sincerity and Authenticity*, comes from No. 434 (p. 121).

42. *Beyond Culture*, pp. 179–208.

43. Robert Boyers, *Lionel Trilling: Negative Capability and the Wisdom of Avoidance* (Columbia, Mo.: University of Missouri Press, 1977), *passim* and especially pp. 56–63.

44. Joseph Frank, *The Widening Gyre* (New Brunswick, N.J.: Rutgers University Press, 1963), pp. 253–274.

45. *The Last Decade*, p. 140.

46. See Irving Babbitt, *Rousseau and Romanticism* (New York: Meridian Books, 1955; first published Boston: Houghton Mifflin, 1919); *Democracy and Leadership* (Boston: Houghton Mifflin, 1924); and especially his translation, with a long introductory essay, of *The Dhammapada* (New York: New Directions, 1965; first issued by the Oxford University Press in 1936). There may be much to find fault with in Babbitt's conception of a New Humanism, but Babbitt's stress fell heavily and consistently on the volitional nature of self-control and the will as crucial in the governing of the passions. Similarly, in contrast to many current interpreters of Asian traditions, especially those of Hindu and Buddhist origins, Babbitt noted and advocated the centrality of spiritual vigor in Eastern religion and thought. He was fond of identifying "spiritual laziness" as the authentic original sin. Frank's charges seem warped a little away from perceptiveness and accuracy by an irritation that may possibly spring from ideological sources.

47. *The Last Decade*, pp. 148–159.

48. *The Liberal Imagination*, pp. 58–92.

49. William Chace, *Lionel Trilling: Criticism and Politics* (Stanford, Calif.: Stanford University Press, 1980), p. 187.

50. Chace, p. 188.

Bibliographic Essay

Although a deeply scholarly man, Lionel Trilling was in no sense a technical or formal scholar. For him, literature represented the most cogent and interesting language for capturing and reflecting upon human experience and the dynamics of culture. In consequence, the study of literature commanded his full seriousness; but the literary discipline enjoyed, in his eyes, far too great an importance to be restricted to discussions among academic peers. Both as critic and as teacher, Trilling drove for the widest audience he could reach, trying to ignite those concerns that literature embodies, that have a singular significance for our humanity, and that contribute to the more effective circulation of ideas in society. Preoccupied with the moral issues and the social dilemmas that he found so well illuminated in literary works, he assumed that thinking people would share his focus because of its intrinsic weightiness. Whether they shared his point of view or judgments was quite a different question that he seldom attended to.

Given his urge for the broadest possible audience, Trilling would be delighted with the Uniform Edition of his works, edited by Diana Trilling and published between 1978 and 1980 in twelve volumes by Harcourt Brace Jovanovich. The books, both in hard covers and paperback, are handsomely and sturdily manufactured, printed in readable type, and—most important—provide ready and pleasant access to all of his work except a few ephemeral pieces and some early articles and stories that add nothing to the riches now so happily available.

The Uniform Edition comprises the eight volumes that Trilling published during his lifetime: *Matthew Ar-*

nold, E. M. Forster, *The Middle of the Journey*, *The Liberal Imagination*, *The Opposing Self*, *A Gathering of Fugitives*, *Beyond Culture*, and *Sincerity and Authenticity*. In addition, it includes a collection of five short stories under the title of *Of This Time, Of That Place, and Other Stories*; *Prefaces to the Experience of Literature*, which include the commentaries that Trilling prepared for his big anthology, *The Experience of Literature*; and two collections of essays—*Speaking of Literature and Society*, which gathers together previously uncollected pieces published originally between 1924 and 1964, and *The Last Decade*, which contains the items that Trilling wrote during the last 10 years of his life, 1966 through 1975.

Only *Speaking of Literature and Society* appeared after the manuscript of *Lionel Trilling: Mind and Character* was completed. The last item in the Uniform Edition to see the light of print (in October, 1980), it would have saved a number of hours in libraries; but fortunately, everything necessary to the present book had been found in periodical form. The utility of *Speaking* rests not only on the increased accessibility of some of Trilling's most noteworthy essays, like those on Dos Passos and on "The Politics of T. S. Eliot"), but on a perceptive and revealing foreword by Mrs. Trilling and her biographical memoir, "Lionel Trilling: A Jew at Columbia," first published in 1977 in *Commentary* and the best publicly available source of information about Trilling's life.

For all practical purposes—and for the purposes that he most honored—the Uniform Edition defines Trilling's canon. But Trilling edited four books in addition to those that he wrote; he served as co-editor of the *Oxford Anthology of English Literature*, and two of the pieces that he later collected appeared originally as small books. For the record, the comprehensive list prior to the issuance of the Uniform Edition includes these items:

Matthew Arnold. New York: W. W. Norton, 1939. (Reprinted by the Columbia University Press, 1949, with a brief preface to the new edition.)

E. M. Forster. New York: New Directions Press, 1943.

The Middle of the Journey. New York: Viking Press, 1947. (Novel. Reissued in 1976 in paperback by Avon Books with a new introduction. The introduction is collected in *The Last Decade* as "Whittaker Chambers' Journey.")

The Portable Matthew Arnold. New York: Viking Press, 1949. (Edited with an introduction that adds nothing to Trilling's insights into Arnold as set down in *Matthew Arnold*.)

The Liberal Imagination. New York: Viking Press, 1950.

The Selected Letters of John Keats. New York: Farrar, Straus and Young, 1951. (Edited with an introduction included in *The Opposing Self* as "The Poet as Hero: Keats in His Letters.")

The Opposing Self. New York: Viking Press, 1955.

Freud and the Crisis of Our Culture. Boston: Beacon Press, 1955. (Incorporated in *Beyond Culture* under the title of "Freud: Within and Beyond Culture.")

A Gathering of Fugitives. Boston: Beacon Press, 1956.

Beyond Culture. New York: Viking Press, 1965.

The Experience of Literature. Garden City, N.Y.: Doubleday, 1967. (A selection of plays, stories, and poems to each of which is attached a critical commentary. In addition, Trilling included a large number of poems "for further reading," without commentary. The commentaries have been collected as *Prefaces to the Experience of Literature*.)

The Life and Work of Sigmund Freud. New York: Basic Books, 1970. (A one-volume abridgment, prepared with Steven Marcus, of Ernest Jones's three-volume biography.)

Literary Criticism: An Introductory Reader. New York: Holt, Rinehart and Winston, 1970. (An anthology of critical writing with an introduction reprinted in *The Last Decade* as "What Is Criticism?".)

Sincerity and Authenticity. Cambridge, Mass.: Harvard University Press, 1972.

Mind in the Modern World. New York: Viking Press, 1973. (The 1972 Thomas Jefferson Lecture in the Humanities, given in Washington, D.C., under the auspices of the National Endowment for the Humanities. Republished under the same title in *The Last Decade*.)

The Oxford Anthology of English Literature. New York:

Oxford University Press, 1973. (Trilling served as one of several co-editors for this edition of a prestigious and widely used anthology. His specific contributions cannot be systematically isolated in the text from those of his fellow editors, a state of affairs both common and appropriate in enterprises of this kind.)

Trilling has himself been an object of critical attention, of course, since the appearance of *Matthew Arnold* in 1939. The first book-length study was Robert Boyers's *Lionel Trilling: Negative Capability and the Wisdom of Avoidance* (Columbia, Mo.: University of Missouri Press), issued in 1977. The most comprehensive to date is William Chace's *Lionel Trilling: Criticism and Politics* (Stanford, Calif.: Stanford University Press, 1980). *Art, Politics, and Will* (New York: Basic Books, 1977), edited by Quentin Anderson, Stephen Donadio, and Steven Marcus, began as a *Festschrift* for Trilling and became a memorial volume when he died in November, 1975. After the fashion of *Festschriften*, most of the essays that it contains develop, in only the most general way, themes with which Trilling was concerned. Anderson's piece on *The Middle of the Journey*, however, and Marcus's appreciative survey of Trilling's career, are directly relevant and of major importance.

Three Honest Men: Edmund Wilson, F. R. Leavis, Lionel Trilling, released only in Great Britain (Manchester: Carcanet New Press, 1980), comprises the transcripts of three radio programs put together by Philip French for the British Broadcasting Corporation. French conducted interviews about each of his subjects with a variety of well-informed persons and then assembled the comments that he evoked in a manner that gives the flavor of first-rate conversation. Contributors to the section on Trilling in this valuable little book are Daniel Aaron, Quentin Anderson, Jacques Barzun, Morris Dickstein, Stephen Donadio, John Hollander, Irving Howe, Alfred Kazin, Steven Marcus, and Norman Podhoretz. Nathan Scott's chapter on Trilling in *Three American Moralists: Mailer, Bellow, Trilling* (Notre Dame, Ind.: University of Notre Dame Press, 1973) has considerable provocative value by virtue of Scott's attack, at once rigorous and sympathetic, on Trilling's "humanism" from the standpoint of contemporary Christian theology.

Although Joseph Frank's judgments of Trilling may be wrongheaded and querulous, both his earned reputation and his clearly established sensibility require the citing of his "Lionel Trilling and the Conservative Imagination" in *The Widening Gyre* (New Brunswick, N.J.: Rutgers University Press, 1963) and his "Appendix (January, 1978)" to that piece in *Salmagundi*, 1978 (Spring), No. 41. Similarly, Robert Warshow's review of *The Middle of the Journey*, which may have turned Trilling away from the career that he coveted as a novelist, has high importance. It appears as a part of "The Legacy of the 30's" in Warshow's posthumous *The Immediate Experience* (Garden City, N.Y.: Doubleday, 1962).

Instructive and frequent references to Trilling appear *passim* in Daniel Aaron's *Writers on the Left* (New York: Harcourt, Brace and World, 1961), Leo Bersani's *A Future for Astyanax* (Boston: Little, Brown, 1976), Stanley Edgar Hyman's *The Armed Vision* (New York: Alfred Knopf, 1955), and Alfred Kazin's *New York Jew* (New York: Random House, 1978). Three essays from the periodical literature have a special utility for identifying the issues with which Trilling was intimately associated: R. P. Blackmur, "The Politics of Human Power," *Kenyon Review*, 1950 (Autumn), Vol. 12; Dennis Donoghue, "Trilling, Mind, and Society," *The Sewanee Review*, 1978 (Spring), Vol. 86; and Delmore Schwartz, "The Duchess' Red Shoes," *Partisan Review*, 1953 (January), Vol. 20. These three unfriendly treatments, like Joseph Frank's and Robert Warshow's, demonstrate something of the impact that Trilling had on the critical community at various stages of his life. For a much more cordial and comprehensive appraisal, see Robert Langbaum's "The Importance of *The Liberal Imagination*," *Salmagundi*, 1978 (Spring), No. 41, and the review by Richard Sennett of the first volumes of the Uniform Edition in *The New Yorker* for November 5, 1979.

Other references, as a representative sample of the extensive attention paid to Trilling, are provided in the Notes to the chapters of the present volume. It is quite possible that several book-length examinations of Trilling may soon appear. In *Three Honest Men*, Philip French remarks (p. 102) that "there are numerous books about him in various stages of completion—anything between seven and a

dozen. Estimates of their number vary." Diana Trilling is
assembling a collection of her husband's letters, and his
papers have been deposited in the Rare Books and Manuscripts Division of the Columbia University Library in
New York City.

Index

MODERN LITERATURE SERIES